PELICAN BOOKS

A891

SYNANON: THE TUNNEL BACK

Lewis Yablonsky

Lewis Yablonsky is Professor of Sociology and Chairman of the Department of Sociology at San Fernando Valley State College. He has taught sociology at the University of California at Los Angeles and criminology at Columbia and Harvard. Educated at Rutgers and New York University, where he earned his Ph.D. in 1958, he is well known for his outstanding work with youth. He is the author of numerous articles on crime prevention and juvenile delinquency, as well as various papers on sociology and psychotherapy.

By Lewis Yablonsky

THE VIOLENT GANG

THE TUNNEL BACK: SYNANON

SYNANON:
THE TUNNEL BACK

LEWIS YABLONSKY

PENGUIN BOOKS
BALTIMORE • MARYLAND

Penguin Books Inc
3300 Clipper Mill Road, Baltimore, Md. 21211

This edition first published 1967 by arrangement
with The Macmillan Company, New York

The author wishes to thank the following publications for permission to reprint copyrighted material;
Time Magazine for an excerpt from "S. S. Hang
Tough," which appeared in the April 7, 1961, issue
of *Time*.

The Nation for an excerpt from Walker Winslow's
article, which appeared in the April 29, 1961, issue
of *The Nation*.

Printed in the United States of America

Introduction

Since this book was first published in 1965, Synanon has grown in size and scope. Despite some surface changes, most of the organization's structure and policy remain constant.

A part of Synanon's character that has become more articulate is its significance as a social movement. The organization has steadily moved beyond the limited work of treating drug addiction and crime. The function of Synanon as a vehicle for constructive personal and social change has become clearer as the theory and method is increasingly utilized by people who were never addicts, criminals or had any history of serious character disorder in their past.

The attraction of Synanon to these people is the opportunity to play the "Synanon Game."* In this intense form of small group interaction, many "square" friends of Synanon find they are better able to comprehend their "existence" as a side-effect of exploring facets of themselves, their relationships to others, and their own human values in the Game. Most participants feel that they

---

* A vital characteristic of Synanon is its flexibility in changing names and methods when this appears appropriate. When Columbia Pictures was filming its movie *Synanon*, what was then called the small-s synanon was demonstrated on location at Synanon for the producer and actors to observe. As Chuck Dederich was leaving the set after demonstrating this form of Synanon's small group interaction—he was approached by a British actor-comedian who had been observing the synanon. He told Chuck, "I must enthusiastically compliment you and thank you for letting me see that synanon. It's the most adult game I have ever witnessed." The term "Synanon Game" clicked with Chuck—since he had always viewed this facet of Synanon as a verbal-emotional game that was actually fun to play. As a result of a directive from Chuck, the small-s synanon (see Chapter 6) name was changed to the *Synanon Game*.

conclude a Game with a greater sense of self-awareness and identity. Some of these people have become so fascinated and intrigued by the Game, the social movement dimensions of the organization and the Synanon way of life that in growing numbers they have moved in, some with their families.

The impact, enjoyment and positive results of the Game can also account for the several hundred college and university students currently involved in campus Synanon clubs. A new development that has formalized the involvement of many so-called squares is the advent of the Synanon Game Club. The Clubs are comprised of hundreds of people who never had any serious emotional problems, but seem to enjoy the thrill of personal discovery the Games seem to produce. The magic and usefulness of Synanon thus seems to be growing and spreading to a wider audience.

Most methods and strategies of Synanon described in the book have not changed in their basic character, but they have become more refined and powerful. The "haircut," the "fireplace scene," seminars and various new forms of intellectual discussion are still useful tools in Synanon for helping people to better understand themselves, become "self-actualized" and mature.

Synanon's philosophical emphasis on self-reliance is becoming more of a reality as its industrial division has grown. (This division of Synanon's activity consists mainly of a specialty sales business.) Synanon Industries increasingly provides meaningful occupational opportunities for its members and has given Synanon an important source of finances in its movement towards self-sufficiency.

The major creative force in Synanon continues in the person of its founder, Charles E. Dederich. Although Chuck still manages the ever-growing Synanon organization as Chairman of the Board of Directors, his central interest is, as it always has been, in social research. His most recent involvement has been with structuring and directing experimental group sessions. In these groups he varies such factors as the time element of a session, and the size and composition of its membership. These group experiments appear to produce some remarkable new insights and potentially valuable discoveries. Chuck's original research along these lines built Synanon and holds great promise for the creation of other significant human inventions that should further validate the importance of this courageous social experiment.

L. Y.
January, 1967

Preface

Synanon is a new social movement and approach to life that has helped more than five hundred people overcome a severe past of crime and drug addiction. It was founded in 1958 by Charles E. Dederich, a layman with a genius for understanding and solving human problems. The creation and development of this novel human experiment is a story of courage. It is about people who moved from the gutters, prisons, brothels, and back rooms of our society into a position of moral leadership.

Although Synanon is a community of former addicts and criminals, this is not a book about deviance. Heroin addiction, the most common past problem of Synanon residents, is a cut-and-dried issue. Getting the white heroin powder through theft or prostitution; cooking it up with water in a bent, dirty spoon; drawing the concoction up through a needle inserted into an eyedropper; and injecting it into a "live" vein tells almost the complete, absurd story of the symptom drug addiction. The criminal behavior that accompanies addiction is also a pattern that has been described in its almost infinite variations. This book is more about the *solution* than the *problem*.

A central part of the Synanon story is an account of the fortitude and creativity of Chuck Dederich in starting a new social movement. Chuck, almost miraculously, first led a handful of addicts out of their formerly encapsulated lives of drug addiction, crime, and prison. With the help of this core group of remarkable people, he has produced a new social constellation of hope which has the potential of benefiting many more people caught in the morass of crime, addiction, and other problems.

The word "synanon" originated with a newly arrived addict

in the early days of the organization. In his attempt to say two "foreign" words, "symposium" and "seminar," in the same breath, he blurted out "synanon": "I want to get into another one of those—symp . . . sem—*synanons*." In this way, a new word was introduced into the language to describe a new social phenomenon.

Synanon is more than symposiums and seminars. It is a new kind of group therapy; an effective approach to racial integration; a humane solution to some facets of bureaucratic organization; a different way of being religious; a new method of attack therapy; an unusual kind of communication; and an exciting, fresh approach to the cultural arts and philosophy. One side effect of intense participation in these diverse human experiences is that people who were criminals and prisoners have found a new existence and now lead constructive lives.

Chuck Dederich is a masterful social planner. He founded Synanon in 1958 with a $33 unemployment check. In 1963, the Synanon Foundation, Inc., spent $200,000 in cash and used up an estimated $800,000 in goods and services. This million-dollar enterprise was supported mainly by small donations from thousands of citizens all over the country. Additional support came from several private foundations.

The central organization of Synanon currently comprises more than five hundred people. They use a variety of living quarters, buildings, warehouses, automobiles, and trucks based in Synanon's five locations throughout the country. There are Synanon establishments in Santa Monica; San Francisco; San Diego; Westport, Connecticut; and Reno, Nevada.

Importantly entwined in the Synanon movement is a cross section of citizens who visit and support the work of the Synanon Foundation. Since the beginning, there have been more than fifty thousand separate visits by citizens from all walks of life to Synanon Houses. In reverse, Synanon members have filled more than one thousand educational speaking engagements to college, university, church, high-school, civic, and other community groups. (In 1964, Synanon, at the invitation of the U.C.L.A. Graduate Student Association, presented a week-long program of cultural art and picture exhibits, a lecture series, Synanon films, and informal discussions in the U.C.L.A. Student Union Center.) This interchange between Synanon's "narcotics experts" and the larger society has been of inestimable value in dispelling many misconceptions and in educating the public about the narcotics problem. This unique pattern of social interaction between Synanon people and the interested public may very well be one of the important secrets of Synanon's success.

Not everyone has supported Synanon. Many segments of society have balked at the spectacle of criminals and addicts living in "respectable" communities and trying to solve their problems in their own way. Cries of fear and outrage have been followed up by a variety of legal maneuvers. The enemies of Synanon have attempted to drive Synanon people and their families (children included) from their newfound homes and their foothold on a constructive way of life. When Synanon's prejudiced enemies could not find anything illegal in the behavior of Synanon people (and they tried), they invoked irrelevant zoning laws in an effort to destroy Synanon's interracial community. (It is interesting to note a paradox: these people invoked what is generally the most corrupt arm of city government—the housing and zoning divisions—in their attacks on Synanon.) In all cases, the zoning boards (in Santa Monica, Westport, and San Francisco), angrily prodded by the supporters of "lily-white" living and by people concerned with property dollars, jumped onto Synanon's back. On the surface, it was zoning; at the murky bottom, it was prejudice.

Countless numbers of addicts who might have lived in Synanon "died" in jails, prisons, and from drugs (an overdose kills) while the enemies of rehabilitation slowed its natural thrust by creating fake zoning issues. Of symbolic interest is the fact that Synanon's leader, Chuck Dederich, who had never been to prison in his life, was locked up in the Santa Monica City Jail for twenty-five days on a *zoning violation*.

Contents

xi

Part I

The Intruders

Oftentimes have I heard you speak of
one who commits a wrong as though he
were not one of you, but a stranger
unto you and an intruder in your world.

But I say that even as the holy and the
righteous cannot rise beyond the highest
which is in each one of you,

So the wicked and the weak cannot fall
lower than the lowest which is in you
also.

And as a single leaf turns not yellow
but with the silent knowledge of the
whole tree,

So the wrong-doer cannot do wrong without the hidden will of you all.

The Prophet—Kahlil Gibran
(New York: Alfred A. Knopf,
Inc., 1923)

Early Encounters

The first time I heard about Synanon was at the United Nations Congress on Crime and Delinquency in London in the summer of 1960. One evening, at an informal gathering, a new experiment for treating addicts was described to me by the noted criminologist Dr. Donald Cressey.

I found Cressey's remarks exciting. In more than ten years of work with the crime problem on the East Coast, I did not know one so-called ex-addict who had totally quit using drugs. If there were more than thirty former addicts and criminals staying "clean" in Synanon, as Cressey had informed me, this was a major breakthrough in treating the problem.

According to Cressey, this small band of former addicts lived together in an old beach house in Santa Monica. They regularly participated in seminar discussions and a new form of group psychotherapy devised by Synanon's founder, Chuck Dederich. Cressey sketched a vivid picture of this group: loudly arguing philosophical concepts and amateur psychology into all hours of the night while a hi-fi blared out jazz music in the background. I especially remember his description of an addict going through drug withdrawal pains on a living-room couch in the center of this bizarre scene.

The human situation described by Cressey seemed strange. But it did make some sense to me that it would probably take a radi-

cal set of circumstances to get addicts off drugs. All other methods
had failed. If this one worked, I wanted to see this sociological
freak of nature.

About a year later, in 1961, when my academic interests
brought me to California, I had the opportunity to see Synanon
at firsthand.[1] Cressey's description bore little resemblance to the
Synanon organization I encountered on my first visit.

First Meeting

When I arrived in Los Angeles, I quickly learned of Synanon's
zoning battle with the City of Santa Monica. Stories were in the
local press almost daily, and several colleagues gave me additional
background information. Apparently, the city officials, prodded
by some irate citizens, wanted to run Synanon out of town.

Other citizens' groups supported Synanon's right to exist. A
member of a pro-Synanon citizens' group invited me to testify
on Synanon's behalf at a City Council meeting. This gave me the
opportunity I wanted to see Synanon at firsthand and learn something directly about the organization. An appointment was made
for me to visit and meet with a "Synanon director," Charlie
Hamer.

My first look at Synanon surprised me. The immense five-story
red-brick armory was nothing like the beatnik beach-house pad
I was led to expect. The large, respectable black-and-yellow
SYNANON HOUSE sign on the front of the building was also
a surprise. Somehow I had expected Synanon to have a more
clandestine face to the world.

The large front door to the building opened into an impres-
sive waiting room. On a bulletin board right inside the door, I
noticed pictures of many celebrities with Synanon members. One
picture showed Chuck Dederich and several Synanon members

[1] Dr. Cressey, then Chairman of the Department of Sociology at U.C.L.A.,
accepted a fellowship to Cambridge University, England, at the Institute of
Criminology. I accepted the opportunity offered me to teach at U.C.L.A.
while he was on leave.

talking to Steve Allen. Also in the foyer was a counter with a variety of Synanon literature. There were reprints of articles on Synanon from *Time, Down Beat, The Nation,* and other publications.

Several feet from the entrance, a young man seated at a desk greeted me in a businesslike manner. He asked me to state my business and then sign a guest register. (I noticed that he had the healed scars of an ex-addict on the inside crook of his arms. This "administrative approach," coming from a former addict, was a startling experience.)

I told him about my appointment with Charlie Hamer. He called my name into an intercom that connected with the "co-ordinator's office." I was now apparently properly checked into the building, and the squawk box answered back, "Send him on up."

It became increasingly difficult to believe that the place was entirely managed by ex-addicts. Everywhere I looked, I saw signs of efficient organization. On my way to the second floor, I passed a sign stating "Business Office." The large room had rows of typewriters, files, and the other accouterments of an office. A small theater marked "Stage One" was at the foot of the stairs. The hall was carpeted with colored rugs, which were well-worn but neat and clean.

On the second floor, I saw men and women bustling around in different directions. They all seemed to be on important errands. With the exception of the sight of several jail-scarred faces and a young man going through drug-withdrawal pains in the center of the living room, I found it difficult to believe this was a "drug-addict rehabilitation center." It seemed to be more of a poor man's version of a co-ed college fraternity house.

Charlie Hamer introduced himself, welcomed me, and introduced me to another "member of Synanon," Jack Hurst. After a brief exchange of handshakes and pleasantries, I was informed that "any friend of Don Cressey's is a friend of ours." They then told me that they really expected a bearded older man and that I didn't "look like a professor." (I thought to myself, "You guys don't look like junkies I have known either.") Both were healthy, bright-eyed, and pleasant men. They were articulate; their conversation contained little of the "hip-addict" talk I was used to and expected.

Hurst was a thin young man, about thirty-two years old. (I later found out that he had been an addict for nine years prior to coming to Synanon.) Hamer was about sixty. He was ruddy-faced and very talky, with a Southwestern twang in his voice. His opening remarks lauding Synanon were very much in the style of many intelligent old "cons" I had met in my past prison work. Most of these old-timers had their theories on treatment. There was one major difference between Hamer's dialogue and what I had heard in the past. He wasn't giving me the usual story of the locked-up *prisoner* and *failure* who now saw the "light." He was talking from the unusual position of a living embodiment of his preachments. This encouraged me to listen more attentively to his story.

(I later found out that Hamer was probably one of the oldest ex-addicts in the country. The first drug he used was opium. This was given to him by a Chinese family in Oklahoma in 1922. This had launched him into almost forty years of leading a life of crime and addiction.)

Both Hurst and Hamer were casually and informally dressed in open-collar shirts, casual cotton pants, and flip-flop beach shoes. This was apparently the style at Synanon. Most of the other Synanon people were similarly dressed. (I felt uncomfortable in my Eastern wool suit, with the accompanying tight shirt, collar, and tie.)

Before Hamer and I could get any serious conversation under way, I observed that most of the people in the house had gathered in the front room. I was informed that the synanons were about to take place and that we would get to talk further "after they were kicked off." According to Hamer, "The synanon is our form of what you probably call group psychotherapy in your business. People here go to these sessions three evenings a week. In the synanon, people can dump their emotional garbage and learn about themselves. It's a kind of pressure cooker for working out what's bugging you."

At this point, a man, whom I later came to know as Bill

Crawford, walked to the front of a large fireplace in the middle of the living room. He took charge of the thirty-five to forty people sitting around the living room. Almost all the people seemed to be smoking with both hands and drinking coffee at the same time. Crawford spoke casually from notations he had on a clipboard: "Sheets go out tomorrow. We're down to rock bottom on money for the few staples we have to buy, and yet some of you keep leaving half cups of coffee all over the place. Knock it off! . . . Let's welcome a new member who came in today, Joe Sommers."

The group vigorously applauded as they looked toward a slim youth about twenty-two years old. He was huddled under a blanket on a couch in the middle of the living room, apparently going through withdrawal pains from his drug habit. He seemed surprised by the attention and managed a weak smile. He was apparently dazed from going through his "withdrawal sickness" and seemed taken aback by the warm response of the group.

The group was young and old, black and white, thin and fat. The girls mainly wore capris. The "kickoff" to the synanons seemed somewhat like a house meeting in the living room of a fraternity house. (Of course, the racial-integration factor was unlike any fraternity house scene I had ever witnessed.) I had, of course, heard (and later confirmed) that all the people had been addicts and had spent varying amounts of time in jails and prisons. (Their past prison-time experience ranged from several months to over twenty years.)

After the applause for the newcomer stopped, Crawford announced synanon groupings for the evening: "Tootsie, Donna, Jimmy, Henry, Betty, Harry, Janis, Candy . . . will meet in the business office." Eight people got up—some went to the restaurant-type coffee urn in the dining room, got coffee, and then went down the stairs. Crawford continued: "Bill, Reid . . ." With each reading of names, another group moved out, apparently assigned to another location in the building.

Hamer showed me one of the rooms set up for a synanon. Chairs were placed in a circle, so that everyone faced everyone else. The room began to fill up with the assigned people.

Hamer and Hurst informed me that they would normally

be in synanons but that they wanted to brief me for the next evening's important community meeting. We began to discuss Synanon and some of its community problems. Hamer told me that before I left he would also give me some literature that described their problems in greater detail.

There were loud curses and shouts coming from the "synanon room" I had just left. I was somewhat disturbed by the voice pitch. I knew, from my institutional experience, that the type of shouting I was hearing was often a prelude to, or accompanied, physical violence. Hurst sensed my reaction and told me about "the two cardinal rules of Synanon. Two capital offenses in Synanon are physical assault and taking drugs or alcohol. The kids are just normally discussing their problems, and they do get noisy. But that's just fine, it helps them get all the pent-up hostility out of their gut and take a look at it. That's what synanons are for."

Hamer suggested that we go to the coordinator's office, where it was quieter. I was informed that the coordinator's office was the "nerve center" of the building and that it "coordinates" internal and outside activities. The office contained squawk boxes, phones, card files, maps, printed directives (for example: "All trips to the dentist are to be cleared through Bill Crawford . . ."; "Meeting of department heads Tuesday at noon in the business office . . ."). The room contained a variety of furniture. I later learned that "everything in Synanon, including the clothes we're wearing, is donated."

In the office was an extremely attractive young lady of about twenty-four. She was on hand to answer phone calls during the synanons. Charlie Hamer introduced Monica to me and invited her to "join in" our discussion of Synanon.

The synanon sessions continued to rock the building with noise. I asked whether this was usual or whether there were calmer synanons. Hurst described a variety of synanons: "The ones going on tonight are the standard floor synanon and are mainly catharsis-type sessions. It helps people get a lot of emotion out of their system. They argue and fight over what happens to be bugging them at the time. Like they think they have a rotten job; why someone had a need to 'look good' all of the time; why someone can't take orders; self-image problems; why someone never talks at all or talks too much."

My own experience in working with addicts in group therapy compelled me to ask Jack what seemed to me at that time an obvious question: "If the people here are drug addicts, why all this discussion about work habits and 'self-image'? Don't you discuss your compulsion to shoot drugs?"

"We're no longer drug addicts. We *were* all addicts, and when we were addicts we talked about dope. We are trying to do something else. We are trying to learn how to live like human beings. I shot drugs for nine years. When I crawled in here two years ago, almost on all fours, I was at the end of the line. My problem wasn't drugs, even though drugs made me subhuman. What I needed, and still need, is to learn more about proper living. There really isn't much to be said about drugs or a yen. We try to get to the 'person' here. Probably the reason group therapy and jail or psychiatry never helped me is because most of the therapy dealt with the symptom of drug addiction.

"This is one of the problems with you professionals. You are all involved with drug addiction. You want to know how an addict uses, how much, and all that crap. Around here we are interested in helping ex-dope fiends grow up, by talking about living clean."

The term "dope fiend" and Jack's hostility began to get to me. I said, "Why do you say 'dope fiend' rather than 'drug addict'? Isn't that what you were, an addict?"

"I call myself an ex-dope fiend, and the noise 'dope fiend' best describes my past behavior. During one of my 'periods' as an addict, I careened around highways on a motorcycle with long hair and a leather jacket—the whole bit. You know, the 'Wild One.' I went through other scenes too. I was even married for a while as a dope fiend.

"Let me give you a real example of my *dope-fiend* behavior. I don't think I told you this ridiculous story before, Charlie. It really describes this dope-fiend thing.

"First get the background. I'm living in Northern California. I went there on one of my runaway geographic cures. You know, I was trying to clean up by getting out of L.A. and away from the scene. Of course, it wasn't working. I would charge into San Francisco on weekends to get my stuff [drugs].

"Anyway, here I am with my wife in this small town. I'm trying to work as a carpenter on a construction gang. My pregnant wife is with me in this burg. It's a city of about ten thousand, with one doctor.

"In the middle of the night, my wife begins to have labor pains. We get into the car, and I take her to this dinky little hospital. The only one there is a nurse, who won't call the doctor till she's sure my wife is going to give birth.

"I held my wife's hand and reassured her that all was well. This goes on for about an hour. Meanwhile, the nurse is preparing my wife, anesthetic and all that. She finally calls the doctor, and he is on his way.

"Now in the middle of this 'beautiful-young-couple-having-a-baby, waiting-for-the-doctor scene,' in the back of my head I'm trying to figure out *how I can get at some of the dope [Demerol] the nurse pumped into my wife's arm!* There's the bottle of Demerol sitting on the medicine table.

"My wife's pains are getting closer together, and the doctor still hasn't arrived. All of a sudden, the nurse let out a gasp. There is the baby's head. The nurse says, 'Let's get her into the delivery room. You're going to have to help. The doctor ought to be here in about fifteen minutes, but put these on.' Then she gives me a doctor's smock, the rubber gloves, ties this mask around my face, and says, 'We got to deliver the child!'

"This catches me off base. Here I am trying to be lovingly concerned for my wife's welfare, help with the delivery, and at the same time get the dope. My wife is screaming her head off. I hold her hand and keep inching my way closer to the anesthetic tray where the bottle of dope I want so badly is sitting. I finally snatched the bottle of Demerol and tucked it safely away in my pocket under the smock. Now I feel comfortable, and I'm ready to help deliver my child.

"At this point the doctor arrives, and I became a bystander. From about seven feet away, I'm watching the doctor deliver the kid, cut the cord, take the crap out of the kid's mouth, give him a smack—and nothing happens. He gives the kid mouth-to-mouth resuscitation, and still nothing happened. He dumped him in hot and cold water and all that. Finally the kid, who had started to turn blue, let out a bellow, and then he was okay.

"But what I vividly remember about the episode is that I couldn't really get concerned about my wife and kid until I had stolen the dope and had it securely stashed away. Now you know why I call people who use drugs 'dope fiends.' " [2]

I had heard the classic true-dope-fiend story of the addict's stealing his sick mother's medicine money many times. The incident described by Jack, however, seemed to top any story I had ever heard.

At this point, Monica, who had been listening in, shyly interrupted: "Maybe a little story about one of my experiences with drug addiction will explain why the term 'dope fiend' seems pretty accurate to me for describing our past behavior.

"If I remember this incident correctly, some guy, a trick [a prostitute's customer], wanted to marry me. I had a very bad habit going at the time, and it's all very vague. I remember this trick had a lot of money. He liked me, and had offered to help me kick my habit. I thought I wanted to clean up, or at least this was one of my attempts. Anyway, I went to his apartment. He hid my clothes, my shoes, blouse, and purse—almost everything—so I couldn't leave. All I had left on was a pair of capri pants and my bra.

"Naturally, when I started getting icky [craving for drugs] after a few hours of kicking [withdrawing from drugs], I asked him for the rest of my clothes so I could go score [get drugs]. He flatly refused to give them to me, and we had a big hassle.

"His apartment was near one of the main boulevards in Hollywood, and I remember running out the door, with him after me, down Sunset Boulevard. I was wearing nothing but my capris and a brassiere. Anyway, there I was racing down the street, with him trying to catch me; he got his car by then. Some guy on a motorcycle was going by. He spotted me and screeched to a stop. You know the type; black leather jacket, helmet, the whole bit. After he stopped, he came on with a wolf whistle. He pulled alongside

---

[2] Jack is currently happily married to the same woman and has been "clean" in Synanon since 1959. Their son Kenny lives at Synanon with his family and seems to be doing fine.

me (remember, I was half-nude), and he 'whoom-whoomed' his motorcycle motor, in a weird wolf call.

"I jumped on the back of the 'cycle and told him someone was after me, and if we didn't move out fast we'd both be in trouble. So we went speeding down Sunset Boulevard and lost the guy following us. I then had the motorcycle cat drop me off at my connection's [drug pusher] house, and I scored."

The thought of this lovely girl with her black hair swept back by the wind, careening along on a motorcycle, inspired a bad joke I couldn't resist: "I dreamt I went to the connection in my Maidenform bra."

Jack's and Monica's stories persuaded me that the term "dope fiend" was more accurate than narcotics addict.

As we continued to talk, I became increasingly impressed with the stark honesty and candor of the Synanon people. Never in my professional experience (certainly not in various institutions or in my research on the "street") had I encountered a more direct and honest response to any questions I chose to ask. I said, "You know, I've done a fair amount of research on crime and in particular with violent gangs in New York. I've never had the experience of such frank responses to my questions. After all, none of you know me that well."

Hurst picked up this point: "Around here, we operate on what we laughingly call the truth principle. If you want to look at it that way, part of our therapy is truth and honesty. We have nothing to hide or creep around about. We aren't proud of our past behavior, but at the same time we can't go around paralyzed with guilt. It would just incapacitate us.

"Perhaps most important, I feel good when I tell the truth and get everything out on the table. By the way, you have been here only a short while, but we may even expect you to tell the truth one of these days. We pull the covers off of our square friends' dirty little secrets from time to time. They seem to like it. We have around thirty squares who attend synanons once a week, and they mix it up with our people."

Hamer said, "Most people in the world can get by with their little white lies and conning each other. We have found we cannot afford to lie at all. Any slips of truth on our part can be deadly. If we do not level with each other, we add more guilt to our already heavy load. This would fester, and we might split [leave] and go back on dope, get ourselves dead from an overdose, or go back to jail. We have to be honest to stay clean."

I was impressed with their articulate responses to my questions and commented on this point.

Hurst replied, "This is not by chance. Obviously, I am no grammarian. I only had a ninth-grade education. But we do work on communication here. That's part of our business. Each noon we have a seminar where we place some concept on the blackboard, and then everyone discusses it. For example, the one we had this noon was, 'We attack in others the evil we dimly perceive in ourselves.' We cut this kind of concept up and argue about it. This helps our discussion ability. Although I may not be too sharp now, when I first came in here I talked out of the side of my head.

"Some of the guys, when they come in here, know one word, 'stickemup.' After a while, as a result of synanons and seminars, they develop their verbal skills. Part of our program involves going on speaking engagements to different community and educational organizations."

Monica showed me what they called a "concept box." It was a standard six-by-six green office card box. On file in it were about three hundred concepts. Emerson, Freud, Thoreau, Nietzsche, Lao-tse, and Russell were some of the names I noticed.

Through the thin walls of the coordinator's office came a bellowing voice from the synanon session next door: "You shucking mother-fucker! When are you going to get off your fat ass and really work in the coordinator's office? Man, you got to give to get. You've been sucking on Synanon's tit for a year now and haven't come up with anything!" The person who was the object of the remarks began to defend his position—and denied the accusation.

I asked, "Is this standard practice in a synanon; are they always this intense?"

Hamer said, "No. In some synanon sessions, we discuss things without dragging in all of our hostility. The longer a person is around here, the more likely he is to have better self-control. Our older members are mixed in with the newcomers and try to get something into the session besides the kind of raw attack you just heard.

"By the way, although we don't make a big thing of it, and profanity is freely allowed in the synanons, we try to keep it to a minimum outside of the synanon sessions. In fact, someone may be pulled up [chastised] for excessive cursing."

As I became more interested in understanding Synanon, many questions crowded my thoughts: "What are some of the other activities around here? How do you get your money? What kind of work do you do?" A few of these questions were partially answered that evening.

Hurst informed me that Synanon was supported by the community: "We get most of our goods and services by donations from the public. People seem to like to help us. We have several trucks on the road. They pick up donations, often made over the phone. The guys who work on these trucks are called the hustling crew.

"We have a service crew that moves and fixes our shaky furniture and keeps up the building. Our electrician, an ex-dope fiend, of course, has the place intricately wired. We will probably blow up any day.

"The automotive crew services our cars and trucks. The kitchen crew provides our meals and has the job of rehabilitating old vegetables and tired meat that comes to us through our hustling crew.

"Hamer and I are members of the Board of Directors. We are part of the administration directly under Chuck Dederich. Our executive staff goes on down to acting directors and coordinators."

"Where is Chuck tonight? I thought I'd meet him."

"Well, right now he is having a meeting with our attorney, Vince Cavanagh, an ex-dope fiend himself, two other lawyers, and our family doctor, Dr. Casselman."

"Who are the other lawyers?" I asked. "Are they addicts too?"

"No. They are squares. Part of a group of local citizens that includes lawyers, doctors, dentists, bakers, and other citizens who like us well enough to donate the goods and services which keep us going."

"Just what is the legal situation?"

The group laughed. Hurst gave me his version of the problem:

"It's too complicated to boil down, but briefly the story is something like this. . . . In spite of the fact that many citizens like and support us, there is a collection of property owners, Birchers, and others who want us out of here. The city administration is composed of a bunch of weak-kneed idiots, who respond to these hate groups. In back of it all, we know there is prejudice. They just do not want a mixed group of whites, Negroes, ex-addicts, and criminals living here. That's the way it is. They plague us, even though we haven't had one illegal incident in our history.

"They trumped up a zoning violation claiming that we are operating, of all things, a 'hospital' out of zone. Of course, we are not anything like a hospital, but this smoke-screens the real issue of ignorance, prejudice, and hatred. That's what we're fighting, really—ignorance. Those people who take the time to get to know us wind up liking what we are trying to do for ourselves."

About this time, the synanons were breaking up and the members were streaming to the coffee urn and a sandwich table. Everyone seemed lively, hungry, and bright-eyed. I was amazed. There appeared to be no animosity at all among individuals who, minutes before, had been viciously screaming at each other. In group-psychotherapy sessions that I had run in prisons and hospitals, hard feelings would persist for days among group members.

Hamer attributed the *esprit de corps* in part to Synanon's common enemy: "We have our petty grievances, like any other family, but we can be friends again. We're all trying to help each other. Although part of our enemy is inside all of us, there's a bigger enemy at our door, trying to smash our right to live clean. We're a pretty tight group."

At this point Hurst and Crawford told me, "Welcome aboard," and excused themselves to attend to other business. Hamer kept talking. I was very stimulated by what he said and wanted to hear more about Synanon.

Charlie's Story

That night I burned the midnight oil in a long talk with Charlie. I was intrigued and wanted to hear as much as I could about him and his experiences in Synanon. He told me about his early encounters in the "club." (At a later date, when I was more "in" Synanon, I had Charlie repeat his experiences into a tape recorder.) As a prelude to Charlie's more complete story, the following statement gives some background picture of Charlie's view of his past criminal-addict life history. He wrote it for me in this summary form:

I was born May 1, 1903, in Henryetta, Oklahoma. My first encounter with narcotics came at the age of nineteen (1922), from association with a local Chinese family in Oklahoma. I was introduced to opium and smoked same for three years. My first hypodermic injection happened in 1925, with the residue from an opium pipe (*yen-shee*). About one year later I began using morphine intravenously. This drug, in the pure form, was obtained from unethical doctors, pharmaceutical houses, peddlers, etc. I built up a large tolerance and used fifteen to twenty-five grains per day. I obtained money for my drugs by theft, robbery, confidence games, etc. Narcotics were cheap in those days, selling from $35 to $75 per ounce. I used morphine and cocaine until 1933, and was then introduced to heroin. I came to California in 1937, and remained free from drugs until 1943, using alcohol to excess during this period. I again started using opium by injection and orally (*samlow*). I shipped out with the Merchant Marines from 1943 to 1945, using many drugs: heroin, cocaine, hasheesh, morphine, etc., throughout the world.

In 1946, I again started using heroin and used it constantly until coming to Synanon.

Family Background: Fatherless at the age of one. Youngest of five children. Reared by mother. Little supervision as mother neither had the time nor knowledge to supply this. Married and divorced three times from 1925 to 1947.

Education: Eight years of grammar school. Four years high school.

Arrest Record: I was first arrested at the age of ten for stealing coal and domestic fowls. At seventeen I was arrested for drunkenness, disturbing the peace, fighting, etc. Until the age of twenty-six, arrested several times for forgery, theft, robbery, vagrancy, etc. I was sentenced to Oklahoma State Penitentiary in 1929, for forgery. Released in 1931. I was arrested for petty theft several times in the next two years. During 1936 and 1937, I was arrested for suspicion of robbery twice. Also found guilty of possession of narcotics in 1943, and was sentenced to eight months in Federal Jail, Oklahoma City. I was arrested in San Diego in 1945 for possession of opium and was sentenced to the Federal Hospital, Lexington, Kentucky, for two years. Released in 1947. From 1947 until 1954, sentenced to Los Angeles County Jail five times for addiction, forgery, and forgery of narcotic prescriptions. Served about four and one-half years. I was arrested in 1955, in Los Angeles, and sentenced to two years in U.S.P.H. Hospital, Fort Worth, Texas. Released in 1956, I immediately returned to drugs and used continuously until coming to Synanon in 1959.

I was skeptical of the Synanon experiment, but desperately searching for some solution to my problems. I was appointed to the Board of Directors in 1960, as Director of Welfare, and since that time have been deeply involved in this program. I am especially interested in any youth program concerning narcotic addiction, and I believe that I can make a real contribution to this particular aspect of drug addiction and antisocial behavior. Synanon worked for me by the fact that I found myself involved with a group that seemed to have a definite goal and that gave me trust, kindness, love, and respect, but, above all, a feeling of acceptance. By learning to verbalize my thoughts and being able to communicate with others, certain things about my particular personality seemed to become quite clear and some of my problems which I considered of the utmost gravity suddenly seemed to be of no consequence.

The fact that I was free to leave at any time had a great effect on me. My relationships with my fellow man, both members of Synanon and the larger society, greatly improved. I sincerely believe that the communication block which seems to exist between the addict and society has been greatly diminished by the Synanon method. With the exception of the brief rundown of my education, this fairly well sums up my criminal and addiction history. Of course, there are many incidents that I have completely forgotten, but I meant this summary to be a real attempt at complete honesty.

ENTERING SYNANON [3]

"I'm not too clear about all this, because my mind was pretty confused at that time, but I was walking down by Ocean Park and I ran into Johnny B., an old dope-fiend buddy of mine. He started telling me he was a director or something of a place for cleaning up junkies. I naturally thought he was crazy. But I thought I'd look into it, because I had a hell of a habit and wanted to clean up. Nothing permanent, mind you, but just to reduce this bitch of a habit I had going.

"He took me down the street to an old store-front building. He told me he was going to take me through the house and over to where a couple-three directors (whatever that was) were going to interview me. I was completely confused, dirty, ragged, and had about $2.50 in my pocket. As I'm going through this room, I saw Billy G., peeling potatoes, a guy I've known for years, been in jails and a couple of penitentiaries with. I go on out the back door on the way to this pad and there's Harry C. out there sweeping up. He was an old friend I used to shoot dope with, and I felt, 'Well, Jesus Christ, as soon as I get back from this interview, I can probably score from one of these guys.'

"I go into this interview and there sits Jesse Pratt. I've known Jesse for twenty years. With him is this woman and Chuck Dederich.

"I said hello to Jesse, and they told me to sit down. Jesse didn't recognize me. That's the point I'm getting at. John says, 'Here's a new prospect, a guy I've known for a long time. I know this guy needs help.' John kind of tried to pave the way for me, so to speak. Chuck says, 'What's his name?' John says, 'This is Charlie Hamer.' Jesse Pratt looked at me and says, 'What'd you say your name was?' I say, 'Charlie Hamer,' and he says, 'No, you're not Charlie Hamer!' I say, 'I am Charlie Hamer, Jesse; don't you recognize me?' Finally, he says, 'Well I'll be goddamned; I've never seen you looking like that. You just don't look like yourself.'

"That's the kind of condition I was in. I was well strung out [heavily addicted], and Jesse couldn't actually believe it was me. So he jumps up and says, 'Well, it is Charlie Hamer and it's an

[3] This longer version of Charlie's "story" was told to me during several lengthy interview sessions.

old, old friend of mine and I have to agree it's him after looking a little closer.'

"I weighed about 118 pounds. It's pretty hard to visualize me at 118 pounds, since I now weigh 170. I looked like I was dead. I get awfully skinny when I get strung out. I had a twenty-eight-inch waist—Jesus, a man of my age.

"Then, Chuck gave me a little talk and says, 'Take him back over there and let him lay down and we'll see what happens.' I lay there a couple of days. Next night, they're having synanon meetings all over the area. When they called the synanons, they said, 'Come on, Charlie, let's go,' and I said, 'Oh, no, not me— I ain't going nowhere—fuck you.' I wouldn't go to a synanon—or anything.

"When I was laying there, I was mainly thinking of getting up and splitting. I was trying to get two or three guys to score for me, like, 'Go get me a bottle of terpin hydrate' [a narcotic cough medicine]. But no one would get me anything. It was awful. There was two broads there—Helen and Rosie. They took a personal interest in me. Those girls actually saved my life. Rose stayed up with me three days and nights. Gave me bed baths and wiped my puke up. I had a bad habit and just couldn't get up off the divan. I was sick as a dog.

"Each night, Chuck would come and shake hands with me. Every night, and he'd say, 'I'll say good-bye tonight, because you won't be here in the morning.' And in the morning, he would say, 'Well, goddamn—are you still here?' This presented some sort of a challenge, and I believe now it kept me there. Nothing else might have worked.

"This big, hairy, uncouth-looking individual with a hole in the side of his head was the main thing that kept me there. Him and the two girls babying me those three days or so. They stayed up with me and never let me alone for a moment. That combination did the impossible. Another thing that hit me was the sight of Harry, Johnny, and Jesse clean. This I refused to believe.

"Harry had a strange approach. I asked him repeatedly, 'What are you taking?' He'd say, 'Nothing, man, nothing. Absolutely nothing.' I'd say, 'Oh, don't bullshit me; I know you're taking something.' 'No, no,' he'd say, 'nothing's happening.'

"Harry told me, even when I was laying there kicking, 'Charlie,

I'm going to be real frank with you. This is the only place for a dope fiend. Believe me. I've been around here for almost five months, and I know it will work. I don't think it'll work for me, but I'd like for you to stick around, because Synanon needs people with a little age on them; guys like you with a long history of addiction.' He said, 'You'll go places in Synanon if you'll just stay here.' Can you imagine that? And me on the divan. Of course, Harry and I were old, old friends—we had lived together. He said, 'This is the place for you.' He said to me right then, 'This is where you belong—you can make it.' He told me this, and it seemed completely ridiculous to me.

"I couldn't imagine at that time that Synanon would ever get anyplace. They were trying to move us out of that old dump at Ocean Park every other day. They would come down one day and cut the electricity off for an hour, then the gas. Christ, they would of cut off the air if they could!

MY FIRST GIG

"I got up off that divan and got my first gig [job] about a week later. I had kicked a real boss habit. I was still alive and still there. Phil Hunt was the breakfast cook, and he had to go to the hospital for an operation. Phil told someone, 'Charlie Hamer will be the new breakfast cook.' When I heard about this, I said, 'No, man, I ain't going to be no breakfast cook. Don't know anything about being a cook and ain't got no eyes for learning how to be one— or anything else for that matter.' But anyhow, Phil said, 'Yeah, I know you can do it.' So he got me over to this old stove we had and showed me how to put hash brown potatoes on. (Incidentally, I was a pretty good cook, but I was denying it.) He showed me the little routines he had, and I got up and tried it the next morning. I did all right for a while.

"I began to notice in those days that some people were chippying [using a little dope]. Nothing important—some terps, pills, a joint [marijuana] once in a while. But for some reason, I stayed clear of it. When I use dope, I can't use a little.

"My dope habit would go like this. When I get in a position where there's a whole lot of dope and no hassle, here's what happens to me: I become completely demoralized. Demoralized in this particular way: When I've got no worry about hustling dope, I get to looking at myself. There's a fear in me that maybe I'm going to sit right there and destroy myself. Nobody loves me. I have nothing to do with anybody. I'm completely alienated from my family. And here I am sitting in a pad with a whole lot of dope. Then I get frightened. It's not the fear of running out of junk, 'cause it looks like there isn't going to be any end to the dope. The only word I can use is 'demoralized.' I'm the kind of guy that does not want just one fix. If I use, I need a lot of dope. If I was in the penitentiary and the guys in the cell next door [had a] fix and I'd be invited, I might refuse. . . . I'm not saying I didn't take a fix occasionally in prison, but I wouldn't give up five packs of cigarettes. Five packs of cigarettes is more important to me in the penitentiary than one fix. I don't like just a little dope, because afterwards I feel bad for days.

"So in Synanon, I stayed away from these few little chippying cliques. But don't get me wrong—I hadn't bought Synanon at that time. I figured I'm there for thirty days to kick my habit. I wanted to get my physical health back and be clean enough so that my habit won't cost half as much money when I get back to the streets. I had no thoughts of really sticking it out for more than thirty days.

WHY DID HE TRUST ME?

"The next big thing that happened to me was enormous to my way of thinking. At the time, there was very little money in the organization. Chuck came around and gave me the function of shopping. He gave me what little money they had to go shop for food! He asked me to go down and get $3 or $4 worth of groceries and get a meal together. He gave me the bankroll. He also gave me the key to the old icebox we used to have, where we kept the keys to the cigarettes (cigarettes and a little coffee were stored there). I couldn't accept it at first.

"Then I took this job where I have to go right past a drug-store. I got this $5 or $6 in my pocket that nobody will miss a buck from. Believe me, this was a goddamn challenge for me to get by that drugstore. I didn't have a yen after those ninety days. I wouldn't call it guilt that stopped me. I wanted to go in there and get a bottle of terps. I don't think I understood the meaning of the word 'guilt' at the moment. But somehow, I got by and I got those groceries and I got back and we got a meal together.

"I don't know why Chuck trusted me. Maybe he did this to me to test me. Maybe he looked at it like, 'Here's a real old-timer who finally got on his feet and looks halfway human.' Chuck works in strange ways. I never asked him about this. Maybe he did say to himself, 'Here's a guy that might have a little moral fiber, but in order to find out, I'm going to give him this $5 or $6—all we got—and see if he comes back with it.' That could have been it; I'm not sure. But whatever the reason, to me it was an important milestone. I gave it a lot of thought. Why did the man do it?

"After that I drifted along pretty good. I performed the kitchen job fairly well and I was more or less completely honest. I didn't take anything, outside of a couple of candy bars and a package of cigarettes. (These things would make me feel guilty now, but didn't bother me then.) Those were about the only infractions that I committed.

THE BIG COP-OUT

"About that time, something important happened in the club that affected us all. It was known as the big cop-out [revealing the truth].

"It kicked off like this. A guy by the name of Kenny, who was a close friend of Reid Kimball and me on the outside, was batting around the club and getting loaded. He took a little here and there. He disappeared one night, and Reid and I nailed him when he came in. He was loaded. This was around twelve o'clock midnight. We asked him where he'd been and said, 'Kenny, you're loaded.' He denied this. He wouldn't listen to reason and was going to split. He's in the midst of packing his clothes, and Reid and I are standing up there giving him a haircut [telling him off]. He's just packing his clothes and saying, 'I don't have to put up with this shit.' Now Kenny and Reid are real tight [good friends], so Reid says, 'Well, you crazy son-of-a-bitch, if you're going, I'm going with you!' And Kenny said, 'Well, you don't have to.' We just can't get him to cop. If he'll just cop, well, everything would have been all right, but he won't cop out. If he cops, we save his life was the way we were thinking.

" 'Jesus Christ—admit you're loaded and unpack your clothes and don't split!' 'No,' he says, 'I'm not loaded.' Again Reid started to go with him. Then Reid and I threatened to fight him. By that time, there are seven or eight people ganged around us, and somebody (I don't remember who) says, 'Well, Kenny, there's nothing wrong with admitting you're loaded. I got loaded the other day. I admit it.'

"That kicked off something. Now, Reid and I ain't copping to nothing yet. Then another guy says, 'Hell, yes, Kenny—I got loaded today.' Chuck's not there at this time, and Reid and I are standing there, hanging tough. Finally we got to the point where we said to Kenny, 'Well, yes, you dirty bastard, we're loaded half the time. Kenny, tell us you're loaded and forget about the whole thing.' He won't do it. Kenny said, 'You can snitch on yourselves if you want to.' Then finally, Reid says, 'You can call me a snitch if you want to, but dammit, I got loaded with you two days ago, and I'm going to tell it!' Then Kenny flipped and said, 'Boy, you dirty fink bastard. . . .' Then every goddamn person there admits to something—to get Kenny to cop. And he still won't do it.

"Finally someone woke up Chuck, and we got all the broads down from their rooms across the street. It turns out that everyone who's come in that room has got loaded since they'd been there. About half had some kind of a beef, and everybody copped out.

"Chuck wondered what in hell was going on in the middle of the night. We explained it to him. 'We're all copping to our sins. We're trying to save Kenny's life here, and he's still packing his clothes.' So then Chuck says, 'Everybody that's gotten loaded since they've been here, tell about it,' and everyone opened up. Everyone except Richie and Portie. Finally Richie cops. And Portie was still hanging tough. 'Not me,' she says. 'Well,' we say, 'you're going with Richie. You ain't going to deny you got loaded with him?' She was the last one to cop.

"Something strange happened from that time on. No one, except in a few rare incidents, used any more dope in Synanon. Something happened to me that night. After the cop-out, I went to Chuck with the keys and money. I told him, 'Here's the money and here's the keys.' And he says, 'What's that for?' I said I resigned. He says, 'Why?' 'Well, man, I can't be trusted with money. You just heard me cop out.' 'Well,' he said, 'what's that got to do with anything? Stick those keys back in your pocket and the money too.' That son-of-a-bitch Chuck just wouldn't give me the chance I wanted to split!

THE CIGARETTE BUTT

"Several months later something even more important happened. I became a director of Synanon. I don't remember how it came off exactly. There was John, Adaline, Chuck, and Dave—four directors, I guess. They called me in there and appointed me a director. It frightened me. 'Jesus,' I said to myself, 'am I capable of being a director?' I think I verbalized this to them. Chuck said, 'Well, you've been *acting* like a director, so now you're *officially* a director.' This did something to me.

"After I was made a director, I still had one foot out the door. But I remember, after everyone had congratulated me and called a general meeting to announce it, I really started thinking. I thought about it for two days and two nights. I even thought of splitting, I was so scared. I really hadn't planned to stay this long. I thought six months, at the most, and here it was getting on to nine months.

"Nothing too much came out of this self-examination. Later, something happened that may sound trivial, but was a very important factor in my decision to stay. Here I am, a director, and I'm still pretty undecided. Well, goddamn, I *am* a director! I've got to either go tell these people I want to resign or I've got to make up my mind to act like a director and do something about it.

"This is the incident. Four or five days after I was made a director, I'm walking down the hallway on the second floor, on my way to the toilet, and I see this cigarette butt on the floor. I reach down, pick up the butt, and put it in the butt can.

"I began to think, 'Here I am picking up butts off the floor! Maybe I finally joined the program? This must be some indication, because I never did anything like that before in my life.' Damn if this thought didn't hang me up for over an hour. I went **out** on the balcony and stood there and thought about it. From that moment on, so to speak, I was with the program. It meant to me, 'I'm going to stay here now. I'm not going to split.' I stayed awake all that night thinking it over. The next morning, I've got a clear look in my eye, and I went down and started sticking my nose in several things that I didn't know anything about, like other people's functions.

THE SHITS WERE TRYING TO KILL US

"A real important incident in Synanon's growth was our move from Ocean Park to Santa Monica. In a way, most of us didn't want to make the move; we were pretty scared. I had a traumatic experience when the move occurred. Everyone went down to take a look at the new building. I didn't go. I knew I was making it where I was, but I didn't know what would happen in the new place.

"I liked it in Ocean Park. I was secure there. We were use to starving. We got use to existing down there without much money. In the new place, we were going to pay $500 to $600 dollars a month rent. Everyone thought we couldn't make it down there; everyone except, of course, Chuck. 'We'll just go down there and fall on our ass. Why can't we stay here where we're pretty secure?' Anyway, we moved.

"There's no way of my describing the building when we first got there. There was grease an inch thick on everything. The grill in that kitchen had a thick coat of crud on it. It was an impossibility. We chipped at it with chipping hammers, like you do at sea, for two or three days. I got so goddamn upset about it that one night I refused to cook supper. I said I couldn't handle it, it was too much. We didn't even have any electricity that first night we were there. We were in the dark, with only candles.

"After a while, things began to straighten out. Except for some people in the community that were dead set against us, we began to roll. Our population began to grow, along with the method. Anyway, we moved, and Chuck was right. We were doing pretty good, even though the shits were trying to kill us." [4]

[4] Charlie Hamer has stayed "clean" in Synanon since 1959. He has been in charge of the young-adult group and for a time directed the Reno, Nevada, Synanon House. More than these direct works, because of his personal success, Charlie has served as a role model to many younger members of Synanon. If someone like Charlie could change, they too had hope.

2

The Community

That night, at Charlie Hamer's suggestion, I read an article written by Walker Winslow (author of *The Menninger Story*) for information on Synanon's zoning problem with the City of Santa Monica. Winslow had lived in Synanon and closely followed the organization's difficulties with the city. His observations, as published in *The Nation* (April 29, 1961), were most revealing:

> . . . The building [in Ocean Park] was condemned and Synanon had to find a new home. Then some members of a prominent theatrical club agreed to pay two years' rent on whatever quarters could be found.
>
> Jutting toward the Pacific Ocean, as a virtual prow for the City of Santa Monica, was an old, three-story beach club of Bedlam Gothic built during one of the booms. Chuck Dederich grabbed it. Just up the beach lived the quality folk of the film and TV world. Overnight, the lost souls who were "fighting their way back to normal society," to quote the *Santa Monica Evening Outlook*, had arrived. But Santa Monica's Chief of Police, Otto Faulkner, made a sudden and amazingly acute discovery. "We don't like the type of people it [Synanon] attracts here," he told the *Outlook*. "The place attracts felons and narco's." [Chief Faulkner admits, however, he has never had cause to arrest anyone from the Synanon House.]

6

A "Beach Front Property Owners Association" had been organized for the general welfare of the beach. The property owners trembled when they heard of this invasion by dangerous "felons." To startle the citizens further, Louise Randall Pierson, an *Outlook* columnist, got out her dictionary and edited the definition of "felony" to read: "usually of greater enormity [in crime], as treason, murder, rape, robbery, arson, etc."

Citizens who had been thoughtfully, and perhaps rightfully, alarmed by drug addicts became genuinely frightened; especially Brian Aherne, a large property holder, and the women, mostly wives of actors, directors, producers and the like. As the property owners circulated a petition for the removal of Synanon, the stories of its potential atrocities developed apace. Synanon has eighteen Negro members, but all petitioners deny that this had anything to do with the issue.

A City Council meeting was swiftly called. The wife of a movie star ran hysterically through the Synanon building, thus becoming an eyewitness.

"People were necking," she reported to the City Council. "It looked like a cocktail party." [1]

---

[1] Another version of this woman's "people-were-necking" story was reported to me by Reid Kimball at a later date: "Chuck gave a demonstration once of a person of such high principles, I still haven't figured it out. When we moved up here to Santa Monica, a group of citizens rushed out and got five zoning complaints against us to get us out of the neighborhood.

"Well about this time, a movie actor came down on a visit. He was a pretty open-minded kid and came down to see what Synanon was all about. He was a very pleasant guy and said that he would certainly wait and see. He took that kind of attitude. He was in Chuck's office for several hours with us, having coffee and yakking about Synanon. We were having a ball. Then his wife (the lady who reported the necking party), one of the leaders of the mob who stormed the City Council, came running into the building like a real nut. She was drunk. She ran through the place yelling and looking for her husband. She then burst unannounced into Chuck's office, where we were talking to her husband.

"Without a word, she smashed her husband in the face with her purse and broke some things on a table. Now, listen to this. She smashed him in the face—he really bled all over—and then went running out of the building like a maniac, screaming and insulting people. She ran out, did a couple of spins in her Jaguar in front of the building. It was real horrible. She was like a real beer-garden dame. Our kids didn't know what to say.

"Now, pick up on this—here's what's important—what a splendid opportunity we had. Here was Chuck, just hauled into court with this zoning-

Citizens broke into tears as they asked that Synanon be removed to protect their children, their homes, lives, and property values from addicts who had already been "menacing" the beach a mile south for over a year without causing alarm. City Attorney Robert Cockins, deeply moved, said, "I intend to file criminal complaints for violations of the Health and Safety Code, the Santa Monica Municipal Code, the Welfare and Institutions Code, and Santa Monica Ordinances."

The only thing the officials and the citizens hadn't reckoned with was that there is no one so contentious as former addicts when anyone challenges their right to cure themselves in their own way and in a place of their own choosing. Slumbering in Attorney Vincent Cavanagh, a former addict and a member of both Synanon and the California Bar in good standing, was the stealthiness of a righteous sidewinder. The battle was joined, as they say.

Both before and after moving from the old store-front building, Synanon has made marked changes for the better in its methods and procedures as a community of ex-drug addicts. This is borne out by the word of reliable observers and by its present status. Even the openly hostile Chief of Police stated to me on January 12, this year, that he had no doubt that "all seventy of the former drug addicts now connected with Synanon are clean" [free of drugs].

Aside from Narcotics Anonymous, which could not supply a live-in situation for addicts, there was no precedent for Synanon; it had to advance by trial and error. Dederich, when he

---

violation thing, and one of the hate mob's leaders comes down and makes that kind of a violent demonstration. She had really conked her husband. He was bleeding pretty bad. When he left, he apologized all over the place for his wife's behavior.

"Before this big City Council meeting, someone hipped Chuck that this kid was getting a big break playing Jesus Christ in a biblical story—you know, one of these big movies. Chuck called a general meeting. He got everyone in the club together and he said, 'Now, look—I don't want this incident to go out of this club. This is a nice kid, and he deserves a break. The fact that he has a crazy wife who hates us is one thing, but we're not going to ruin his career in order to make a few points at the City Council meeting.' . . . That night, of course, this woman slavered with the mob to drive us out of our home, while her jellyfish husband sat there looking ashamed."

moved his clan up among the "squares" whose society he was sure they were now fit for, ordered that new members would not leave the building unless escorted by older members. Good taste was enforced within and without the walls. The old building was repainted inside and outside and redecorated. Dormitories for the girls were arranged on the lower floor; those for the men two floors above. The living room, dining room and a legal office, rest room and kitchen were on the floor between. But since *sex* and *dope fiends* have emerged in press-fed folklore with a twinship more binding than *initiative* and *free enterprise*, the neuter second floor ceased to have any existence for rumor mongers.

In the meantime Dederich had developed seemingly workable methods for helping dope fiends abstain from dope. (1) Synanon House was a real home for people who were dedicated to staying off drugs and finding themselves; (2) at daily seminars, they whetted their appetite for learning; (3) in small, leaderless groups they met three evenings each week to "release hostilities" and expose and discuss dangerous thinking and tendencies as they saw them—in themselves and others at Synanon.

Dederich made no extravagant claims, but he wanted the addicts of Synanon House to pride themselves on the fact that they comprised the largest group of abstaining addicts living behind open doors anywhere on the planet. This seems to have been continually true.

Synanon took dope fiends as they came. It required that they kick their habit "cold turkey"—without drugs or medical help. Twenty-four-hour-a-day sympathy was available, as were massage, eggnogs and observation. Even after the organization acquired Bernard W. Casselman, M.D., as a family doctor, he treated the illnesses and injuries that might occur in any family and he did this without charge. Had an addict become dangerously ill during withdrawal, he would have been taken to the emergency hospital. The total stock of drugs at Synanon was some vitamins and aspirins. A visitor to Synanon might have thought it to be anything but a hospital.

And yet, on August 28, 1959, Synanon was cited with five misdemeanor counts of violations of codes having to do with operating a hospital: (1) operating an establishment for the care and treatment of the insane; (2) operating a hospital without a license; (3) treating an addict for addiction; (4) violating fire regulations pertaining to hospitals; (5) operating a hospital in an R-4 zone.

The members of the famous theatrical club withdrew their offer of rent for Synanon as soon as the charges were filed. More people from Synanon simply went out to work and made up the deficit.

The trial dragged along for two months. It took place in the Court of Municipal Judge Hector P. Baida. The proceedings were casual in the extreme. Sex was at once introduced, although it had no bearing on the matters at hand. When an objection was made, the judge said disarmingly, "It may not be pertinent, but it's interesting." After that he often remarked that where "women are living on one floor and men on another, something is bound to be going on."

. . . The judge was now remarking amiably, from time to time. "I know they [Synanon] are not operating a hospital and that the work they are doing is commendable, but something is wrong." As Dederich and the Synanon board members appeared in their own defense, he was overtly friendly. He also seemed pleased when State Hospital Inspector, Charles Feldman, testified that Synanon was not a hospital in any sense of the word.

In the middle of the trial, the Santa Monica City Council called another meeting to zone Synanon out of existence. But as member after member of Synanon got up, after the manner of Salvation Army "testifiers," and told his or her story, tears began to flow on both sides. Even the *Outlook* editorial writer was softened. The council decided against creating an ordinance against narcotic rehabilitation as had been planned, and decided to license Synanon as a boarding house for five dollars a year. For once, the City of Santa Monica and Synanon embraced and mingled their tears. The beach set was absent from this meeting.

As the trial drew to a close, the arguments for both sides having been heard, Judge Baida turned to Vince Cavanagh, the ex-addict who had taken over Synanon's defense, and asked, "What shall I do?"

"Find us not guilty on the basis of the evidence, of course, Your Honor," Cavanagh replied genially.

"There is something wrong somewhere," the judge said. "I have to find you guilty of something."

"In that case I'll appeal, Your Honor," said Cavanagh.

"Then what charge shall I find you guilty of?"

"Of the third count, if it pleases Your Honor," replied Cavanagh, deeming that the third count, that of illegally treating an addict, offered the best grounds for an appeal.

The judge thereupon found the defendants, Dederich and two Synanon board members, guilty of counts three and five, the latter having to do with a zoning ordinance that would enable the court to order vacation of the premises. Later, the defendants were sentenced to vacate the building by May 10, 1960.

At the time I arrived (September, 1961), Synanon was still fighting this complicated legal holding action. The City Council meeting at which I was asked to testify was another attempt at somehow "reaching" the city fathers in an effort to prevent Synanon from being evicted from its home.

Santa Monica Versus Synanon

The next evening, I returned to Synanon for the preliminary conference organized to present Synanon's position once more to the City Council. This was my first meeting with Chuck Dederich.[2]

Despite comments I had heard to the contrary, I was surprised

[2] Later I learned that Chuck had been born in Toledo, Ohio, in 1913; grew up in the Midwest; attended Notre Dame; for a time worked as a corporation executive for the Gulf Oil Company, and in his own words, "Roared up and down the countryside drunk, for over twenty years." Chuck defies description in capsule form. Over the long haul of this volume, his intellectual viewpoint and personality will be revealed in action. The story of Synanon provides the best description of Chuck Dederich.

to find that Chuck was a gentle person. He could become arrogant, even hostile, when the situation demanded. (At later events, I observed him throw his five feet ten inches and 240 pounds into an argument or to make a point.) However, at our first meeting I was taken aback by his quiet, even shy, manner.

Chuck ran the preliminary dinner meeting that evening. About a dozen prominent members of the community were on hand to testify on behalf of Synanon. Chuck made some preliminary comments to the group, prior to our trip to the Santa Monica City Hall Auditorium: "All we can hope to accomplish tonight is to give our viewpoint. This isn't really a fight. All we want is the right to live here in peace and do our work. This is really something that local citizens and the community ought to handle without Synanon. I don't plan to speak unless it seems necessary.

"The opposition, as usual, will be out in full force. I appreciate your taking the time to say a few words on behalf of Synanon. It might help get these people off our back so we can devote all of our energies to the job of cleaning up addicts and the neighborhood. That is our main business. Unfortunately, some people challenge our right to exist and we, of course, have to react. Fred here will quarterback the order of speakers. Thanks for your help."

(I was very impressed with Synanon's supporter, Fred Nicholas, a prominent Beverly Hills lawyer. Fred had volunteered to enter this legal arena for Synanon's right to exist. He later told me that his close appraisal of the legal situation revealed that the zoning case against Synanon was a real travesty of justice.)

Chuck and I went to the meeting in the same car. I told him of my interest in carrying out some research on Synanon. We agreed to get together when we both had more time.

Chuck saw the necessity of attending the City Council meeting as one that interfered with Synanon's real business. He said, "All we are trying to do is clean up some dope fiends. I hate like hell to have to get all dressed up to fight the nuts in the community trying to smash our organization. Some people really believe we thrive on conflict—that these problems help Synanon. This is sheer nonsense. We hate to waste our energy on this kind of thing, but we have to defend ourselves. At least until there is a large enough segment of the community organized on our behalf—to keep these people off our back."

Chuck continued to discuss Synanon's friends and enemies: "All of the supporters of Synanon have taken the time to come down and get acquainted with us and what we are trying to do. The nuts trying to kill us never put their foot in the door."

(At a later date, a Chamber of Commerce group opposed to Synanon actually put into the record of a meeting the statement that they had voted against visiting Synanon because they feared that a visit would prejudice their already decidedly negative opinion! No one from this group ever visited Synanon. The president of this same Chamber of Commerce later responded to a TV interviewer's question, "How can you be against an organization you've never seen firsthand?" by stating, "Do I have to visit Russia to know it's bad?")

THE TESTIMONY

The City Hall Auditorium bustled with an overflow group. Almost everyone there had come to hear testimony on both sides of the Synanon issue. From my point of view, it promised to be an exciting evening. I wanted to learn more about Synanon, and I tried to keep an open mind; although I had to admit that I was already somewhat pro-Synanon's basic right to exist. I felt that Synanon's civil rights were being violated.

The mayor called the meeting to order and announced that the first order of business would be to hear from citizens who wanted to testify on the "Synanon issue." Before allowing any testimony, the mayor talked at considerable length about the tolerant attitude the city had taken toward Synanon. In summary, he stated, "We aren't against Synanon, but they are illegally out of zone for operating a hospital and will simply have to move."

I had an excellent seat for watching the action, next to Chuck in the back of the room. Chuck educated and entertained me with his personal running commentary on the "realities" of the situation: "The zoning-regulation business is pure bull. The whole opposition boils down to a prejudice against Synanon's interracial living and the fact that we have ex-dope fiends and criminals living along their Gold Coast."

The first person to testify was Dr. Bernard Brandchaft, a U.C.L.A. psychiatrist. His main theme was an assertion that if he, as a medical man, knew of a situation where a formerly incurable disease, such as cancer, was being successfully treated, he would feel compelled to defend the right of the organization to continue its work. It was his opinion that Synanon was successfully treating the heretofore incurable disease of drug addiction, and he urged the city officials to allow the organization to continue its important work.

In a later statement before a California State Assembly Interim Committee on Criminal Procedure, he presented a similar argument on behalf of Synanon. His statement was published in the official report of the Committee:

My observations upon the operations of Synanon over the past 8 months have convinced me that there is something new, worthwhile and important in this experiment. I think that this is irrefutable from the evidence at hand. More than 70 confirmed and, in most cases, chronic addicts have been enabled for the first time to remain narcotic free voluntarily, for periods of time ranging from a few weeks to more than 2 years. Many of them no longer have to be supervised in any way and some are able to tolerate all of the stresses of ordinary community living without resorting to narcotics. Since the vast majority of these people have tried numerous ways of attaining these goals in the past without success, it is obvious that there must be something new to which they are able to respond.

That the experiment is worthwhile is also, I believe, evident from the facts. Here is a large group of addicts who are being reclaimed to useful citizenship and, in the process, are keeping themselves out of jail or hospitals, out of any antisocial or criminal activities, many for the first time in as much as 10 or 15 years. For similar purposes the government expends very large sums of money. For Synanon and its members, there is no government or public expenditure of any kind. I do not believe that it is necessary to contend that Synanon works for all addicts or that it permanently cures any addict to establish its value and to argue for its survival. . . . The operation of Synanon is based upon sound psychiatric principles in their essentials. . . .[3]

[3] *Report of Assembly Interim Committee on Criminal Procedure*, published by the California State Assembly, January, 1963, p. 100.

The next speaker for Synanon was the Reverend C. Mason Harvey, a minister of the First Presbyterian Church of Santa Monica. He delivered his statement with great personal feeling. His remarks were similar to the verbatim comments he made before the same State Assembly Interim Committee:

When I came here [to Santa Monica] two years ago I hadn't been here six months when I began to find that there were some young people, kids, I call them, who were experimenting with dope. And something else that bothered me was the thing that they called "sniffing the sock." That is, they dip a sock in this airplane glue and inhale it and this gives them their kicks.

I don't know and never have known very much about the dope problem and I became quite concerned within a few weeks after I was informed about this "sniffing the sock." There were two young people, one boy and one girl, both in their teens who told me that they were taking pills and that the girl had actually done some shooting. She had some heroin and she was very frightened and I asked her where she got it—and she got in the car and we drove up right across the street from ——— High School. This shocked me and she pointed out several other kids that she knew that were experimenting with this.

In my counselling I began to ask some of the young people who were more responsible and very active in my youth group if they knew anything about it. And I would suggest that at least one-fourth of them said they knew one person who was playing around with this. I had my ninth graders—at this particular time. About now, I had been here a year. I had a group of ninth graders that numbered between 65 and 75 and I asked one night at a meeting how many of them knew anybody that was sniffing the sock and over half of them raised their hands.

Then I heard about Synanon and I decided that I had better if I was, one, going to be responsible and, two, if I was going to have anything to say to these kids I should know something about the problem. I heard about Synanon and I came down here, and I must confess I came down with many fears. I am pretty naïve as far as dope addiction is concerned and my image of a dope addict, I suspect, is what the television and motion picture people imagine a dope addict to be.

I came down here not knowing what to expect but I certainly didn't expect to find what I found. This was over a year ago. Since that time I have had the people from Synanon come and speak with the junior high church school classes—if you want to call them that—in the evening meetings. I think I could safely say that when these addicts came and spoke to my young people, the response was electric. I don't believe, in all my experience with kids, I have ever seen the kind of response that these kids gave. The thing that was so effective, I think, was what one young kid said . . . "You know when you get up and you make the noises like a minister, we say, 'Sure, he's got to say this.' But to hear someone who's been there, and knows what they are talking about and who can make us realize how dangerous it is to become involved, this really got to me." They requested that they [the Synanon people] come and talk to other classes that we had.[4]

Reverend Harvey ended his statement with the announcement that, after considerable soul-searching, he had decided to move his wife and three children into residence at Synanon as a demonstration of their faith in the organization and its right to exist.

This caused quite a stir throughout the assembly. A woman, close by, apparently oblivious to the fact that Chuck was within hearing distance, proclaimed, "This is a disgusting exhibition— the mayor should stop this nonsense and get on with the business of clearing those degenerates from our neighborhood."

Chuck was accustomed to this type of comment. "This is exactly the insanity we keep running into," he said.

My name was called. I went to the bar in front of a platform where the mayor and six City Council members were seated. The rush of experiences I had encountered in Synanon over the past twenty-four hours crowded my thoughts. I tried to make three points: (1) that my experience in working with addicts over the past decade and the accumulated social science research knowledge revealed addiction to be an almost incurable social problem; (2) that a community of ex-addicts treating each other could pos-

4 *Ibid.*, p. 101.

sibly be a breakthrough in the entire approach to addiction and a variety of other social problems; (3) "Why don't you leave these people alone?"

The latter point was developed by the next speaker, Dr. Page Smith, U.C.L.A. history professor. He related his several personal visits to Synanon and how he had developed many positive impressions of the organization. Dr. Robert Wilson, a political scientist who had visited Synanon many times, followed Dr. Smith. He discussed the organization within the context of the civil rights problem. He cited the need for "constitutional protection" for all citizens, regardless of their past life. He felt, on the basis of the evidence, that Synanon was being treated unfairly.

Dr. Bernard Casselman, a physician who had donated his medical services to Synanon almost since its inception also spoke in a laudatory fashion about Synanon. He confirmed the fact that people with long addiction histories were staying "clean" in Synanon—most for the first time in their lives outside prison walls. He reported on the great personal gratification he received from being "Synanon's family doctor."

As "anchor man," lawyer Fred Nicholas spelled out the legal situation in detail. He concluded that the city had no proper legal ground for evicting Synanon.

Next came the opposition. Chuck had a biased viewpoint of them: "Wait until you hear the opposition. See that woman over there with the dead bird on her head?" I followed Chuck's gaze to a thin pinch-faced woman wearing a straw hat with an artificial bird on top. "At a recent meeting on Synanon, she got so angry at us, she threw some of our literature on the floor and jumped up and down on it. She is a member of the local John Birch Society. She is opposed to fluoridation, a local health program, Synanon, Chief Justice Warren, and mental health—especially her own."

The first opposition spokesman was a man I will call Bill Sheep, a tall, distinguished-appearing gentleman. He told how he had first heard about Synanon from his daughter. She had participated in a church youth group run by Reverend Harvey. He noticed her reading literature and various articles about Synanon at home and felt it was time to investigate the situation.[5]

"I found," he shouted at the mayor, "that my daughter was participating in a church youth program involving group counseling. I have evidence that this treatment emanates from a Communist-inspired approach known as group therapy. This brainwashing method encouraged these adolescents to freely discuss their personal life. I found that this group demanded that my daughter express what they called her 'true feelings' about her parents!

"When I learned about this 'program,' I pulled her out of this so-called youth group and began a further investigation of Synanon. First, men and women lived there together. There are Negroes and whites mixed, and they were all drug addicts and criminals!"

The next opposition speaker was a mother who feared for her children's safety on the beach. She claimed that since Synanon had come to Santa Monica, the beach was overrun by degenerates. "I'm a mother with four children," she said. "We cannot tolerate this kind of situation." She continued on this theme and became increasingly hysterical.[6]

---

[5] I later learned that Sheep had never visited Synanon. He was also, co-incidentally, the local John Birch Society leader in Santa Monica. His role in Santa Monica was emulated by a Dr. John DeTar, a John Birch Society leader in Reno, Nevada. DeTar published a twenty-page pamphlet, entitled "A Study of Synanon," that in part attempted to imply that Synanon was a leftist movement. The pamphlet sold for twenty-five cents in Reno at about the time that Synanon was being established in Nevada.

[6] This woman's testimony conflicted sharply with the views expressed before the California State Assembly Interim Committee by the owner and neighbor of the rented Synanon building, Ephraim Ralph. Mr. Ralph's testimony (p. 109 of the Committee's published report) was as follows:

"My name is Ephraim Ralph. I live at 1343 Ocean Front, Santa Monica, next door on the north side of the Synanon building. I am the owner of the Synanon building and I can honestly say that I had some qualms at first about renting to former drug addicts as narcotics users are commonly called. I inquired about them of former neighbors of Synanon when they were located on the oceanfront in Ocean Park. I was told that they were well behaved and honest in their dealings. I therefore decided to rent to them and my trust in them has not been misplaced. The people at Synanon have proved to be good neighbors in the full meaning of the word. They are well behaved, always willing to be of help and service. They take care of

Dederich told me that they had had no police incidents at Synanon. At the time, there were ten children of Synanon members, including Chuck's daughter, who lived at Synanon and used the beach in front of the building. The only problems they had were created by an occasional drunk who wandered into the area. "We would politely but firmly ask him to leave. On one occasion," he said, "we had to call the police regarding some noisy drunk neighbors."

The next speaker was a member of a "property owners' association" who feared that property values would drop. He had "nothing personal against Synanon." A member of the City Council asked the mayor for time to comment. The councilman revealed that he had checked on property values and incidents regarding Synanon and had found no evidence to support the negative allegations of bad behavior or a drop in property values. At this point, a disturbance occurred in the auditorium. A well-dressed blond woman in a mink coat rose, pointed a finger at the councilman, and shrieked, "You are on *their* side. I can't stand any more of this!" With this, she stalked out of the auditorium. (She later came up to me in the hall outside, reeking of alcohol, and started to dress me down for also being "on their side.")

The mayor gaveled the group back to order, and the parade of Synanon opposition continued. It was more of the same type of argument. A dominant mood was fear. A housewife testified that she hesitated to answer her doorbell; a mother feared for her children; a property owner feared land devaluation. In summary, the arguments presented against Synanon were: a fear of the corruption of the young people by drug addicts; a fear of the lowering of property values; and the fear of alleged sexual

---

their obligations. It has been stated by the detractors that they constitute a menace to the young people with whom they come in contact. What a ridiculous charge! I have an only child, a 13-year-old girl, and I can testify that Synanon has been no menace to her or to any other of the neighborhood children or young people when they come to the beach. In closing, I would like to remind you gentlemen of the ancient wise saying which goes as follows: 'Anyone who comes to purify himself should be given every encouragement and help.' I feel that those at Synanon are there to purify themselves and should be given encouragement and help by all people of good will."

immorality in Synanon. One opponent took the position that "Synanon may even by 'good,' but make them go do it some-where else." The meeting ended on this note, with the mayor assuring everyone that he would take all the testimony into ac-count in the City Council's future deliberations on Synanon.

Later, returning to Synanon in the car, Chuck gave me his reactions to the hearing: "This is the usual performance. On our side, we have the more logical, informed minds in the commu-nity—the lawyers, psychiatrists, sociologists, professional people. The opposition is usually a traveling band of haters. Just look at them and then listen to their stories. They are full of fear, hate, and ignorance about Synanon.

"Their main criticism is that we are running a hospital out of zone. How asinine! That is what is published and said; but I know as a fact, from personal interviews in my office, that the *sub rosa* issue is the fact that we have an integrated 'family' here in a segregated neighborhood. We have Negroes, whites, Mexicans, Jews, and Anglo-Saxons. We have all kinds of people, tall and short, black and white, and young and old, living to-gether. This seems to offend some people."

The City Council meeting, I later confirmed, was typical of a whole set of Synanon encounters with officialdom (for ex-ample, the Los Angeles County Zoning Commission, other zon-ing hearings, the State Board of Medical Examiners). The cast of characters, with some slight variations, was usually the same. Synanon would lead off with an array of distinguished professional and nonprofessional citizens who attested to the positive value of Synanon on the basis of their firsthand observations. Then the critics would appear, spewing hatred. In some cases, they would reveal the fears which generated their hostility.[7]

[7] In several cases of testimony that I later heard and witnessed, there appeared to be a projection of personal problems onto Synanon's situation. For example, at a Los Angeles County Zoning Commission hearing, a young man (who identified himself as a leader of an American Legion Chapter) testified: "I went down there for a Saturday night meeting. First they dis-cussed a concept. Then later a band began to play. Men and women began to dance together! The music was sensual, and I was disgusted by the ex-hibition." The young man began to shriek about "sexy dancing." He became visibly hysterical, to the point where he was gaveled down by the chairman of the Zoning Commission and asked to leave the hall.

THAT EVENING AT SYNANON

When we arrived back at Synanon House, there was considerable activity. The people who had been at the hearing were greeted like conquering heroes. The main question asked was, "Did we have a chance to present Synanon's point of view?"

Many close friends of Synanon had attended the meeting and returned to the club. There were about forty "squares," in addition to the speakers, and about a dozen Synanon people. (There were more supporters in the group of four hundred at the auditorium, but the people who returned to the club were Synanon's closest friends from the community.)

Food was served and the house was buzzing with ". . . then he said . . ." and ". . . this drunken woman stormed out of the room . . ." and ". . . Sheep was there with his hate group. . . ."

The *esprit de corps* in the group reached me. In a conversation with Jeanne, a Synanon member who had attended the hearing, I asked her opinion of the scene.

"Well it was fairly typical," she said. "The usual 'hate-Synanon group' was there in full force. I just wish they would understand what we're trying to do. I agreed with that vicious housewife on one point she made, though."

"What was that?" I asked her.

"I don't want to live with junkies or degenerates either!"

Monica, who was nearby, joined our discussion. She asked me, as an outsider, why these people were so set on destroying Synanon. She told me how she had tried Lexington (twice) and other cures, and nothing had worked for her. "Here we have something that finally works for addicts and they won't let us live."

Of course, I had no answer to her questions. As we talked further, she began to tell me something of her past. Her painful life as an addict had run the gamut of jails, prisons, and an attempted suicide. Her response to one question I asked stopped me cold. I asked her, "Where would you be at this moment, if there never was a Synanon?"

Without any hesitation she said, "Dead."

Her definite reply shook me. If what she said was true, and I had no reason to doubt her, it logically followed that Synanon's existence was a life-or-death issue for many people. If Sheep, the fearful mothers, bureaucracy, and the officials of Santa Monica succeeded in their efforts to destroy Synanon, they could literally kill people like Charlie Hamer and Monica.

Monica's Story

These first encounters with Synanon motivated me to devote my energy to understanding and revealing the Synanon story. Certainly, Monica's life experience was part of this story. That night, and on other occasions (with the aid of a tape recorder and note-taking), I compiled part of Monica's drug-addiction past and her later Synanon experience.

Monica had the textbook brand of problem family: a mother and father who were excessive drinkers, continually fighting and separating. Their destructive parental approach drove her out of the house into a search for the thrills and kicks that she mistakenly believed could assuage her emotional tensions.

"They were never there when I needed them," she said. "They would just go away and leave me. I remember being alone most of the time, as a child. They would always lie, on top of it, and this made it worse. They said they would be right back, and then they would go away, sometimes for a day or more.

"I still don't know how to explain it, but I began running away from home at the age of two. When I was three, I ran away so much they made a chicken-wire fence and put me in this cage. I burrowed under it and ran away again. I remember a cop brought me back on his shoulders.

"When my parents did take me anywhere, it would be to a bar. I remember how the drunks would call me cute. Sometimes, they would put me to sleep in one of the booths in a bar while they got drunk.

"I was bad and rebellious from the first grade on. I wouldn't behave, and my parents were always being called to school. They seldom came, because they were always out either working or drinking. I don't blame them now; they were like children themselves, always arguing and fighting with each other. (In spite of this I always remember that they were basically kind.)

"During my early teens, my mother and father separated several times. I seldom saw either of them, since both were dating and drinking. I lived with my mother some of the time and then with my father. I didn't have a home, since we were always moving around. I changed schools several times a year, and I never really got going in any school. It seemed that just when I would begin to get interested in a school, we would move. I began to play hooky most of the time.

"At fourteen, everything seemed to happen to me at once. It was really a weird year in my life. I began dating older men; going to bars, nightclubs, and jazz joints. That year, I began drinking, smoking pot, and taking pills. I had my hair dyed red, black, and finally silver-blond. I had few problems in getting almost any man I wanted. But I still felt all alone. One day when I was home alone, I slashed my wrists. I didn't cut myself too deep. Just enough, I guess, to get some attention. But it didn't work—my parents were still not there for me, nor was anyone else.

"The year I was fourteen, I also got involved in another ridiculous scene. I ran away [from Los Angeles] to San Francisco. I had taken tap- and toe-dancing lessons on and off since I was five, and thought I could easily get a job dancing. After finding a room, I put my tap- and toe-dancing shoes in a bag and set out to find a nightclub. Never having been to San Francisco, I asked someone where I could find a nice nightclub. I was directed to the International Settlement, to a club called the Barbary Coast (unbeknownst to me, a strip joint). I saw the manager and asked him if he could use a good toe or tap dancer. He replied, 'No kid, but can ya take it off?'

"He nodded toward a girl on stage who was doing the bumps and grinds. I had never tried this kind of dancing before, but I was running low on money, so I told him, 'Sure.' 'Okay,' he said, 'you start tomorrow night.'

"For the rest of the night, I sat and watched every move the strippers made, until I was sure that I could do the dance. The next night, in a borrowed costume and wearing gobs of makeup, I danced through the motions of having sex—a virgin. I couldn't bring myself to remove every article of stripper's costume as they expected (down to the G-string). After two weeks of stalling and saying I'd do it when I was used to it, I was fired.

"When I returned home, I was taken into custody by the juvenile authorities. This woman cop who looked like a bulldagger [Lesbian] came right into my class, put handcuffs on me, and took me to the lockup. I'll never forget that humiliating experience as long as I live.

"I was miserable in Juvenile Hall. That's where I received my basic training. There I was told about heroin, sex, and things I had never heard of, and all in a very glamorous light.

"After I was released from Juvenile Hall, I continued going around with the same crowd. We were different, we were hip. We had our own language, our own way of dressing, and what we thought was our own music—jazz and lots of it. Sundays were spent smoking weed [marijuana] and then making it to a club for an afternoon session of jazz and coasting.

"I always had the idea I wanted to lead a glamorous life. Maybe become a movie star. I thought I was on the right path. Inside I always felt twisted and unsure, but outside I always managed to look good. I always played a role and kept an image. I became known as 'Countess.'

"At sixteen I was turned on to heroin. I knew nothing of getting hooked or the sickness and degradation that goes along with being addicted. I just knew that other people in my clique were fixing [using drugs] and that it was supposedly the hippest kick to be on.

"In my early addictive period, I still looked good. I began working in Hollywood for a photographer, posing in bikinis and sheer nighties. I made a fair amount of money posing, and I blew most of it on clothes, hairdos, and heroin.

"Shortly after I started using heroin my mother caught me with my outfit—my spike [hypodermic needle], my spoon, my eyedropper—the whole thing. She called the police and turned me in! Right or wrong, I hated her for what she did.

"I was finally sent away to a great finishing school—the Ventura School for Girls. In the reformatory, I learned about everything I hadn't learned about on the streets. My 'Countess' handle stuck with me. I ran with the hippest and the toughest girls in the place. Once I got a weekend leave, scored in Los Angeles, ran drugs back into the place, and fixed with my girl friends.

"When I left Ventura, in no time flat I was back using [drugs]. That's when I met Bill. He was known around our group as an important pusher. I thought I was in love and latched onto him. We lived together for several years, using all the time. He kept me like a baby at first. I wore sheer nighties most of the time and just laid around up in the pad. I would deal drugs for him if any customers showed up when he was out. He kept me well supplied with drugs.

"Our wedding, as I look back on it, was really absurd. One day, after we had lived together a while, Bill said, 'We're going to get married.' I thought I loved him and that this was a swinging idea. We got some of our junkie friends together and went to this Church of the Mind—or some name like that. Before the wedding ceremony, I thought it was strange—but I was glad to join in—when everyone cooked up and fixed. I was shocked but thought it was wild when I saw the 'minister' (whom I later found out was a junkie) fix with us.

"Looking back, that episode isn't too strange, when I think of other experiences I had in my marriage. Sometimes I used to go across the border to Mexico with my husband, where he would buy dope to sell. I was his helpmate in his business. We'd go once a month or so and bring back two or three pieces [ounces of heroin]. I would keep some of it in my box [vagina]. In fact, that's how we always smuggled it across the border. One time, after we had just returned from a border run, my old man wanted to go peddle some of the stuff. I, of course, wanted to go with him. I had silver-blond hair at the time, and he said I couldn't go because I'd be too conspicuous. Anyway, I insisted on going along and refused to give him the stuff out of my box unless he'd take me. I remember I had on brand-new capri pants. He began to tear them off me and said he'd get the stuff if I wouldn't give it to him. I finally gave it up but managed to hide the car keys on him. I don't exactly remember how it turned out. I don't think he left me, but it was sure an insane scene.

"Another time, I had threatened to leave my husband, and he locked me in a hotel room, in downtown Los Angeles, so I couldn't get out. He took my shoes away from me and told me he'd be back shortly. I tied some sheets together and crawled over the transom. I vaguely remember walking around downtown in my bare feet, looking for my connection to score. These were only some of the episodes in the 'happy marriage' of a dope-fiend couple.

"As bad as things were with him, they were worse without him. One time, I decided to go to Lexington and try to kick. After a few weeks there, I decided it wasn't for me and split.

"On my way back to L.A., I got involved with some dope fiends in Chicago. I don't remember the incident clearly. All I know is that I almost died several times in Chicago. At first, I scored with these people and got an overdose of drugs. I don't remember it all, except I fixed and passed out. The next thing I remember was waking up in this Chicago hospital with a tube in my throat. I was being fed intravenously with wires and oxygen tanks and things. They had to open my throat to restore breathing with a tracheotomy.

"As if this wasn't enough, tube in my throat and all, I ran away from the hospital for a day and scored. I fixed and went back to the hospital. The doctor told me by all rights I should be dead, and then they strapped me to the bed to prevent my running away again.

"Somehow, I got back to L.A. and my husband. He was still in action, and I, of course, went right back to using. Then a real bad scene happened.

"Some broad set us up. We had just come back from a big border run. We hadn't even cut the stuff. The next thing I knew, the heat [police] came in with their guns drawn. My old man's partner Ed and his girl were in the bedroom asleep. I screamed, 'Ed, it's the heat!' But it was too late. The man [policeman] was already headed toward the bedroom. The stuff was in the drawer, and the cop got to it. He asked, 'Who owns it?' I claimed it was mine, to protect my husband. I was on Youth Authority parole and figured I wouldn't get as much time as the others. They were all over twenty-one.

"A few minutes later, they brought in my husband. He was handcuffed and bleeding from the temple, where he had been grazed by a bullet. (I later found out he tried to split, and they shot to stop him.) My husband said the stuff was his, and we argued over it in front of the heat. He told me to shut up, since they already had him on a sale. At the trial, I was cut loose and he was sent to the state prison with a five-to-life sentence.

"I was now really all alone, and I had to support my habit completely on my own. I began to earn money the only way I knew how. I was still attractive and had clothes. I began to develop a call-girl book, with the help of an older established Hollywood call girl. At first, I had good $50 and $100 tricks. Mostly they were older men in the garment industry. But I was a bad whore. I only earned enough money to keep up my habit. I would miss lots of appointments. I hated what I had to do and could only turn a trick if I was heavily loaded. I always fixed before I turned a trick.

"Because I was unreliable, my business began to fall off. I began to get skinny and badly strung out. Without going into the sordid details, I wound up in downtown Los Angeles as a common street hype [addict], doing what I had to. For about a year, I made this horrible scene. It was like a nightmare. I would turn a trick, score, fix, and nod.

"I was all alone. I never tied up with any other person. I sometimes just walked the streets for hours all alone at night. I got busted [arrested] a few times and did some small jail bits. They never really pinned me. Finally I was sent to the Terminal Island Prison for a year.

"When I got out of there, I naturally went back to the streets. It was the only life I knew. I was desperately trying to quit. One day I heard about Synanon from a connection. Somehow I got down there, and that was it. I've been clean since 1959 because of Synanon. The main thing I was given there was a new direction.

"Down deep somewhere, I guess I always wanted to do something better for myself. I'm now tremendously happy. I'm married to a wonderful man who knows all about my past and understands me. I have a lovely child, a real home for the first time, and my life is strangely beautiful."

3

Origins

Synanon began within Charles E. Dederich. It seems that Chuck was able to plunge into the development of a new approach to life as completely as he did because of his lack of commitment to any specific system of ideas, yet a limited belief in many. His involvements with philosophy had included the study of Freud, Thoreau, Lao-tse, Buddha, St. Thomas, Catholicism, Plato, and Emerson. At the time that Synanon was founded, Chuck was a man with no firm position, searching for a meaning to his own life.

He had been an alcoholic on and off for twenty years and had been through a variety of jobs and wives. Alcoholics Anonymous had accomplished its mission of symptom removal; however, Chuck's restless urge continued. His life lacked completion and was generally self-defeating. When he felt that he could win or succeed in another man's land, he would smash the track he was on and begin anew. This happened to him when he quit college as a sophomore at Notre Dame; as a junior executive in the Gulf Oil Company; and later as an employee of Douglas Aircraft in California. Immediately before founding Synanon, Chuck had been a devotee of A.A., and although it helped him quit drinking, he found it limiting. In retrospect, it seems that any approach not *completely* developed by Chuck himself was too binding for his roaring ego needs. The development of Synanon confirms this speculation. Chuck appears to need an "empire" based on his own ideas, and Synanon has fulfilled this prescription.

Origin 1—January 1958

Chuck's financial situation, when he began what became Synanon, was rock bottom: "I had no job, two cents in my pocket, and was living off unemployment benefits, in a small apartment near the beach in Ocean Park, California. With some friends from A.A., I had set up a Wednesday night 'free-association' discussion group. The group was set up to explore 'a line of no line.' The meetings were loud and boisterous. Attack of one another was a keynote of the sessions, with everyone joining in. I could detect considerable lying and self-deception in the group. I began to attack viciously—partly out of my own irritations and at times to defend myself. The group would join in, and we would let the air out of pompously inflated egos, including my own. The sessions soon became the high point in everybody's week."

At first, the group meetings had a rotating moderator. Chuck's bellow and his apparent analytic ability projected him after several meetings into the permanent-leader role. The group sensed that he could attack and defend better than anyone in the group. The group process seemed to carve the attacked person down to a sense of reality, and this was felt to be therapeutically beneficial. Chuck said, "Because most of the people had some psychoanalytic orientation, the early sessions were focused around sexual problems. Some of the group had analytic couch work. Our language was psychoanalytic, and there was much ten-year-old-kid talk. It was loud, dirty, and wild."

Chuck noted some positive changes in people in the group. It seemed to him that these resulted more from the intense verbal attacks than from the analytic approach. "As a result of these vicious haircuts, people seemed to grow before my eyes."

Origin 2—March 1958

The meetings were held once a week. The disaffiliated group of about seven men and six women increasingly looked to Chuck for leadership. With their growth, he grew. His attacks were at first disorganized and "almost exclusively from the gut." He began increasingly to measure them for positive therapeutic effect. With his own growth and greater feeling of personal security, Chuck felt that he was developing a new method of therapy. He became further involved in building an organization or structure for administering the therapy. The organization produced several more clean addicts, and this further reinforced Chuck's belief in the verbal-attack method.

In May, two female addicts, fresh from jail, appeared at the front door of Chuck's small apartment, which became known as the "clubhouse." They asked for help. With no direction or place to go, they became part of the movement. The girls moved into apartments close by, as did others who became attracted to the growing organization. This was the beginning of a female wing of Synanon.

The financial operation continued to rely heavily on Dederich's $33 unemployment checks. About this time, several older A.A. people on pensions and others in the group began to provide funds for a collective type of food and rent arrangement.

One of the group was an older woman. She served as a mother surrogate for many early members. She gave money, cooked meals, and generally counseled new members. Her past psychoanalysis experience was part of her approach. Although the organization was essentially a patriarchy, with Dederich at the top, this hard-working woman was important to the early Synanon situation.

The first addict was brought into the group by Grey, an A.A. member and friend of Dederich. "Grey brought Whitey into my little bit of a room," Chuck went on. "It had a slide-out bed. When you pulled out the double slide-out bed with the couch and one big chair, the room was full. Grey brought him in this night, and he turned me on. He said, 'I want you to meet an old friend of mine—Whitey. We know each other since boyhood and blah, blah, blah. Let's try to straighten him out. I want you to talk to him.'

"I gave Whitey a real verbal blast. He went into a bona fide positive father transference that night. I actually didn't think of him as anything frightening or glamorous. I didn't connect him with any of the myths of the addict. I looked at him as I did the others: as a person with problems."

Origin 3—July 1958

Around this time, there were about twenty people living in various apartments close to the hub of Chuck's personality and apartment clubhouse. He had crystallized in the thoughts of most of the people as a wise father figure. His developing inner strength appeared to be the cohesive force that held the cluster of general misfits and alienated men and women together. At that time, the direction of the "movement" was not clear, not even to Chuck. He was, however, very conscious of several more addicts who had cut down on drugs and of some who were "making noises in that direction."

A store-front building was rented about this time, and this was used as a larger clubhouse. Chuck still lived in his small apartment, but went to work at the "club" each day. It was his job. The group of "ex-addicts and ex-alcoholics" met regularly in the clubhouse. Most of them were ex-alcoholics.

Chuck said, "They were all kind of mixed up, and everybody was relating pretty well, although there was a subliminal conflict. Addicts think alcoholics are squares, and alcoholics think about addicts like squares think about addicts. I would say it was around that time, in July, that I knew it was possible to clean up a dope fiend. I knew that Whitey had been clean maybe for about four months. It was made possible by the emotional talks and, secondarily, by screaming in catharsis-type synanons. Some of these guys and gals were staying more clean than not, and it was happening in a free environment."

Origin 4—August 1958

Being a businessman, Chuck incorporated the club. An organized structure and "set of motions" for "staying clean" began to evolve. Group sessions were held regularly on Mondays, Wednesdays, and Fridays. In addition, there were readings from Emerson, Thoreau, and Freud, combined with intellectual seminars. "Sometimes we had all-night 'philosophical and psychological' discussions," Chuck said.

At this time, the first "incorrigible addict," Jesse, moved into the building. When Jesse moved in, he had a vague desire to quit using drugs and to get his parole officer's approval. Chuck said, "He was a big-time loser, with a lengthy addiction and prison record. Jesse had a criminal jacket [label] of complete incorrigibility. He had just been released from prison. His parole officer got him a job, and Jesse was working about ten hours a day and going home to sit in front of a television set, trying to stay clean. He was in terrible shape not using drugs. He came down to the club one night, and I told him about our club. He came back the following night or maybe two nights later. We laid it on the line. We said, 'You have to quit your job and have to come down here and move in.' This was the first addict with whom we pulled this stunt. Jesse went back and thought about it and moved in the next day."

After Jesse had been in Synanon thirteen months, his own "story" was reported in the Santa Monica *Independent* (June 19, 1959):

I was a gutter hype. I have known guys who could fix two or three times a day and be content. Unfortunately for me, I couldn't. I was greedy. I was sicker; my need was greater. I don't know for sure but I managed to spent around $100 a day for dope and I had to steal the money to buy it.

I wasn't a big-time gangster-type guy who made his money in lump sums; I was a scared, cautious, short con, petty-thieving dope fiend and my money was mostly acquired in dribbles or small amounts.

A typical day in my life started in the morning when, with tears in my eyes, sniffles in my nose and sweat oozing from my pores, I'd make it to my stash and put my "get-up" in my veins [take a fix]. When I leave the pad I know I am on my way to commit a crime to get some money. Most of the time I don't have the slightest idea what type of crime it will be or where. Sometime within the next two or three hours I would commit a crime, get some money, buy some dope, get "fixed" and get on the move again and repeat this all over and over through the day.

Recreation and pleasures, big or small, are luxuries I could not afford because all my money is set for the "connection man" and there doesn't seem to be enough hours in a 24-hour day.

I used narcotics about 16 years and I spent about 10½ of the 16 years locked up in jails and other kinds of institutions.

Before I came to Synanon I had given up on myself. I had tried almost everything in the way of therapy and nothing worked. I had private consultation with a psychiatrist, group therapy with a psychologist and sociologist, and until the day I walked into Synanon the longest period of time I was "clean" on the streets was 60 hours.

I have been here at Synanon 13 months and I have been "clean" since the day I arrived. Staying clean is a necessary part of the therapy here at Synanon, but the complete picture is much broader and deeper. I have gained insights into my personality that it would be impossible to put a price tag on.

I am learning to accept myself, I am learning to love and understand other people, I am learning to be honest and truthful. If you can picture yourself buried alive for 16 years in a deep, dark, slimy pit with no way out and, after resigning yourself to your fate, suddenly see a little daylight where before there was none, then you know how I feel about Synanon.

(Jesse has been "clean" since 1958 and has been working steadily since 1960 as a salesman in an electrical appliance store.)

Jesse was the first voluntary "formal commitment" to Synanon, and his parole officer was the first professional contact. After that, many parole officers came down, and Chuck felt that he now had a position in the world: "I knew I had a career for myself. I was tremendously stimulated. I never had a job that really satisfied me. Even though I had once been a young man in a big oil company for ten years and I had promoted two corporations, that work didn't do it for me. I got them going and then drank myself out of them. I made and lost money in my life, but never at any time had a career mapped out for me that I could see myself doing for five years in a row. With Synanon in motion, I was no longer concerned with what I was going to do with the rest of my life. I now had a career."

Jesse was the first successful "cleaned-up dope fiend" produced by Synanon. He was an important and highly useful symbol, because he was the first one to enter with the avowed purpose of cleaning up and because he succeeded. Others hovered around but were not too sure of what they wanted. Jesse was the first role model for others to emulate. He had an important effect on Charlie Hamer's staying "clean." As Charlie told me, "I knew him in jail and on the streets. He was a boss hope-to-die dope fiend. I thought that if Synanon worked for him, maybe it would do the same for me."

Origin 5—September 1958

With an influx of drug addicts and with Dederich leaning in their direction, a battle welled up between the addicts and some of the members of A.A. "The break with Alcoholics Anonymous occurred about the middle of August," Chuck said. "It happened right in the middle of an A.A. meeting. Our whole gang had taken over the Saturday-night meeting of the Santa Monica A.A. group at Twenty-sixth and Broadway and built it up from its attendance of ten people to an attendance of about forty-five or fifty. There was some objection on some issue by the members of the Board of Directors of the A.A. club. I recall the leader stopping the meeting. They didn't like us. The alkies didn't like the addicts, and they didn't like me in particular, because, among other things, I had been through an L.S.D. experience. I had committed the unpardonable sin—I had taken a drug. In fact, I had even participated in an alcohol experiment up at U.C.L.A. So they didn't like me up there, and they didn't like my gang because they were mostly addicts. They made things difficult for us. I remember getting up in the meeting and saying, 'All right, let's go home— the hell with this.' So the whole meeting got up, and we all got into our automobiles and came down to the club, and we never went back to A.A. again.

"We were building something new and different. Although I will always be grateful to A.A. for helping me personally, Synanon has nothing to do with A.A., any more than a rowboat compares with an airplane. We have a live-in situation, with family characteristics. We emphasize self-reliance rather than dependence on a higher being."

The complete break with A.A. threw all Dederich's weight and energy into Synanon, on the side of the addicts: "After incorporating, and the break with A.A., I began to lay down the law. We were a California corporation, and we had to be law-abiding. The very fact of our existence as a corporation said it was doing something. We assumed a responsibility; we had to get up the rent, we had to feed the people when they came in, and so on. This was the point at which the few alcoholics in the club began to fall out. They didn't want any responsibility. They were afraid of it. In fact, it was even verbalized. 'We don't want to do this; we want to have a lot of fun; we want to have a club as a club.' The alkies began to say, 'Well, it's our club; it's my club,' and I said, 'No, it's my club.' I became the champion of the addicts, chucked the alcoholics out, and Synanon was then fully launched for addicts."

Origin 6—October 1958

About this time, Chuck began to pull together the loose ends. With incorporation, and several clean role models like Jesse Pratt for assistants, Synanon entered the public domain. Publicity, good and bad, true and untrue, began to propel the organization into recognition by the outer world. Chuck said, "Paul Coates picked up on us. He printed the first publicity in his column. We went

on the Paul Coates show as a sensational thing. Some of the girls
were blindfolded, given bongo drums, and all that kind of mishmash. The Paul Coates program man actually wrote the drums
into the Synanon show. We had never seen a bongo drum before
we went down there, but we used them on the show. This introduced bongo drums into Synanon. We then got hold of some
and began to play them every night, until the neighbors began
to complain."

Some professionals became interested in Synanon, and they
invited Chuck to talk to a group of Southern California parole
officers. For this event, he wrote a speech that could be considered
"Synanon's Manifesto" (the principles incorporated in this original statement are the backbone of the current larger, more stream-
lined Synanon organization):

The Synanon Foundation is a non-profit corporation which
has emerged as part of an overall phenomenon which is taking
place on the beach at Ocean Park, California. At this time it
appears that an environment has been created which seems to
have a beneficial effect on some narcotic addicts.

We have here a climate consisting of a family structure
similar in some areas to a primitive tribal structure, which
seems to affect individuals on a sub-conscious level. The structure also contains overtones of a 19th century family set-up
of the type which produced inner-directed personalities. It is
the feeling of the Synanon Foundation that an undetermined
percentage of narcotic addicts are potentially inner-directed
people, as differentiated from tradition-directed or other-directed
people.

A more or less autocratic family structure appears to be
necessary as a pre-conditioning environment to buy some time
for the recovering addict. This time is then used to administer
doses of an inner-directed philosophy such as that outlined in
Ralph Waldo Emerson's essay entitled "Self Reliance." If it
seems paradoxical that an authoritative environment tends to
produce inner-direction, it must be remembered that the inner-
directed men of the 19th century, viz., Emerson, Thoreau,
Oliver Wendell Holmes, Longfellow, were products of an authoritative family structure. It might also be remembered that

intellectual, emotional, and spiritual food fed to the recovering addicts while in the climate is rather carefully selected, as cited above.

The autocratic overtone of the family structure demands that the patients or members of the family perform tasks as part of the group. If a member is able to take direction in small tasks such as helping in the preparation of meals, house-cleaning, etc., regardless of his rebellion at being "told what to do," his activity seems to provide exercise of emotions of giving or creating which have lain dormant. As these emotional muscles strengthen, it seems that the resistance to cooperating with the group tends to dissipate. During this time a concerted effort is made by the significant figures of the family structure to implant spiritual concepts and values which will result in self-reliance. Members are urged to read from the classics and from the great teachers of mankind—Jesus, Lao-tse, Buddha, etc. These efforts have been successful to a rather surprising degree. The concept of an open mind is part of a program to help the addict find himself without the use of drugs.

Another device which has seemed to produce beneficial results is the "synanon." The synanon can be defined broadly as a kind or type of group psychotherapy. Synanon, which is a coined word, is used to describe a more or less informal meeting, which ideally consists of three male patients and three female patients plus one Synanist who is himself an addictive personality, but who has managed to arrest the symptoms of his addiction for some considerable length of time, or seems to be progressing at a rate somewhat faster than his colleagues in the meeting. The Synanist acts as moderator and, by virtue of an empathy which seems to exist between addictive personalities, is able to detect the patient's conscious or unconscious attempts to evade the truth about himself. The methods employed by a Synanist in a synanon meeting may include devices or weapons which appear to be unorthodox, but such surprisingly beneficial results have occurred in an encouraging number of cases that we feel we must further explore the method.

The Synanist leans heavily on his own insight into his own problems of personality in trying to help the patients to find themselves, and will use the weapons of ridicule, cross-examination, hostile attack, as it becomes necessary. These synanon sessions seem to provide an emotional catharsis and seem to trigger an atmosphere of truth-seeking which is reflected in the social life of the family structure. The Synanist does not try to convey to the patient that he himself is a stable personality. In fact, it may very well be the destructive drives of the recovered or recovering addictive personality embodied in a Synanist which make him a good therapeutic tool—fighting fire with fire.

The sharing of emotional experience in synanon sessions seems to encourage in the family structure a tolerance and permissiveness within rather loosely defined limits in which the addict who wants to recover feels sufficiently comfortable to stay and buy himself time. This permissiveness, of course, does not include the taking of any form of addictive substance. It is stressed, for instance, to everyone that no addictive personality can take anything which will have an effect on his mind. The ingestion of alcohol, opiates, barbiturates, tranquillizers, psychic energizers is strictly forbidden. Permissiveness in the area of verbal resistance or rebellion to authority is rather encouraged than discouraged. The insistence is on performance. For example, if it is suggested that one of the boys or girls help in the kitchen, he is free to "gripe," "beef," as loudly as he wishes, but it is required that he comply in the area of action. It has been observed that the verbal rebellion towards authority seems to relieve inner tension, and that compliance in the action area seems to exercise the "muscles of giving."

Another device which in the opinion of the foundation has been successful, and which is paradoxical in the extreme, is the "haircut." The "haircut" is a session which is attended by relatively new patients and four or five of the significant figures of the family structure, during which the patient is . . . "taken apart" and his performance to date, both constructive and destructive, is pointed out to him, together with suggestions for his future behavior. These sessions may even contain tones of the "third degree" and may become quite brutal, on a verbal level, of course. Surprisingly, the patient's reaction has been almost 100 percent favorable. As one of our members put it, "When the word gets around that 'haircuts' are being given, people seem to get in line."

It might be that this device awakens in the subconscious of the patient a realization that someone cares about him. It may satisfy a desire to be the center of attention. It may help to make him realize that a loving father must also be a firm father. Many of the people who have experienced these "haircuts" reported a change in attitude or a shift in direction almost immediately. There is, of course, no policy as to timing, and many times a "haircut" session will be in no way critical. They seem to be guided only by intuition.

We feel that it should be pointed out at this time that the growth of this group on the beach has taken place under conditions having much to be desired in the area of tangibles. The movement has been in no way self-supporting, but has been financed by individuals interested in the problem of addiction. It has not been possible for us to induce an ideal environment in our living room for various reasons. For instance, we are of the opinion that addiction is contagious, and it has not been possible for us always to eliminate contagion from our environment. We have had much over-crowding into apartments in the beach area, and we have not been able to exercise what we feel to be proper control of these living quarters. We feel that what has occurred here has been under conditions which could be improved considerably, when, as, and if we are able to control the degree of permissiveness in the family structure.

The Synanon Foundation is anxious to continue this work which it considers to be in its very earliest stages. The phenomena have occurred under conditions which leave much to be desired and which we feel can be corrected as time goes on.

Origin 7—November to December 1958

Around this period, many Synanon members were not completely "clean." There was, with the exception of several people, considerable "chippying around" [occasional use of drugs]. The "chippying" pattern varied in the group. Some were sneaking an occasional marijuana cigarette, some pills, a bottle of terpin hydrate, or "red-dog" wine. Apparently no one, however, was "strung out" [heavily addicted].

Chuck told me, "Nobody at that time had anything approaching a habit—nobody. People came down and they kicked and then they would cheat on Poppa. They would smoke a little stick of weed, sometimes—on rare occasions—some weak heroin would get into the place, and then maybe somebody might fix. But this was very rare. There was a little cough-syrup cheating and an occasional pill, but there were no habits. They wanted to believe Synanon worked, yet they couldn't believe it. Naturally, they were all a bunch of crazy kids. They would come in and try to cheat, like dope fiends do. They would come in and say, 'I'm tired, Dad, help me.' Their lines were beautifully written, and then they would cheat. Of course, I was aware of what was going on, but I had to build the organization. This was more important, at that time."

Origin 8—January to February 1959

Given his basic executive training, Chuck began to attempt to develop an organizational structure. He said, "My first real executive officer was George the Turk.[1] He could get things done because he was a good organizer and everyone was afraid of him. He was a definite extension of me. He was the 'executive officer' when we moved from Ocean Park up to Santa Monica."

Despite all the development of Synanon at the time, the only fully trustworthy person in the group was Chuck. Whether the Synanon fetus would survive was highly tentative. The embattled group managed to get through the spring partially be-

[1] George the Turk was an unusual addict. He spoke several languages and had a "business background." Raised in Lebanon, he began using various drugs at an early age. In his career, he was a gun and dope smuggler in the Near East. George has been "clean" since 1958. He has lived away from Synanon since 1960 and has been successful in the wholesale and retail dress business.

cause of an influx of newcomers, whose initial zeal for staying "clean" apparently helped the momentum, even though they did not substantially contribute to operating the organization.

Origin 9—Spring 1959

"December up to around April and May had a very dark-green look," Chuck said. "The place was cold, and a draft came in under the door. Everything was damp, and we had a rough time with food. It was at this time we began to do some serious hustling. One of the original hustling jobs happened when I took Jerry Hampton down to a former employer of his and his father's. We hustled some old sandwiches off a catering truck—you know, the kind that goes to the manufacturing plants. We made a connection where we could go down there every couple of days and get a barrel of this stale junk off the catering trucks. Stale pies, doughnuts, sandwiches, and so on. We would take the sandwiches apart and pull the meat out. Some had mustard and pickles. We would throw all this junk into a pot and make some kind of a stew out of it.

"Also around that time, somebody connected with the Mormon Church found out about us. They brought us a whole pickup truck full of gallon cans of homemade stew. It was awful stuff, but we ate it. We would throw some extra potatoes in, pepper it up, and eat it.

Origin 10—Summer 1959

"By June we had reached a population of about forty people. We abandoned the dormitory store front on Main Street and acquired our first old dump of a house, which we had for about three months. It was later condemned and torn down. We also had a big double-apartment girls' dorm with twelve girls living in it."

The program settled down to a routine. An early member,

Bettye (now Chuck's wife), described the routine and the tone of the establishment at that time:

"There was a morning meeting that kicked the day off at about 10:30 A.M. The committee would go down to Chuck's office. We would anxiously await their return to give us the word on what job we were on and what synanons to go to, and so on. Marion got the work list. We would kind of wait for Marion to read it off to see who was going to clean which pad or who was going to cook that day.

"In those days, all jobs were rotated around. Each member had to wash dishes and cook. Everyone had a little job assignment. We would wait for the word.

"Then we'd have lunch of some sort, and people would do their various little jobs. If it was your day to cook, you would kind of get with Charlie Hamer and get back into the kitchen part of the place. We had kind of a counter deal. We kept the coffeepot going and the cups washed up during the day. Then at four o'clock every day, there was this reading. We would all go to a reading for an hour. They would read something out of philosophy or something. This was interesting to me at that time. I can remember yakking it up. It was my only means of expression. At that time, I couldn't talk to the kids. Being the first Negro woman in the club, I felt very isolated and kind of alone.

"There would be the readings, and then three nights a week, Monday, Wednesday, and Friday, we had synanons. The people in these rotated too. Ricky had an apartment. Chuck, Jr. [Chuck's son] had one. Adaline had one too. You know, you would go out to the synanons in each of these pads on different nights.

"The synanons were very frightening to me. Those old synanons were just pure id hostility and yelling. It was a real catharsis thing. They were really frightening. People would get together and they would have no ego or anything. They'd just yell and scream at each other. Jesse used a lead-hammer attack in the girls' synanons. I never did get over the fact of Jesse. Even though he was telling home truths, he would conduct the girls' synanons, calling the girls bitches, and, 'You know, you phony mother-f———, you're going to sit there and tell me you were doing such and such, blah, blah, blah.' It was the truth, and it would hit you with big impact.

"When a new prospect would come into Synanon, sooner or later the phone would ring and they would get called up to Chuck's place. He would write down a little information on a card. Who they were and all that. I never got that phone call. He never did talk to me, and I felt real rejected. I wanted to go. I wanted him to call me up there, but this never happened.

"When I walked into the club, I walked into the midst of a big father transference. Everybody seemed to be having it. This man [Chuck] was God up there. They would anxiously wait to hear what the old man had to say. If it came from him that's the way it was. That was the beginning of a lot of imitation too, that I can see now. They would actually quote things that Chuck would say. Everybody would try to be a Chuck Dederich and pattern themselves after him.

"Of course, some had mixed feelings. For instance, Paula, she used to swing hot and cold. Others hated him, just about as much as they feared him. They accused him of getting all us dope fiends down there and feeding off of us. They would recognize that Synanon was going to move and they would think that Chuck was taking something from them. We know now he was just taking our dope from us, but everyone seemed to think it was something else."

The father transference Bettye referred to comprised both love and hatred toward the man who claimed he wanted to help them. Paula, who had been an addict for fourteen years before coming to Synanon, recalled several episodes with Chuck that affected her deeply.[2] (She has currently been clean since 1959, is a housewife, happily married to Hal, another Synanon graduate.)

"Of course, in the early days, I didn't have any trust in Synanon, or Chuck, or anybody else for that matter, and I acted that way," Paula said. "I kept acting it out.

"One time I remember I had an argument with Chuck in the dining room. Charlie Hamer was just made a board member, and I was working on the dishes or the counter. I had set up the dining room and was very pleased with the way I had set it up. I felt it was the first time it had ever been arranged correctly,

[2] Paula's "story" is described in more detail in Chapter 5, "The Women."

and I went into the living room to smoke a cigarette. Charlie, who was feeling his oats in his new position, bellowed about something. I cursed him out pretty raw in the living room. About that time, everybody had become 'cursing conscious.' You know, Chuck had put down the word to cut it out and start acting like grown-ups.

"Of course, I went in exactly the other direction. I cursed out at Charlie, 'What does that old bastard want?' or something like that. Chuck happened to be in the kitchen. He walked up right behind Charlie and let me know where he felt Charlie was *at* and told me where I was *at*.[3] He called me into his office. There were a lot of words passed. I was a 'nasty little bitch' and 'wouldn't listen to reason.' Chuck completely lost his temper. He told me, 'Well, if you don't like it, pack up and go!' I was mad, and I started to walk down the stairs. Then I snapped to something. I turned around and said, 'You can't kick me out of this house. *This is my house*. You leave. You're nothing without me and your other dope fiends!'

"Know what he did? He turned red—deep red. I remember that the guys who were around lifted me bodily and took me out to the hall in fear of my life. I walked back in, right in front of him—courting death—and poured myself a cup of coffee. He looked at me, scratched his head, and then broke into a loud roar of laughter."

The organization at this time began to solidify further with a greater definition of roles. According to Bettye: "Jesse was real important. Jesse was the boss model ex-addict. He was the addict who was saying the words, dropping the concepts. The kids would really identify with Jesse. I don't think Chuck could have sat there without him as proof that Synanon worked. I've heard a lot of old-timers, like Phil and George and all of them, say Jesse was the one who kept them in the club. Jesse was real important. Jesse was the addict, Adaline was Momma, Chuck was Poppa."

The power images that emerged, like Jesse and Adaline, were apparently manipulated into useful positions in the club. At dif-

[3] "*At*" doesn't simply refer to position in space or the club. It refers to one's psychological-emotional posture as well.

ferent points in the development of the organization, different images were required. As they ran their course, and served their purpose, Chuck would move on to the next person.

"Let's take a look at every person who was directly under me from the very beginning of Synanon," Chuck said. "First there was Grey. He was a crazy alcoholic. A young guy, enormous physically, tremendously id driven.[4] Grey was the only person I've ever met that I felt impact with when we had verbal battles. Then I had this relationship with Adaline, who never actually filled a role in the organization. It was a personal thing. Immediately following Grey was the first dope fiend, Whitey. Whitey was the first example before Jesse. Whitey got Jesse there. Then my first real assistant in the business of Synanon was Jesse. Later, George was kind of an executive."

Appropriately different individuals and personalities were maneuvered into vital positions. Through all this period of organizational manipulation, it was hard to keep close checks on drug use. This was partially due to the scattered buildings.

Origin 11—July 1959

A major turning point in the establishment of Synanon was the shift of the balance of power to a majority of "clean" addicts and to an antiaddiction tone. Up to this time, there was some drug use in the club, with members operating on an "as-if-clean" basis. One member recollects this period: "I remember George the Turk crawling around under the houses looking for stashes. It was really a thing when I came to Synanon if you were caught with any kind of pills or anything. I remember big Trina getting busted with sleeping pills. There was a belief that if you got anything here, we're going to find it; and you can't use it and stay here."

The so-called big cop-out [telling all] was a potent experience. It shifted Synanon to a totally "clean" organization. Chuck's

[4] Chuck's philosophy accepts the Freudian concept of unconscious drives as being a basic force in self-motivation. "Id driven" here refers to Grey's underlying motivations.

version gives another perspective to Charlie Hamer's description of the "big cop-out": "Kenny got loaded, and he was brought back to the dorm. The shit hit the fan. Everyone began to yell at him. The dorm filled up. I suppose there were a dozen people in it when I got there. Then others began to drift in. I told the head of the committee to get the girls. Pretty soon there was a big crowd in this dormitory. They were all draped on top of double-decker beds and peering out from the lower bunks, standing around and all yelling. Then I gave a real emotional talk about their childish games of self-destruction.

"The copping out started to gather momentum. Kenny finally copped out, then somebody else. Then somebody else copped on somebody. It's hard to describe. It was one of those snowball things; each revelation created more tension in someone else to talk up.

"Someone would stand up and say, 'Yes, I got hold of some pills last Thursday.' Then somebody would say, 'Well, who'd you take them with?' 'Well, I gave some to Joe and so and so.' They all began to confess and tell on each other. It was fantastic. One guy, Henry Cotton, when he came back from a trip had about twenty indictments. He didn't know about the big cop-out. He was the connection man. Everybody squealed on him. 'Yes, I shot some dope.' 'With whom?' 'Henry.' 'Yes, I had some pills.' 'With whom?' 'Henry.' He had been in on all scores.

"The only one who was completely clean was Arline. She had never indulged in anything, in the midst of all this. It was nothing serious. A bottle of terps, a bottle of wine, a couple of Equinols, and so on. After it was all over, I felt it was great stuff. This was what the synanons had been banging away at. I thought it was great. They all opened up. It was a turning point."

Despite the fact that some drugs had been used, the formation of a "clean" organization had now been achieved. In the beginning, Chuck had been dealing with random individuals. He now had a sizable cohesive group to manipulate—a core group intensely committed to antiaddiction. Dederich didn't take their early misadventures too seriously, since "we were now really embarked on our new method in uncharted waters."

According to Chuck: "All the dope that was used in the club

from July, 1958, to July, 1959, wouldn't have kept one dope fiend loaded for four days. It was really a vestige, a little hangover. The will of the group to stay clean and get clean was apparent from the very beginning. That was the important issue. The big cop-out indicated to me that the synanons had finally worked up to the point where guilt forced out honesty. The clean will of the group was there all the time. The purpose of Synanon became increasingly sharper following that night.

"The group became involved in another goal that I initiated. It was to get out of the slums of Ocean Park. I located a new building in Santa Monica. I described it as if it were some kind of castle. I built this new building up as being the most gorgeous beach club on the West Coast. We'll never make another move that will be as much of a contrast. If we move from the way we are living now up to the finest thing that could be designed in the Swiss Alps, it couldn't compare with the move from Ocean Park to the Santa Monica oceanfront."

The move from Ocean Park to Santa Monica was later written up in *Time* magazine (April 7, 1961) as follows:

S.S. HANG TOUGH

Early in August 1959, homeowners along the stylish Pacific Ocean Beaches in Santa Monica, Calif., were dismayed to get a new set of neighbors: a bedraggled platoon of half a hundred men and women, who moved into a run-down three-story red brick building that once was a National Guard armory. White and black, young and middle-aged, criminals and innocents, artists and loafers, the unlikely assortment shared one trait: they were narcotics addicts determined to kick their habit for good.

Scrounging lumber, paint and old furniture, the troupe converted the top floor of the armory into a barracks-style men's dormitory. They turned the second floor into offices, kitchen, dining hall and living room, and the main floor into women's sleeping quarters.

Over the door in the living room they hung their emblem: a life preserver with the words "S.S. Hang Tough," slang for "don't give up."

Such was the formal dedication of Synanon House, a self-run, haphazardly financed experiment in human reclamation whose success has been hailed by Dr. Donald Cressey, University of California at Los Angeles sociologist, as "the most significant attempt to keep addicts off drugs that has ever been made."

Origin 12—1960 to 1961

The move produced as many problems as it solved. It seemed to "kick off" Synanon's problems with the community. When Synanon was based in the slums of Ocean Park, the organized forces of society viewed it as an interesting, almost charming, experiment for addicts. They were in their "proper place" in the slums of Ocean Park. Even the local paper, The *Santa Monica Evening Outlook,* had written a very positive series of articles in the early days. However, when Synanon dared to barge into "polite society," the cry became loud and vicious. The *Evening Outlook* turned on Synanon in a series of negative articles demanding the expulsion of the "undesirables."

Various orders to vacate were not complied with, and after several stays of execution and habeas corpus legal moves, Chuck was sentenced and spent twenty-five days in the city jail, on a zoning violation. I was with Chuck the night he was locked up. I clearly remember one comment he made on that night as the big iron doors of the cell slammed shut: "For many years I tore up and down the highways drunk, endangering my own and other people's lives, without serving a day of jail time. Now that I'm in the business of attempting to help people, the community locks me up. Maybe on a deep level, some people don't want addicts to quit shooting dope."

Chuck took his twenty-five days in jail hard. He reacted as I suppose any average American citizen might who was unfairly locked up. I visited him regularly and felt a great identification with his frustrations. (I had never had a friend of mine go to jail and took it rather hard myself.) I noticed that the Synanon people, although outraged by the atrocity, accepted his sentence with resignation. Their reaction stemmed from a long experience of having had friends in jail. Chuck was released at Christmas. It took him several months to recover. The experience damaged him physically and emotionally. He was physically ill in jail with a severe cold, and the impact of the injustice was difficult to assimilate emotionally.

After Chuck's return from jail, a truce developed between Synanon and the city. (Perhaps the city officials developed some vague guilt feeling for carrying the entire matter too far. The Synanon group was really guilty of nothing except an attempt to live in peace, and to the best of my knowledge, people seldom go to jail for a zoning violation.) The city attorney and Synanon lawyers met in a series of meetings, and it was agreed that Synanon would seek another location.

Recent Developments—1962 to 1964

With the City of Santa Monica temporarily off their back, a new location was sought in an isolated section of Malibu. Chuck attempted to comply in every way possible. He said, "We tried our best to comply by selecting a location on the far side of the moon. We picked a spot zoned for agricultural use, but even this did not satisfy our enemies." The bigoted fringe of the Malibu community went into action against Synanon. In one meeting before the Los Angeles County Zoning Commission to determine Synanon's right to locate in Malibu, hysteria was rampant. Some excited citizens talked about buying dogs for protection, doubling the police force, and expressed concern for the safety of their children. All this developed in spite of the fact that (aside from the "zoning violation") Synanon had not been involved in one illegal incident in its four years of existence in Santa Monica.

About this time (April, 1963), I wrote a letter to the press, summarizing my views, in an attempt to counteract the wave of public hysteria:

> Over the past year and a half, I have had the opportunity to make an objective survey of the Synanon organization. My

preliminary findings seem to conflict sharply with Synanon's opposition. I have spent, conservatively speaking, 150 research days (roughly 900 hours), utilizing a systematic field-survey method, studying the Synanon organization. The attackers of Synanon base their opinions on hearsay. To the best of my knowledge, not one member of the opposition has visited Synanon once. The following observations may be of some usefulness to the rational citizens of Malibu in evaluating Synanon's planned movement to Malibu:

1. Synanon has been effective to date with 150 individuals —who encountered clear failures with many other methods for solving their addiction problem.

2. Those people, who have been helped by Synanon, partially as a consequence of the intensive educational and intellectual tone of the method, are positively motivated and concerned with community problems. They qualify to be of help to the community in which they reside when given a chance. This is amply demonstrated in the Reno, Nevada, Synanon, where political and community support has helped Synanon members to make a vital contribution to the mental health and correctional program in that state. (Legislative appropriations for Synanon in Nevada were given for Synanon's prison work.)

3. The presence of a Synanon in a community appears to marshal the support of many citizens who take the time personally to investigate the organization. In almost all cases they draw positive conclusions and become supporters of Synanon. (Synanon can exist only through community support.) At the same time it enlists rational support, Synanon appears to incite many members of the community to anger and fury. I would urge citizens of Malibu to withhold judgments based on rumors spread by citizens who find themselves violently opposed to Synanon with no evidence other than their personal phantasy of the way in which the organization functions. In some cases, condemnation has taken the form of elaborately described sexual phantasies. Synanon's morality is no better nor worse than the standards operative in middle-class society, and is certainly healthier than that of these attackers who seem morbidly preoccupied with the sexual activity of Synanon members.

4. Synanon in over four years of operation in Santa Monica has been a model law-abiding organization. In fact, the norms for behavior at Synanon are necessarily higher than those in the general community of Santa Monica. Of course, violence, drug use, alcoholism, neurotic acting out, illegal behavior and other manifestations of emotional disorder exist in Santa Monica; however, these patterns *are not* permitted at Synanon. Good behavior is demanded. It is the heart of the program. No member of Synanon has been arrested in the four years of its existence for illegal behavior. The only violator was Charles E. Dederich, its founder, who was held in custody in the Santa Monica City Jail for twenty-five days on a zoning violation for attempting to maintain this constructive community. Contrary to wild belief, Synanon does not produce problems for a community, except those stirred up by its own negative forces.

The accusations hurled at Synanon by some segments of the community had little validity. There was no increase in drug addiction in Santa Monica, nor was there any increase in the crime problem within the Santa Monica–Synanon area. (This fact was confirmed by an extensive statistical analysis that appeared in the January, 1963, *Report of The California Assembly Interim Committee on Criminal Procedure*, pages 142 to 149.)

Hysterical people in the community continued their attack. Mr. Sheep, described earlier, went so far as to make trips to New York and Washington, D.C. to argue his case against Synanon! Despite these impediments, the Synanon operation continued to develop.

The State and Federal Evaluations

Several governmental bodies closely investigated and came to positive conclusions about Synanon. One significant objective evaluation came from the California State Assembly Interim Committee on Criminal Procedure. Another was made by the United States Senate Subcommittee on Juvenile Delinquency, headed by Senator Thomas W. Dodd. Both analyses resulted in laudatory reports that wholeheartedly approved Synanon's pioneer work.

THE STATE REPORT

The State Assembly Interim Committee on Criminal Procedure held a full day's hearing in Synanon House, Santa Monica. In addition, there were several visits by individual members of the Committee. This Committee published a lengthy report on Synanon in January of 1963. On the first page, they summarized their findings and recommendations as follows:

FINDINGS

The existence of Synanon serves several useful purposes:

1. It is keeping approximately 100 former addicts off of narcotics. This feat in itself benefits not only the persons directly involved but also the community at large by preventing crimes committed to finance addiction.

2. It saves the taxpayers a sizable amount of money which they would otherwise have to spend to keep these people in jails or state hospitals.

3. It provides a valuable educational service by sending speakers to any requesting school, church, club or other facility.

4. It provides an unparalleled opportunity for research on every aspect of narcotics addiction. These possibilities are not being adequately exploited at the present time.

5. There is no known "cure" for narcotics addiction. An essential part of addiction is the tendency to relapse and return to the use of narcotics. Judged in comparison to other narcotic treatment programs, Synanon appears to be a most promising effort to rehabilitate narcotic addicts.

RECOMMENDATIONS

1. Recognizing that there are many approaches but no proven formulas for addict rehabilitation, we recommend that the State of California take a friendly but nondirective interest in Synanon and any other private attempts to rehabilitate narcotic addicts.

2. We recommend that one of the publicly supported universities in Southern California co-ordinate a research program to study the causes of addiction and to appraise the various

rehabilitation efforts, both public and private, being made throughout the United States.

3. It is hoped that such a study might enable California to develop effective methods to prevent addiction.

A FEDERAL ASSESSMENT

Senator Dodd, after conducting hearings on drug addiction throughout the country, delivered an address from the floor of the United States Senate on Synanon. His address was based on Synanon's testimony in hearings conducted in Los Angeles, combined with a personal investigation by Senator Dodd and the Senate Subcommittee's staff director, sociologist Carl Perian. The last part of Senator Dodd's more comprehensive report summarizes the results of this inquiry into Synanon by one of the nation's most important judicial investigative committees:

. . . The [Synanon] program has survived now for several years in spite of mistrust and attacks by the public, by some professionals, and also by the State on several occasions. The participants have organized into a foundation finally recognized and incorporated as a nonprofit corporation and have maintained their existence through public support, through donations of food, furniture, and other equipment by business concerns in the community and through the faith in the program of the members and the directors, most of whom were confirmed drug addicts a few years ago.

Today they are productive members of their small community. They all have worked hard to turn the old armory building into a home and they have maintained themselves by organizing the collection of food and clothing in the larger community. Every day they send a truck into the city to pick up unsold bread from bakeries and other food items that can no longer be sold by the stores and restaurants for one reason or another. Together they have built an institution as peculiar, but as courageous, as the individual men and women who live there. Because of this unique method of self-maintenance, Synanon can be operated at a cost of some $60 per patient a month. This is a fraction of what it costs to maintain patients at one

of the Federal hospitals for drug addicts, and the more than
200 addicts helped at Synanon, that is, individuals who have not
relapsed to drug use to date, compare favorably with the 40
patients that, by the hospital's own admission, were helped in
the Riverside Hospital in New York City after an expenditure
of 4 million dollars.

I want to emphasize that the people at Synanon, as many
other addicts, at one time used $25 to $50 worth of narcotics per
day. They often had to steal $100 worth of goods daily to sup-
port the habit, and their crimes, together with the court processes against them and their upkeep in public institutions, cost
the community virtually millions of dollars.

Increasingly today the Synanon project is being studied by
criminologists and sociologists, and it is my hope that it will
spread and expand with chapters being organized in all parts
of the country with high addiction rates. It is also my hope that
Federal agencies, such as the President's Committee on Juvenile
Delinquency and the National Institute of Mental Health, will
consider the program as a source of study and as a source of investment of some of the funds available for testing new ways of
fighting crime and delinquency.

I have recommended that the director of Synanon, Mr.
Dederich, apply for funds to the National Institute of Mental
Health so that he can expand his program and introduce it in
correctional and other institutions throughout the country. I
propose also that social scientists and heads of treatment institutions for addicts request funds to experiment with the Synanon idea. It is my belief that we have found something new
and workable in this project and we must develop it to the
fullest extent.

Mr. President, there is indeed a miracle on the beach at
Santa Monica, a man-made miracle that I feel can benefit thousands of drug addicts.

4

New Patterns

Some of Synanon's "philosophy" corresponds closely with "square society"; other Synanon viewpoints represent unresolved vestiges of the addict-criminal underworld; and still other ideas are unique human imprints developed in this new community. The common bond of these often disparate social elements is that they collectively reflect Synanon's new way of life. "In front," [1] the Synanon approach has caused many friends and enemies to see Synanon varyingly as excessively brutal, totalitarian, "communistic," beautiful, loving, corny, naïve, vicious, and constructive.

The process of building a constructive society with the varied "characters," misfits, "boss criminal-addicts," and others who form the Synanon amalgamation has produced many unusual thoughtways. Synanon has not evolved too many *completely* new positions or postures in life. The social system of Synanon, however, has shifted and modified standard philosophies to fit its own needs.

Chuck's viewpoint as Synanon's founder and major creator looms large and important in this new "social construction." Obviously, not all Synanon's ideas are his alone. Part of Chuck's power in Synanon emanates from his ability to tune in clearly to the demands and feelings of "his people." Although Synanon was

[1] An expression used in Synanon is "in front." Someone will say, "Let me tell you, in front," or, "In front, I know such and such." An "in-front" statement intensifies all that follows.

built mainly by Chuck, Reid, and other leaders of the "movement," it is in great measure a reflection of the people to whom they have listened with great awareness. In fact, few other social organizations have listened to the needs of the alienated person with greater sensitivity. This is attested to by Synanon's unprecedented success. As a result of living "Synanon style," compulsive individuals intent on "self" and "other" destruction, no longer find it necessary to act out these drives, and they have learned how to live constructive, happy lives.

The following discussions or brief essays on important Synanon patterns of life attempt to elaborate and illuminate the various Synanon processes, viewpoints, and "philosophies" expressed by people at all levels in the Synanon hierarchy.

Synanon's Government and "Politics"

The criminal-addict, when he is acting out his plight, tends toward anarchy. He lives outside the law most of the time. He even rejects the confines of a coherent ego; for to accept a "self" is, in some measure, to accept society's norms and recognize boundaries for behavior. The criminal-addict in the raw tends to be almost apolitical.

If not antisocial, his awareness of the mainstream of political life is minimal. One person at Synanon told me: "When I was using dope and going to jail, I was really a hick. I hardly knew or cared who was President. Someone once mentioned the name Adlai Stevenson to me. I actually thought they were talking about a connection."

In Chuck's opinion, because of the criminal-addict's free-floating past, his actions must be completely controlled when he first becomes part of Synanon. This is believed to be necessary until he shows some signs of being able to think for himself in a constructive direction. Therefore, when he moves into Synanon, he must, at first, accept a kind of autocratic government, run by Chuck and a select few.

Chuck describes it this way: "We were able to get Synanon off the ground because, basically, most people who come here are apolitical and tend toward some kind of anarchy. Their behavior is anarchistic. This is what they have acted out as criminals and addicts. Because they think anarchistically, they wind up being separate and apart from society. They usually have few ties and are, therefore, quite easy to organize into the autocracy that we have here. As they grow up within this autocracy, they tend, with exceptions, to be liberal in their broader political views.

"There are very few kids here who have any brief with the Republican Party. Those who vote later on (and quite a few now do) vote as Democrats.

"In overall organization, we can also be looked at as a corporation that produces 'clean-man days.' Like a corporation, our flow of power comes from the select few. Most corporations are autocracies with a Board of Directors. American corporations are not democratic, and neither are we."

ACCEPTING THE AUTOCRACY

Synanon is most attractive to people who need help and seem at rock bottom. People who have a drug habit but who are more established in the community show a resistance to accepting the "necessity" of placing themselves (at first) totally at Synanon's disposal. When they have something "going for them" outside, this interferes with their desire to accept the total commitment that Synanon demands.

In one case, a twenty-eight-year-old physician showed up at the foundation one day "begging for help." He said that he had become hopelessly addicted to drugs and wanted to quit. He was told that he would have to give up his medical practice and his family for a time and move into Synanon. He was informed that he needed the complete program and that this was the only way Synanon could help him.

According to Chuck: "We told him he was, of course, welcome to Synanon and explained how we worked. But when he found out he'd have to live here to get well, he apparently decided his business and family came first. He said he had some things that he had to take care of, and he left. A couple of days later the papers carried the story. He'd gone home and blown his head off with a shotgun."

(Synanon has had some success with two ex-addict medical doctors who accepted the requirement of moving into the total program. One teaches the youth group in the Synanon school. The other worked for a time in the business office. At about a six-month point, it was determined that he had made sufficient personal progress to resume his medical practice in Synanon. He is currently Synanon's doctor and at this time looks upon this job as a possible life plan.)

In general the anarchistic and alienated person who comes to Synanon seems to be helped with greater success. He is more apt to feel that he has less to lose by totally joining Synanon. He has usually hit rock bottom several times in the past. (Close to half of Synanon's members have an attempted suicide in their background.) More recently, however, the Synanon method has been successfully utilized by people with less severe problems.

SELF-GOVERNMENT

Synanon experimented with a "gamesmanship" effort at a democratic organization. A committee of seven was elected periodically to handle a measure of self-government. (The idea originated with Bettye Dederich, who passed the motion on to some of the older members.)

Election conventions patterned after the Republican and Democratic conventions were held, with most of the Santa Monica House population turning out. Political speeches were made by candidates representing the youth group and other factions in Synanon. Confetti was thrown, humorous and pompous political speeches were made, and the band played. Anyone who had more than six months' residence in Synanon was eligible to vote in the elections.

According to Dederich: "This is great stuff. It gives our people a chance to learn about political maneuvering, elections, and the like. But it has little to do with the major policy decisions in Synanon. At this time,[2] we continue to make decisions related to Synanon's operation at the top.

---

[2] The term "at this time" is continually used at Synanon. It reflects the belief and practice that all is flexible; what applies "at this time" probably will not at a later date. In Synanon, change is always imminent. A highly regarded quotation, which is posted on several bulletin boards in Synanon, is Cromwell's statement: "If you are not getting better, you are getting worse."

"The political activity here is turning into more of a guild or union within our corporate structure. We are interested in what everyone has to say through the committee, but we have to run this corporation from the top. This is where most of the clearer heads are found in our particular kind of organization."

I have observed that the Synanon members' involvement with the "outside world's" government and politics is in direct proportion to their length of time and position in the organization. The leaders are necessarily more in touch with the larger society, since more of their business is transacted with the outside world.

The newcomer is usually more provincial and self-involved. His first motivation to read a newspaper often comes from his interest in a newspaper clipping about Synanon. As times goes on, and his head clears, his interests shift to involvement with larger political issues. American foreign and domestic policies are subjects hotly argued by older Synanon members.

Greater awareness, as indicated, appears to be in direct proportion to the individual's degree of freedom from the encapsulation of his past addictive life. The continuum of political awareness ranges from the minimum of the "anarchistic" newcomer to the maximum of the upper administration, which must necessarily deal with the "real world" of community issues, politics, and government.

SYNANON'S PRESIDENT

Synanon's indirect process of "attaching" people to the larger body politic was revealed in the reaction to President Kennedy's assassination. The day after the tragedy, despite a tremendous flood of grief felt throughout the House by almost all members, Synanon held its regular Saturday-night discussion meeting for the public.

The meeting was an especially somber occasion and revealed a tie with the larger society that had previously been hidden from the conscious awareness of many Synanon members. Chuck, in a prelude to introducing member John Peterson's two-year clean birthday in Synanon (part of the Saturday-night program), gave a talk. These excerpts from Chuck's overall statement reflected the feelings of many Synanon members, whose new ties to the larger society came into focus as a result of the tragic event of November 22, 1963.

". . . I was surprised at my reaction to yesterday's tragedy. Twenty years ago when Franklin Roosevelt died, I was puzzled and could not understand the extent of other people's grief. I felt very little as a result of that President's death. For me and my human condition at that time, it provided an excuse to not work and to possibly drink a little more than usual.

". . . Fortunately for me, I came out of the fog in which I lived for many years, a few years before John Kennedy came into the public eye. The ideas presented by this man captured my imagination. He has been a tremendous inspiration to me in what I've been trying to do the past few years.

"As President, he threw himself almost immediately into a cause which might very well have led to his political crucifixion. He recognized and acted on the fact that all human beings are parts of our own body. He entered the civil rights arena full blast. He did what was necessary on the basis of principle, rather than political expediency.

"The immortality conferred on this man yesterday will accomplish the things he stood for. The civil rights bill will have to pass. I don't think there's any question about it. It's probably not accidental that two martyred Presidents, separated by one hundred years, were required to get this thing done.

"While John Kennedy was starting and getting his stride in his new job, another man—who, let's say, was not so well endowed—was beginning to find himself. He owes much to the existence of the late President. I think he knows this now. Two years ago this month, another John entered Synanon. John Peterson is a Negro. He was a human pincushion, scarred emotionally and physically, when he came to this door. Today, John is celebrating his second year birthday in Synanon off drugs and all it entails."

John said, "While Chuck was just talking, I had a very interesting experience. Emotionally, something happened to me. I learned something about what happened to me yesterday. I never knew that I had a connection with a human being whom I had never met. A person whom I actually knew very little about before I came to Synanon. On the streets, other people in this world, on this earth, were beyond my vision. I had no feeling of their existence in reality; therefore, what happened yesterday came as rather a surprise to me.

"I had a powerful feeling of grief when the news of our President's brutal death reached me. This feeling was shared by all those that I talked to around the house. It came as a great surprise to all of us that the death of the President could shock us and give us this strong feeling of sorrow. It came as a surprise to me that I could feel this way.

"A lot of things have come as a surprise to me in my two years at Synanon. My first year at Synanon left me speechless up here. I came up here a year ago and was unable to say hardly one complete sentence. What happens to a person here in Synanon, through their close loving contact with other human beings—for the first time in their life—is a very, very moving thing. I had never had any real contact with human beings in my life before I came here. I owe this to Synanon, and I'm grateful. I'm grateful for being free of drugs for two years—and I hope for the rest of my life. And I'm also grateful I could feel sorrow over what happened yesterday."

The tragic event seemed to emphasize for many Synanon people their new ties with the larger society. As both Chuck and John described it, the assassination produced a double shock for most Synanon members. First, they were greatly shocked by the death of a person who was an important hero at Synanon. (A large oil painting, done by one of the Synanon members, hangs over the fireplace in the living room.) The second shock was the awareness that they *could be* shocked by the loss of a person they had never met.

One Synanon girl told me: "When I was on the streets, my only reaction to the tragedy would have been my concern with the closing of the Mexican-American border. [This occurred right after the assassination.] I would have been worried about a panic [a stop in the flow of drugs across the border]. The death of this wonderful man has made me feel more emotion than I've ever had for anyone in my life."

The Administration

The noted sociologist Max Weber delineated three types of leadership.[3] One was "traditional authority." This derived from inherited leadership or the appeal to tradition. Another was "legal" or "bureaucratic leadership," which derived from law based on formalized rules and standards of justice. The nature of Chuck Dederich and of Synanon's development precluded these two patterns and left it with the third alternative that Weber described, "charismatic leadership."

The charismatic leader depends on emotional appeal and personal magnetism for his power. He controls through an almost magical force of personality. And since "nothing is sacred," partly because there are no precedents, decisions are made by the charismatic leader on the basis of his immediate inner urges and personal conclusions.

Charismatic leaders function in a highly personal manner, and their subordinates derive almost all their power and authority from the leader. Because Synanon had no traditional or legal base at the outset, it depended heavily (and still does) on the qualities of Chuck's charismatic leadership. Chuck's charismatic capacity remains the basic element of leadership and power in Synanon. Increasingly, however, there is a movement toward the development of bureaucratic leaders. This pattern of leadership has emerged with the organization's growth in size and as its internal social norms have become more articulate.

With Synanon's growth and movement toward bureaucracy, Chuck has increasingly delegated responsibility and power to his subordinates; however, he remains in final control of the power structure. Chuck's charismatic leadership largely derives from the "consent of the governed." The members have given him the right to control their future. At this time, Chuck is the only leader with the vision to dream and plan with reality; although several others, particularly Reid Kimball, Jack Hurst, and Bettye, are

[3] Max Weber, *Basic Concepts in Sociology*, New York: The Citadel Press, 1962.

rapidly developing this kind of independent leadership ability. Chuck continues as the central leadership force in the organization, although some of his charismatic quality has been transmitted.

SYNANON'S LEADERSHIP STRUCTURE

Synanon is currently structured as an autocratic pyramid with Chuck as the Chairman of a National Board of Directors, composed of Reid Kimball, Bettye Dederich, Jack Hurst, and Vince Cavanagh (Synanon's lawyer). This central group is responsible for major policy decisions. These include the broad expenditure of funds, changes in therapeutic practice, fund raising, relations with various groups, and the opening of new Synanon facilities. These and other overall policy matters are discussed by this group at least once a week. (Members of the National Board serve as advisers to Chairman Dederich, who invariably makes the final decisions. Recently several prominent square friends of Synanon were added to the Board.)

Working directly for the administrative staff is the accounting department. Also directly responsible to this Board are about ten acting directors. These executives, most of whom have been in Synanon for more than two years, essentially run Synanon's facilities in Santa Monica; Reno, Nevada; Westport, Connecticut; San Diego; and San Francisco. An acting director is in charge of either a location or a particular function.

On the next rung beneath acting directors are department heads (for example, the automotive, maintenance, and coordinating staffs). Below this level are individuals with special talents, such as electricians, auto mechanics, and good cooks. They are like straw bosses or foremen to others in training, even though they do not run the departments. Then there are the "troops." These include newer people, who are floor moppers, cleaners, furniture movers, car drivers, office clerks, and typists.

THE "LETTING GO"

Chuck was the basic therapeutic agent for the first thirty to forty people with whom Synanon succeeded. He necessarily carried the power, glory, and responsibility of this type of therapeutic leadership role. He said, "The addicts who gravitated around me in the early days wanted a superbeing. I tried as best I could to fill this difficult role for them. You know, the 'all-knowing, all-understanding' bit. That's what they wanted.

"People that submit to this type of leadership not only give you the right to help them, they give you the responsibility for their destiny. You can't really accept one without the other.

"At first, it's fun and ego gratifying to have the power and the feedback of gratitude. Then it becomes commonplace and gets in the way of business. People crawling all over you physically and emotionally becomes tedious. You begin to set up guards. You try to cut them loose. People who go overboard like this become overly dependent and you have problems like sibling rivalry, and this sprays out into the organization.

"It isn't as much strain in a secondary group organization. The people who have come into Synanon in the last year or two are not in the direct rays of my efforts. They look at me as a big shot and figure I must know what I'm doing. 'Look at what he's done and blah, blah.' But I'm not their salvation. The whole organization has helped them. Their growth is not all on my back as it was with the early group. There isn't much jealousy and sibling rivalry among the two-year-old people, but there is still a helluva-lot between the four- and five-year-old Synanon people."

When Synanon's membership went over the hundred mark, Chuck could no longer maintain direct contact with all residents. The organization moved from a primary to a bureaucratic secondary group structure, and the pattern of Chuck's therapeutic contact with the members shifted accordingly. He could no longer be a significant figure on a face-to-face basis. The organization was now too large.

This was not much of a problem for the newcomers. Their "therapy" came from leaders down the line, but it became a real problem for the first thirty to forty people to whom Chuck was chief "poppa," therapist, and charismatic leader.

Despite the fact that Chuck's role as an administrator changed from essentially that of a therapist to dealing with necessary real-estate rentals and other matters related to running a national corporation, the "early group" continued to come to him with their problems. These included marital difficulties, raising their children, and many other basic life decisions. Despite Chuck's attempts at encouraging the break of this dependency or transference and an effort at giving them back self-reliance and self-government, this group continued to look to him for most answers to their important life problems.

In addition to the problems presented to him, Chuck was also held responsible for the joys as well as sorrows of this original group. In many synanon sessions, efforts were made to unburden Chuck from this responsibility. The ancient Chinese tradition that if you save a man's life, you are responsible for him, seemed to apply here. At least it applied to the first group "saved." Chuck finally succeeded in divesting himself of some of this dependence on him through a method that he invented and labeled the "synathon." In two lengthy sessions (one ran twenty-one hours and the other seventeen hours), this dependent emotional tie was apparently snapped for quite a few of these people.

The newcomer now receives this "treatment" from the overall organization and its processes. Although he finds particular people of importance to him, his destiny does not rest as completely on Chuck as did that of the original group. The "letting go" of Chuck by the original group was an important milestone in Synanon's development. Although Chuck's charismatic leadership role continues, he is less beleaguered by individuals and small groups and is freer to develop the overall corporate entity of Synanon.

With a few exceptions, none of the people in Synanon had any prior ability in a constructive leadership role. The Synanon system is able to train many members to assume a variety of leadership roles in the organization. At first, as might be expected, many were carbon copies of their role-model leader, Chuck. Some of the first group talked, walked, and even looked like Chuck at work. Increasingly, their own individual traits intruded upon their actions, and they developed their own style of leadership.

Some Synanon leaders maintained the antisocial leadership traits they had in the past. The essential modification is that they now use their "method" for constructive goals. Charlie Hamer, as a case in point, still sounds like an old con man, but it is apparent to him and others that he is now selling a legitimate product. He sells Synanon with honest conviction.

The feelings that many members have about Synanon, because it worked for them where all else failed, foster a conviction about their work that results in an almost magical leadership quality. This quality of intense personal belief in Synanon work amplifies a charismatic leadership quality. For example, Reid Kimball, who tried to free himself of an addiction problem for most of his eighteen years as an addict, has become a Synanon leader with a sincerity and conviction that springs from his own personal triumph.

THE BENEFITS OF STATUS

In almost all hierarchies, rank has its privilege, and this is true in Synanon. Members of Synanon enjoy the benefits of the Foundation in proportion to their contribution. The Board of Directors and their families, for example, have more private and better living quarters. But in addition to their regular work, they (in Synanon jargon) "sit on top" of a facility. This involves working around the clock somewhat as House parents. It includes counseling, seeing to it that "their home" is clean, behavior is proper, and the meals get cooked and served.

In general, there is equality in the distribution of donated clothes and food; however, older members (who contribute more to the running of the organization) have greater freedom and access to goods, services, and transportation facilities.

Despite this distribution of material goods according to rank, regardless of status any Synanon member is helped by the full power of Synanon in the event of a personal emergency. This has included such help as paying off hundreds of dollars of a newcomer's "bum" checks, providing for health services, and securing legal aid.

No one in Synanon, Chuck included, receives any pay at this time. However, Chuck foresees a future in which the professional Synanist would receive some kind of salary commensurate with his leadership position and contribution to the administration of the organization.

At this time, everyone who has been in Synanon for at least

six months receives two dollars a week as "walk-around money." Members of the upper administration get additional funds for the various expenses they have related to their executive position.

A Synanist's compensation is indirect. According to Chuck: "Those of us who are working, thinking, and grunting about Synanon get paid indirectly for our efforts. We eat, smoke, and have recreation. We have the toys that other people have, such as TV sets, and we ride around in company cars. We don't own our homes or cars, but we have the use of them. Actors, musicians, theatrical groups, in addition to our own, like to perform for free at Synanon, and we have excellent entertainment and recreation.

"Perhaps, it's just as well that our employees don't get paid for a while. The people who come to Synanon, in front, know very little about money and its uses. Addicts don't know how insurance companies, mortgages, or even rents work. Addicts and criminals look at money like a child looks at it—for buying candy and goodies. They usually don't know what a checking account is; they only used other people's accounts to forge their names. So, for a while, until they are around a few years, money is no problem to them.

"We're having an increasing problem with some of our older Synanon people who have climbed the ladder to important positions and want to continue to work for Synanon and commute to their own families and homes. At this time, we cannot afford to give our executives rent money and the rest to live outside Synanon. But we will, of course, solve this in time, as we have the other problems that are tied in with our occupation."

The fact of Synanon's contribution to their past and present life growth is the bank of *esprit de corps* upon which the organization's leaders continue to draw.

Patterns of Religion

Every Saturday night, immediately preceding the evening's events, what is known as the "Synanon Philosophy" is read. It contains some of the elements of Synanon's "religious" position:

The Synanon philosophy is based on the belief that there comes a time in everyone's life when he arrives at the conviction that envy is ignorance; that imitation is suicide; that he must accept himself for better or for worse as is his portion; that though the wide universe is full of good, no kernel of nourishing corn can come to him but through his toil bestowed on that plot of ground which is given to him to till. The power which resides in him is new in nature, and none but he knows what it is that he can do, nor does he know until he has tried. Bravely let him speak the utmost syllable of his conviction. God will not have his work made manifest by cowards.

A man is relieved and gay when he has put his heart into his work and done his best; but what he has said or done otherwise shall give him no peace. As long as he willingly accepts himself, he will continue to grow and develop his potentialities. As long as he does not accept himself, much of his energies will be used to defend rather than to explore and actualize himself.

No one can force a person toward permanent and creative learning. He will learn only if he *wills* to. Any other type of learning is temporary and inconsistent with the self and will disappear as soon as the threat is removed. Learning is possible in an environment that provides information, the setting, materials, resources and by his being there. God helps those who help themselves.

Synanon emphasizes *self-help*, with a focus on individual self-reliance. This attitude reflects one of the major areas of contrast between Synanon and Alcoholics Anonymous. The latter builds upon man's reliance on a higher being. Synanon's emphasis is upon the individual's self-help and "actualization." This theme is further revealed in the formal Synanon prayer that is read each day at Synanon's morning meeting:

Please let me first and always examine myself.
Let me be honest and truthful.
Let me seek and assume responsibility.
Let me have trust and faith in myself and my fellow man.
Let me love rather than be loved.

Let me give rather than receive.
Let me understand rather than be understood.

Some Synanon members carry a backlog of hostility toward formal religions, based on their life experience with most religions. According to one member: "The religious hypocrites and holy Joes have had a shot at us. On the streets, most hypes don't consider religion at all. In prison, most chaplains are looked at as lames. The 'take-Jesus-into-your-heart' bit is a joke. But since I came to Synanon, I've thought about religion differently. I'm beginning to examine it—and myself—even though it isn't part of the program."

THE GOLDEN RULE

Hank Anderson, an old-timer in Synanon, looks upon Chuck as a kind of religious leader: "Chuck, of course, has never preached religion as religion or even the Bible or Jesus Christ or anything else like that directly. Once in a while, he would come out with something like, 'Love thy neighbor,' or I've heard him refer to Jesus as 'that great Jewish philosopher'—kind of half-joking. But whatever he said religiously, I've felt he meant exactly what he said—and really believed it. When Chuck, for example, says, 'Judge not lest you be judged,' or, 'Cast your bread upon the water,' Chuck really believes this.

"Now there's so damn many people who consider themselves devout and read the Bible and all that, but I don't know anybody that literally takes the word of Christ and practices it as Chuck does. Sometimes he'll say something religious in a joking light and it could sound like blasphemy to a 'good,' religious person. But I think when Christ said something, I really believe that's what he meant—he didn't mean anything else. I believe Chuck talks this way too—and, of course, he sure lives by the Golden Rule."

Dederich takes religion very seriously, despite his limited practice of any formal, organized religion: "Here at Synanon, we try to practice the Golden Rule. For example, in a synanon session, 'doing unto others what you would have them do unto you' is a major theme."

An older member described Chuck's beliefs in the following way: "Chuck is always the person who will forgive and accept someone when everyone else has put him down. Take Henry Cotton for example. Henry was a real problem in the very early days back in '58. He tried to smash Synanon, brought dope into the club, and tried to undermine us, just when we were beginning. Henry is Negro. On top of everything, he had a problem of always feeling persecuted and discriminated against in a real sick way. Finally he split. Naturally he went back to dope and jail. Around two years ago, in 1962, we heard he had an incurable disease and had both of his legs amputated at the hip.

"Henry called up and wanted to come back into the club. No one really wanted him. We were in the coordinator's office discussing him. Here's a guy with no legs, dying—and on top of that a boss dope fiend. We were discussing how we couldn't take care of him; you know, get him up and down the stairs—he needed medicine—and all the other problems he had.

"Chuck happened to be passing by the coordinator's office and heard our conversation. Without any hesitation, Chuck said, 'Of course we'll take Henry back in. He's a member of the family!' "

(Since his return, Henry has become an important member of Synanon. Back in the club since 1962, his health has miraculously improved. He works at least an eight-hour day, assisting in Vince Cavanagh's law office. In addition to this, he is studying to pass the California bar exam for practicing law. Henry's wheelchair condition is ignored by practically everyone, including Henry. He gets around fine and is leading a constructive life for himself and Synanon.)

RELIGIOUS OBSERVANCE IN SYNANON

Although Synanon is essentially a secular organization and there is no emphasis on any specific religion, many religions and religious holidays are voluntarily observed. Christmas, Passover, and Easter are some of the holidays regularly observed at Synanon by many members.

According to Chuck: "At Synanon we try to probe beneath the surface of concepts and philosophy, and we do the same thing with religion and religious holidays. We try to look at the holiday and its meaning on many levels."

Christmas at Synanon is observed with an intense spiritual feeling, and many people attend formal church services. Gift-giving is observed in an interesting way for a financially poor group of people. Each member receives a dollar and the name (which they pick at random from a jar) of someone for whom they will purchase a gift. The Christmas evening program includes caroling and, what has become a traditional practice, presenting acted-out satires on life in Synanon. These observances, combined with a sumptuous Christmas Day dinner, give the house a pleasant aura of gaiety and a happy spiritual feeling.

One Jewish Passover holiday, I attended a Seder at Synanon. (A Seder is a long meal with many rituals to commemorate the exodus of the Jews from Egypt. The story of Passover is read at the Seder from a book called the Haggadah.)

Synanon's Seder was a fantastic religious event. Jewish women, friends of Synanon from the community, came to the Synanon kitchen and cooked a delicious meal. The Seder was opened by Dederich, a former Catholic. Frank Lago, a New York Puerto Rican, read from the Haggadah. He was followed by Candy Latson, a Negro from Texas. The overall Seder was initiated and supervised by Zev Putterman, a Jew from New York City, whose father is a cantor. Zev's personal description of the Seder provides some interesting insights into religion in Synanon:

"This Seder experience really begins with the day I came into Synanon. About twelve hours after I got here, I was still pretty loaded from a fix I had taken before I arrived. When I'm loaded, I talk even more than when I'm on the natch—also, I'll talk to anybody who will listen. Well, there was this big fat guy, and I go over and talk to him. Someone pulled me aside and put me on about the fact that Chuck doesn't talk to anybody until they're around the club for six months.

"When I came down off of medication, it really hit me gut level that I had talked to Chuck. Since Synanon was a strange land to me anyway, I took this 'don't-talk-to-Chuck-for-six-months' ban literally, and it really shook me.

"It was several weeks before the holiday, and I started thinking about Passover and about how many Jews were around the place. I found out that there were about twenty or thirty. I don't remember for sure. I talked to Reid about it and told him we would like to have a Passover thing and I'd like him, Reid, to run it. You know, be the father of the Passover feast. He said, 'Why don't you talk to Chuck?'

"I said, 'Well, he doesn't talk to anybody for six months,' and Reid broke up. He laughed and told me to talk to him anyway.

"So the whole Jew thing—the prejudice thing—came right up in my throat, and I said to myself, 'Well, I'm going to ask Chuck, that son-of-a-bitch, that German Kraut, that fat murderer!'

"That was my attitude towards him—and, 'If he won't do it, well, I'll shoot some dope and show him!' So I got my little book—I have this little Haggadah Passover book—and I went over to him and hurriedly said, 'We're going to have a Passover here, and Reid said you should do it.' He was patronizing and said, 'Very good, lad,' and walked away.

"Passover was coming, and I went back to Reid and said, 'Chuck doesn't know how to run it—he doesn't know what's happening.' So Reid said, 'Just grab him about half an hour before the thing.'

"By that time, we had the matzoh-ball thing swinging and everything was going on. Forty chairs were set up in the dining room. All the non-Jews were putting more into it than anyone else, of course, and there it was dress-rehearsal time. Curtain was half an hour away. By this time I was trembling about all the Passovers that ever happened—and the whole thing.

"I look and Chuck's there and he's dressed up. He's around and he's dressed up! He's got on a white shirt, a jacket, and blue trousers. Pick up on this. I got the Haggadah—which is now drenched from my sweating hands—it's absolutely wilted, but I've got it. I mark it—like Chuck's lines and the response. I underlined the whole thing in English. I'm going to give him five thousand years of Jewish history in thirty seconds—quick, before he runs away. I go up to him and tell him I've got the book and, 'Here it is—you do the thing.' He said, 'Come on into the office.' But he didn't say 'come in' like he did 'very good, lad.' He gives it a different reading.

"So we go into the little office there and we sat down and

I don't know what happened, but in about two minutes he wasn't German and he wasn't outside of it. Like he looked at me at that moment with, 'I don't know anything about this, but I feel that it's important, because it's got something to do with slavery and freedom, and if it's important to you (I was here six weeks), let's do it right.' Then he said, 'Sit over here' [motioned next to him].

"I said, 'Well, you do the washing of the hands, the drinking of the fruit juice, etc.' And as I ran it down to him, he turned into about a twelve-year-old kid. His eyes got big-wide interested —and, oh, well, you know how he gets. . . . 'Oh, is this what you do?' He was dead serious, and then he asked, 'Is this all right? Should I wear a hat? And is it all right if I do . . . ?' He was open—wide open, and it threw me. I just poured the data into him.

"Later, he got up there in front of the group and gave a solemn reading, with heart. There was a lot of room for laughs, lots of room—and he usually takes advantage of this. He didn't, and he didn't give it a grim feeling. He gave it an especially nice, warm feeling—warm as when my old grandfather did it, with the beard, when I was a kid—and it deeply affected all of us."

Prejudice and Discrimination

Synanon is confronted by problems of prejudice and discrimination both from within and from outside the organization. Synanon is an "integrated community" in the fullest sense of the expression. There are Negroes and whites, Jews and Gentiles, Catholics and Protestants, young and old. Focusing on the Negro-white situation in synanon sessions, accusations are often hurled in both directions. Negroes accuse whites of prejudice and vice versa. Synanon members have helped reduce their problems in this area by a direct and open discussion of their feelings in synanons.[4]

Candy Latson, a Negro (and one of the developers of the

[4] A selection from a synanon on prejudice is presented in Chapter 6, "The Small-'S' Synanon."

Nevada Prison Project), described his prejudice in this way:
"When I first got here all white people looked alike to me. You
see, I hated them all. Before I got here, I belonged to the Black
Muslims and even roomed with Malcolm X for a time. At Synanon, in one of my earlier group sessions, some white guy looked
me in the eye and called me a black mother-fucker—just to stir
me up and check my prejudice. I wanted to kill him right there.
After a while, I saw it for what it was—just a noise. I began to
look at my own prejudice. I began to communicate with the
'enemy' about problems. I'm still prejudiced, but I'm beginning
to see things differently." (Candy recently married Janis, a white
girl, who is also a Synanon member.)

From the other side of the aisle, many whites arrive at Synanon hating Negroes. According to Chuck, the prejudice part of
the problem in Synanon is quite similar to the problem in the
larger society. However, Synanon handles the discrimination aspect of the issue differently. "We can't stop feelings, but we
can direct behavior." Despite the feeling of prejudice, the behavior component, the act of discrimination, is controlled in
Synanon.

Negroes and whites occupy the variety of status positions in
the organization. The individual's position is essentially related
to his ability to do the job. There are two Negroes on the Board
of Directors. Also, Chuck's wife, Bettye, is a Negro. These facts
have a powerful demonstration impact on the Synanon community. Among other things, it turns the word "integration" into
action at the top of the pyramid. For Synanists, the first step
toward becoming "clean" is to "act as if" they are no longer
dope fiends. In a similar way, starting with overt nonprejudiced
behavior, many people in Synanon seem to lose their internal
feelings of prejudice.

Feelings of prejudice are honestly discussed in the synanon
sessions. Bringing these feelings in the open seems to diminish
the usual negative consequences of prejudice. Many Negroes who
used the fact of their victimization by prejudice as a rationalization for using drugs often stop using this as an out. This seems
to occur after an open synanon discussion and frequently produces some resolution of prejudice feelings. Also, when the individual's general life problems are helped (Negro or white), his

tendency to be a bigot seems to diminish. (Many social science studies reveal a correlation between extreme bigotry and mental disorder.)

Most criminal-addicts, white or Negro, have been exposed to prejudice and discrimination of some kind because of their criminal label. The criminal-addict has usually been stereotyped by his family and to a great extent by society. Those who attempt to "go straight" may run into prejudice on the job or in personal relations. This adds another dimension of sensitivity to feelings about prejudice.

The bigotry issue has been a primary problem for Synanon in most communities in which they attempt to reside. On the basis of Synanon's problems of acceptance and rejection in several cities, Dederich has postulated a theorem about prejudice and resistance to Synanon. Dederich believes that "resistance to Synanon is in inverse proportion to the social maturity and enlightened nature of a community."

Although zoning and building violations are invoked as the legal mechanisms of resistance, there is strong evidence that Synanon's interracial life situation stirs up the bigots. (*It is interesting to note that the generally most corrupt arm of city governments —the zoning and building departments—is usually brought into the attack on Synanon to legitimate the underlying force of bald prejudice.*)

Synanon seems to encounter the problem of prejudice whenever it moves into a new community. Bigotry and discrimination was behind and produced the Santa Monica battle; prevented an attempted move to Malibu; and caused a zoning battle for Synanon in Reno, Nevada, and Wesport, Connecticut. Even in the seemingly enlightened community of San Francisco, bombings and other threats of violence came to the fore when Synanon moved into town.

THE "INSPECTORS"

A typical case of the kind of prejudice that Synanon encounters is revealed in Dederich's review of one situation in which Synanon attempted to rent a building to house and service its automobiles and trucks. They rented a garage that seemed reasonable, in Venice, about two miles from Synanon's main building in Santa Monica. Soon after they rented the garage, the bigots in the community responded.

Chuck said, "The Venice slum area, where we *had* to rent this garage, because we could not rent elsewhere (we tried six places), is patrolled by more police cars than any area of its size outside of Fifth and Main Streets in Los Angeles—maybe even more. This slum area is loaded with busted-up buildings that lean on their foundations. We finally rented this old building, a brick structure about thirty years old, for the purpose of using it as a garage for our cars.

"Before we rented the garage, it was a community eyesore. There were always around ten or so broken automobiles strung around the driveway. Some with three wheels, some with five, some with four flat tires—a real junk shop. After we leased the place, the first thing we did was open up the doors and windows and let some fresh air in. Right off the bat, we had to take out a whole truckload of crap and grease from thirty years back. It was almost a half inch thick—all over the floors.

"We hustled a steam cleaner and had twenty-six Synanon guys crawling all over the inside and outside of the building. We scraped and wire-brushed and began to put on paint. We swept and scrubbed the driveway. We even swept the streets in front of the building!

"While this was going on, what was the neighborhood reaction? Little old ladies in tennis shoes, crazed red-necked types, both male and female, were peering into our windows. Then there was a meeting of the 'Venice Betterment League' or something of that kind. What it came down to was, 'Get them out of there. There are niggers in the place.'

"Day and night these people were peeping in our windows. We should have sworn out a complaint for peeping-tomism. We could have done that, but we didn't. We continued steaming the floors and minding our own business. Then they started to send in city building inspectors. They came down with orders to demolish the two offices in the building because they didn't appear on the last inspection report on the building—which was in 1952. No inspector had been in that building for twelve years prior to Synanon's occupancy!

"Nothing was wrong with the building for twelve years, but now the inspectors came in droves. But that's okay—we're replacing everything as fast as we can. Then they started to send down another bunch of inspectors who were not even from this area. The case was somehow taken out of the local man's hands and was now with the L.A. County Conservation Department. Over a dozen of these inspectors came down and were poking around, looking for trouble spots—anything they could hang on us.

"Here's how far they went. When they found out they were not going to stop our using the place as a garage for work on automobiles—because we complied with all of the necessary changes—one of the inspectors came back and said, 'I saw a man down there fixing a television set. You can't do that in that building.'

"In the first place, we are not in the business of fixing television sets commercially. If a license was required for that, there is no license required to fix our own television set. As an American, I will fix my television set on my kitchen table, my front porch, or anyplace I wish.

"This just gives a brief description of the ignorance and bigotry we keep running into. We've been at Synanon for five years now. We don't have to be geniuses to know that the reason we have these problems is that pressure comes from these bigoted, ignorant people.

"Somehow they can always use the camouflage of zoning violations, with backing from the zoning department. *Maybe the zoning departments know they can't shake us down for money. They may want someone in the building who will comply with a payoff. Of course, we won't.*

"They don't like Negroes, some don't like Jews, and a lot of them, I guess, do not want people who *were* at one time junkies or thieves in their neighborhood. All we want to do is fix our cars, our TV sets, keep our people busy, and try to cure them of narcotic addiction. The bigots keep trying to stop us!"

The day I visited the garage I was tremendously impressed with the activity described by Chuck. Various work crews were all over the garage putting this formerly old, dirty building in shape. Men were painting, fixing cars, and generally cleaning the building.

I began to chat with Jack W., whom I had met several months before when I visited Nevada State Prison. Before his release from the prison on Synanon parole, Jack had been a member of the Synanon prison program. (He had spent two years in the prison for armed robbery.)

Jack told me about an incident that occurred earlier that day. It added an interesting angle to the Venice "get-Synanon-out-of-the-neighborhood" issue. That morning, Jack observed a car illegally parked in the Synanon garage driveway. He further noticed a wallet on the seat of the car that had some bills sticking out of it. This was reported to Jack Hurst, who was in charge of the garage cleanup. Jack promptly called the police. About the same time that the police car arrived, so did the owner of the car. The police officer reprimanded the car owner as he pointed to the bulky wallet on the car seat: "You sure are lucky these men [pointing to the Synanon contingent] aren't a bunch of thieves."

Interactions with the Community

A "square," in synanese, is a person who was never an addict. The more common slang usage of the term "square" to denote a "corny," not too bright person does not apply to Synanon's squares. In fact, the square friends of Synanon are considered to be very "hip" and "in." Prior to their Synanon experience, many members had a stereotyped idea of squares, which is exemplified by the following definition provided by a newcomer: "Squares are dull people who don't have much fun and are slaves to conformity. They are puritanical and don't have any real serious personal problems, because they don't feel as much as someone who is hip."

This stereotype of nonaddicts is often maintained by "using" criminal-addicts, possibly for the same reason that squares stereotype "dope fiends." In a sense, prejudice is fought with prejudice. Stereotyping is a shortcut way of looking at a category of people, and it may give the "viewer" a false sense of superiority. It may have helped the criminal-addict to rationalize his own behavior as the best way of life. For the drug-using criminal-addict, having squares to scoff at and ridicule enlarges his own "sharpness."

The fact that the addict may at times regard the square's "straight" life as desirable only deepens his negative reaction formation. In his "game," he cannot give square life any credence. One possible reason why he condemns it in a "sour-grapes" way is that he desires it. Underneath, he believes that "going straight" is a state of being that he can never attain.

Hal, a criminal-addict for fifteen years prior to Synanon (now "clean" and a "square" salesman for more than four years), put it this way: "Although I would never openly admit it, when I walked the big yard at San Quentin and ran the streets for fourteen years as a boss dope fiend, I wanted to change places with the squares I saw. I remember lots of times riding down the street, half-loaded, even with a pocketful of cash from a big score, I would see a healthy, clean-looking guy driving a truck. It would well up in me: 'God, I would like to change places with that man!' "

Part of growing up in Synanon involves a clearer, more realistic view of squares. In reverse, Synanon provides the opportunity for many squares to meet "live ex-addicts." Each group finds that the other comprises human beings with a range of problems and viewpoints not too distant from their own. When the veneer of the criminal-addict hipster falls away, a person usually appears who is not so remote from most squares. In reverse, with communication and closer interaction, the Synanon member discovers that squares have problems similar to his own. One of the devices that facilitates a better understanding and communication between squares and Synanon people is the Saturday-night meeting.

SATURDAY-NIGHT MEETINGS

Synanon people, in the normal course of life at Synanon, interact closely with squares, and this is considered an important part of the program. The Saturday-night meeting is an especially important function for interaction with the community.

Saturday evening is open house, and everyone gets dressed

up to meet the many citizens who come to visit the organization. The meeting begins at around 8 P.M., and on the average about 150 to 200 people come to visit. (Including those who came during the week from the community, there were more than 2,500 visitors to Synanon in 1963.)

The evening's program begins with a member reading the "Synanon Philosophy" (previously quoted). Then, for about an hour, the Synanon people and the squares get acquainted through discussing or arguing a concept placed on the blackboard in the living room. After this discussion, Dederich or one of the directors takes over and "runs down" the week's main events. At this time, such items as news from other Synanon Houses, progress or lack of it in various legal battles, the announcement of a member's marriage or engagement, special Synanon news coverage or TV appearances, and other pertinent information relevant to Synanon's progress are discussed.

What do the many people who visit Synanon see? In one case, I gave a student (a "middle-class square") the assignment of recording her observations of Synanon. Her written report reflects the typical observations made by many squares who have visited Synanon:

On Saturday night, January 11th, a girl friend and I made a most rewarding visit to Synanon House.[5]

On the main floor as you come in, there is a reception desk and an area for your coats: also a tape recording room, clerical office, discussion center and a very interesting little theater that the residents use to put on their own programs. After walking up a flight of stairs, one comes to a kitchen area, a dining room and the main reception center.

There are various other features I noticed on a tour I was given later in the evening. They have a beauty shop run by the girls for giving an added lift to the female residents. There is also a barber shop for men. I also saw a beautifully furnished office where all the so-called "big wheels" meet. I was very pleased and impressed with the facilities created by the residents' own sweat and sheer determination.

[5] The two students, Meryle Epstein and Teena Ente, made several visits to Synanon to confirm their initial observations.

When my girl friend and I first arrived, we were met by a very attractive young lady, who looked like a college co-ed. She escorted us up the stairs and took us to seats in the living room. At approximately eight o'clock a young man came into the room, sat in front and started the program by introducing himself to the audience. He wrote a quotation by Cromwell on the blackboard: "If you're not getting better, you're getting worse." This we were told was a seminar, to put everyone at their ease and break the ice.

Most of the people who participated in the discussion were residents of Synanon. Probably the visitors were shyer and more reticent than the Synanon members.

After the quotation had been discussed for about an hour the founder of the organization, Chuck Dederich, was introduced. He gave us a brief résumé on Synanon's latest activities. He spoke about the branches in Westport, Connecticut, San Diego, California, and the one they hope to establish in San Francisco. Chuck mentioned that within a year or so they hope to be able to help three times as many members.

The highlight of his talk came when he introduced one of the residents, Lena, who was having a four-year birthday at Synanon. She told of her many years of addiction—her search for a cure, and finally finding Synanon and help with her problem. She thanked Chuck for all he had done for her. I got the feeling that Lena was truly a remarkable woman, and I couldn't stop the tears stinging my eyelids as she walked off the platform, clasping her two little children in her arms.

After this part of the evening, over cake and coffee, we got into a discussion with an attractive, twenty-year-old Negro girl. She had only left New York two months previously but she said she was very happy and felt fortunate to be living at Synanon. When she left, two gentlemen came over and sat down. Their names were Danny and Shelley. Danny, forty years old, was an addict from New York, who now wanted to become an actor. Danny seemed to be in the advance stages of getting well and he gave me the impression that he was more or less able to come and go as he pleased. We discussed a variety of topics, including college, professions, etc. We also found out that Danny had been in prison many times for drug addiction, been to Lexington, Kentucky, and nothing had worked for him—prior to Synanon.

At this time we were handed song-sheets and a loud sing-along began, led by a girl named Jeanne. Both "squares" and Synanon members participated. However, as I scanned the room, the members seemed to be enjoying themselves considerably more than the "squares." The "squares" appeared rather inhibited and less inclined to let themselves go. As if reading my thoughts, Danny said, "Don't you wish you could live here?" For one fleeting moment I was almost envious. It was like one big, closely knit family who shared each other's joys and problems.

When the sing-along was over we were joined by two other young men who seemed to take over where the others left off. The one I spoke to was Dick, who had been at Synanon only three weeks.

Dick was a twenty-five-year-old college graduate who taught high school chemistry and physics for two years. When he was twenty, and still in college, he had a brief unsuccessful marriage. He believed this was a major reason for turning to drugs. I asked him why, since he obviously had knowledge of the consequences, he started on drugs in the first place. He told me that when he first tried dope he was just looking for kicks. He didn't bargain for the "whole package."

An interesting factor which I had become increasingly aware of throughout the evening and which was particularly manifested in Dick was a kind of brainwashing that the residents seemed to have undergone. By this I mean they seemed to have incorporated the ideas of Chuck Dederich, Reid Kimball, and the other directors of Synanon as their own. They accepted these ideas wholeheartedly. When I mentioned this to Dick, he said that "brainwashing" was the exact term used when he first arrived at Synanon. He said that when he relayed his sentiments to Chuck, he was told that "brainwashing" was precisely what they hoped to accomplish; they at Synanon wanted to wash out things in the brain that had caused his trouble up to now, and start fresh with new ideas, attitudes and values.

Later, I met another young man called Dave. Dave was a

very tall, nice-looking boy who seemed to be a little nervous and a little fascinated that he was carrying on a conversation with a twenty-year-old girl who attended college. He talked about his past and gave me the impression that he wanted very much to be an "intellect," and go to college. Instead, he had only received a ninth-grade education. Dave told us a narcotic addict played many pseudo-roles. Sometimes he would dress like a hoodlum and other times he would try to dress and act like a college student, in order to get money for drugs. Dave used words like "intelligence," "inevitably," and a few others, as if they were new to him and still strange to his way of talking. Dave told us that most ex-addicts have difficulty speaking correct English, and are taught vocabulary and spelling at Synanon. It seemed obvious to me that Dave had just recently acquired these new words in his vocabulary.

I noticed that probably to take the place of drugs, these young men and women smoked to an extreme and drank gallons of coffee. I was very curious as to where the latest fashionable clothes some residents wore were being acquired. Dave told us practically everything was donated by outside sources. I felt pleased that this young boy who had had such an unhappy childhood was being given a new lease on life and a chance to achieve something.

We later met Reid Kimball and told him of our assignment in Dr. Yablonsky's class. He told us we could come to a noon seminar in order to get "another angle on Synanon."

My girl friend and I thoroughly enjoyed the whole evening. We met many interesting people and learned a great deal. I left that night with a warm feeling for Synanon and the important work they were doing.

NOON SEMINARS

On January 14th, at noon, I returned to Synanon with my girl friend. We noticed that everyone was dressed much more casually than at the Saturday meeting. Each person seemed to have a "job" and nobody idled around. A young gentleman met us at the door and escorted us upstairs to the dining area. I was glad we were early and had a chance to observe different people at work. A young lady invited us to go into the kitchen and help ourselves to lunch. As we were eating, I felt that lunch wasn't the organized ritual I had expected. Instead it looked as if everyone was eating in shifts and making room for the next batch. While eating, John Maher, whom I met when he talked to our [sociology] class, came over to join us. He talked about everything from psychological theory to the theories of Albert Camus.

While waiting for the afternoon seminar to begin, we were told something special was going to happen that noon. Instead of the usual afternoon seminar, Chuck Dederich, or the "big man" as John called him, was going to give a talk.

I was still curious about what a noon seminar was. I was told that the members were divided into two groups. The first group was given a quotation, similar to the one used the previous Saturday night, and then the quotation was discussed in every conceivable way.

The second group met in a "public speaking seminar." Different people would be selected at random to stand up in front of the group and talk spontaneously about assorted topics and subjects. In my opinion, this was an amazing system and appears to be working miracles. I had heard John and others speak in class and I was surprised to find them such polished speakers. I now understand why they were so good at it.

I was with the group in the dining room. At approximately one-thirty, Chuck appeared and gave what turned out to be a most carefully planned talk. I'm sure every one of us finally gained the point of his speech after due consideration. First he put the following nouns on the blackboard: Eros, Agape and Charis. His talk became increasingly understandable each time he put up a new set of words:

NOUN	VERB	NOUN	ADJECTIVE	ADJECTIVE
Eros	takes	child	uninformed	stupid
Agape	share	adolescent	informed	smart aleck
Charis	give	adult	wise	wise man philosopher

He explained that every one of us has some measure of the above ingredients. Addicts have too much eros and too little agape to begin with, and much too short a dose of charis. As time goes on, Chuck said, he hoped everyone there would learn to share and give more of themselves, and that this was important to their human growth. . . .

The Saturday-night meetings, the noon seminars, and other such events at Synanon provide the opportunity for considerable interaction with squares. It places Synanon people in the community and gives them an opportunity to interact with the larger society in their own home. In reverse, the square has an opportunity to learn something about Synanon. The process seems to be mutually beneficial for both squares and Synanon members.

Cultural Arts

Many Synanon people in their leisure time paint, dance, and play musical instruments. For most Synanon members, artistic expression is a new experience. However, some members were outstanding professionals in their field prior to arriving at Synanon. Joe Pass (a Down Beat award-winning guitarist) and Arnold Ross (a pianist) had national reputations. Arnold recently toured Australia as an accompanist to Jane Russell. His main job at this time is as an acting director in the San Diego Synanon. Oscar Camano and Frank Lago are art students. Oscar received a scholarship to the Chouinard Art Institute. Another younger Synanon member, Monte, had a scholarship to a dance school.

THE PRODUCTION OF A FILM

A case in point of Synanon's involvement with artistic enterprises is the Synanon production of a film called *Some Sort of Cage*. Herb Rosen, who had had no prior success as a writer, wrote a play called *Nostalgia Never Hangs Its Hat*. The story was largely taken from his own experiences as a patient in a mental hospital. The play was developed "Synanon style" into a

film that was good enough to be shown at the San Francisco
World Film Festival. A summary of the film appeared on a program written by its producers:

> *Some Sort of Cage* is a film dealing with drug addiction
> and the difficulty of its cure. It was made at Synanon House,
> a unique rehabilitation community for former narcotic addicts
> in Santa Monica, California. The screen play was adapted
> from a one-act play by a resident of Synanon, himself a former
> addict. *The cast consisted totally of former addicts.* The set
> was constructed at Synanon and the technical film crew was
> augmented by residents.
>
> The film serves a two-fold purpose: the expert and authen-
> tic examination of a critical failure in dealing with a major
> problem in the United States; as well as the real therapeutic
> value derived by the cast and crew, indeed the whole Synanon
> community, in the making of the film. A short synopsis of the
> film will aid in illustrating these points.
>
> JIM, a drug addict, is committed to the closed ward of a
> mental hospital in an attempt to cure his addiction. He is
> the only addict in this ward and his daily attempts and failures
> to contact and communicate with the psychotic patients for
> eight months leaves him totally uncured at the time of his
> release. Thus, although he was denied the use of drugs during
> all this time, the continuance of his alienation from a healthy
> environment with a society—either inside or outside the "cage"
> —will surely lead him back to his addiction.
>
> The film was shot utilizing some of the "techniques for
> living" employed at Synanon. Group therapy sessions or "syna-
> nons" were held throughout the rehearsal and shooting days,
> combining the residents of the house and the film professionals.
> Problems, suggestions, personal conflicts or fears—anything that
> would hinder or help production were dealt with. The life
> experience of the cast, many of whom had been locked up in
> jails and institutions very much like the one depicted in the
> film, were extroverted and utilized in the acting experience.
> It was thus that the co-directors, Peter Baldwin and William
> Allyn, were able to make their first filmmaking effort "Synanon
> style." As co-producers they petitioned the entire Hollywood

industry to donate services and equipment gratuitously—no salaries were paid and all the moneys earned by the film will go to Synanon Foundation. The response was overwhelmingly enthusiastic in all areas and truly lent the film an importance and quality beyond expectations. *Some Sort of Cage* represents a valuable collaborative effort combining the Synanon dynamic with creative filmmaking.

As indicated, Bill Allyn and Peter Baldwin, the producers of the film, were the only professionals involved in making the film, although many others contributed film equipment and technical aid.

According to Peter Baldwin: "Making this film was one of the most fantastic experiences of my life. We had to convert a cellar into a movie studio, and in some remarkable way, with everyone giving their all, it happened in Synanon's basement. The usual temperamental problems of actors and production pressure were handled in the many synanon sessions we had to have. It went beyond making a movie. We all had a profound human experience."

JAZZ MUSIC AND DRUG ADDICTION

Despite pronouncements to the contrary, by vested interests, drug addiction seems to be linked with jazz music and the places where it is played. Most former addicts "dig" jazz, and consequently jazz music has been an important part of the Synanon milieu.[6]

Synanon has its own jazz band and has successfully treated many jazz musicians. In the process of helping musicians like Joe Pass, Arnold Ross, Charlie Haden, and others, Synanon has developed a new position on the relationship between jazz music in the United States and the drug-addiction problem.

In an early article on Synanon, John Tynan of *Down Beat*

---

[6] It is interesting to note that intense involvement with jazz music seems to disappear with length of time in Synanon. Chuck and I once discussed the hypothesis that "using" addicts *don't really listen* to jazz music. The dark setting where it is played and the audience role permit them simply to sit without being disturbed by anyone. One older Synanon member added to this speculation: "Sitting with shades [dark glasses] and digging jazz is part of the dope-fiend image."

magazine wrote: "Jazz and narcotics are unfairly linked in the public mind. Addiction is rare among jazzmen and, reportedly, actually runs lower than in the medical profession. Yet there is a small minority of musicians who suffer from this terrible illness, and the problem cannot be solved by pretending it doesn't exist."

Synanon takes an opposite view. Extensive experience with this issue and the information that Synanon has been accumulating since 1958 reveals that a close link does exist between the jazz musical world and drug addiction.[7] For example, many Synanon residents have told me that "where you find jazz music, you will find dope fiends and dope pushers." They further relate that at any jazz concert or jazz nightclub, there is a plentiful supply of dope and dope use. According to one Synanon resident: "When I was using, if I hit a new strange town and wanted to find a connection, the first place I would go to would be some nightclub featuring jazz music."

In 1963, Joe Pass hit a peak in his musical career. He made several record albums, was hired for national jazz tours, and played with some of the top jazz musicians around. According to Joe: "Many musical groups contain using addicts. These people may use anything from pills to heroin. This 'unfair-link' idea between dope and jazz just isn't true.

"I did forty-four solid months in prison for addiction. Another bust and they would throw the book at me. I have to continue my musical career, but I have to be careful. Some guy playing right next to me might be a junkie—and with my past record, any arrest and I'd be dead. I've been clean since 1961 at Synanon, and the experts tell me I never played better in my life. The myth of playing better with drugs is bull. I'm now happily married, and life looks real good to me at this time."

Chuck has strong feelings about the problem, based on the knowledge accumulated by Synanon: "Contrary to the myth per-

[7] This supports the conclusion of several sociological investigations. Charles Winick, in a paper entitled "The Use of Drugs by Jazz Musicians," based on his interviews of 377 jazz musicians, revealed that 82 percent had tried marijuana at least once, 54 percent were occasional users, and 23 percent were regular users; 53 percent of those interviewed admitted using heroin at least once, 24 percent were occasional users, and 16 percent were regular users.

petuated by music unions, *Down Beat* magazine, and others that there is no tie-in between dope and jazz, when you 'pull the covers off,' we in Synanon have found that most jazz musicians use some kind of illegal drugs.

"The fact that the jazz musician is a national hero to many of our susceptible young people is a vicious factor in encouraging and supporting drug use by many adolescents. The glorification of the dope-fiend horn tooter contributes greatly to the drug addiction problem. Those 'heroes' are negative role models.

"If they want to make a dent in the problem, let's have a national conference with the major union leaders in the music business. We could hold it here, at Synanon. Get some honest testimony on the subject. Then I would suggest something which may sound brutal at first glance—lift the union cards of all known drug addicts in the music business. This would force them to do something about their problem."

THE "ARTIST" IN SYNANON

Synanon has developed a do-it-yourself approach to the cultural arts that appears to have great significance for its members. Dederich describes it this way: "We encourage people, as much as possible, to make their own recreation. I like to use the word in its basic sense. It literally means re-creating or renewing oneself. We are aware of the dangers of people sucking up entertainment, movies, TV, or even some reading, where you are just kind of a big mouth. Participation is good. I think it's better for a kid to toot a horn then for him to sit around listening to a record and snapping his fingers and repeating over and over, 'Go, man, go.' Even if he can't carry a tune, it's good for him to toot his horn. The arts have the same place in Synanon that they *should* have in the larger society—for re-creation and creative expression.

"We try to avoid the hero-worship syndrome of looking at a person only in terms of his talent. Joe Pass, they tell me, is a great guitarist. But we know him here as a guy who works for Synanon.

"We really don't get too excited about stars and celebrities, unless they are also nice people. For example, in this past year [1963], we've been visited by James Mason, Jane Fonda, Steve

Allen, Rita Moreno, Rod Serling, Milton Berle, and James Whitmore, among others. We meet them person-to-person. They seem to like this better than the usual ridiculous fawning that they find elsewhere. When a so-called celebrity comes down to visit us, we have a cup of coffee, blow smoke at each other, and get acquainted, like people do.

"We do not permit the so-called artist's volatile temperament in Synanon. We don't reinforce bad behavior. When our first band was bickering and backbiting, I had them all in and told them to knock off their temperamental bullshit. I said, 'Making music isn't that different from mixing cement. Let's do it. Don't take yourselves so seriously—nobody else does. You can tell that by the fact that no one pays most jazz musicians enough money to earn a living. Play the music, blow the wind through your horns, in sequence. Get to work and do it.' In sixty days they had a Pacific Jazz record album—a good one—called *Sounds of Synanon* on the stands."

The varied cultural activities that take place in Synanon often express new emotions. Somehow their bottled-up feelings come out in Synanon and new discoveries are made. A girl finds she can sing; a young man decides that artistic dancing isn't "queer" and that he likes to do it; another fellow fulfills a lifelong ambition to act in a play. Many inhibitions seem to disappear in Synanon. This frees the person to express himself in some cultural art form.

The person who is a professional in some artistic field when he arrives at Synanon poses a different problem. The already established person in the field of art or music is allowed to use his special professional skills only after he has demonstrated that he is growing *first* as a person.

Dederich commented as follows about an ex-addict jailhouse poet, whose poetry was described in laudatory terms by a visiting sociologist: "The fact that Jackie writes good or bad poetry is exquisitely unimportant, *at this time.* Jackie wrote considerable poetry while using drugs and going to jail, two things we do not want him to do any more. At Synanon he will work at jobs good for his emotional growth. Let's knock off rewarding him for throwing good lines together. This approval may be the very thing that reinforced his addiction symptom and kept him sick."

At first glance, this statement may seem antipoetry and harsh, yet Chuck's point is well taken. It may be that it is precisely the same approval that the person received for his artistic ability that allowed him to "get by" without growing up as a person. Chuck's logic is confirmed by Synanon's experience with several jazz musicians who have succeeded in Synanon. Joe Pass and Arnold Ross were told to put aside their music until they had matured. They went along with this directive. According to several important jazz critics, they are now playing better than ever.

In several other cases, in the early days of Synanon, when musicians were handled differently and were allowed to play when they were newcomers, most "split" soon after they arrived. Several went back to long jail terms; and in one tragic case, a "splittee" musician died of an overdose of drugs.

Encouraging the artist to grow up first as a person, and considering this more important than his area of special competence, seems logical. It may very well be that the emotional disorders of many artistic people are nurtured by an assurance of public approval in their one area of ability. Because they can get by with their talent, they are allowed to remain immature as people. Their typical symptoms of emotional immaturity, childish tantrums, excessive drinking, and rudeness are aggravated by the doting approval they receive for their artistic competence. Their bad behavior is tolerated, and in this way it is reinforced.

Synanon is concerned with the emotional growth of the total person. The artistic individual is forced to grow up first as a person, then as an artist. The Synanon experience, so far, has indicated that when he grows as a human being first, his creative and artistic abilities also seem to develop.

The Value of New Patterns

Synanon members are busy people. Their participation in cultural arts, work, and seminars and their encounters with people from all walks of life seem to strengthen their constructive "emotional muscles." When they are, in Synanon jargon, "doing the thing" (this was the title of a musical show put on in Synanon), there is little time left for their former destructive inclinations. Chuck considers the variety of Synanon activities crucial: "Part of our approach is to buy time for the recovering addict. The more time he spends at constructive activities, the greater the time-space distance between the person and his past symptom." An important side effect of the Synanon member's active involvement in synanon sessions, Synanon work, cultural arts, religious activities, and intellectual probes is that he stops using drugs and committing crimes.

5

The Women

When women enter Synanon, they generally present two kinds of appearance. At one extreme, they show up with heavy makeup, overdressed, and "looking sharp." Others arrive in a state of personal disarray and openly reveal feelings of confusion and fear. Many women later admit that their fear partially stems from the imminent prospect of having their inner world exposed in Synanon.

Women who come to Synanon have many problems similar to those of the men, yet their difficulties are compounded by special complications. Compared with men, most women who have been criminal-addicts carry a more intense guilt about their past lives. The women who had to resort to prostitution to support their drug habit, as many did, also developed considerable confusion about their female identity. The role of a prostitute involves dealing with incompetent, often "freakish" men in an almost ahuman relationship. As a consequence, many of the women developed hostile attitudes toward men. Those women who had to spend time locked up were apt to have further confused their female identity with some homosexual experiences.

Further complicating the women's problem is the simple yet profound fact that women have the responsibility of bearing and raising children. One of the additional consequences of getting caught up in the criminal-addict-prostitution whirl is the physio-

logical and psychological damage that often results from the violation of their reproductive organs. Most women caught in the
criminal-addict treadmill have one or more abortions.

Another complex problem that the women face when they
"straighten out" is their conscious and unconscious guilt responses
to the generally held cultural attitude toward women criminals
in American society. The criminal as a heroic figure is a popular
American image—provided the criminal is male. Although the
male criminal's behavior is often condemned by society, at the
same time he is generally viewed (at least in the mass mind) as
a courageous and adventuresome hero. (A casual look at TV or
movie advertisements any night in the week confirms this assumption.) Many "American heroes" of the past (Dillinger, Capone)
and of modern times (Costello, Luciano) have been criminals.
A reverse response is accorded women who become criminals.
They are looked upon more critically—especially by themselves.

This double standard of judgment regarding the criminal-
addict has a significant impact on male and female roles in Synanon. The woman in Synanon is often her severest judge. Her
criminal-addict past provides the fuel for severe guilt feelings.

Guilt

When the female addict-criminal is compulsively in action,
although there are times of great depression (and even suicide
attempts), she has some mechanisms for self-defense. One set of
rationalizations includes the "righteous-dope-fiend" syndrome.
Here the women convinces herself—with peer group support in
and out of jail—that she is leading an exciting "kicks"-filled life
of freedom and excitement. In some cases, if the woman is attractive enough to be a high-priced Hollywood-type call girl, she
can convince herself for a while that she is leading a "glamorous"
existence. (This image, of course, often falls apart when she
finds herself degraded and compromised by certain "depraved
acts" she must carry out in the course of her "professional" work.)

Her most important method of self-defense is, of course, her drugs. Here she uses, in a certain sense, a quick, fairly inexpensive form of self-therapy. Relief is just a "fix" away. She doesn't have to have anyone else involved in her private therapy (except a "connection"). The drug she puts into her arm bathes away her depressions, problems, and guilts in one shot. Although each "fix" may in reality drive her deeper into despair and confusion, she does get the "temporary relief" so heavily advertised in American society.

Unlike the average prostitute, women who become prostitutes because of their addictive compulsion do so under great emotional pressure. One Synanon girl, who has been "clean" since 1959, put it this way: "For two solid years I was completely miserable. I hated what I had to do. I hated the coquettish act, I hated the tricks, I especially hated myself. I saw no way out except suicide, and I tried that a few times. Whenever I turned a trick, I always made sure I was heavily loaded."

Most women in Synanon had similar feelings about what they "had to do." Surprisingly, despite their "atrocious behavior" (by their own judgment), most of the women seemed to maintain, underneath it all, a standard middle-class attitude about their behavior. Consequently, their compulsive, and apparently necessary, prostitution and criminal acts were judged harshly. One girl said, "I saw myself, almost as if in a dream, doing these horrible things and then pushing drugs into my arm to block it all out." Because of these severe self-judgments when they "clean up" and when some of the superficial rationalizations about past behavior are removed, most of the women at first experience deep depression and feelings of guilt. A typical comment: "I felt I could never be clean again, as if I was stained for life."

Prior to my encounters with Synanon people, I had concluded that psychopathic behavior, asocial acts without any apparent conscience, was carried out by psychopathic personalities. I have revised my concept of the psychopath on the basis of knowledge I have since received, particularly from Synanon women. It is apparent, from the profound guilt they manifest in their early days in Synanon, that while they were "doing what they had to do," there was a highly critical conscience evaluating and judging their "horrible" behavior. When their self-defense mechanisms, their drugs, and their rationalizations are taken away, their inner conscience takes over and considerable guilt, accompanied by depression, appears. It is almost as if a time-bomb conscience has been ticking away inside, recording and judging their behavior. When the "covers come off," the time bomb of conscience is revealed in Synanon, and it has to be dealt with in some therapeutic fashion.

The female criminal-addict in jail or prison can maintain a semblance of rationalization and the self-image of being a "hip broad" or a "righteous, boss dope fiend." In other settings, such group-shared rationales bolster the criminal-addict in continuing on a path of self-destruction. In Synanon, and the synanon sessions, this kind of self-deception is not acceptable for rationalizing any *continuance* of the past behavior. In Synanon, although the woman's past behavior is not approved, the person is not condemned. An attempt is made to have her examine her past "stupid" behavior and look ahead to a better way of life. Despite emphasis in Synanon on "forget what was and let's go from here," many women experience a torrent of guilt.

In some cases, there is dramatic evidence of this profound guilt. One girl had repeated dreams of being covered with feces. In addition, she dreamt of throwing up feces. No matter what she tried to do in the dream, including talking showers and baths, the cover of feces would not disappear. In her dream, when she tried to bathe or shower, it poured out of the water spout.

One conclusion that might be drawn from the manifestations of extreme guilt is that the women are *not* the callous psychopaths that they seem to be when they are acting out their criminal-addict role. On the contrary, underneath the tough shell that the ravage of addiction (and such concomitants as jail and prostitution) produces is often a deep and sensitive person who views with horror the compulsive acts connected with her drug habit. The presence of this sensitive conscience is amply demonstrated by the compassionate and loving behavior of Synanon women after they have worked themselves out of their previous difficulties. This process seems to take several years of intensive Synanon experiences.

Attitudes Toward Men

The woman newcomer at Synanon often brings with her many feelings of confusion about proper male-female roles. Also, a residual of past prostitute behavior may be a general hostility toward men. The addict-prostitute on the street seldom has a constructive relationship with a man. The image of a romantic love affair, which many arrive with, is quickly shown up as a sham under the bright lights of reality. "If he *loved* you so much, how come he turned your ass out to hustle on the street?" is a standard question that many of the girls have to examine.

In another case, a girl described the great romance and love affair she had been having with a particular man for seven years. A closer examination revealed that she had, in fact, lived with this man for about six months out of the seven years. Either one or the other or both were imprisoned for more than six of their "beautiful seven years" of romance. When they were "together," they used drugs and she turned tricks.

The relationship between a dope-fiend pimp and his woman is somewhat revealed by Frankie Lago's [1] description of his "divorce" from his wife, Carmen: "We both had habits like oil burners. I was doing some petty thievery, and occasionally with a gun or knife I would get some money by armed robbery. Mostly, I laid up in the pad watching television and waiting for my wife to come home with the dope. It was a beautiful love affair. I would lay up in the pad and she would be out on the corner all night, and sometimes in the afternoon, peddling her ass for us. Of course, in our total insanity at the time, we actually thought we were in love!

"We got 'divorced' this way: One night, I think it was New Year's Eve (it was very 'romantic'), she calls me up and says, 'I don't want any more to do with you. I want to stop using dope. I want to straighten up and get my kids back.' So I told her not to worry about a thing, I'd be right there. Before she hung up the

[1] A more complete description of Frankie's "story" is presented in Chapter 7, "Institutions."

phone, I had already crossed town by cab. Of course, I tried to talk
her out of her insane idea. I think I hit her once or twice. She
wouldn't listen to reason. Later that night, back at the pad, I
said, 'Let's do this thing right!' Now this is the way a dope fiend
thinks: We took all our family supply of dope and split it down
the middle. 'Two spoons of heroin for you and two for me; 150
Nembutals for you and 150 Nembutals for me. There's $20 left
in the kitty; you take $10 and I'll take $10.' Then we sort of
kissed and wished each other good luck. Of course, each of us
had a stash [drugs they had hidden from each other] and thought
we were holding out on the other!"

(Frankie and Carmen have now been "clean" in Synanon since
1960. They have one of their children back with them, and both
are doing well—together.)

Carmen told me that she had a little guilt about her past relationship with Frankie: "When I was turning tricks, sometimes
I didn't give Frankie all of my money. I felt a little bit bad about
it, but I overcame this with the extra fixes I would take with the
money I 'stole' from him."

The past role of an addict-prostitute often produces in her a
rigid, stereotyped perception of men as objects of exploitation or
as exploiters. A male, to most prostitutes, is either a "trick" (a
revealing term) or an emotional infant (the pimp whom they
support).

Pimps are apt to be dependent, physically abusive, and sometimes both. Some pimps appear to help expiate some of the prostitute's guilt by abusing her in some fashion. The physical abuse
seems to feed the prostitute's lowly, masochistic self-image. Other
pimps sit at home like spoiled children, waiting for the dope to
be brought home by their "old lady."

Some of the women were extreme loners. These women would
not involve themselves in a relationship with a pimp. Their only
relationship with any man when they were addicted was that of
"whore and trick." The results of these complex and destructive
set of male-female "experiences" are observable in much of these
women's early confused behavior in Synanon.

One response is, as described, extremes of guilt. Another is an
exaggerated attempt at proving "femininity" by validating their

attractiveness to men. Many of the girls act like adolescent flirts and attempt to capture as many male "scalps" as possible. Any girl in Synanon who acts out this "seductress" role is viewed with some amusement. Her romantic inclinations are, in most cases, an exaggerated effort to prove to herself that she is a desirable woman.

This phase is often most useful to the girl in the process of climbing the ladder of maturity. Her behavior is considered outrageous, draws attention, and she is exposed to considerable attack in synanons. The response to her behavior during this period often involves many "in-depth" counseling sessions conducted by women who have been in Synanon a longer time and are more mature.

In summary, the women who come to Synanon have had considerable exposure to a set of severe and destructive emotional forces. They carry the stigma placed on them by society and themselves for having been criminals, whores, and addicts.

The results of their past way of life include a dependence on a set of false self-images and rationalizations, feelings of confusion about their female self-identity, and—as a consequence of their primary relationships with infantile men—a distorted perception of most men.

There is strong evidence in most of the women of a strong superego, or conscience. Although buried deeply in the woman, it judged her past "outrageous" behavior. This self-judgment appears to produce considerable guilt in the woman. Her flimsy rationalizations of having been a "righteous dope fiend" or "a glamorous call girl" or involved in a "romantic love affair" are exposed to the light of reality. She is permitted these illusions in the dishonest settings of jails and prisons, where a group rationalization is used. In Synanon, however, she must confront the realities of her past and current existence.

Paula

One woman who traveled the dope-fiend path and recovered in Synanon provides a living example of the process. Paula, now in her late twenties, was an addict for fourteen years before her arrival at Synanon. She has been "clean" in Synanon since 1959 and is now happily married. (This report on Paula's "life and times" was compiled from several lengthy interviews, note-taking, and tape recordings.)

"I was born by mistake twenty-seven years ago. According to what I'm told, since I don't recall too much before I was nine or ten, I was a problem child. I was put into a problem child's institution at a very early age. I think I was a year or a year and a half old when I was placed. I progressed from there to different institutions until I was sixteen. The last reformatory I was in was a so-called treatment center. Here I got my final street education.

"Most of the kids there, including myself, were considered incorrigible. Most of the guys had criminal records. Some of the girls had been whores from the age of ten or eleven, and a couple of the boys had committed the act of rape (or what was called rape) and even murder. They were accomplished thieves and con men. I absorbed all of their teachings readily. I enjoyed it.

"I think I always knew I was going to use drugs. I used my first form of drugs when I was twelve. There were two guys who lived in the same apartment house with my family. I admired and looked up to them. They were about seventeen or eighteen at the time. I was allowed home visits once or twice a year for a weekend (when my behavior, in the institution I was in at the time, was good enough).

"Whenever I did manage a home visit, I looked forward to hanging out at night in front of the house with these guys. They seemed to know I was hurting inside and tolerated me. One summer night I saw them going to the roof of the house, and I followed them. They were smoking (I found out a few minutes later) some weed [marijuana]. It smelled good to me, and I asked for a drag. I turned on [was introduced to drugs]. I remember that I felt it was the most beautiful thing that had ever happened to me. I was very happy and started to imitate all the singers I liked. The guys gave me lots of approval for my singing. From then on, I was one of them and could get all the pot [marijuana] I could use.

"After that year, I was introduced to cocaine by the same two guys and horned [sniffed] it whenever the opportunity arose. For fourteen years I enjoyed all the drugs I ever used. Heroin crept up on me. I normally weigh 125 pounds. There was a period when I was badly strung out [addicted] on heroin and weighed 90 pounds. I thought my clothes had stretched!

"I had a six-year period of using every form of narcotic and everything that went with it. Maybe if I describe the average life of an addict in New York City, you will get an idea of what my life was for the years before I got to Synanon.

"My hours were from six to six. That is, six in the evening to six in the morning. (It took me a year to go to sleep before 2 A.M. at Synanon.) I'd get up as late as possible, because the sun hurt my eyes. I didn't want to look at people. You know something's terribly wrong. You're different. Squares are scurrying around, bumping up against each other. They look insane to you. Addicts talk a lot about how crazy squares are.

"You get dressed, and if you happen to have some drugs you take your morning fix. From there on in, you begin to scramble for bread [money] and drugs, and anything goes. I would buy or sell drugs. Most pushers [drug sellers] are addicts. They're not the big-time people you read about with beautiful apartments. The heavier pushers [those with large quantities of drugs] are usually addicts too. That's the reason they're pushing. It's a simple matter of economics. You buy a quantity. You cut the drugs yourself. You sell a little bit. You make a little money to buy more dope.

"Most of the time you're broke, so you use your wiles. You'll use anything you've learned. You con, and being a female you have a few tools that guys don't have. I did a few nasty things in my time. I turned out as a whore. I participated in many degrading acts. If you check Krafft-Ebing, you will find a pretty good catalog of what I had to do to make my money.

"When I could, I worked with people who were experienced in different con games. I especially liked one con game called a Murphy. Someone fronts for you [acts as a pimp] at a bar. The trick gives your front some money on account: He thinks he's going to meet you in a nearby hotel. As soon as the money changes hands, you, of course, disappear. There's a lot of men like that who come into New York from out of town. They're dying to have their money taken away from them.

"Then there's till-tapping. One person diverts the storekeeper's attention and the other one puts his hand in the cash register. Then there are vending machines you can always break into when you get desperate. And when all else fails, there is a gun—if you happen to have one and the weight to hold it and not shake so you can get what you want.

"You're constantly looking for a good connection. Yours is never there. If you spend a lot of money, you might have a good connection. One that lasts for three months or so. But there's always a shortage of drugs. Something always happens. Like there's a bust [arrest] in the neighborhood and everyone who's holding [has dope] gets off the street. On some days, you might travel on foot for miles with $50 in your pocket and not touch a penny of it because you don't want to go to the man [connection] short. You want to get to him with the full amount so you'll be sure to get as much drugs as you can buy. There is very little sleep involved.

"If you get drugs that are pretty strong, you can go along on them for a few hours. But usually drugs are so weak and cut down, you have to fix six or eight times a day just to feel normal. When you have a real habit going, you don't really get loaded like you see acted out in the movies or read about.

"After the first few months of addiction, the stuff takes over. The demand builds higher and higher and the supply is never enough. You need more and more drugs and money. I spent as much for myself as I did for my old man. (You would call him a pimp—I didn't think he was.) If I made $100 a day, it would be spent on drugs.

"The first three years that I used drugs, I didn't try to kick. At that time, the situation was ideal for a junkie. My old man was a connection. He had a lot of dope, and I stayed in our apartment most of the time. As a matter of fact, when I was taken care of, I stayed in once for nine solid months. I went out about once a week—at night.

"Then, of course, the drugs ran out and a little reality crept in. My old man sent me to some people he knew in another part of town, who were running a call house. They had a large apartment and a telephone for appointments. The place was closed down a few months later, and I hit the street, uninitiated in street bargaining. But I had to take a chance, and that's when I got my first arrest for soliciting.

"I almost died the first time I was arrested and put in the tank [cells for addicts only]. When I landed in the jail infirmary, I knew something *was* wrong. I got a suspended sentence the next Monday and, of course, went right to a connection.

"I don't think I really seriously thought about kicking for five years. I felt that dope was my fate, that I had to be an addict for the rest of my life.

"In 1957, I went to Lexington [the Federal Hospital for addicts] to try to quit. I heard that it was a hospital. I found out it was also a lockup. I left in ten days, sicker than when I arrived. In Lex you're given a purer form of drugs to 'help' your withdrawal pains. That year, methadone was given orally. You, of course, exaggerate the extent of your habit so you can get as much 'M' and goofballs [sleeping pills] as possible. If you get any kind of a habit from these drugs, they are a lot worse to kick than a heroin habit. I was pretty disillusioned with Lex.

"By the time I got back to New York, my old man had been busted and was sent to a federal prison. Most of the people I hung out with in New York were connected with jazz in one way or another. Most of the junkies and their wives were connected with the jazz-music business. One of these junkie musician's wives got a letter from another musician's wife in California describing a bunch of addicts living on the beach in Ocean Park, California. They were supposedly trying to do something for each other and their drug problem. My family had moved out to California, and I thought I'd see what it was all about. I didn't believe Synanon really existed. But I'd see what it was all about; and, anyway, I would find a 'Broadway' in Los Angeles. I knew if there was one, I'd find some stuff. I didn't think I was taking a real chance by going to the Coast.

"Earlier that year I made my first real effort to kick. I did this in different people's apartments. Every Saturday, for months, I would not use any stuff. Of course, by Sunday morning I would realize how stupid it was, especially if there was any money or dope around.

"On one of these weekends, I almost killed myself, accidentally. The girl whose apartment I was kicking in that Saturday gave me a bottle of goofballs to help me. It was ridiculous, because all these pills do is leave you *immobile*. You may think you're moving, but you probably haven't budged an inch. I tried 'escaping' from this fifth-floor apartment by climbing out of a window. It was separated by four feet from a fire escape. I somehow managed to get down one flight. I burst into someone's apartment through their window, to get out their front door!

"I was really running scared and alone. I called a trick I knew who had liked me and who I thought would help me if he knew my problem. I guessed right. He said he'd come over. I decided to shoot all the stuff I had, together with some goofballs. By the time he arrived, I was in a coma. He got a chambermaid to open the door to my hotel room, threw me in the shower, and they did the best they could to revive me.

"He contacted my sister (whom I'd seen twice in five years) and with her arranged for my plane fare to the coast. He also gave my sister a check for a couple of hundred dollars (to be mailed to my parents' home in thirty days), with the stipulation that I *promise* to stay in Los Angeles at least six months. That's how long he thought it would take to straighten me out!

"I was put on a nonstop flight to Los Angeles in May of 1959. When I landed in California, I was a physical and emotional wreck. I wanted a fix very badly. I called this musician's number that the girl in New York had given me. His wife, who wasn't an addict, answered the phone. I told her who I was, where I got her number, and asked if her husband was really clean and at Synanon. She told me yes and to hang tight until she could pick me up.

"She picked me up in her car and brought me down to the beach [Synanon's old building in Ocean Park]. All the way there, she had to keep assuring me that she was taking me to a connection or I probably wouldn't have gone. She pulled up in front of this place and just left me there and cut out. (I found out later she had gone to Chuck's apartment to let him know I was in the clubhouse and to get someone over there right away.)

"I was three thousand miles away from my connection, with $6 in my pocket, so I thought I'd better stick around for a while.

A big healthy-looking guy with balding blond hair and a seaman's walk came in from a side door. He asked who I was. When I told him, he put me in a huge overstuffed broken-spring lounge chair. The chair faced what I thought was an oil painting of bleeding testicles. I was told to sit there until someone could talk to me. He said that the synanons were going on and told me to hang tough.

"I made a crack about the painting and asked him if I could find another place to sit. I told him that image in front of me didn't help my withdrawal pains any. It turned out to be one of his artworks, and I made my first 'enemy' in Synanon!

"Of course, he wouldn't allow me to move. After he left, I doubled up in the chair, stashing my small overnight bag next to me, and peeked out from under my trench-coat collar. I thought from the looks of the place, junkies *had* to live here and if I acted right I could get turned on sooner than I planned. There were a lot of couches and chairs like the one I just described all over the place, a few tables, and fewer ashtrays. The walls were painted different colors. Murals were plastered on top of that. A particularly ugly mural showed something labeled a geeze [slang for the ritual of "fixing"].

"When the Board got around to interviewing me, I was escorted through an alley to a small apartment behind this building. The first person I saw inside was a man whose frame completely covered the largest sitting chair ever made. He was using a Chinese back scratcher on his toes. He looked across at me with a kind of half grin. (This was, of course, Chuck.) He was soon joined by a round black man, the blond seaman type, and an older woman, who shouldn't have been wearing the tight capris she had on. I explained as carefully as I could that I was sick and would need some stuff very soon. They all looked at each other and laughed. I was asked some questions about my background and the extent of my habit. They told me the two rules of the house: no drug use and no physical violence at any time.

"I tried to push my case with Chuck, thinking he was the man [connection] around there. He finally told someone to put me on a couch in the club to kick my habit and he'd see me in a few weeks or so.

"By that time, I was drenched and shivering. I had on a blouse, capris, tennis shoes, and a trench coat. My hair was very long then. It was uncombed since the night before and flying all over me. I suppose I looked like a scared Gravel Gertie. I felt like a cornered wild animal. Ten days later, I began to sleep.

"In my early days in the club, there wasn't anything that anyone could tell me. In my past I had been exposed to all types of clinical tests and psychiatric treatment. I was somewhat familiar with the terms they were using in Synanon then, and I thought the psychological discussions were part of a continuing farce. I split the second week.

"The money my sister had been holding was sent to my parents' home, and I went to get it. I found a connection in downtown Los Angeles and scored. As soon as that money was gone, I went back to Synanon. To this day, I do not know why—aside from the obvious fact that I was in a strange town, half sick all the time, and didn't know anyone. After a mild hassle, they accepted me back. This time the place seemed different . . . something odd had taken place.

"Lois, a girl I had gotten a little friendly with, ran the story down to me. Two or three days before I got back was the night of the big cop-out. Copping out is telling on yourself or anyone else. This is something you just don't do. Your so-called underworld image says that if you're a whore, act like you're a high-flying whore. If you're a thief, you're the best thief there is. And if you're a junkie, well, you shot the most dope.

"One thing that Synanon does, the thing it started to do the night of this big cop-out, was to tear these images to pieces. The junkies did it themselves. Of course, with Chuck's help. Most of the kids were *trying*, and a few others were getting drugs from peddlers in the neighborhood. That night, a few people gave up the code of the streets and their images, and it started a chain reaction.

"Everybody (about thirty people) was pulled out of beds at three o'clock in the morning. Everyone began telling who they had used with. One tough nut finally put his head down and said, 'Well, I fixed with anybody who said I fixed with them.' The stories were out. From then on, everyone really made an effort to look out for everyone else. They tried *together* for the first time, and that was when I got back to Synanon. That was around July of 1959.

"After many years of being a hope-to-die dope fiend, something happened to me then. I don't know what it was. But the people that I had been conniving with the previous two months seemed awfully serious. Also, they didn't have religion, and this impressed me. I was always afraid if something like this were to come about, it was going to be like A.A. Being a rebel of sorts, I couldn't stand the similarity or the smell of it. But the hard-core dope fiends were now dead serious, and this reached me.

"The people, Chuck, Jesse, and all the rest, sounded like they were interested in me and wanted to see me clean. I began to listen, instead of talking all the crap I used to. In fact, I was put on a talking ban for a while. I almost choked to death keeping quiet, but it helped tremendously. For one thing, I think I found out what quiet people are like *inside*.

"Shortly after this, we moved to the larger building in Santa Monica. Chuck did something then that really hit me. I had gained a lot of weight fast. In fact, so much that I had nothing to wear that fit. I got the outrageous idea that if I was allowed to leave the house for a week, I could turn a few tricks and make some money for a new outfit of clothing!

"I walked into Chuck's room, which served then as boardroom, library, sitting room, and gave him my story. I told him about my plan to get money for clothes. I wouldn't use much [dope] and would definitely be back.

"Reid, Chuck, Jesse, and Adaline were in the room. They just stared with obvious disbelief at what I said. Now, Chuck had a double army-type locker in the main hallway outside the office. It held all the clothes he owned, which consisted of three or four sport shirts and some wash pants. He walked out to this locker and came back with one of his few shirts and handed it to me. He gave me his sport shirt to wear! This shook me up. I didn't know how to act. He just told me, 'Run along, child,' and something that added up to, 'Think over what you just said, and for God's sake, don't let me hear anything like it again!'

"I really got with the program from then on. About a year later, I got a job with a meat company as a clerk. After a few months, I ran the meat company's small advertising and mail office. I worked there successfully for almost two years. This was the first real job I ever held in my life.

"Now I'm a housewife and I'm married to a wonderful guy I met at Synanon. Hal was the first guy I ever met in my life who treated me like a woman. The guilt of my past life as an addict-whore hit me hard for a long time. But Hal treated me as a good person. This really reached me. He came into Synanon about the time I did.

"He's a guy who had quite a record. He was an addict for fifteen years and was in with what the underworld considered big time. He began when he was about eighteen or nineteen years old. He's now thirty-seven. He did time in various places, including San Quentin. He too is working for the first time and independently. He's now a successful salesman. He has the respect of everybody he knows, squares as well as the people at Synanon. People love him. He's one of the people who don't seem to fit in the junkie category—not to me, anyway. We've both been clean since 1959, and the world looks pretty good to both of us."

This is the story of one of the women with whom Synanon has been successful. Of course, Paula's story is not exactly the same as the other girls. However, there are many threads of similarity. The confused early childhood; the belief in drugs as an answer; the turning to prostitution; and the dark, painful life of an addict-whore appear in almost all the women's stories. The jails, the failing efforts at change, often resulting in a suicide attempt, are common elements in Synanon women's background—then Synanon and the possibility of a new direction. What happened to Paula at Synanon has happened, to date, for more than a hundred women.

Working with the Women: Problems and Program

Synanon has a special division for women. At the top of the female pyramid in Synanon is Bettye Dederich, who handles the overall administration of the Women's Division. Several other women work along with her on a more direct-action level. Arline

Gutierre and Jeanne Camano, among others, handle indoctrinations, job placements, and the special counseling of the women.

There is an *esprit de corps* among the women that appears to be helpful to the newcomers. The more mature Synanon women members maintain an "older-sister" protective atmosphere. This protective and therapeutic approach is notable in the Women's Council, an operational body of the Women's Division.

The Women's Council was described in the following way in a statement made by Bettye:

"The Women's Council, among other things, protects women's rights in a predominantly male society. The women on the Council have the greatest seniority in Synanon and wield the most power. In addition to the senior Synanon women, we have two women directors on the Council. In a way, we are the inner circle of the women. We serve as judge and jury in certain cases or problems in the House. For example, one girl, Connie, was on her way out the door as a result of some hassle. We stepped in and took over her treatment, so to speak, set up a work program for her, and she's still here. We also have the power to decide if a mother is emotionally ready to get her child back. We'll have the girl into our Council meeting. We'll talk to the girl, get information, and then advise her. We handle both general and specific women's problems that come up in the House.

"The Women's Council is also a tension-release situation for the older girls. Sometimes our meetings turn into intense synanon sessions—where we cut loose on each other. We feel freer to do this among ourselves in what is, for us, our peer group. Several of the senior Synanon women in our Council are married and live outside of Synanon. This provides us with another view of our internal problems.

"Generally, the Women's Council equalizes the male-female power balance in the House, provides counseling for all of the girls, gives the older women a place to blow off some steam, and keeps us up to date on the changing roles in Synanon."

EARLY PROBLEMS

According to Arline, the women bring with them into Synanon "a mess of problems that have to be worked out. The woman newcomer has to kick a habit. She is generally underweight, very sensitive, and apt to get hysterical. When they first get here, they present themselves as dependent, helpless infants, desperately seeking aid. First, they will say or do anything necessary to get them into Synanon. They are quick to accept the necessary contract of not communicating with their past 'husbands,' or lovers, for a few months. These men in their lives were usually their crime partners or pimps. They are also willing to accept the fact that the children they have accumulated over their drug addiction and prison careers, will stay put for a time. They say all this in the beginning, but in about a week or two they are whining to get all these relationships back, when it is obvious they can't handle them."

Their "loving-mother role" is usually a fake image. According to Bettye: "The girls try to hold up an image of themselves as loving mothers who, in spite of their troubles, always took care of their kids. This is, of course, 90 percent untrue. Their kids were usually shuffled around many different homes."

Lena, an attractive thirty-year-old woman, arrived at Synanon after a long addiction history. Her dealings with Synanon with reference to her children followed a common pattern. Chuck knew her typical background: "Lena was an awful baby when she got here. She was always spouting tears. She had a terrible background. Many years of addiction and whoring. She's now quite solid—runs our nursery and does a terrific job." (Lena recently married Wilbur Beckham, one of Synanon's acting directors.)

Lena received considerable counseling from Chuck. She told me: "When I first came to Synanon, I was always withdrawn, and I was never one of the people who talked a lot or talked very loud. When I did get into a hassle, I would end up in Chuck's office. He had always kind of manipulated me in there, some way or another. I'm one of those people he has never given a haircut to. I guess he senses the kind of people he has to give haircuts to and the people he just talks straight to. He would always make it very easy for me to talk to him. He's the first human being I ever met I could really talk to.

"When I was here a few months, I was always having trouble with my mother about my children. Chuck would go out of his way to see that I could visit my kids or get somebody to bring them here. He would tell me, 'In a couple of years, we will have a nursery and you can have your children here.' I didn't really believe him. I just sort of went along with the dream.

"I had given myself three months to stay, and I wasn't going to stay any longer than that. After three months, I found myself still here. He use to pull me in the office every so often to find out what was going on with me and how I was doing. I would start wondering. Why was he going out of his way to do all this for me? Was he really concerned about me?

"A turning point came when I was here about nine months or a year—something like that. I got a frantic call from my mother. She was always hysterical and complaining about something the kids did. I went to Chuck and told him about it. He simply said, 'Go get your kids and move them in.' Just like that!

"He also told me we'd have a place for a nursery. Of course, we do and I run it."

WORK PROBLEMS

In the early months after a woman kicks her habit, she is given basic tasks to do such as kitchen work, cooking, cleaning, or housekeeping. In time, some of the women move into other jobs. At this time, many women in Synanon occupy significant administrative roles in the organization.

The early work pattern of many is often compulsive. Their overwork almost appears to be a reaction formation to their underlying feelings of guilt. At the opposite extreme, some women are slovenly and have to be "pulled up" (reprimanded) about their appearance. One of these women explained it this way: "I think one reason I dressed like a slob was because, underneath, that's the way I felt. Also, the way I looked was an attention getter. I always wanted to be the center of attention."

The compulsively clean "hard workers" explained their behavior to me as a possible attempt to expiate their guilt or "wash their troubles away." Two girls, in their early days in Synanon, would take four and five showers a day. Others compulsively washed and ironed clothes, with detailed attention to removing all spots.

These extreme manifestations of guilt and attempts at expiation and rationalization for past behavior were not exclusively a female pattern. Many of the newcomer men also manifest some of the described patterns. The women, however, seem to experience a deeper and more pervasive guilt reaction.

THE ROLE OF WOMEN

The role and problem of women in Synanon are discussed in weekly meetings held by the Women's Council. Some selected excerpts from one of these special "women's-role-in-Synanon" sessions provide some insights:

BETTYE: I guess the responsibilities of women in Synanon are what they are in any family. We have to take care of our more helpless citizens—the newcomers, the children, and old people. We are also, of course, part of the total organization.

[An interchange developed on some special problems related to a new girl who wanted to leave. She was talked to and stayed. Bettye then gave what she called a "lightweight haircut" to the older girls for their indirect mistreatment of several newcomer girls.]

BETTYE: The newer girls are *newer* girls. They are *not* servants. They are not to be ordered around because you have a couple of years' seniority in Synanon and they are available to you. They should be fed Synanon information and Synanon concepts. That means you personally take the time to talk to them, take them on walks, and guide them.

Let me repeat what I brought up at the mothers' meeting last week. [This was a special synanon session for the problems of mothers in Synanon.] If anybody has the right to go into a "thing" [a period of depression and emotional confusion], it should be Chris [a newcomer], not any of you old-timers. The new girls are going to have bad feelings. They are going to be rebellious. They are going to act out. Of course, we shouldn't encourage them or feed their sickness. But I guess of all the girls living at number five [the nursery building], if anybody is under the bed wailing and moaning, it should be the new girls, not any of you older girls.

[The next issue that came up was the proper handling of work assignments. The group concentrated on the problems that the women seemed to have in organizing their work. Jeanne Camano, a three-year member and Women's Division executive, described her own difficulty.]

JEANNE: I don't know whether it's a feminine trait or whether it's a special problem of mine, but I have a problem staying organized. Lena doesn't seem to have this problem. Somehow Lena demonstrates consistency. She has completely a different personal orientation to work compared with mine. Maybe it's a personality thing. I have a feeling that it is necessary for me to make a list, because I can't keep myself organized long enough to accomplish anything in my work. It's my own personal lack of organization which makes for my work problem. It's not my inability to do something or my inability to have enough energy or strength. It's just my lack of organization.

When I have a strong male figure telling me how to work and what to do, I can function beautifully. I do okay as long as there is a tight rein on me. As soon as I am put in a position where I am my own boss and have to take care of my own business, I really go to pieces.

When I am given a job, like the one I have now, keeping records of donations, stores, and things in our warehouse and am told, "It's yours; do what you want to do with it," I get confused.

BETTYE: I can identify with you, Jeanne. When I first got here, it was easier for me to do things in the kitchen. I could put my hands on the pots and pans and cook and that kind of thing. When I got an administrative job here, it threw me too. Thrown on my own, here's what I learned to do—as one aid.

I have a folder—it's a dictation file for things to be done. When I think of anything to be done, I immediately write it down on a piece of paper and throw it in there. Lena picked this up as a hint. I gave it to her. This file is kind of a crutch you can lean on. It's impossible to keep everything in your head, and very important details get overlooked many, many times unless they are written down.

They are a reminder to you. For example, its impossible for me to keep in my head how many girls want to talk to me, when I should have a meeting, or if this is going to happen or that is going to happen. I have to start organizing my routine or my day on a workable level, then I can check it off, you know, check myself.

[The ensuing discusion concerned women who wanted their children back and what to do about it, handling special problems of women acting out their rebellion, and other such matters.]

The weekly meetings keep up with and handle many of the women's crucial problems in the organization and also serve the women as a continuing check on "where they're *at*." This important work on the special problems of women in Synanon is accomplished through the compassionate help and support of women who themselves have experienced the psychic pains of the addict but have successfully worked their way out of the morass.

THE ROAD BACK

The woman who has been entangled in the addiction-prostitution web has been far down and has a long distance to travel back. Many explain their early sensitivity to pain as the force that drove them to try to escape life through drugs. Conceivably, it may have been their early strong feelings of compassion and love, in most cases rejected, that caused them to regard the use of drugs as a way out of their painful emotional condition.

The women who succeed at Synanon are remarkable people. In addition to developing strong feelings about being truthful and loyal, they see no special glamour in the "hip-party-girl" pattern. They have sampled that life and have clearly rejected it.

The sum total of their past intense emotional experiences seems to leave them, after they turn their behavior completely around, with an unusual capacity for compassion and love. It may be that the security and direction they find at Synanon permits them to act as they always felt underneath. The Synanon process demands a positive set of values. Synanon's emphasis on truth, loyalty, and honesty seems to be effective in encouraging the women to assume their responsibilities as wives and mothers. To date (1964), there have been more than twenty successful marriages of Synanon people. Also, there are now about twenty-five mothers, with about thirty children living at Synanon. (This does not include the mothers and children among the "graduate" families.)

Synanon gets involved in the marital counseling of its members. This may account for the fact that, to date, only one marriage has failed out of the more than twenty marriages of Synanon people. Paula describes her Synanon experience and its effect on her marriage in the following way: "Going steady at Synanon gave Hal and I a relaxed opportunity to closely examine our thoughts and feelings for each other, in a way that many squares never get. In synanons and other activities, while we were busy cramming ourselves with the growing-up process, we found ourselves and each other.

"The many people whose lives are intimately shared had a genuine concern for our welfare. I think because of this, we learned how to air our problems, our inadequacies (real or imagined), and our fears about responsibility. We had the time to discard some of the unrealistic ideas and unbased fears about each other (and people in general) that seem to get in the way of living. Although Hal and I have been married now for almost three years, we still seem to benefit from the information we received in many synanons in the past. And, of course, unlike most of our married square friends, we have an understanding family of friends at Synanon we can turn to when things go wrong."

The people in Synanon, partially in compensation for their past, are apt to develop positive qualities in an intense measure. Growing up "the second time around" appears to be a powerful and productive human experience for both men and women.

Synanon provides a rounded human experience for women, through work and various cultural activities; however, their background and their reason for coming to Synanon are things they try not to forget.

Jeanne told me: "The first thing I don't want to do in my life is ever use drugs again. I don't want to be a dope addict. It makes everything so simple. If I start from the basic premise that the one thing I don't want to do is shoot dope, then anything else I do is better than that. And anything else I have in Synanon is frosting on the cake."

As might be expected, female Synanon members develop close

ties with their "brothers and sisters." At times, these loving emotions are forgotten in the fray of a synanon battle. At the end of a rugged session, Chuck put the girls' relationship to one another back into focus: "Why shouldn't the girls in this room be tremendous friends, closer than any sisters could ever get? It's incredible to me that it isn't true right now. It has to be, because you have shared experiences that no one else has shared. You've approached death and insanity as close as anyone possibly could and you've come back again. You've done this together. What greater common meeting ground or bond can any people have?

"There's nothing stronger. There can never be anything stronger. It's right there. It's right in the palm of your hand and sometimes you don't see it. There isn't a person around here that isn't full of faults and character defects and everything else. I'm the worst one of the whole damn bunch. But you know, we're all a pretty damn lovable crew. Obviously, we're better than we are bad. We've got to be better than we are bad or we wouldn't be sitting here today. We'd all be in jail—or dead."

6

Small-"S" Synanon

The small-"s" synanon is the group psychotherapy of the total Synanon social structure.[1] In a sense, it is the force that drives the wheels of the overall organization. Information is fed into these intensive group sessions for treatment purposes. Also, the content of a synanon tells a great deal about the Synanon organization at any given point in time. Synanons are run regularly as part of the total therapeutic process. In addition to the basic-problem-oriented synanons, there are special ones on different topics. Among these are synanons on status-seeking, organization, prejudice, education, and work problems.

In its basic form, about three times a week each member of Synanon participates in a synanon with ten to fifteen people. The groups proceed to different parts of the house. Everyone in the group settles down, as comfortably as possible, in a circle, facing one another. There is usually a brief silence, a scanning appraisal as to who is present, a kind of sizing one another up, and then the group launches into an intensive emotional discussion of personal and group problems. A key point of the sessions is an emphasis on extreme, uncompromising candor about one another. "No holds or statements are barred from the group effort at truth-seeking

[1] Throughout this volume Synanon refers to the overall organization and synanon refers to the special type of group psychotherapy described in this chapter.

137

about problem situations, feelings, and emotions of each and all members of the group," I have been told.

The synanon is, in some respects, an emotional battlefield. Here an individual's delusions, distorted self-images, and negative behavior are attacked again and again. The verbal-attack method involves exaggerated statements, ridicule, and analogy. The "attack," paradoxically, is an expression of love. As one Synanist told a person in a synanon: "If I didn't like you and also feel that you could change, I wouldn't tell you the things I do. It would be foolish to attack a cripple you don't like for limping."

Attack therapy in synanon has the effect of "toughening up" the person.[2] It helps him to see himself as relevant others do. He gains information and insights into his problems. If, at the conclusion of a synanon segment, an individual who has been under attack is able to hang on to any of his defenses, they are probably, in Synanon terms, "valid defenses." A participant in a synanon is forced to examine positive and negative aspects about himself, as well as some dimensions he would never have considered on his own. This often leaves him with a clearer view and a greater knowledge of his inner and outer world.

The process of a synanon also involves learning something about the norms of the overall Synanon society. The synanon helps to socialize the person and fosters a learning of interpersonal competence. This set of experiences seems to be useful for interaction situations both in Synanon and in the larger society.

The Synamaster

Synanon groupings are constructed by a "Synamaster" (usually an older Synanon member), who draws his lists from the overall population sheet of the house. The Synamaster puts together a group with a variety of considerations in mind. He may separate an "employer" and his "employee," or he may put them in the same synanon, with a "therapeutic hypothesis" in mind. He considers time in Synanon and chronological age as factors in constructing synanon groups.

[2] The rationale for "attack therapy" is presented in greater detail in Chapter 16, "The Newest Profession."

Ideally, a synanon should have a chronological and "Synanon-age" range, a correct male-female balance, and a senior Synanist to spark the session. These are only some of the many possible variables taken into account in constructing a synanon group. The Synamaster makes use of both knowledge and "hunches" in his consideration of the possibilities of each group's structure.

In some cases, the Synamaster will receive requests from an individual who wants to be in a synanon with a particular person in order to work out a special problem or because he has some data on the other person that he wants to reveal or discuss. Often two or more people, because of a particular situation, will request admission to the same synanon (for example, people who work together and have an interperson problem). These requests are usually granted and tend to have constructive consequences.

Some synanons are "rigged" in advance. Here a group or some key person is given a preliminary briefing about someone's problem, often with a suggestion as to how it might be worked out. Also, a combination of people with very similar problems may be placed in "fighting range" of one another in the same synanon. "Big talkers" and "screamers" may be mixed in with "quiet types" in order to give balance to the group.

Employer-employee problems and on-the-job problems generally are handled in the synanon. The synanon provides the opportunity to understand better a person's combined "official" and personal role. When an individual is thrown in with someone with whom he works, he has to relate to the individual's role both as a worker and as a person. The synanon provides an opportunity for an employee to confront his employer (or vice versa) on a personal level three times a week.

An important characteristic of synanon construction is the mathematical probability that no one group will meet intact more than once. This fact helps defeat the problem of the "therapeutic contract" that emerges in many professional therapy groups, where the same people meet regularly in the same group. A "therapeutic contract" involves a conscious and unconscious reciprocal agreement between two or more people not to expose one another's psychological "Achilles' heel." The unstated "contract" might be, for example, "If you don't expose or attack my embarrassing and painful mother problem, I won't bring up your problem with your wife."

Although synanon groups shift, as an individual builds up "synanon man-hours" his particular emotional problems and weaknesses become well known. This information is consciously exchanged and passed around the organization. A person may get a "jacket" (or personality inventory) that becomes well known. It is standard operating procedure *not* to maintain confidences expressed in a synanon. Personal data are Synanon property. An effort is made to use the information for the benefit of the individual and the group.

This "fallout" of personal information helps to ensure the continuity of an individual's "treatment." In synanons, a well-known "tough guy," "lazy slob," "momma's boy," or other type of personality may be continually attacked on his specific problem until he "straightens out." The continuity of treatment is also maintained by proper use of the person's "jacket" and the Synamaster's group arrangements.

Some Types of Synanons

The content of a synanon session is not usually predetermined. The group's spontaneity is called upon to bring out a timely and significant problem. An individual's problems may be introduced by the comment, "Hey, Jim, how come you look so guilty?" (or "nervous," or "happy" or "bored"). This may then trigger an investigation by the total group into the individual's feeling state. The person on the "hot seat" (or receiving end) is the primary focus of attention at the time and usually defends or counterattacks. In the interaction process, information about feelings, attitudes, and his life situation emerges for him and the group.[3]

[3] The synanon process has some of the characteristics of the adversary approach to justice in the courtroom. The judicial assumption is that the process of prosecution and defense interaction as adversaries will reveal the truth. A similar procedure operates in synanons. In the synanon situation, an attempt is made to bring to the surface the delusions and faulty self-images that have kept the "defendant" in trouble with himself and the world around him. In the synanon, the adversary truth-seeking method is employed for the purpose of self-realization. An effort is made to have the person know himself, in accord with a much-quoted concept in Synanon, "The truth shall set you free."

SURFACING A PROBLEM

The following is an oversimplified example of the way a segment of a session begins and unfolds. Jack, age twenty-four, in Synanon for four months, is accused of an excessive dependency on his mother. It is then alleged by the group that this has prevented him from identifying with Synanon and becoming part of the processes that could help him. He counters by stating that the accusations are ridiculous and unfounded. "It's a bum beef." It is pointed out to him that he has been observed to do very little else in Synanon but wait for phone calls and mail from his mother. (The accusation is somewhat exaggerated, since Jack *has* been working and participating in the program.) After about fifteen minutes of group cross-examination, he admits to an extreme, depressing loneliness and a desire to see his mother. He claims that she is the only one in the world who truly loves and understands him. He has thought of "splitting" to go back to New York to see her.

His claim of his mother's exclusive love for him is scoffed at and ridiculed. In reply, as proof of her love, he points out that "she always gave me money for the commissary when I was in prison." This is ridiculed by the group as "guilt money." Jack cites other examples of her "mother love," including the fact that "when I was up tight, she would sometimes even give me money for a fix!" His arguments are battered by the group.

He concludes, "Maybe I am sucking a dry tit and ought to let go." The group advises him to "go through the motions" of forgetting her for a while and "joining Synanon." They point out how he can resume his relationship with his mother under better conditions when he "straightens out." Jack admits to seeing his relationship with his mother in a somewhat clearer light. He "feels better" now that his feelings are "out" and agrees to "get with Synanon."

This is obviously a highly oversimplified glimpse of a slice of a synanon. However, it illustrates something of the kind of interaction used in an attempt to produce facts about a situation, the types of defenses used, some of the insights into behavior, and some of the suggestions for change. Not all dimensions of a problem are worked out for an individual in any single session. Over a long period of time, however, many Synanon members benefit from the help of a group that is familiar with their difficulty, since others in the group have had similar problems.

SOME DIMENSIONS OF PREJUDICE

Jack's dilemma related to a mother-lover problem. The following is a verbatim account of part of a synanon that probes the issue of prejudice. It reveals some of the dynamics of the direct-confrontation approach to underlying feelings in a synanon session. Wilbur and "Pete" (John Peterson) are the only Negroes in the session (involving about ten people).

PETE: I want to ask Wilbur something. Wilbur, what did you react to so much in synanon the other night?

WILBUR: Oh, I got triggered off. We had a synanon and talked about prejudice.

PETE: You're not prejudiced are you?

WILBUR: Yeah, I'm prejudiced.

NANCY: [Sarcastically] Oh, Wilbur, are you really prejudiced . . . really?

WILBUR: [Jokingly] As bad as I hate to say it and as much as it hurts me, I'm prejudiced, and I got triggered off and I started yelling and screaming.

PETE: What triggered you, Wilbur?

WILBUR: When Danny called me a black nigger I got very, very mad—and I just blew.

PETE: I hear you went around the room and said fuck you to every white face in the room. How do you feel about the white faces in this room?

WILBUR: Well right now—when I'm not prejudiced—I like everyone in this room. I don't have any hostility right now towards anyone in this room. But I imagine if they start throwing hostility at me, I probably would react.

HERB: If people don't try to communicate with you everything is hunky-dunky. But if people start communicating with you, then you have hostility for them.

WILBUR: I don't think that's true. I like to communicate with people. You know, communicating is communicating. I don't feel anything about talking to a person, which means communicating. But hostility, I react to hostility. What I think is hostility, I meet with hostility.

PETE: You mean to tell me nobody in this room brings your prejudice out in you.

WILBUR: No, not just like this. If someone starts talking about prejudice and calls me a black nigger, where I'll feel something, then watch, you'll see.

PETE: What about this sucker right here that goes around the house all day spewing his prejudice shit out of his mouth all the time. [Pete refers to Don, accusing him of spreading anti-Negro prejudice in Synanon.]

NANCY: Yes, Don always is dropping his prejudice around the building.

WILBUR: I've never heard it.

PETE: You've never heard it? Call him a black nigger, Don, like you do other people everyday of the week.

NANCY: Like you do everybody else, when they're trying to eat dinner.

GEORGE: Yeah, you always talk about these spick [Spanish] meals!

DON: Yeah, well, I don't like spicks, but I didn't say anything at dinner.

WILBUR: Well, you see, that triggers me, hearing about this son-of-a-bitch and what he does all the time.

PETE: [To Don, sarcastically] You say you don't like spicks. How do you feel about niggers?

DON: Well, I don't dig them like I dig Jewish guys, you know. [Don is Jewish.]

PETE: Who's talking about Jewish guys, sucker?

DON: I'm prejudiced, all right. I'm prejudiced like Wilbur.

PETE: I asked you a question. Why don't you answer it?

DON: Hey, listen, I don't want to scream in synanon. Wilbur has a bigger prejudice problem than I do.

WILBUR: No, look, I get mine out in synanon. No one can tell you that they hear me around the floor talking the shit that I talk in synanon. I talk about my prejudice in synanons, and I'm talking to a mother-fuckin' white face like you. You see, I call you a mother-fucker, but I do it in synanons.

DON: So what does that prove—what does that prove?

WILBUR: That proves you ain't got no goddamn guts.

NANCY: Don, you can do the right thing in here by spewing your prejudice garbage in a synanon, where more people can look at it with you. Get it out here and now. Then maybe you won't be spreading it all over the house.

PETE: You gutless mother-fucker, you won't call him [Wilbur] anything to his face. You'd rather go behind his back and call him something. Why don't you call it to his face?

DON: We've spoken about my prejudice already in synanons.

PETE: Tell it to him now.

DON: I'm not going to tell it to him again. I told him how I feel about him.

PETE: How do you feel about him, then?

DON: I can't see a colored guy doing executive work or in charge of me.

JACK: What did you tell Sherry [a Negro woman] the other night? You know, all colored broads ain't supposed to do nothing but clean up, you know?

DON: When did I tell her this?

JACK: In synanon the other—

DON: Oh, you say a lot of things to trigger the guys.

JACK: That's how you feel. Man, why not admit it? Get it out. You might feel better!

GEORGE: This is how you feel. You know you've had this all your life. All colored women coming and cleaning your house and so forth, once a week or every other week, you know? And this is the conditioning you've had.

PETE: You fat, ignorant slob. That's exactly what you are. And you don't have any guts, man—not a gut in your whole fuckin' body. . . . You're the biggest asshole in the house and the biggest coward.

DON: [Trying to act unprovoked] Right.

PETE: I could probably get up and spit in your face right now and all you'd do is wipe it off.

DON: Go ahead and try it.

PETE: You fuckin' coward.

DON: Go ahead and try it.

[Here the "no-physical-violence" rule is tested. It permits Don and Pete to express their real feelings, without the possibility of physical retaliation.]

PETE: What do you think of me right now?

DON: What am I suppose to do, get mad at you, man?

PETE: I'm mad at your crazy ass right now. You know what you are to me right now?

DON: What?

PETE: You're exactly like them suckers down in Birmingham last week that turned dogs loose on people to do what they couldn't do. That's exactly what you are to me right now. You're like that prejudiced mother-fucker, Governor ————.

DON: That's good; that means you respect me, you're afraid of me.

PETE: Yeah, I respect you all right.

DON: Definitely.

HERB: Do you think anybody in here respects you, Don? Forget about the prejudice—do you think anybody in here respects you?

DON: No.

HERB: Now they put you down all the time and ridicule you.

DON: They can't down me all the time.

HERB: *This is the world, Don, this is the world!*

DON: Herby, I'm in a world of my own. Jack here goes to the other extreme with his prejudice. [Jack is Jewish, and Don accuses him of getting "too close" to Negroes. He implies that Jack's fraternizing is reverse prejudice.]

JACK: My bed's in his [Wilbur's] house and it don't bother me, but a Jew prick like you [Don] bothers me more than a black guy like Wilbur, see?

WILBUR: It's all right for you if you have to feel this way, Don. No one is indicting you for your feelings.

DON: Then what's all this bullshit about?

WILBUR: What I'm indicting you for is taking these feelings out everyday in the building and spreading all this goddamn garbage and hate into our house. Dump that prejudice garbage here in a synanon, where you can get some help and change, and maybe you'll understand it better, and maybe I will too. Let's use the synanon to handle these vicious prejudice feelings. Maybe we can work the problem out here together.

Senior and Junior Synanists

Built into the synanon sessions is an awareness of each group member's ability to take a bombardment of truth about himself. The Synanon *newcomer* is often handled lightly (given a "pass") until he becomes trained into the method. Old-timers in Synanon and synanons are considered fair game for all-out attack. With them, there is an assumption that the synanon experience has toughened their emotional hides. They can defend more capably and are better prepared to handle the group's biting appraisal of their personal problems.

The senior members of Synanon, who have been through many synanons, are more sophisticated in their ability as Synanists. When they get together in a "senior-members' synanon" (as often occurs), they use less profanity, throw up fewer "smoke screens" to obscure their problems, and waste less time on irrelevancies. Their synanon fighting style is more like a rapier than a bludgeon. When a point is made, the group does not dwell on it and savor its "great success"; they move into another problem area. At least one senior Synanist is injected into each basic "floor synanon" to facilitate the interaction, pace, and productivity of the session.

When newly arrived individuals dominate a group, the synanons are more apt to be cathartic sessions that involve excessive "emotional vomiting" and wild verbal fighting. As an individual grows and develops in the Synanon organization, he usually develops better control and has greater insight. Older members tend to be more intellectual and in many respects more productive in a synanon.

According to Chuck: "Individuals who are more adult in the Synanon organization and whose attention span is greater are able to sit in a synanon longer. The emotional babies can't keep to a subject too long, or they get ground up on an irrelevant item."

Chuck maintains that the subject and focus of a session needs to be varied and gave this instruction about the use of the synanon method: "There is a tendency, if you don't vary the synanon material, to run out of gas. When you shoot your wad with one person or topic, then move on to another. It's a refreshing experience. You have new strength, you have new data to work with. It's very tiring to go on and on and on with one person. After you've pushed someone for ten minutes or so, move over to someone else. Everyone can learn more from using a different set of emotional muscles." The senior Synanist is able to set the pace of a synanon in terms of these principles.

THE ROLE MODEL

A conscious dimension of the synanon situation is the use of the senior Synanist as a "role model." The role model is a synanist who has been in the situation of the newer person and has made progress to a higher level of performance. The role model is a living example of what the newcomer can become. Often the comment is made by the senior Synanist, "I remember when I was like you when I was here X amount of time." The role model (or as Bach [4] calls him the "senior patient") then points out why and how he is no longer deviant or misbehaving. This permits the newcomer to identify with someone who has experienced the same internal conflicts that he is currently facing. In addition, the role model provides some preliminary information about the problems that the newcomer can anticipate when he reaches the older member's level of functioning in Synanon.

Self-revelation by the "therapist" in a synanon is a factor not usually found in professional group therapy. Professionals seldom use their own problems as examples for the patient. In fact, it is counterindicated in most therapeutic methodology. In synanons, however, it is standard technique for the acting "doctor" to "cop out" and identify himself with the "patient's" problem. In synanons, therefore, an individual has pointed out to him an achievable, positive goal, exemplified by a person who can guide his growth from the successful position of his own personal experience.

The role-model concept is openly discussed in synanons as

[4] George Bach, *Intensive Group Psychotherapy*, New York: The Ronald Press Company, 1954.

a basic socialization process for developing personality. It is comparable to the family unit of the larger society, where mother, father, and older brothers and sisters are the role models whom the child emulates. This same process operates in Synanon for socializing its "children" into adults.

Combating the Phony Insight: Pseudopsychology

One ruse that is counteracted by the use of shifting synanon groups and the senior synanist is the "therapeutic contract" for a "dramatic insight discovery." The "dramatic insight discovery" is a fake insight that is used by a patient to give the appearance of making therapeutic progress, thus avoiding the pain related to true self-examination.

The phony-insight game (avoided in synanon) takes the following form in standard group therapy. A group member in a therapy session makes the "remarkable discovery" that he shoots drugs (or acts out other deviances) to rebel against his proper, respectable father. The "insight" occurs as a result of a series of interchanges with the "therapeutic-contract" partner, who may in a later session reveal a remarkable "insight" of his own. The two involved in this kind of reciprocal deception (in some cases, a third person gets a "piece of the action") nurture and manipulate each other over several sessions into revealing their smoke-screen "discoveries." These "insights" (even when they have some degree of validity) enable the individuals who have revealed them to get the group off their backs, since they are "obviously making progress" in understanding themselves. They can then spend the rest of their therapeutic-interaction days feeding each other soothing lines such as, "Of course, that relates to your admitted rebellion against your father," and therapeutic progress founders. In synanon, shifting groups and the trained synanists tend to deter the development or continuation of this pattern of psychological masturbation.

Also, in synanon group therapy, pat pseudopsychological answers are viciously attacked when they are used as rationales for bad behavior. As Chuck told a newcomer trying this old game in a synanon, "In one sense, we don't really give a damn if your grandfather was an alcoholic, your mother hustled, and your father slugged you daily. None of it is an excuse for *bad behavior in Synanon!*"

In the synanon system, good behavior is demanded on the implicit assumption that it affects internal (intrapsychic) processes. Synanon uses an approach that is the reverse of that commonly used in psychotherapy. In most therapeutic practice, the starting point for treatment is the internal world of the patient. Generally, in professional therapy, the assumption is made that if a person's inner problems are somehow adjusted, he will stop "acting out" his "bad" behavior. Synanon starts with an attack on the reality of overt bad behavior.

ATTACKING THE INSIGHT DISCOVERY

In the annals of Synanon, a particular incident helps to reveal the synanon approach to the phony "insight discovery." Thereafter, this kind of situation became known as a "Lefty" (named after the member involved). The episode was described by Reid Kimball in the following way: "Lefty committed several offenses of the following type: He would bully or threaten another member, usually a smaller guy. He never used any violence, because he knew that he might get kicked out for it. On about his third offense, Chuck and I were in a synanon with him, and the two of us began to work him over, with the group's help. What happened in this particular case was that he had picked up a tire iron and threatened Bill Crawford. Bill had ordered him to do something in the course of a work project. Compared to Lefty, Bill is a physical lightweight.

"Well, in the synanon, we confronted Lefty with his atrocious behavior. He began to use a psychological mishmash of terms to defend. He said that he had a psychological block, that he was displacing aggression, and a whole bunch of other rationalizations and bullshit.

"Chuck and I glanced at each other and decided to really put him on. Chuck said something like, 'Well, let's examine the psychological implication of your behavior with Bill.' Lefty brightened up, and we went at it. Chuck said, 'Let's analyze it. Is there any significant figure in your earlier life or is there any situation that comes to your mind when you think about the Crawford incident?'

"Lefty's eyes began to glitter, and he said, 'Let me think.' Chuck saw him take the bait and said, 'This may explain the whole thing, think hard.' Lefty pursed his lips, acted pained, wrinkled his brow, stared up at the ceiling, and went off into a reverie of deep thought.

"He then said, 'Gee, that makes a lot of sense. It certainly brings something to my consciousness. At one period, when I was a kid, and I use to wash dishes—'

" 'Who did you wash dishes for?'

" 'It was my grandmother! She had a certain way of talking to me and a nasal twang and . . .'

" 'And perhaps this reminds you of Crawford?'

" 'That's it! Crawford sounds just like my grandmother. She use to make me wash dishes and nag at me when I wanted to go out and play. She really used to incite my hostility.'

"Then Chuck said, 'Well, maybe we've hit on it. Crawford, with his particular approach and his voice tone, seems to trigger you, and you associate his behavior with hers.' Everyone in the session joined in to confirm Lefty's exciting insight discovery.

"Lefty picked up on the group's approval and went on further: 'By God, that's it exactly—when Crawford comes on like he does, it's my grandmother all over again. No wonder I blow up and . . .'

"At this point, Lefty was beaming—carrying on and everything—and then Chuck pushed him right off the cliff, 'You lying son-of-a-bitch, you're so full of shit, it's ridiculous!' With that, everyone in the group broke up in a loud roar of laughter.

"Here he was trying to rationalize away his bad behavior with this bull story he had dug out of Psychology I. Of course, he couldn't get away with it in Synanon. The Lefty story spread all over the club; and from that day on, anytime anyone tried to pull that crap to avoid personal responsibility for their behavior, someone will say, 'You're pulling a Lefty!' or, 'It sounds just like Lefty's grandmother.' "

The synanon makes it difficult for an individual to hide behind a false insight, complicate a simple behavioral situation
with pseudoanalysis, or maintain a "therapeutic contract" for any
length of time. "Insight discoveries" are placed under close scrutiny in a synanon. If they do stand up after a synanon group
barrage, they probably have validity; and in the process, every
facet of the insight or situation has been tested and examined.

Professionals tend to lean more heavily on the psychological
insight. Within the framework of standard professional psychotherapy, insight discoveries (valid or not) are the "bread and
butter" of the trade. The professional may, in fact, encourage
insight discoveries to validate their own success. Chuck takes
this position on the issue: "These are, of course, the professional
stock-in-trade. When someone comes into Synanon loaded with
all kinds of psychological mishmash, for a while we have a hell
of a time breaking through to the person beneath. Of course,
many psychological principles are valid—and are useful later on
in his growth process. But at first we have to deal with the
person and his actual behavior at that time. We cannot permit
him to use psychological explanations to rationalize his bad
behavior. He might shoot dope behind it."

SYNANON AND PROFESSIONAL GROUP THERAPY:
SOME COMPARISONS

Synanon sessions operate within a social scheme and under a
set of conditions different from those of standard professional
group therapy.

First: The sessions are administered by a group of peers who
have similar problems. Because of a similarity of life experiences
and identifications, a fellow Synanist is more likely to be acceptable as a "therapist" than the usual professional. Also, compared
with the usual professional therapist, the synanist is *not* seen as
an *authority figure* in the usual sense.

Second: Synanists can and do reverse roles as "patient" and
"therapist" in synanon sessions. The Synanist who plays the role
of a therapeutic agent in a synanon expects, and often does obtain, some insights into his own problems in the process of help-

ing the other person. He often projects his own problems into the situation. This kind of cooperative therapy facilitates the realization of a true total therapeutic community.[5]

Third: Synanon involves a democratic approach to "psychological interaction." There is an absence of the usual status differences between "patients" and "doctors." This condition of equality among group members seems to facilitate a deeper intensity and involvement than does standard group therapy.

Fourth: The emotional growth of each person in Synanon is of concern to everyone in the group. Everyone's success and personal growth is part of Synanon's overall development. An enlightened self-interest in helping the other member is a significant motivating force for all participants. There is a "gut-level" recognition that no man *can be* an island in Synanon. Involvement with Synanon entails involvement with the success or failure of other members.

Fifth: The session material is timely, pertinent, and important to all members of the group, partly because they live together in the same community. The use of material and events in a synanon that have been experienced firsthand by other members of the group is a most significant element of the synanon. The problems dealt with are vital to all the members.

In contrast, in professional group therapy, the group members usually come from various walks of life, convene for a session, and then return to their private worlds. This kind of treatment can become a therapeutic game, not closely related to basic life situations, since the group members do not live in similar environments. In Synanon, a person locks horns with others who are part of his actual primary group. Everyone is a "significant other" to him in his life space. The "other" confronting him in the synanon may be his roommate, employer, lover, or wife. Having them understand or get a "correct" self-picture of himself is of crucial importance. The synanon encounter is therefore a potent interaction, and the outcome of a session has real mean-

[5] This type of society is a live demonstration of Moreno's concept of the *total* therapeutic community, where everyone is a therapist (and at the same time a patient) to everyone else. See J. L. Moreno, *Who Shall Survive?*, New York: Beacon House, Inc., 1953.

ing for all participants. When a decision is made in a synanon session, the person has, in fact, acted. The synanon is not a game. It is live and meaningful behavior.

Synanon's Social Structure and the Synanon

As Synanon increased from a small, "face-to-face" primary group to more than forty people, it began to take on the characteristics of a secondary, more impersonal group structure. Chuck began to delegate and transfer leadership and power to some of the older members. Department heads were appointed and began to meet "in committee." The interoffice memo was discovered, and more complex files were developed. The organization began the natural drift toward bureaucracy and a degree of dehumanization that often results from increase in size.

It became apparent to Chuck that it was becoming physically impossible for him and the Board of Directors to indoctrinate or handle all persons and problems directly. The lines of communication in the organization shifted, and power was increasingly relegated and delegated to different people and divisions. A head of women in Synanon was appointed to handle their special problems; another woman was placed in charge of the nursery. Also, as each new location opened, a member was appointed to the role of acting director to "sit on top" of the new establishment.

Chuck recognized the possible ill effects of bureaucracy on an organization that is primarily devoted to human problems. In a tape-recorded discussion, Chuck and I talked about the matter of Synanon's drift toward bureaucracy. The following excerpts from our talk reveal the important role of *the synanon* in maintaining the primary group force of Synanon.

L.Y.: Sociologists have made many theoretical observations about the important qualities of primary-group organization. They have noted that face-to-face personal communication, identity of goals, and real concern for another, as exemplified in the ideal family, are basic to the proper socialization of the "child." Special prob-

lems seem to develop in a human organization when it becomes
a more machine-like, secondary form of group structure. The
secondary pattern of relating could pose some significant difficulties for a milieu like Synanon. Here, if people become automa-
tons, placed in certain status boxes and expected to function
with limited personal orientation, it could defeat Synanon's
human-development goals. Bureaucracy can be extremely functional in a technological way in Synanon if it doesn't compromise
the basic "human" quality of the organization.

Synanon, in a microcosmic way, seems to be confronted with
the problems of the macrocosm. In the larger society, the threat
of large-scale industrial organizations and a shift from small community to urban area, with its concomitants of dehumanization,
creation of anonymity, and the loss of personal identity, have
been major American dilemmas. Bigness and mass production
are functional and economical, but gains in this direction have
been counterbalanced by the creation of many severe new social
problems. These include crime and addiction, the very problems
Synanon is attempting to solve. Now that Synanon has moved
into this somewhat bureaucratic secondary-group pattern, how
do you plan to maintain the vital primary-group orientation of
the organization?

CHUCK: The small-"s" synanon is the contrived, constructed primary-group formula for the maintenance of our secondary organization. The two put together, I believe, produces a most
effective kind of human organization. It has become axiomatic in
Synanon that the triggering mechanism in the whole dynamic
was, is, and always will be the small-"s" synanon, in its expanding
form. The synanon started as being peculiarly suited to its time
and place and is, of course, growing, expanding, and taking on
dimensions that it didn't have before. I guess the original in-
vention, the innovation, of Synanon was not the living together,
it was not the preparing of meals together. The innovation of
Synanon was the devising of the so-called synanon.

Preserving, adding to, and expanding the synanon has the effect of ameliorating some of the so-called evils that are associated
with bureaucracy. The synanon is, in a sense, a floating primary-
group situation that impregnates the whole secondary-group
structure of Synanon.

L.Y.: You imply that Synanon attempts to utilize the best properties of both primary- and secondary-group relationships. The synanons, then, are the formalized primary groups called into action and adapted to the requirements of the total organization.

As Synanon has moved toward a secondary-group structure, the synanons have been adapted to a variety of needs of the organization. The therapy synanon focuses on personal therapeutic-interaction problems and helping people to "grow up." Other synanons are useful for investigating and solving organizational problems. Another type of synanon is useful for educational purposes.

Synanon seems to have produced an approach to bureauacracy that might well be adapted to business or industry. A group of business executives or management people might very well benefit from taking off the straitjacket of their *organization status* and talking to each other person-to-person. Of course, this is done in some measure. However, the synanon facilitates a deeper level of communication.

CHUCK: Definitely. As an ex-corporation executive myself, I can look back and see how it might have been most effective. Who knows, if there had been synanons in the corporation I worked for, lots of guys, including myself, operating at low efficiency because of alcoholism might have been reached and made more productive. It would have had a hell of an effect on the total organization if executives and others could communicate person-to-person, synanon style.

Getting back to large-growth problems at Synanon, a new trend is now developing. It occurred to me a few weeks ago that it would be a good idea to explore the possibilities of setting up or introducing into the environment what we might call the "house synanon." We now have over ten separate residences here in Santa Monica alone, each containing from five to twenty people. I selected one and called a meeting of the residents of what we call "house number 6," or "Hank's pad." We sat down and we had a helluva synanon right in that house.

L.Y.: In other words, you built a "family synanon" into their life situation. So, despite the fact that they are part of a larger organization, they have a primary-group mechanism built into their lives, right in their own home.

As I mentioned before, in looking at the organizational problems of Synanon, we are in some measure discussing a broader problem characteristic of American society. Bureaucracy has produced an increasing problem of family disorganization, partially as a result of work patterns in the large automated factory.

It has dehumanized the worker. As a cog in the large industrial machine, the active use of his primary-group faculties is increasingly diminished and lies fallow. At work on the "assembly line," whether it's in an office or at a lathe, he is in a machine-like situation for eight or ten hours a day. At home there is usually another kind of secondary-relationship situation. Here the machine (for example, TV, electrical gadgets, and so on) also dominates interpersonal relationships. The result is limited primary-group communication. People living this way seldom exercise their primary human mechanisms for relating to another person. It might be effective to have synanons held several times a week in some American homes. Imagine the possibility of parents, wives, sons, daughters, and husbands putting aside their roles and openly talking to each other person-to-person?

There seems to be a desperate need for the revitalization of a primary-group pattern of relationship. The ahuman processes of socialization that many children in American society are exposed to seem to produce a high rate of sociopathic individuals. The absence of deep primary-group relationships produces people with a limited social conscience, unable to relate effectively to one another. The extreme example of this is the "kicks-oriented," violent gang kids, with their destructive motivations and inability to relate to another person.

Part of the problem is that a child growing up in an anonymous society seldom sees people engaging in primary-group relationships with one another. They don't know what sympathy, empathy, or concern for another is, because it is seldom within the range of their human experience. They grow up looking for something to change their feelings of emptiness and alienation. The symptom of this problem can be anything from empty TV-watching to "kicks." This would include the very symptom you are working with here, drug addiction. That's why I believe that the synanon is such an important method. The synanon seems to get people to interact on an intense personal level and counteracts the ahuman conditions of alienation and separation.

For example, synanons on prejudice and discrimination are powerful tools for getting people together. In the discrimination synanon, Wilbur and Don, black and white, put their deeper emotions on the subject out in the open. This person-to-person, eyeball-to-eyeball, deep primary-group interaction in a synanon facilitates the solution of these problems. I strongly believe that almost any kind of human problem can be resolved through a deep primary-group kind of interaction. The synanon is a device that produces this level of interaction.

CHUCK: In times of greater stress, in matters of life and death, we always go back to the primary group. For example, if we wish to put a commando team together in time of war, we get a small group of men together, put them in a primary-group situation, and they seem to function with great effectiveness.

The large corporation could benefit from the use of synanons as floating primary groups. For example, in a corporation, the small accounting department on the third floor may have some primary-group aspects in it. Perhaps some of the guys get together on weekends, play golf, or even have parties together. They may even cut up their personal problems in the office. They do this, but how do they communicate with the operations department on the fourth floor, people who are essentially doing similar work? Here's where the temporary, fluid synanon can come into play. In Synanon, in a synanon session, you have two people out of primary-group A, four people out of primary-group C, and three people out of primary-group G. All these people, from different parts of our total organization, get together in a synanon. This is what our Synamaster accomplishes by putting the groups together properly. The synanons, therefore, put some primary-group juice into the total organization.

Let me try to summarize our analysis of the role of synanons in counteracting the so-called evils of bureaucracy. The big pyramid, *Synanon*, is composed of many small *permanent* pyramids within its context. There are many face-to-face primary groups in Synanon. The secondary group, the Synanon total, thus comprises many primary groups. In order to make the overall organization more cohesive, we developed the phenomenon of the small-"s" synanon. The synanon is a small *temporary* pyramid within the boundaries of the large, inclusive pyramid. Every night, we create many small synanon pyramids composed of ten to fifteen people. The synanon pyramid is in existence for a couple of hours. The people who are members of that pyramid, which disintegrates and goes into eternity at the end of about two hours, gather together again in other pyramids on other days.

The fluidity factor is important. Most organizations are a pile of small permanent pyramids. We have that, but in addition to that, we have planned small temporary pyramids that have the short life-span of a few hours. They go out of existence after they have served their purpose. The proper use of synanons is our most important method for solving some of our large-group problems. The synanon is, of course, not only a tool for dealing with organizational problems; it helps our people learn how to communicate and relate on a deeper human level. After all, Synanon's primary goal is to help our people "grow up." The synanon is one of our primary tools for accomplishing this main goal of human growth and development. Also, secondarily, we try to use the synanon to neutralize the destructive elements of bureaucratic organization.

7

Institutions

The criminal-addict has a close familiarity with the traditional "correctional" systems. For him, reformatories, prisons, jails, mental hospitals, and addict hospitals are all familiar institutions. Even on his first "bust" (arrest) and incarceration, he has usually been equipped with a set of attitudes for handling encounters with society and its "administrators of justice." He learns the proper set of attitudes and responses on the streets, and these are reinforced in jail.

The "bad guys" are the cops, "squares" (nonaddicts), judges, jailors, and prison administrators; on the right side of the fence are "righteous dope fiends" and "stand-up guys." The criminal-addict learns quickly to trust the "right guys" and to hate and distrust all squares. He can "smell a cop a mile away," and he can pick a "dope fiend" out of a crowd.[1]

In prison, if he's a "right guy," he lives according to inmate rules. He believes "thou shalt not squeal," he engages in petty larceny (stealing food, especially nutmeg, which supposedly gives

[1] At a probation conference that I attended with Candy Latson, he picked out an individual in a crowd of several hundred people and said to me, "What's that using dope fiend doing here?" I later confirmed that Candy had, in fact, picked out an addict who was being claimed as cured by several psychiatrists in the group. The psychiatrists seemed to derive some emotional satisfaction from their "success," although it was Candy's opinion that the person was still using drugs and was high at that time.

him a "charge"), and he gets some homosexual kicks from the prison "punks." All these activities and others are supported by the "right guys" in the inmate system.

If he is a "solid" member of the ingroup, he uses, or "cons," the staff whenever he can. They are the enemy inside the walls who represent the enemy (square society) outside the walls.

According to the inmates' code, the hospital or prison therapist is considered, *at best*, a stupid square. When a Synanon member mentioned "a fantastic psych [psychiatrist] at Lex," I wanted to hear more, since this was the first psychiatrist I had heard discussed in positive terms by an ex-inmate. I was told, "Oh, he was a stupid shit about helping me with my problem, just like the rest of them. But, man, he took me off a bad drug habit and I didn't feel a thing. I had practically no withdrawal pains."

Almost all members of hospital and prison officialdom are stereotyped by the inmate code—at best as inept, at worst as proper targets of extreme rebellious hatred. For most inmates, they represent objects to be manipulated for quicker release, or they are "tricks" to beat for small "scores" to relieve the boredom and monotony of custody. In the chess game of manipulation, the institution's officials are pawns. This inmate code tends to confirm and reinforce criminal-addict ethics and behavior.

By contrast, the criminal-addict entering Synanon is bound to be baffled by what he finds. *Everyone is a "right guy," including the administrators.* If he tries to play his usual prison games, he is laughed at. He can't hate the officials, and he can't even hate squares, because they are the "good people who support our organization."

If he wants to "break out" (a common subject of conversation in prison), he is invited to "get lost" by the staff. At every turn, he discovers new responses to old situations and, most important, other people who know how he feels. Instead of a callous reaction, he is told, "I remember how I felt when I first got here," and this is followed by a detailed description of the feeling he is experiencing at the time. This is often disconcerting and frightening, because it is a new and strange situation. Yet, at the same time, the sight of others like himself who "made it" gives him confidence.

In Synanon, he finds a new society. He encounters understanding and affection from people who have had similar experiences. He finds a community with whom he can identify, toward
whom he can express the best human emotions that are in him,
rather than the worst. He finds friends who will "pull him up"
when he begins to slip or fall short of what he has set out to do:
to develop and mature. In the new society, he finds a vehicle
for expressing his best human qualities and potentialities.

Entrance and Indoctrination

A "prospect" (the Synanon term for someone seeking entrance) must voluntarily present himself and must prove to an
indoctrination committee of older Synanon members that he truly
seeks help and wants to change his behavior. He does not enter
an organization that is compelled to accept him, as in a govern-
ment-run jail or hospital. His acceptance comes from a peer group.
He is both puzzled and intrigued by the Synanon indoctrination
process.

In the following portion of an interview of an addict-prospect
fresh off the streets of New York, Jack Hurst reveals some of the
attack-therapy approach used in one kind of indoctrination.[2] The
prospect had not been helped in any of the several jails and addict hospitals he has been in and came to Synanon with an air
of belligerence. Jack forcefully presented Synanon's "contract."

JACK: If we decide to take you in, you'll be the new element in
the family. You'll be kind of like the new baby. We'll talk in
terms of family structure—it isn't bad. You'll be told when to
get up and what to do when you do get up. You'll be told when
to go to synanon, what kind of work to do, when to go to seminars. You'll be told when to talk and when not to talk. You will
kind of be told what to do for a while. I guarantee that if you go
through the motions that we describe and prescribe for you, you'll
end up being a man, not the sniveling, whining brat that you
are now. You'll be a man!

[2] The complete process is presented in Chapter 9, "Indoctrination."

PROSPECT: What makes you think I'm a sniveling brat? You only know me for five minutes and . . .

JACK: You see, people that use drugs, people that steal hub caps, people that go in and out of jails, people that go to nut houses for help are sniveling brats in my opinion, and my opinion carries a lot of weight in this house. Get that gut level. Try to understand that, and if you don't understand it, act as if you understand.

When you make a lot of noise in our environment, it's not very nice to listen to. Arguments are something we save for synanons. You can argue your ass off in a synanon. When you're being talked to around here and when you're in our office or in our dining room, you kind of behave yourself and keep your big mouth shut. Listen to what's going on around you—you might learn something. Don't be so frightened about learning something. You see, you almost learned something a moment ago—the fact that you are a whining, sniveling brat. But you fight it.

That's your big trouble with life—you fight information that could help you. If you could start to accept some of these things about yourself and learn to live with them, you know, you may outgrow it. I guarantee you, you will if you stay. There's no question about that in my mind. No question whatsoever. If you stay, if you listen, and if you do as we say, I guarantee it.

Now you're not going to be expected for a couple of months to do our banking, for instance. This would be like asking a four-year-old child to do our shopping. You're not going to be expected to get into our car and go to Bridgeport to pick up donations. You're not going to be expected to make big decisions concerning what will be policy around here. We have other people to do this. What you're going to be expected to do, at first, is to wash the toilets, wash the floors, do the dishes, anything that we feel that you should be doing. As you learn how to do these things well, *well* mind you, then you will gradually get to more and better things, or let's say more responsible jobs. You'll graduate up the power structure. Pretty soon, you know, in a couple of years, maybe even a year, you just might be a big shot around here—or Santa Monica or Reno.

This reflects only one kind of indoctrination—and a rather tough one. Jack felt a tough line was called for with this individual, because he came with a chip on his shoulder. Jack attempted to test him out to see whether he was willing to accept some of the verbal attack he would later receive in synanons. With other prospects, a more conciliatory, warmer approach is used. Women are usually indoctrinated by other women. The tone of their indoctrinations is generally softer; although the facts and expectations of life and work in Synanon are clearly and forcefully set forth to all "prospects."

The newcomer thus enters voluntarily into a community of people who formerly had his very problem. They clearly inform him that the primary basis for being accepted is proof of a desire to reorient his life. This situation is the reverse of the one in which an offender arrives in police custody at a jail or a mental hospital. In Synanon, the prospect is also clearly told at the outset that if he does not live up to the organization's rules, he will be asked to leave. He is expected to fulfill the "contract" he accepted when he arrived.

Caste and Stratification

It is well documented in published theory and research on prisons and mental hospitals that a patient or inmate subculture usually develops within the overall institution. This tends to produce a "we-they" conflict and split between the professional administration and the inmates or patients. The underground inmate society has norms, patterns of behavior, and goals different from and, more often than not, in conflict with the overall institution.

The inmates and officialdom are divided into two segregated strata, or camps. The inmate system tends to be a caste of "untouchables." They are restricted to an inferior position in the hierarchy, and there is no possibility for them to move up. It is conceded by most correctional administrators that this inmate-administration conflict situation contradicts and impedes therapeutic progress with the inmate.

The inmate subsystem helps the patient or inmate cope with the new set of problems that he finds in most institutions. He feels rejected by the larger society and tries to compensate for this rejection. One way he does this is to reject and rebel against the administrators of society's rejection—the prison staff.[3]

Synanon does not have a "we-they" caste system. It provides an open-ended *stratification* situation. A full possibility for upward mobility is available in the organization. (As Hurst states in the indoctrination ". . . in a couple of years . . . you just might be a big shot around here—or Santa Monica or Reno.") There is not only upward social mobility in Synanon, but healthy status-seeking is encouraged.[4]

Synanon assumes, with some supportive evidence, that a person's position in its hierarchy is a correlate of social maturity, "mental health," increased work ability, and a clear picture of the Synanon organization. Stated another way, there is a correlation between one's position in the hierarchy and a clear perception of the organization's dynamics. Another assumption is that the social skills learned in Synanon are useful within the larger society. (The reverse appears to be true of the "skills" learned in prison society.) The "we-they" problem is nonexistent in Synanon, since the "administration" and the "inmates" are one and the same.

"Tough Guys" and Synanon Status

Synanon attempts to discourage the "tough-guy" criminal attitude. There is no symptom reinforcement of "tough-guy" behavior at Synanon as often occurs in jails and hospitals. In other settings, the offender receives approval from his fellow inmates and, to some extent, from professionals for being a "tough guy."

In a "haircut" session, Reid Kimball partially reveals the way Synanon attacks this tough-guy syndrome. The following com-

[3] Lloyd McCorkle and Richard Korn, "Resocialization Within Walls," *The Annals: Prisons in Transformation,* May, 1954, p. 88.

[4] In Synanon, one set of indoctrination sessions was devised for encouraging residents to seek status and its "rewards" inside and outside the organization. See Chapter 13, "Status-Seeking."

ments made by Reid are taken from a more extended attack approach used on a "newcomer–tough-guy" group:

"Some of you guys in here will make it, whatever that means. I guess on some level, you want to quit being real nuts, lunatics, and locked up. It seems quite obvious that before that happens, you will have to quit doing what you've been doing. If this place was San Quentin or Sing Sing, I might agree with your tough-guy act. In prison, I suppose you have to let it be known that you were a hotshot on the streets and that you're a bad guy inside the walls. This is what you do to get status in prison. But think of how ludicrous it is when you come here to this place and you try to be tough guys or gangsters. In this place, if you make progress, you act like an adult. . . ."

In the complete session, Chuck and Reid attempted to point out graphically to the new "tough guys" that status is achieveable in Synanon through constructive behavior.[5]

Group and Personal Identity

Dederich was once asked what he called "Synanon inmates," and he replied, "We call them people!"

Synanon members are not identified as "wards," "prisoners," or "patients," and this makes a big difference in their self-identity and outlook. Also at Synanon, the "person" can identify himself with the constructive goals of the organization for which he works. After he kicks his habit, he automatically becomes an employee in the organization. In this capacity, he is encouraged to take part in Synanon's management and development.

In the traditional institution, the reverse is generally the case The inmate or patient feels helpless and hopeless about his destiny. He has limited control over the institution, since it is run by administrators who are usually indifferent to his opinions about its management. Moreover, as indicated, hospital and prison administrators tend to be representatives of society's rejection of the patient or inmate, and this sets up additional blocks

[5] The full session is presented in Chapter 11, "The Criminal Mask."

to correction. Inmates have a clear authority object for their frustrations and hatreds—the prison staff. At Synanon, there is no such split, since the administration consists of co-workers and colleagues. There is no "they" to hate within the organization.

Involvement in the Synanon may help to foster empathy in a person whose problem is partially alienation. (As an example, Charlie Hamer, for the first time in his life experience, began to identify with a constructively oriented group of his peers.) Identification with Synanon involves feelings of concern for the other members and for the destiny of the Synanon totality. The development of these empathic qualities reverses the addict's past sociopathic lack of social concern. (A period of intense *esprit de corps* appeared when Chuck went to jail and the organization's existence was seriously threatened. There was a heightened involvement in Synanon's future and the usual humorous banter gave way to a hardworking, dedicated spirit.)

The work pattern at Synanon is "real" work, unlike the often contrived jobs in prisons and mental hospitals. There is no "basket weaving" at Synanon. All work activities are tied in to the real needs of the organization. This includes the functions of the "hustlers" of food, the office staff, the maintenance and service crews, the automotive crew, the operations crew, and the coordinating staff. Since its inception, Synanon has been shorthanded for carrying out the many dimensions of its necessary work. Therefore, everyone in Synanon works in a meaningful fashion, and the work is built into the organization's needs.

Recently Synanon has successfully developed what is known as "Synanon Industries." The organization has acquired several warehouses and factories. Synanon now accepts industrial contracts for manufacturing machine tool parts. It is hoped that this program, using Synanon personnel, will eventually make Synanon financially independent. The program has already shown a profit.

Also, at Synanon, cultural activities are more in accord with the wishes and desires of the residents. There are no special rewards for participating other than those that the individual gets from the activity. He participates in lectures, seminars, theatrical groups, semantics classes, and other types of activities in Synanon voluntarily. He doesn't participate, as he might in prison, for a "good time," or earlier parole.

There have been attempts at self-government in prison and hospital situations. In these settings, however, the inmates recognize that final decisions on important policy matters remain with the administration. In Synanon, perhaps for the first time in his life, the member assumes a significant role in controlling his future. Leadership in a constructive situation is a new experience for him, and it appears to develop responsibility.[6] The residents at Synanon, unlike patients and inmates, are involved with the growth and development of their own organization. Because there is a generally held belief by the residents that "Synanon saved our lives," the *esprit de corps* in the organization is quite powerful. Few inmates would give "three cheers for dear old San Quentin"; however, Synanon people seem to enjoy praising their alma mater at every opportunity, and work hard for its growth and development.

Group Psychotherapy in Prison and at Synanon

As indicated, one major difference between synanons and the usual institutional forms of group psychotherapy is that the synanon sessions are not directed by professional therapists. Perhaps even more important is the differential setting of the two approaches.

There is some evidence that in prisons, individuals participate in group psychotherapy with an eye on the front door. Consciously and unconsciously, the prisoner may verbalize "insights," seemingly indicating therapeutic progress, in an effort to convince the therapist and prison officials that he has changed and is ready for release. (At a group therapy session that I attended in a California prison, I noted an obvious "therapeutic contract" between several inmates who were attempting to "look good" in their therapy session. They were all getting wonderful "insights," and as one fellow put it, "This program really makes me see life

[6] Anita arrived at Synanon in 1961, at the age of nineteen. She currently has the responsibility and power, as the Synanon accountant, to place the final authorized signature on check payments for the Foundation. This involves the responsibility for the expenditure of thousands of dollars per month.

more clearly." Several admitted to me in private, "Of course, I want to look good to get out of this dump.")

Synanon sessions are more closely related to the "real-life" problems that confront the member in the community in which he resides. Given the lack of caste division, lines of communication exist throughout the organization. This, plus a "goldfish-bowl atmosphere," is conducive to a more extensive reevaluation of underlying problems. ("We tell all our dirty little secrets.") The synanon sessions intensely attempt to surface all possible data, since they are vital to the protection and growth of both the person and the organization. There is a strong belief at Synanon that a person who has been an addict and a pathological liar cannot be allowed to lie at all, not even a little bit. The synanon sessions are, in part, "emotional-first-aid" stations where members must be completely candid and truthful. Unlike the usual prison or institutional group therapy situation, the synanon member has nothing to lose and everything to gain from telling the truth.

Synanon in the Community

Synanon members have a qualitatively different relationship with the community than "prisoners" or "patients." The almost total isolation of the prisoner from the outside world is a major impediment to correction. The institutional setting isolates the confined offender from socially beneficial contact with individuals "outside." This prevents the formation of relationships that might help him make the necessary transition to life outside the walls.

Synanon is in the community, and its members interact with outsiders. Synanon people meet members of the community on equal terms. There are more than three hundred visits each week, from both professionals and laymen, into Synanon's various homes. Unlike prisoners, Synanon people are not "caged animals" on display for curious observers. They are not visited involuntarily, as in a prison, where approval for a visit is given by an administration and the inmates have no control over the situation. People who live in Synanon can be selective about their guests, and they sometimes exercise this right. On rare occasions, visitors who do not behave properly are asked to leave.[7]

All Synanon residents have significant experience in closely interacting with a variety of people from all walks of life. This type of experience seems to socialize Synanon people to function effectively in the larger society.

Cross-Comparisons and Conclusions

In summary, the following elements reflect the significant difference found between Synanon and the traditional institutions:

1. There is a qualitative difference between indoctrination at Synanon and in other settings. The contractual arrangement for therapy and the "prospect's" expectation of success in Synanon are different. The indoctrination of the "prospect" by people who have themselves been in "his shoes" and succeeded appears to be a significant element that differentiates Synanon from other institutions. It provides the newcomer with a role model of what he can become.

2. Synanon provides the possibility of upward mobility, whereas prisons and hospitals have caste systems. Becoming a Synanist provides incentive for modifying one's procriminal motivation to an anticriminal motivation.[8] The Synanon resident

---

[7] As an interesting case in point, one Saturday evening, at Synanon's traditional "open house," a visitor, a Hollywood movie producer, was engaged in an intense conversation with a Synanon resident. The discussion was cordial until the producer revealed that he had a "pill habit." The situation changed dramatically. He was brought into the coordinator's office, where he was clearly told that "no using addicts could be permitted or tolerated in Synanon." He was firmly told to leave. It was suggested to him that if he wanted to enter Synanon to deal with his problem, he would have to apply like any other "dope fiend." In another case, a large financial donor attempted to visit one evening under the influence of alcohol. He was promptly asked to leave. There is no compromise with the use of any drugs or chemicals in Synanon by *anyone*, including visitors.

[8] Unlike the standard professional, a trained Synanist has at least two kinds of experience that uniquely qualify him for work with other offenders: (1) He has a lengthy history of personal criminal experience. He has himself made the "scene." He knows the crime problem in its many dimensions firsthand. (2) At Synanon, he has deeply experienced the emotions of rejecting one way of life for another. He has, "in his gut," gone through the resocialization process. He knows something about the set of experiences and pain involved in the transition.

can actually achieve any role in the organization. In contrast, in the institution, an inmate or patient is locked in position.

3. There is a qualitative difference between the synanon and the form of group therapy carried on in prisons and hospitals. This is partly a function of differences in the overall social-system context. The Synanon resident, as a voluntary participant, has little to gain from faking progress, whereas in prison the appearance of "getting well" may be rewarded by an earlier release from custody. The Synanon person is encouraged to reveal and deal with his problems honestly, by others who have traveled the established Synanon route to recovery.

4. The Synanon subculture is more like the larger societal structure than traditional settings. The flow of members of the community through Synanon and the participation of Synanon members in the larger society place it closer to the "real-life" situations of the outer world than do the artificial communities of traditional institutions. In addition, Synanon residents have an involvement with and a commitment to their organization, whereas traditional institutions usually engender hostility and rebellion.

The Synanon Process in Action [9]

The Synanon developmental process is partially revealed in the following account of the movement and growth of Frankie Lago. In this description, in part, Frankie's encounters with Synanon are compared with his past interactions in traditional institutions. Frank has been "clean" in Synanon since 1960.

Frankie first came to my attention in an unusual fashion. While listening with Chuck to some tapes that I had on the Egyptian King gang killing (an incident described in my *Violent Gang* book), he detected a familiar voice. Hearing one King comment, "I kicked him in the head; it was the least I could do," Chuck remarked, "That sounds like Frankie." I later confirmed, when I met Frank at Synanon, that he was that Egyptian

[9] This section is a revised version of a statement that originally appeared in my book *The Violent Gang*, New York: The Macmillan Company, 1962.

King gang member's older brother. I also learned that Frankie's early case history and violent-gang life pattern paralleled his younger brother's. After his violent-gang youth, Frank turned to a criminal career of using and selling drugs. This life resulted in his "doing time" in a federal prison (Danbury), New York City's Riker's Island Penitentiary (five times), Bellevue Hospital in New York City, and the federal hospital in Lexington, Kentucky.

In addition to a pattern of drug addiction, pimping, and theft, Frank had a violent streak. "Frankie would never use a knife, unless he had to. Mostly with his fists he would beat a guy down and try to kill him right there. They pulled him off this big guy one time—he wouldn't stop punching him in the face." This was the casual observation made by Frankie's ex-crime partner, the girl with whom he had lived for five years in New York.

Frankie's first reaction to Synanon was confusion: "The first thing they hit me with flipped me. This tough-looking cat says to me, 'There are two things you can't do here, shoot drugs or fight.'" Frankie said, scratching his head, "I was all mixed up— these were the only two things I knew how to do."

Frank went to the West Coast at the insistence of his parents "to try a new way of life." "The family chipped in, gave me a plane ticket, and told me to straighten out or drop dead." He accepted the plane ticket they bought and left under the assumption of continuing his old way of life. In Los Angeles, he had trouble getting a good drug connection and stealing enough money to supply his habit. He heard about Synanon and decided to try it. His initial motives were not pure. His thought was "to get cleaned up a little" and either get organized for a new onslaught on Los Angeles or steal enough to return to New York and his old criminal pattern. Something happened at Synanon to make Frankie stay "clean."

He found the Synanon environment interesting and exciting. There were, in the addict's jargon, "lots of hip people," such as Jimmy the Greek, who at forty-eight had been an addict, a criminal, and a con man for more than thirty years;[10] Jimmy

[10] Jimmy's personal statement in a special Synanon issue of the *Terminal Island Prison News* reveals his criminal background and current view of life: "My addiction history goes back to when I was 12 years old (I am close to 50) but up until the time I came to Synanon, 31 months ago, I never knew

Middleton, who ran the kitchen in Synanon at that time, where Frankie got his first job, scouring pots and pans and mopping floors. According to Frankie, Jimmy Middleton could not be "conned" or manipulated out of position like the guards and therapists that Frankie had encountered at Riker's Island Penitentiary. Jimmy, of course, knew the score; to him Frankie, with all his exploits, was a "young punk," who could give him no trouble. "I've met kids like this all my life—in and out of the joint," he said.

According to Frankie, "I hated this bastard for no good reason. I used to sometimes sit and plan ways to kill him." When Frankie wanted to fight Jimmy over a disagreement about work, Jimmy laughed and told him that if he wanted to fight, he would be thrown out of Synanon.

The usual prison situation was reversed, and this confused Frankie. In the "joint" (prison), if Frankie got in trouble, confinement became increasingly severe, with the "hole" (solitary confinement) as an end point. In the Bellevue Hospital psychiatric ward, where Frankie had also "done time," it was a straitjacket. What made Frankie behave in order to stay at Synanon, with its open door?

The fact that Frankie was exported from New York to Los Angeles was a significant initial force in keeping him in Synanon. As he commented: "At times I felt like splitting, then I thought it would be hard to make it back to New York. I didn't know Los Angeles and was afraid to make it out there, because I didn't know the people. Synanon was better than anything else I could do—at the time.

---

about what it was to be 'clean' on the streets. I have done just about everything illegal to obtain money; work was not a part of this life, for I could not support a habit working. I have spent almost 10 years in county jails, the Lewisburg federal penitentiary, and chain-gangs. I can go so far as to say that I had never met a 'clean' dope fiend until I came to Synanon. . . . I have been a resident of Synanon since 1959. I plan on staying for some time to come. For the first time in my life I like what I am doing—Synanon is growing and I am a part of it. There is a group from Synanon attending meetings at Terminal Island every week, for the past 4½ months; I am project director of this group. There are plans in the making to start Synanon meetings on the women's side at T.I.—and eventually, men and women together. I am sure with the cooperation we have been getting this plan will come about in the near future."—*James (the Greek) Georgelas.*

"Also, Synanon House was at the beach, and the meals were good. In the evening, many ex-addict top musicians played cool jazz." [11] Also, there were, according to Frankie, "broads to dance with and get to know." But highly important in this anticriminal society, there were others who understood him, had made the same "scenes," intuitively knew his problems and how to handle him. He respected people he could not "con." He belonged and was now part of a "family" he could accept.

At Synanon, Frankie could also make a "rep" without getting punished or locked up. In prison, the highest he could achieve in terms of the values of "his people" was to become "king" of the inmate world, acquire a "stash" of cigarettes, obtain some unsatisfactory homosexual favors, and land in the "hole." In Synanon, he could achieve any role he was "big enough of a man" to deserve, and "growing up" carried the highest approval of his fellows. He could actually become *director* in this organization, which was now in the national spotlight. (Articles on Synanon had been published in national magazines such as *Time*, *Life*, and *The Nation* and were coming out regularly in the press.) For the first time in his life, Frankie was receiving status for being "clean" and nondelinquent.

Of course, when he first arrived at Synanon, Frankie attempted to gain a "rep" by conniving and making deals, in accord with his old mode of relating. He was laughed at, ridiculed and given severe "haircuts" by other "old-time con men" of the organization. He was accused of "shucking and sliding" (not performing adequately). The old-time Synanists were ferocious about keeping the organization, which had literally saved their lives and given them a new life status, operating smoothly.

Frankie found that "rep" was acquired in this social system (unlike the ones he had known) by truth, honesty, and industry. The values of his other life required reversal if he was to gain a "rep" at Synanon. These values were not goals per se that someone moralized about in a meaningless vacuum; they were means to the end of acquiring prestige in this tough social system with which he increasingly identified.

In the synanons, three nights a week, Frankie participated

[11] The Synanon band produced a widely acclaimed commercial record album, appropriately called *Sounds of Synanon*.

in a new kind of group psychotherapy, unlike the kind he had "fooled around with" in prison. In synanons, the truth was viciously demanded. Any rationalizations about past or current experiences were brutally demolished by the group. There was an intensive search for self-identity. He found that, in the process, he learned something of what went on beneath the surface of his thoughts. Frankie admitted that for the first time in his life he had found other people who had some idea of his underlying thoughts. He had had individual and group therapy in prison, but there he could "con" the therapist and most important, "I said what I thought they wanted to hear so I could get out sooner."

Frankie at first followed his usual pattern of self-centered manipulation of others. However, a new element was introduced into the situation. He began to care about what happened to others at Synanon. This was, at first, selfish. Synanon was for him a good, interesting way of life. He identified with the organization and learned at "gut level" that if any Synanon member failed, in some measure he too had failed.

Frankie began to get some comprehension of what others thought in a social situation. The concept of empathy, or identifying with the thoughts and feelings of others, became a significant reality.

In the status system, Frankie's rise to the role of coordinator was neither quick nor easy. He first moved from the "dishpan" to serving food at the kitchen counter. After several months, he began to work outside on a pickup truck that acquired food and other donations. With two other individuals who worked with him on the truck, a group decision was made one day that "a few pills wouldn't hurt." They acquired some pills from a connection known to one of the group.

When they arrived back at Synanon, their slightly "loaded" appearance immediately became apparent to the group. ("They spotted us right away.") They were hauled into the main office and viciously (verbally) attacked and ordered to "cop out" (tell) or "get lost." A general meeting was called, and they were forced to reveal "all" before the entire group.[12] Frankie was back at work at the "dishpan" that evening.

---

[12] This process, known as a "fireplace scene," may be called at anytime, day or night. The "transgressor" is placed at the fireplace in the main living

Frankie learned the hard way that the norms of Synanon society are the reverse of the criminal code. On one occasion, Frankie, with two other members of Synanon, went for a walk into town. One individual suggested buying a bottle of wine. (Of course, no drinking is permitted.) Frankie and the other member rejected the proposal. However, no one revealed the incident until two days later, when it came up in a synanon. The group jumped hardest on Frankie and the other individual who had vetoed the idea, rather than on the one who had suggested buying the wine. Frankie and the other "witnesses" were expected to report such "slips" immediately, since the group's life depended on keeping one another "straight." For the first time in his life, Frankie was censured for not telling. The maxim "thou shalt not squeal," basic to the existence of the usual underworld criminal culture, was reversed at Synanon and was ferociously upheld.

The no-physical-violence rule was at first difficult for Frank to grasp and believe, since his usual response to a difficult situation was to leap, fists first, past verbal means of communication into assault. As a result of the synanons and other new patterns of interaction, Frankie's increasing ability to communicate began to minimize his assaultive impulse. Although at first he was kept from committing violence by the fear of ostracism, he later had no need to use violence, since he then had some ability to interact effectively. He learned to express himself, in what was for him a new form of communication, on a nonviolent, verbal level.

On occasion, Frankie would regress and have the motivation for assault, but the system had taken hold. In one synanon session, I heard him say, "I was so fucking mad yesterday, I wished I was back at Riker's [prison]. I really wanted to hit that bastard Jimmy in the mouth."

Frankie had a sketchy work record before joining Synanon. Since most of his time was taken up by gang fighting, pimping, armed robbery, or pushing heroin. Aside from some forced labor in prison he was seldom engaged in anything resembling formal

---

room, in front of all other residents. They are ridiculed into an honest revelation of their "offense." The group then decides to evict or to give the individual another chance. There have been only about a dozen "fireplace scenes" in the history of Synanon. In the past year, there have been three.

work. His theme had been "work was for squares." He learned how to work at Synanon as a side effect of his desire to rise in the status system. He also learned, as a side effect of working, the startling fact that "talking to someone in the right way made them do more things than bawling them out!" One of Frankie's past positions involved the overall supervision of the Synanon building where twelve mothers (ex-addicts) lived with their children. Frankie supervised a budget, the care and feeding of those in the establishment, and the inevitable daily counseling of his "wards." (Although it is not apparent on the surface, Frankie, underneath, is amazed about his new role in society.)

As a consequence of living in the Synanon social system, Frankie's social learning and ability continued to increase. His destructive pattern of relating to others seems to have withered away—it is no longer functional for him in this new way of life. Synanon developed his empathic ability. It produced an attachment to different, more socially acceptable values and reconnected him to the larger society in which Synanon functions as a valid organization.

Frankie, reunited with his ex-wife Carmen and their child, continues to live and work in Synanon. He has developed an active interest in becoming an artist. His Synanon affiliation has placed him in position to train with such noted artists as Rico Lebrun and Keith Finch. They consider him to be a promising potential professional artist. More important than this is Frankie's development as a mature human being.

The Principal Social Forces at Work in Synanon

The following elements were selected from Frankie's experience to reveal further the essentials of the Synanon process:

Involvement: Initially, Synanon society is able to involve and control the newcomer. This is, in part, accomplished through providing an interesting social setting comprising associates who understand him and will not be outmaneuvered by his manipulative behavior.

An Achievable Status System: Within the context of this system, the newcomer can (perhaps for the first time) see a realistic possibility for legitimate achievement and prestige. Synanon provides a rational and attainable opportunity structure for the success-oriented individual. He is no longer restricted to inmate status, since there is no inmate-staff division and all residents are staff.

New Social Role: Being a Synanist is a new social role. It can be temporarily or indefinitely occupied in the process of social growth and development. (Some residents have made the decision to make Synanon their life's work.) This new role is a legitimate one, supported by the ex-offender's own community as well as by the inclusive society. With the opening of new Synanon Houses and increasing development of projects such as the one at the Nevada State Prison, Synanon-trained persons are more and more in demand. Since the Synanon organization is not a hospital or an institution, there is no compulsion to move out of this satisfying community.

Social Growth: In the process of acquiring legitimate social status in Synanon, the offender necessarily, as a side effect, develops the ability to relate, communicate, and work with others. The values of truth, honesty, and industry become necessary means to this goal of status achievement. After a sufficient amount of practice and time, the individual socialized in this way reacts according to these values naturally.

Social Control: The control of deviance is a by-product of the individual's status-seeking. Conformity to the norms is necessary in order to achieve. Anomie, the dislocation of goals and means, is a minimal condition. The norms are valid and adhered to within this social system, since the means are available for legitimate goal attainment.

Another form of control is embodied in the threat of ostracism. This too becomes a binding force. The relative newcomer in Synanon usually does not feel adequate for participation in the larger society. After a sufficient period of Synanon social living (Dederich estimates about two and a half years), the individual no longer fears banishment and is adequately prepared for life on the outside (if this is his choice). However, he may remain voluntarily because he feels that Synanon is a valid way of life for him. In Synanon, he has learned and acquired a gratifying social role that enables him, as a coordinator or a director, to help others who can benefit from the Synanon approach.

Another form of social control is the synanon session. Here, the individual is required to tell the truth. This helps to regulate his behavior. Transgressions are often prevented by the knowledge that his deviance will rapidly and necessarily be brought to the attention of the Synanon community in a synanon session. He is living in a community where others know about and, perhaps more important, care about his behavior.

Empathy and Self-Identity: The constant self-assessment required in his daily life and in the synanon sessions fosters the consolidation of self-identity and empathy. His self-estimation is under constant assessment by relevant others, who become sensitive to and concerned about him. The process provides the opportunity for the individual almost literally "to see himself as others do." He is also compelled, as part of this process, to develop the ability to identify with and understand others. A side effect is the development of self-growth, social awareness, the ability to communicate, and empathic effectiveness. When these socialization processes are at work and take hold, the individual becomes reconnected with the larger society and personally develops within the constructive framework of both Synanon and the larger society. The total combination of Synanon processes provides what Chuck Dederich has aptly called "a tunnel back into the human race."

Part II

The Tunnel Back

Synanon is a tunnel back
into the human race.

Chuck Dederich

8

Welcome

Chuck considers direct and personal contact with people to be the heart of Synanon business. Although his role as Synanon's administrative head involves, among other responsibilities, the maintenance of several national locations, constant financial problems, and proper manipulation of the overall organization, Chuck attempts and does maintain a direct contact with the people of Synanon. "In the complex bureaucracy that Synanon seems to be developing, we can't forget our main job is helping people who come here to grow up," he said. "We have to stay close to our basic principles and what we are trying to do in Synanon."

Chuck makes a point of talking to newcomers whenever he can. He does this as a constant reminder to himself of what Synanon is attempting to do, as well as for the benefit of the newer people. The talks keep him close to the lifeline of the organization and seem to refresh his own sincere belief in the Synanon way of helping people.

In the following talk to a group of ten newcomers (in Synanon less than a week), Chuck attempts to communicate Synanon's basic philosophy. The group members (white and Negro) were fresh from the "streets," various jails, and prisons. They ranged in age from nineteen to fifty. They sat in a circle around Chuck in his living room and listened attentively to his statement on Synanon.

181

Trial and Error

"What we are trying to do here will dawn on you in time, and that's extremely important. We're not going to measure your psyche or find out who your grandfather got mad at. This has been the approach that I guess has failed. The fact that you came here, and have had a narcotics problem, is enough.

"We are not rich. As a matter of fact, we are expanding way ahead of our bank account. We're looking for other houses in addition to those we now have. We can see to it that it doesn't rain on you and that you have all the food you can possibly eat. You will get plenty of cigarettes, and you will have a nice, clean place to live. You will also meet a lot of people that share your problem, but are further away from it than you are by one to five years.

"All of you are different. I haven't yet found anything in common about drug addicts except that they use drugs. We are not going to examine the broken homes in your background. You are more familiar with this information than I am. I don't know too much about those matters. I would like to give you an idea of where we are heading and what we have to offer you.

"I have met hundreds of people in the past years who were exactly as you are today. You sit here at the end point of your thinking, feeling, your genetic and cultural backgrounds. This is the end point right here. The values that you have accumulated through life for your own protection, to get what you want, or what you think you want, have brought you here. This is pretty clear, isn't it?

"We don't have sitting in this room ten people who have been successful, creative lawyers, ministers, toolmakers, or anything like that. We've got some people that have spent time locked up in various playpens—jails, penitentiaries, nut farms, and things of that nature. In other words, you've landed periodically, or at least once, on your part. We have a starting point if you can concede that the set of values and the things that somehow you've built up, the things you learned and absorbed through your skin from your parents, teachers, friends, siblings, and others, brought you somehow at loggerheads with things as they are.

"I don't know what you want. Maybe you want a couple of Cadillacs. You guys probably want a broad. You girls probably want a husband and possibly some children. I don't know what you want; it really doesn't make too much difference at this time. This may very well be part of your trouble. Maybe you don't know what to want. I didn't for a much longer time than most of you.

"You are now living in a place with several hundred people who were addicts like you and have not used any drugs for over a year, many for two years, and it goes into the hundreds of those that haven't used any drugs or alcohol for three to five years. In addition to not using drugs, these Synanon people have not been in trouble. They haven't bumped heads with the police, they're not starving to death, and they haven't run out of the things that one needs to live. They managed to get around. There are automobiles here, and they get from one place to another and do pretty well.

"You must have tried to grow up as I tried. I bloodied my head, fouled up my environment, and screwed everything up in a real boss way. I conned people out of more money than all of you put together. It never did me any good. You have tried somehow to go after the things you wanted. When you were a baby, you wanted the red fire engine that the kid next door had. When you got into high school, you wanted the wardrobe or the little Chevrolet roadster that the guy across the aisle had, and you wondered how in the hell you could get it. Possibly, you tried to help yourself to success, but you haven't been too successful. You've gone after things, position, status, more or less directly, and they have all slipped through your fingers. I venture to say that every one of you can think of the time you got right up to the point where you thought you had it. You thought, 'If I just had an apartment, that woman, that car, everything in life would be swell,' and—boom—there you were back in a tank of some kind. 'What the hell happened this time?' you say to yourself. You say, 'Well, I made a little mistake,' and then you go out and do it again and again and again.

"Now, suppose we assume that in the process of chasing *di-*

rectly after the things you wanted, the situations you wanted, the material things you wanted, made you somehow miss the boat. I'm going to draw a little analogy. Suppose that in taking in your food, in the eating process, which if you are healthy is a very enjoyable one, instead of sitting down at the table and tearing into your steak and having a good time with it, you said the following to yourself, 'Well, now, let's see, this mouthful I'm going to have to send over to this arm, because I want this bicep to be bigger.' Fine, so you chew the steak and concentrate on getting it over so that your arm can get stronger for you. Now you reach over and take a mouthful of carrots, and you think, 'These carrots I want to send to my eyeballs so that I can see better.' Then you have some Jell-O and send it up to your head so that your hair will get nice and lustrous. You then want to send a glass of milk to your feet because you have too many corns. You think, 'If I can get the milk down here to my foot, it will dissolve my corn.' This is kind of ridiculous, isn't it? You see, you can't do this. There's absolutely no way of doing this. If you sit down to a good meal, dive in, and eat it with enjoyment, with good companions and everything that is set up properly for a meal, you digest it. I guess there is a process in your body that will see to it that four ounces of the Jell-O go to the head and two peanuts go to the brain. Better still, let's send a sardine there; fish is good brain food.

"There isn't a damn thing that you can do about this process. Of course, if I wanted to, and if I could do this, I would probably be in a hell of a mess, because, you see, I couldn't keep track of all this. I would get up one morning and look into the mirror and find out that one arm was twice as long as the other. I had inadvertently put too much food into it. I would find that one foot was beginning to shrink, because while I was concentrating on my hair, I had forgotten about the foot. I couldn't possibly keep track of all these details. I couldn't eat this meal and then divide it up and send it where it was supposed to go.

"Now, suppose we take the analogy in the living of life. You don't know how to live life very well, I guess, because here you are. You have tried, somehow, to distribute the good things in life that you saw, or have had hold of, or that someone else had and you coveted. Somehow, you have tried to acquire these things for yourself. You have concentrated on the getting without going at the process of getting. Here we will teach you how to get the things you want constructively. If you can admit that you don't know too much about life—because not knowing got you here, and there has been a lot of psychic pain and nonsense and trouble in your background that you would rather not experience again— then you might accept this intellectually. Don't believe it, accept it intellectually. Say to yourself, 'I'm going to act as if he knows what he's talking about.'

"Look at it this way: you have everything to gain and nothing to lose. In the beginning, because you have no power of decision that's any good, you use somebody else's power of decision. You use the power of decision that pervades the whole Synanon Foundation. You are going to find people in here you don't like, and you are going to find people in here you like. You're going to find smart people in Synanon and dumb people in Synanon and everything in between. We have a pretty good cross-section in this microcosm of the larger society. We have just about every social, educational, and economic background in here. We have every color, size, shape, and age.

"After you've been here for a short time, you will learn how to use the synanons three times a week. You will have one tonight, and you will be able to yell and throw your emotional garbage all over the floor. Everything goes. That is, everything short of physical violence. You can call anyone around here anything you wish in synanon. During the day, when we're trying to have a nice home, this kind of profanity gets in the way. It's a lot of nonsense. Who the hell wants someone to curse and swear, look sour, whine, and throw tantrums in the living room or dining room. It's asinine. We have an emotional bathroom three times a week: synanons—the most powerful form of group therapy that any of you have ever experienced, this I assure you. You will begin to use them pretty soon, and the gang will begin to nudge you a little bit, try to hurt your feelings, stir you up so that you can get this crap out. The rest of the time, do the best you can and try to control yourself.

"You'll have a gig [job] pretty soon, but nobody works too hard in Synanon. We don't have time. We have a lot of other things to do. We have seminars, synanons, semantics classes, music classes, bands, choirs, art classes, and photographic studies. We're always doing something. You're only asked, or required, to go to the synanons three times a week, turn up at noon seminars, and do your job. That's all you have to do.

"People are going to get mad at you, because the whole house is full of other people just like yourselves. They are going to make all kinds of noises at you. If you're nuts, if you are totally insane, you will run out the door like children do and fall down a manhole or slide merrily back into the penitentiary or whatever nut farm you were enjoying yourself at before you came here. That's what you will do. Remember what I'm trying to tell you. You're going to hear a lot of noises, and noises never hurt anybody. When you were a little kid, you used to stand on the corner and shout out at the kid next door that you were mad at, a very, very deep form of philosophy which you've probably forgotten. You said, 'Sticks and stones may break my bones, but names will never hurt me.' You see, you understood more about semantics then than you probably do now.

"Remember the analogy of trying to send the six delicious flavors to your calf muscles and the steak to one foot? You can't do this anyway. I want to tell you something. You can't do it in life either. You see, you have found this out, but you don't know it yet. If you live your life and live fully in a point in space-time and do your work, you will begin to find yourself. As you eat the meal of life, the Cadillacs pop up here in one corner, and the woman that you've been looking for—boom—here she is. The money that you need to live like a dignified human being, well, something sneaks up and jams it down in your back pocket. This is the way it is whether you believe it or not. I say to you again, don't believe it; think about it, keep it in your head, and say to yourself, 'Well, I did come down here to Synanon to get help.'

"Two of you people must have the same writer. Your reasons for coming here are beautiful. They're good. No criticism intended. It sounds nice, but you've probably sat in a police station or the Lexington narcotics farm and told them the same story. I don't believe it; it's a lot of nonsense. And you and I, one of these days, if you stick around and grow up, will have a good laugh over that kind of nonsense. It might be fun to sit down and listen one day to this tape of what you said.

"Right now, though, say to yourself, 'I came to Synanon, and I went to considerable trouble to get here. I ran around shooting dope and went to jail and got roughed up and degraded. People said to me, "Get out of that car; stand over against that wall." ' Guys like you and me, drunks and dope fiends, we're always sitting around saying, 'By God, nobody's going to tell *me* what to do.' *The paradox is that there is no class of people in the galaxy that get told what to do more than nuts like us!* [Laughter] Isn't that true? You go over there and live in San Quentin for two years. When you get to San Quentin, you might say, 'By God, did I put it over on that judge! He must be nuts—he *only* gave me two years!' Man, oh, man, isn't this fantastic? [Sarcastically] Nobody is going to tell *me* what to do!

"Don't let noises bother you. Nobody will paste you in the mouth. It's never happened in Synanon and never will. We have a few verbotens here: you don't get loaded in here, and we don't have any physical violence.

"There it is. From then on, you can do anything you are big enough or smart enough to do. You put your head down and you do what you're told, and pretty soon you find out that nobody is telling you what to do at all any more. You will have begun to grow up. Nobody has to tell adults what to do, they already know what to do, and they're doing it.

"Suppose we assume that our problem as a category of people is that we didn't grow up right the first time; something is missing. We didn't get the brass ring, there's a piece missing out of the pie. The psychiatrists say that people like you and me have a character disorder. We're not neurotic, but we have a character disorder. This means that we act out our pain and our rebellion to our own detriment and to the detriment of anyone who happens to get in the way. Now, our character disorder, the one that I shared with you until a few years ago, the one you have right now, doesn't really do too much harm to other people in the larger society. There is nothing big time about our problem. We run around loaded, maybe engage in petty thievery, prostitution, or pimping. It's really kind of an annoyance, just like a fly that society has to put up with. So they drop us in a cage and wonder what the hell we're going to do next time. They say, 'We had better take care of him or he will kill himself. He will overjolt or fall down a manhole. He might smash up an automobile, and he might smash up somebody else while he's doing it. We had better confine him, because we don't want him to do harm to the rest of society.' The point is that we don't do too much harm to the rest of the society—but we do tremendous harm to ourselves. Our behavior is self-destructive.

"We go through life in a state of terror most of the time. We rationalize it into resentment or rebellion. We tell people what big guys we are. We even get into aggressive behavior sometimes. We hurt ourselves because we are motivated by an immediate self-interest. We want what we want when we want it. We want other people's property, we want their position, we want relief immediately from any kind of psychic discomfort; so we get drunk or we get loaded on drugs immediately. That's the kind of people we are.

"We merely have to develop an enlightened self-interest. We have all these disadvantages and negatives behind us. We have, however, a tremendous advantage that many people do not have. Let me tell you what it is. We have inadvertently put ourselves through the most powerful learning process that is possible. The most powerful, that is, by doing things *wrong* the first time around.

"Let me give you an example. Two guys are given the responsibility of painting the two opposing walls in this room. We give each one of them a can of paint and a paintbrush and say, 'All right, Number 1, you paint this wall, and Number 2, you paint that wall.' One guy is a kind of a normal son-of-a-gun. He somehow has not grown up as a nut. He looks at the can of paint and reads the directions. The paint is a little thick, so he reads down to where it says, 'Mix paint with solvent X-42.' Fine, he proceeds to do that, according to the directions, and he paints his wall.

"The other guy is sort of like you and me. He looks the paint over. Of course, he's probably a compulsive worker. He's so damn guilty, he wants to get it done right away. He opens up his paint, he jams his brush in, he sees that the paint is too thick. He grabs a can of turpentine, throws it in there, mixes it all up, and starts to paint his wall. He has used the wrong solvent because he didn't read the directions. He stands there and looks at the paint, thinks it looks swell, and sits down and lights a cigarette. He looks up. All the paint has started to run down the wall and all over the floor. He says, 'Oh, my God! What's happened to me?' And somebody says to him, 'Why didn't you read the directions?' If he can listen, just this once, he will, later on, *always* read the directions.

"I'll tell you something. It would almost be impossible, with this lesson under his belt, for this guy ever to paint a wall again without reading the directions. If he is capable of learning, you see, he couldn't do this again. Now the other guy, he knows that what he did worked, doesn't he? He knows it worked, but he doesn't know yet that it wouldn't have worked if he had used another kind of solvent. He doesn't know it yet. Now who has the deepest learning experience? The loser really has. He's done it wrong and right.

"Expand this experience. You have had thousands of experiences—most of them errors. The basis of the learning process is trial and error and 'don't do it again!' The trouble with nuts like us is that we keep doing it wrong over and over and over. We won't listen. This is our only sin in the cosmos. Our only sin, as far as I'm concerned (and I've made a rather deep study of sin for damn near fifty years), is stupidity. And there you have it—stupidity! You are at the end point of conscious and unconscious stupidity.

"We assumed when you first came in here that you were emotionally a baby. I don't blame a baby because he sits in ashtrays, jams his fingers into light sockets, puts his hand on a hot stove, or walks out of the window instead of down the stairs. No, one doesn't blame a baby. But when a baby begins to grow up a little bit and has been exposed to a learning process, people are trying to teach him all the time, and then this person becomes responsible for his own actions.

"As a result of things that are inside yourself, I would say that out of the ten here, at least two of you will be gone in less than thirty days. You will be strung out on drugs again within six months. Within a year, you will be in another playpen, or you will be dead. It used to be that I could say that out of ten, four of you would be writing me from some jail within X period of time. We're getting that down now, our learning process is better and bigger. As our social dynamic whirls around, we've got a stronger centripetal force.

"I'll say to you again that two of you will be back on that old merry-go-round within thirty days. Now, your reason for that may be that somebody made a face at you in the dining room, or someone will say to you, 'What the hell's the matter with you, Buster? Why are you sitting in the ashtray?' And you will say, 'Fuck you,' and run out the door. You will go running back to the street. That, of course, is the path to whatever playpen you prefer, and that's the way it will be. Two of you will miss the boat. Out of those two, one of you might get buried for about ten years in prison before he gets another crack at living. I may miss it, three of you may have to take a walk. But you may surprise me. You may up the average. All of you may be leading creative, happy lives and feeling better than you ever did in your lives a year or two from now.

"You are reaching for something and shooting for something that you can not imagine. There is no possible way of anyone communicating to you how it feels to be a grown-up human being with a grown-up body and brain. You don't know about this. You've had no experience with it. We're faced with a problem similar to this one. For instance, trying to explain how a chocolate soda tastes to an Eskimo who's been eating whale blubber for thirty years. There is no possible way this can be done. It is out of the realm of his experience.

"You can enjoy the experience of living as a creative adult with a grown-up body and brain. All of you basically have the potential. None of you are congenital idiots, none of you have hydrocephalic heads, none of you are morons. There's one main thing wrong with you. You don't know how it feels to be an adult and you're scared to death of the responsibility and even the rewards.

"You think, way down in your deepest gut, that somehow you're kind of a little kid playing with the big guys. You've got a feeling that all these people know things that you don't know. You feel something like the eighth-grader feels in relation to high-school boys or the high-school boys feel in relation to college boys. You feel somehow like the nineteen-year-old feels when he looks at his friend who is a lawyer with a couple of kids. You've got that feeling buried deep in your gut, that feeling of unworthiness, of inadequacy. It isn't true, but you don't know it yet. We'll teach you all we can about life here in Synanon.

"I love to talk about Synanon. The very second somebody comes into our door, at the club, I immediately accept the challenge, and it becomes very personal to me. I am speaking only for myself right now, but it has the same meaning for many other people around here. In some way, we hope to be able to put a crack into that wall of stupidity that surrounds people. We want to help get them living again. *There is nothing more charming, nothing more satisfying to me than watching people toss away their blinders and begin to live.*

"This has been and is one of the greatest experiences of my life. When you get past your childish stage, you will find out that you have a lot of tremendous friends here at Synanon. There are other human beings here with whom you will be able to share many deep emotional and philosophical experiences. You will learn more about this as time goes on. As for now—welcome to Synanon."

A New Direction

This informal talk by Chuck to a group of newcomers reflects the spirit in which they are met in Synanon. An attempt is made to establish clearly that "I myself was like you, but I have worked through a large part of my own problems—in Synanon." Also, an effort is made to assure them that their basic needs of food and shelter will be taken care of and that there is a real concern for their welfare.

The newcomers are informed in advance about some of the "noises," or attack therapy, they will encounter. And it is suggested that they take it in the spirit in which it is intended: they are asked to view verbal attack as a *method* to help them see their problems, rather than as a personal assault on their dignity.

The emphasis on "doing the thing and the rewards will

emerge" is another important aspect of Synanon that is pointed out by Chuck. In some ways, this theme reflects a recent trend in psychology that emphasizes *positive behavior* as a modifier of intrapsychic processes. Rather than working first on underlying emotional problems directly (as in psycholanalysis), Synanon concentrates *first* on the person's acting out of constructive behavior.

The underlying assumption is that people mature psychologically after a sufficient period of constructive behavior. In short, positive behavior eventually affects internal psychological adjustment. This process reverses the usual professional approach.[1]

Chuck's wall-painting vignette communicates an important image to Synanon people about their past negative behavior. It emphasizes the notion that if they straighten out, they have the double advantage of both negative and positive past experiences. They are told, in effect, that they can convert their negative past into an asset if they "straighten out."

Repetition, analogue, and caricature are continually used in Chuck's approach. The assumption is that colorfully and dramatically repeating the same idea in several different ways eventually gets the message across. Parallels, the use of personal experiences, and dramatic vignettes are employed to convey information to the somewhat emotionally encapsulated newcomer. There is an assumption that he doesn't hear too well on an emotional level.

The newcomer is asked to accept several facts of his condition "at the time" as a prelude to his potential growth in Synanon. His past failures are emphasized, not to demean him but to help him fully *accept* that his past approaches to life have repeatedly failed. This may convince him to accept the different approach offered by Synanon as a reasonable possibility and a starting point for a new way of life.

In a sense, they are asked to accept Synanon on the basis of a faith in their own potential as human beings. Implicit in what Chuck tells them is a faith in their ability to succeed. ("None of you are morons," and so on.) The constant reminder is that "people like us can make it."

[1] A fuller discussion of this theoretical point is found in Chapter 16, "The Newest Profession."

Some of their past behavior is ridiculed, not as "sick," but as stupid. The absurdity of the convict who outsmarted the judge and received *only* a two-year sentence instead of five is held up to the ridicule it seems to deserve. Also, the theme of the rebellious criminal who is a "free spirit that nobody tells what to do" is caricatured. Chuck dramatizes how people who take this posture in life find themselves pushed around harder and confined more than most other people. He attempts to get the group to laugh at some of their past "ridiculous behavior." In Synanon, criminal behavior is viewed as an absurd pattern of life rather than as pathology.

The newcomer is also offered a concrete new direction in Synanon. In an almost mystical fashion, a *possible* new way of life is held out to him. ("You are reaching for something you cannot imagine.") The experience of becoming a "creative adult" is held out, in exchange for the newcomer's recognition of past failures, giving up a variety of false personal images, and conforming to a new "set of motions."

Synanon offers the newcomer this new direction for life, with clearly patterned ways for proceeding. The fact that Synanon's philosophy has already been *successfully demonstrated* by several hundred people gives the message power. The spirit of Chuck's "welcome-to-Synanon" talk is an important part of Synanon's overall approach to involving the newcomer in the Synanon community.

9

Indoctrination

"Most addicts arrive at Synanon filthy, running from both ends, with one shoe off, no underwear. They stumble in with their phony little story and say, 'Dad, please help me.'" (This was a comment made by Chuck in a lecture to a group of college students.)

The indoctrination, or initial interview, establishes a "contract" of conditions for Synanon's intervention. At first, some token roadblocks are thrown in the way of the person who is attempting to enter. He may be given an appointment and made to wait. If he is even a few minutes late for the appointment, he is told to come back another time. ("He has to begin to learn some discipline in front.") Sometimes money is requested as an entrance fee. An effort is made to have the individual fight his way in. All this is a new experience, since, in the past, he was usually involuntarily brought into a prison or hospital.

According to Chuck, "When the addict arrives in his usual dazed condition, he feels more secure meeting the firmly defined situation provided by Synanon. Slobbering affection is something he can't handle at this time. His enormous guilt might activate him to run out the open door and smash himself once more."

The "firm hand" of the ex-addict experts he meets at Synanon is puzzling and attractive. Often the newcomer's curiosity is piqued by the spectacle of people with whom he did time or shot drugs functioning as executives!

A typical reaction: "I couldn't figure it out. I figured there must be a gimmick. I didn't really want to stop being a dope fiend. I wanted to rest for a while. First, I began to look for the connection in the joint. They laughed at me. I think I stuck around at the beginning because I couldn't believe it was true, and I was curious. Live dope fiends not shooting dope—behind an open door!"

After he kicks his habit, the addict is given a job commensurate with his limited ability at the time (for example, washing dishes, cleaning, mopping). This seems to give him a sense of security, satisfaction, and participation. Before his mind can race too far in the wrong direction, toward drugs, "he is involved in group-therapy synanons, where everyone laughingly exposes all his silly little plots and devices." He is confused and kept off balance by the "experts."

At the same time that this firm approach is going on, the newcomer also meets friends who are trying to help and understand him. With many newcomers, there is an outpouring of deep personal emotion that may have been pent up for many years. In other settings, he had to be a "tough guy" to get by and gain status. However, at Synanon, he is encouraged to let his hair down. At almost any time of the night or day, there is a friendly, understanding person available to hear about the newcomer's current and past difficulties. In certain cases, someone may be especially assigned to help the person become integrated into the "club."

Synanon views the newly arrived addict in terms of his generally distraught emotional state. At first, he is likely to be limited in his ability to communicate meaningfully. The words he spews forth at that time are generally ignored for all practical therapeutic purposes. As Frankie Lago put it, in response to a compliment on his present verbal ability (he had just delivered a lecture to a group of Los Angeles parole and probation supervisors): [1] "When I got to Synanon, I would begin a sentence in the middle,

[1] As previously mentioned, Synanon residents have filled more than one thousand speaking engagements with professional groups, college and university classes, high-school assemblies, and other community organizations since 1958.

and I didn't know which way the words would go, forwards or backwards."

Combined with this usually confused emotional state, the newcomer is likely to be physically sick on arrival. When his drugs are withdrawn, he may suffer not only the pain of withdrawal illness, but the pain resulting from deficiencies of the kidney, liver, and other vital organs. There is some evidence that heroin holds certain physical problems in check. When the addict's "medicine" (heroin) is withdrawn, he tends to reveal a variety of illnesses. This is attested to by the many medical doctors who treat Synanon newcomers. Concomitantly, a variety of psychosomatic symptoms emerge, which may, for the newcomer, serve as a partial rationale for him to "split." He may break out in a nervous rash or complain of pains that have no physical basis.

Withdrawal

At Synanon, the addict withdraws from his habit without the support of any drugs or chemicals. Despite the popular misconception of withdrawal sickness (as depicted, for example, in the movie, *Man with the Golden Arm*), "kicking the habit," although uncomfortable, is not reported to be an extremely painful experience. This has been attested to by most of the addicts who have come to Synanon and "kicked cold turkey."

The ease of withdrawal from drugs at Synanon may be attributed to several factors. In the first place, drugs sold on the "street" have been significantly cut down by each link in the distribution chain, from the major crime-syndicate importer to the street addict. The "cap" (gelatin capsule) or balloon (literally a rubber balloon or condom) of heroin that ultimately reaches the average addict has been reported to be, on the average, 10 percent heroin and 90 percent milk sugar (a white powder that gives the appearance of heroin). Thus, to a great extent, the use of heroin is a combined physiological and psychological "fantasy fix," with considerable emphasis on the psychological response.

The procedure of obtaining and using drugs becomes for the addict a compulsive circular nightmare. He "scores" (buys the drug) from a "connection" (seller) and goes through the addict's ritual. He finds an isolated place, ties up his arm, cooks up the drug (mixed with water or saliva in a bent spoon), draws the concoction up through a needle inserted into an eyedropper, then shoots it into a vein. He then experiences the *expected* psychological euphoria, a release from his anxieties and concerns. The process of getting and using drugs seems to be as much a part of his habit as the actual emotional or physical impact of the drug. Part of the cultural experience of using drugs also seems to be embodied in the pain of withdrawal. There is an expectation of withdrawal "sickness," and it is usually confirmed.

In situations other than Synanon, the expectation of pain from drug withdrawal is often compounded by the setting. In many hospitals (and in some jails), dosages of drugs are prescribed for the withdrawing addict in decreasing quantities. The assumption here is that the addict will slowly withdraw physiologically. In many places, during medical withdrawal, the addict receives the purest and most powerful drugs he has ever had. According to Frankie Lago: "At Lexington, I first learned about powerful drugs. I was never so well fixed in my life. I floated for two weeks. Just when I began to come to, the doctor would fix me again. I remember at breakfast once, I was so loaded my head kept falling into the oatmeal."

Withdrawal in a jail setting involves several factors in addition to the sheer physical illness associated with drug withdrawal. First, the addict is in a stressful human situation. He is locked into a steel and concrete jail and is confronted with the dire consequences of an imminent court experience. He is usually visited by distraught (often admonishing) friends or relatives. He faces the real possibility of a long-term prison sentence. This set of difficult possibilities seems to blend with the physical discomfiture of drug withdrawal and cannot easily be separated out of the total negative situation.

Moreover, among criminal-addicts, paradoxically, prestige is derived from having had a "boss habit." The criminal addict may therefore literally climb the wall, moan, and complain to validate for his cell mates the degree of his past addiction. This pattern is more characteristic of the younger criminal ("gunsel") who wishes to signify the intensity of his habit. The older criminal-addict is more apt to play his withdrawal "cool." One older female criminal-addict described the typical pain of withdrawal and her reaction this way: "When I was arrested, I usually had a real oil burner ["large" habit] going. I always preferred to kick in isolation. I knew that I would be running at both ends [vomiting and diarrhea] and didn't want anyone to bug [bother] me. Also, when I felt that every nerve in my body was exposed and coming to life, I would masturbate. This relaxed me and offered some relief even if it was just for a few minutes."

In contrast with the difficulty of withdrawal symptoms under other conditions, Synanon provides a unique social setting for withdrawal. The withdrawing addict at Synanon has already taken the first step by making a voluntary decision to attempt to eliminate his habit. He is placed on a couch in the main living room, where he is in full view of all members. Also, he is in a position to visit with residents, observe the activities in the House, and become better acquainted with Synanon. Although he can leave, the newcomer voluntarily remains because of a commitment he has made to himself and partially to the people in Synanon. Moreover, he is in a reasonably pleasant environment, entirely different from the jail or prison situation.

The hi-fi is usually playing, children may be around in the room, he receives warm drinks (eggnog, hot tea), and he is physically soothed with occasional shoulder rubs. People will come over, shake his hand, welcome him, and chat. Most important, he can literally see live evidence of success at Synanon. He may see "clean" ex-addicts with whom he personally used drugs. He is encouraged to achieve the healthy physical and emotional condition of the people he sees before him. He begins to learn about Synanon from people who have experienced his current emotions. He sees role models of achievable success around him. He is interacting with people who understand how he feels, since they themselves were all at one time in his shoes. In addition to understanding his feelings, they sketch for him a positive future which they themselves are literally experiencing. In his confused state, these solid reference points provided by other Synanon members help to minimize his psychic and physical withdrawal pains and speed his involvement in the group.

The Synanon Contract

After physical withdrawal, there are a series of indoctrinations and discussions with the newcomer. These are *not* rigorously formalized sessions (as are interviews in a hospital or jail). Some newcomers go to work and are not talked to for several weeks. Others are subjected to many discussions in the first few days. Informal attention is paid to the newcomer, and this is geared to his needs. The indoctrination is not carried out in the institutionalized, bureaucratic style of a narcotics hospital or other kind of formal setting. It is adapted to the emotional condition of the newcomer.

A characteristic of many newly arrived addicts is their limited ability to locate themselves in time and space. When they attend their first synanon, they may mistakenly project the familiar image of a jail or hospital onto the situation. Some react as if they were in a police station. Newcomers are often confused by Synanon members. Even though they know intellectually that the synanists are not wardens or professional therapists, on a deeper emotional level they may view Synanon personnel as the "keepers of the keys" of the traditional institution. Synanon is faced with the difficult task of divesting newcomers of these delusions and at the same time acquainting them with Synanon.

INDOCTRINATION 1—CHRIS

No indoctrination is typical. Each is geared to the newcomer's special human situation. The following indoctrination session was administered by Chuck, since the set of talks this newcomer had received from other Synanists did not seem to get through to her. The girl involved had some apparent special problems. She was fat (she weighed more than two hundred pounds) and emotionally disturbed. On top of these problems, she thought she was a lesbian. She had arrived several days earlier from New York (1962) with an addicted "girl friend." Both had made motions toward the door and leaving. Chuck delivered this indoctrination of the "Synanon contract" with the aid of several associates.

CHUCK: How much of a habit have you got?

CHRIS: Since 1957.

CHUCK: Since '57? How much have you been using recently, like over the last month?

CHRIS: About sixty or seventy dollars' worth of stuff a day; cut, you know.

CHUCK: Have you been locked up since 1957?

CHRIS: Yes, I've been locked up.

CHUCK: When was the last time you kicked a habit?

CHRIS: 1960.

CHUCK: 1960! You have much trouble kicking, comparatively?

CHRIS: Just the weakness; that's what gets me. I get real weak.

CHUCK: What were you using on the way out here, pills or anything?

CHRIS: We were both kicking on the bus; we used some pills and Dolophines.

CHUCK: What else did you use, any barbiturates?

CHRIS: No! Not Seconal or anything like that; a few Equinols, some Dolophines that I got from the doctor. We tried to use Dolophines, but it just didn't work. We tried to kick before we came out here on Dolophine; it didn't work, so we used Equinol and phenobarb.

CHUCK: You apparently are confused about Synanon. This is indicated by your behavior. You do not seem to know where you are. You think you're in jail or something. Maybe you could understand what we are trying to do here if I described it this way. Synanon is a corporation; it's a nonprofit corporation. It's a private enterprise; it is not supported by public funds. It is *our* business. It is sort of like the Standard Oil Company, owned by the stockholders. All the people in this room except you are directors, and we own this corporation.

Now, here's what we offer an addict, in simple terms. We offer an addict an opportunity to go to work for the Synanon Foundation. When you work for the Synanon Foundation, you get the necessities of life: you get shelter as good as we have, you get all the food you can eat, you get cigarettes, you get a pretty nice place to live; and if you continue to work for the Foundation, a month, two months, four months, or a year, eventually you'll be a pretty well-integrated human being. You've seen quite a few of them around here since you arrived, whether you recognize them or not. The small amount of work that you'll be required to do, any adult could do standing on his head in a hammock in about two hours a day. Your job will probably run from four to five hours a day.

You will get the only therapy that works, more often than not, for narcotic addicts. In addition to your work, we demand certain standards of behavior around here for reasons known to us; not to you, yet. Someday you quite possibly will understand it; you will if you get well, and then you'll see why we are insistent on certain standards of behavior. There is no "we-they" situation here like there is in a prison.

The minute you kick your habit, you become part of the staff. You become one of some hundred or so doctors, and then you yourself are a patient and you've got about a hundred doctors around you. This is a new concept.

[Chuck now brings up her bad behavior of the evening before.]

In Synanon, we don't, for instance, permit women to go into the men's john and then, when they're reminded of it by another woman, say, "I ain't afraid of no mother-fucking man." That's not the way to operate here. If you want to operate that way, then you go someplace where they work that way.

We insist that you do your work and that you go to synanons. We insist that you stay clean and that you, to the best of your ability, behave like an adult human being. We provide synanon meetings three times a week, where you can have catharsis sessions.

You can sit there and call somebody a mother-fucker. There you can say to someone, "How do you stand that mother-fucking Chuck who runs the joint?" That's fine. I want you to do that, in that situation; but not in the building or in the men's john. You will behave yourself and you won't throw your weight around in this place, because you're an amateur. You don't know how to throw your weight around yet. Someday you'll learn how to assert yourself in a constructive manner. Now your behavior is quite obviously destructive.

Here you are, you're a mess, aren't you? The end point of your thinking and your attitude. Aren't you kind of a mess?

CHRIS: Yes.

CHUCK: Okay, now we can get you out of this mess, if you do it exactly our way. We insist on this; first, for the Foundation and, secondly (always remember that), secondly, for the salvation of your soul. We only have one Foundation—that's why we put it first—but we have tens of thousands of dope fiends out there, so you are more expendable than the Foundation.

Now this ought to make some kind of sense to you. We want you to watch your behavior, watch your language, except in the synanons. Blow off in the synanons, great stuff; but not on the floor. If you decide that you want to run off again, nobody is going to stop you; they're going to get right behind you and say, "Bye-bye, Jake," boom, boom, boom, right out the door. That's the way we operate around here, and it's successful, whether you think so or not.

Your equivocations and all the nonsense about your name and your relationship with this other girl are of no consequence in themselves. But they prove to me what a nut you are. I suppose you came out here because you wanted to stop being a nut; is that true? Or did you come out here for the ride? Why *did* you come out here; do you know?

CHRIS: Because I want to straighten out.

CHUCK: Very good! See if you can get going in here. You can't have very much of a habit. I'm going to assume you don't, because it really doesn't make a damn bit of difference. I'm going to assume that you told me the truth about your ride out on the bus.

CHRIS: We didn't use any junk [heroin].

CHUCK: Junk, schmunk! You didn't use very much because you're really not in very bad shape. My God almighty, you look like a crowd!

You know, dope fiends, as a general rule, are four or five inches wide and weigh about eighty pounds. You can't be in very bad shape. We don't take a little mickey-mouse habit seriously; in fact, we don't take any habit as an excuse for behaving like an animal, not around here.

You're in with the experts; all of these people, every single one of them in this room, were addicts. I watched them kick in the Synanon Foundation. They didn't kick in a nice, beautiful building like this; but in a filthy store-front that we opened up in. While we were working, getting this place ready for nuts like you, you were out using drugs. You will keep a civil tongue in your head when addressing your betters, right! Does it make sense to you?

CHRIS: Yes.

CHUCK: How old are you, by the way?

CHRIS: Twenty-eight.

CHUCK: By the time you're thirty, you can be a grown-up. This is what can happen to you if you decide to stick around and do it the way we do it here at Synanon.

This is it! No more nonsense; every person that comes in here doesn't get this kind of attention. I, for instance, don't even know anybody's name, as a general rule, until they've been here two or three weeks. They usually get indoctrinated by coordinators; but your behavior made it necessary for us to get some information out of you.

The people who talked to you yesterday couldn't even get your right name. It's all so asinine. You're behaving like a child. If you behave like an adult you'll feel better immediately. You don't know how to behave like an adult, so we tell you how to behave like an adult. If someone asks you a question, answer the question! We are deserving of this courtesy, because you have no right in here at all, only on our sufferance. This is not a government lockup. That's why I bring this thing up. We're a private foundation; we're in the business of making life smooth out for nuts like you. Do you have anything to say? What about this girl you came up here with; what is her name, and what is your name? What name did you start life with? Give us this information, we want to know it!

CHRIS: You have my name; you have my identification. Her name is Rae Edwards.

CHUCK: What is your name?

CHRIS: Joyce! You have my driver's license, I'm quite sure.

CHUCK: I asked you a question. What is your name?

CHRIS: Joyce Mathews.

CHUCK: Joyce Mathews! I see, and this girl's name is Rae Edwards. What does Rae stand for?

CHRIS: Rae, Rae!

CHUCK: Rachel? That's what I'm trying to find out; Sugar Ray? Rae doesn't mean too much to me. Hoo-ray? Sugar Ray?

CHRIS: Rachel Edwards.

CHUCK: So her name is Rachel Edwards? I see! Then you are not genetically sisters.

CHRIS: No.

CHUCK: Very good! See how easy it is? You and I have got to be pretty good friends for about the last forty seconds; I now know your name. It's rather important that human beings know one another's name. You sat up here for an hour or so and sparred like you were in some kind of a police station. One of your problems, my dear, is that you always think that things are something they're not. This isn't a police station; your name isn't Chris Jones or something; you're not this girl's sister. You go dragging a bunch of delusions like this around with you all the time and there is only one escape for such nonsense—drugs!

Both Chris and Rae have been in Synanon since they arrived in 1962 and are doing well. Chris discovered that she is a woman; she has changed her hairdo and dress. She has a melodic voice and sings with the band. Since this session, she joined the organization to the degree that she has not required any additional severe "haircuts" of this type. She works in the coordinator's office in Santa Monica. Rae has been working at the Reno facility and has also "joined the program." (Rae recently married one of Synanon's acting directors, Ted Dibble.)

INDOCTRINATION 2—FRANK FROM NEW YORK

Following is another example of an indoctrination. This one was administered by Jack Hurst and Jimmy Middleton in the Westport Synanon installation. Interestingly, Jack Hurst's approach reflects a combination of phrases and comments similar to Chuck's. This is, of course, to be expected, since Jack learned the approach from Chuck.

At the time, the Wesport facility had been open only a few months, and there were only ten people in residence there. It was necessary to indoctrinate the prospect totally at the outset, since the organization was busily engaged in the usual zoning battles thrown up to block Synanon. There was an urgency to indoctrinate the newcomer more quickly, and this is reflected in the comprehensiveness and toughness of the indoctrination. There was no fencing. The points of importance were driven home rapidly and forcefully in this first encounter.

PROSPECT: I didn't want to waste another call, and there were no trains until later. This was the earliest train today. Except the eight o'clock in the morning, and that was not good.

JACK: Why are you talking right now? You arrived on time; that's all that we insist upon.

PROSPECT: Oh, all right. I thought I was late.

JACK: If you were late, we would have, of course, put you back on the train and sent you back to New York and told you to come back tomorrow. But you arrived on time.

PROSPECT: I thought the first thing I should do is tell you that—

JIM M.: The first thing you have to learn is to listen. Now you're talking. Listen! That's the first thing you have to learn when you come in here.

JACK: You keep thinking that because other people are talking, this is a sign for you to talk. It's not true. It's one of the things that's wrong with you. What brought you up here today? Now you can talk.

PROSPECT: Well, a series of things brought me up. I was introduced to Mr. Ross and—

JACK: No! My question is why are you at our front door? Why are you at the front door of our home? What do you want from us?

PROSPECT: I want to stay here and I want to get away from New York City and I want to change my way of life.

JIM M.: Why?

JACK: Why do you want to stay here? Why do you want to stay

away from New York? Why are you at our front door? You still
have not answered the question.

PROSPECT: Because I'm sick of the rat race I've been going through.

[Jack attempts to get him to state that (1) he is an addict and
(2) he wants help. However, the prospect keeps skirting this
issue.]

JACK: What kind of rat race? Do you chase cheese? Are you on a
merry-go-round? What do you do? Are you a bricklayer that
doesn't like laying bricks any more? Or are you a carpenter
that doesn't like driving nails, like I didn't? What is it? What do
you do that you find so obnoxious? You're unhappy. What makes
you unhappy?

PROSPECT: Well, I'm in and out of jails, taking narcotics. I'm just
trying to get off it. I've been trying for years to get off it, in jails
and hospitals. Other places accept me for a couple weeks, they
detoxify me, they throw me back out in the street, and they say,
"Go ahead, stay off."

JACK: How long you been shooting dope, or sticking it in your
arm or up your nose or whatever else you do with it?

PROSPECT: Well, since the first time, it's been close to ten years.

JACK: And how old are you?

PROSPECT: Twenty-six.

JACK: So you started using at sixteen, in high school?

PROSPECT: About sixteen and a half. No, I quit school, and right
after that I started.

JACK: Why did you quit school?

PROSPECT: I don't know.

JACK: But at the age of sixteen were you getting bad marks and
running around with the nuts that were slashing tires or stealing
hubcaps, kind of like the rest of us?

PROSPECT: Yes.

JACK: Were you living at home with your parents?

PROSPECT: Yes.

JACK: You still live with your parents?

PROSPECT: No, I had to move to my sister's house. You know,
when I'm up tight and I have no place to go, she takes me in. As
soon as I have enough money, I go out on my own again.

JACK: But you keep returning to some kind of family life. You keep returning to your momma or a momma substitute. That's one of the things wrong with guys like *you and me and the rest of us* in the room. The fact that we all have a great big need for momma. We do not have mommas around here. You are not going to be mothered. I hope you understand that. We're going to expect you to act like a man. In fact, we're going to insist upon it.

We know, in front, that you have some problems. Your problems are not what you think they are. Your problems are something that will come to you in time. It's going to take a year, maybe two, maybe never. We don't know. Eventually you're going to discover what your problems are. You have no idea what they are at this moment. None. If you knew what they are, you wouldn't be in the shape you're in.

We are a place established for guys who can't seem to understand the way the world works. I'm beginning to understand the way the world works. I'm the resident director here. You'll do as I say and as all the rest of the guys say. I have an assistant here, Jim Middleton. The rest of the guys are all kind of equal. If you come in here, you'll be part of a family of ten. You'll be the new element in the family. You'll be kind of like the new baby, I suppose. We'll talk in terms of family structure; it isn't bad. You'll be told when to talk and when not to talk, for a while. You will kind of be told what to do for a while. I guarantee you that if you go through the motions that we describe and prescribe for you, you'll end up being a man.

We may ship you off to Santa Monica. Drive you back there in a great big fine Cadillac that we own. We don't know quite yet which way you'll be growing up, but I guarantee you this again, if you stay and do as we say, you will grow up. There is no question about this in my mind. Every single one of us, hundreds now, are growing up today. They are well today and continuing to grow up. Some will leave, some will stay. More will come to us. Those that stay, those that are here today are growing up. If you wish to join us, if you wish to buy this as an assumption for yourself—I don't ask you to believe it; you can't believe anything right now, you're too confused—but if you come in here and act as if it's true and go through the motions, it will come true.

JIM M.: What do you think about everything that's been said so far?

PROSPECT: I've been fighting all my life for everything I wanted, and I *had* to fight for it.

JACK: You fight for what you want? What is it that you wanted that you fought for? Do you want the womblike atmosphere of your sister's house, or the womblike atmosphere of the jail or of narcotics? This is what you've been fighting for? Now, we're going to get you to stop fighting for all these destructive things. We're going to get you to start fighting for the finer, more mature aspects of life. We'll teach you how to scrub the floor, we'll teach you how to drive the car, we'll teach you how to meet people. We'll teach you how to understand others—and yourself, more importantly than anything else—and, you know, pretty soon you'll start to feel like a man.

JIM M.: I think we better straighten something out here in the beginning. We have two cardinal rules here. There is no physical violence, and there is no using of drugs, chemicals, or alcohol anywhere in this house or on this property. No physical violence, no chemicals whatsoever.

JACK: You will find out another thing. We are in the business of saying No. That's our business. Pretty soon we expect you to say, "I want to visit my sister." *No!* "I want five bucks." *No!* "I want to go to the movies." *No!* "I want to shoot dope." *No!* You know, that's the business we're in. We're going to tell you no for a long time. Pretty soon you're going to learn how to say no to yourself. Then you're going to find that there is nothing in the world that you really can't do, if you so choose. This takes time. In a couple of years, you'll be in a position of being able to live anywhere in the United States and be a respected member of the community. This I guarantee you. But it's going to take at least a couple of years, maybe longer—maybe shorter, but I rather doubt it.

You know there's a big chunk missing out of your life. Since the age of sixteen you've had some kind of chemical rattling around in your bloodstream. This has caused you to miss all the world's activities, all of life's stream has just kind of passed you by.

You were encapsulated down into a dope fiend. A dope fiend is the kind of guy that knows nothing of his environment other than where he is going to get his next fix from, or where the [prison] screws tell him to go eat. That's about the end point of a dope fiend's life. That's what you are. So, you know, we're going to widen you out. We're going to open up your awareness, using Synanon mechanisms. You are not going to agree with anything we say for a while. But you're going to act as if it's all true. Take what we say on blind faith for a while. Say, "All right, you goddamned dope fiends yourselves, I'll go along with it, but I don't think none of it's worth a damn."

I don't care how you think. I don't care what you say in synanon, but on the living room floor or in the everyday business of life here, you kind of *go through the motions* or you'll get lost. Just that simple, you'll get lost. We'll throw you out, or you'll just split [leave].

You'll join us 100 percent, you know, with everything you got. But you have so little to work with. Please don't bother your brain with trying to figure out a way to smuggle drugs in here or trying to figure out a way to con someone here into going to New York and scoring with you. Don't waste your time trying to fight the authority. You will not win. I guarantee it. I know the kind of guy you are, because I was one once myself. You will want to fight all the authority symbols in here. There's only one top authority symbol, and that's me. You are not going to whip me. I guarantee that. Tougher guys than you have tried.

So, you see, here you are. We offer you life as an adult in comparison to the life of a sniveling, whining dope fiend from the gutters of New York. You arrived here in a fine suit and a taxi cab. But I know what you are. You have no money. You have no property. You have nothing of any value. Your mother had to pay your way in here. You see, I know the facts. Now, you know, work from that point. There's nothing wrong with this if you accept it as being true and grow up from there. You'll become a man. Don't fight the knowledge that's so clear to everyone in this room. Please. It just gets in the way of your progress.

JIM M.: So how do you like it? Now what do you think?

PROSPECT: I'll tell you, in the beginning you got me a little sore, but now he's talking sense. Now it's making sense.

JACK: We don't expect you to make too much sense at first. In time, if you stay, if you listen, open up your ears, open up your eyes, kind of look around and see what's going on, you'll begin to make sense. Not only to me but to yourself. That is more important than anything else in the world. You'll begin to make sense to yourself, and you'll find a little peace, a little comfort in life. You'll find that you can enjoy things. You'll find that you will enjoy the fact that Synanon goes to visit the President in the White House [referring to a Synanon group trip to the White House Conference on Addiction in 1962, by invitation of the President]. You will find that you'll enjoy your brothers and sisters in Synanon. We have dance bands and dance classes and many of the finer things in life. You'll enjoy the fact that we have some wonderful friends in the community. Yesterday we were visited by a local narcotics officer. How do you like that? He sat around, had a cup of coffee, dropped five bucks in the till to help us eat. He related with us, man to man.

Everybody in this building knows more about life than you do, everyone. That includes the boy that we just took in a week ago off the streets of Bridgeport. He's one week ahead of you. That's the way it is. Everyone here knows more than you, at this time. You know, here at Synanon we kind of laugh at tough guys. For Christ's sake, here's a tough guy [points to Middleton], if you want to meet one. There really aren't any tough dope fiends. There isn't any such animal. They're just little children trying to act like adults, and they're so pathetic. Really they're so ridiculous. *Here, we paint them as the comic figures that they are.* You may be able to teach the guys that follow you in here. Within a short time, you're going to be telling some guy what to do and how to do it. There is no job in the Synanon Foundation that you can't achieve if you have the balls for it. I offer you a challenge; I tell you, you can have my job. If you have the balls for it.

PROSPECT: I'd like to get your job.

JACK: I bet you would. Well, you have a nice long row to hoe. We'll teach you to channel this rebellion of yours into a constructive way of competing. You are on the ground floor of one of the fastest-growing social movements around. We'll teach you how to channel this drive of yours, that somehow comes out all distorted. You will learn to channel it into a constructive drive to create things. Things that are worthwhile. At first, you're not going to understand a lot of things that go on around here. Don't try to understand our zoning problems. We got a little zoning hassle going on right now with the city. Don't let it even bug you, because you can't understand it. I barely do myself and I have excellent advice from a local attorney.

You see, I know how a dope fiend's mind works. You're going to read the newspaper tomorrow or the next day or look up on our bulletin board and say, "Hey, this place is out of zone. Well, shit, I think I better split so I can go shoot dope."

Any rationalization in your mind that takes you out that front door will be only a very cleverly disguised attempt to shoot dope again. There's nothing in the world out there for you this time. This is where you belong. Don't start thinking for yourself yet. You know, when you try to think, you attempt to use a muscle that hasn't been developed. You haven't any muscle there yet. You have a little quivering fiber that just buckles if you try to think. It gets so confused and tired. It just all relaxes when you put dope in your arm. Don't try to think for a while. Let us do the thinking for you, for a while.

When was the last time you fixed?

PROSPECT: What?

JACK: When was the last time you injected some kind of narcotic?

PROSPECT: This morning.

JACK: What did you use?

PROSPECT: I mainlined—shot up.

JACK: You fixed this morning? Do you have any drugs on you at this moment?

PROSPECT: No.

JACK: Do you have an outfit on you?

PROSPECT: Not a pill, nothing.

JACK: If you do, we're going to find it. You have nothing on you at this moment?

PROSPECT: Nothing on me.

JACK: Go shake him down. [Jim finds nothing.] Welcome aboard, Frank.

After the indoctrination, Middleton engaged Frank in a friendly conversation about various matters. This was surprising to Frank. However, he later learned to distinguish between the contentious, "tough" approach that is used during an indoctrination, a "haircut," or a synanon and the more friendly, affectionate tone generally operative in a Synanon House.

THE RATIONALE OF THE INDOCTRINATION

The indoctrination attempts to pare the newcomer down to his real emotional size. From Synanon's point of view, as Hurst describes it, "the addict who runs up and down back alleys, goes to jail, lies and cheats is an emotional infant." There is an attempt to get the newcomer to accept himself overtly the way he really thinks of himself inside. The mutual recognition of his low self-image is a first step toward progress. Jack once told me that when he was indoctrinated by Chuck, "his perception of me as a punk made me feel secure. I felt good in the presence of someone who really knew me and the kind of guy I was."

Another characteristic of the indoctrination is to tell the newcomer clearly and forcefully what will be expected of him: that he will have to work (at first on a menial level) and that he will have to follow the rules of Synanon. In addition, he is given some information about the nature of the organization.

He is further informed that he automatically becomes part of the staff. This tends to give him a sense of belonging. Also, as Jack put it, the addict "can achieve any status in the organization." He can see this as a real possibility, because the individuals confronting him (although they may not look like it) were once themselves "dope fiends."

Another element of an indoctrination is to anticipate and prevent rationalizations and excuses for failure. Jack made reference to the zoning situation and other problems. The newcomer was vigorously apprised "in front" of the set of rationalizations he might use to go out and shoot drugs. This seems to have the effect of involving the newcomer more quickly. It helps him to become increasingly aware that he is dealing with individuals who know him and *anticipate* his thoughts and drives. In the indoctrination, the assertion is repeatedly made that the newcomer has a limited superego, or ability to control his impulses. He is told that this self-control must initially be handled by the organization. ("You do not know how to say no yet, but you will learn.") After the prospect's low self-image is brought out into the open, he can relax about being "found out." The indoctrination has already exposed him—and it is not necessary for him to keep up a "front."

Another impression made on the newcomer is that he is in an environment wholly different from any he has known. He is told that he is not in prison or in a hospital, that he is in Synanon. This is repeated and forcefully driven home to him. Since the newcomer has probably failed in other settings, Synanon's uniqueness and difference may give him an expectation of hope.

Although tough, the indoctrination is honest. Despite the seemingly harsh quality of the "attack method," the newcomer is accepted and explicitly informed that he can change. This technique is a most important part of the indoctrination. It helps the newcomer feel that he has overcome an obstacle "in front." He is encouraged to believe that the tough, honest people who indoctrinate him must think that he can change or they would not waste their time. A successful indoctrination transmits a feeling of hope to the newcomer and a belief in his own ability to succeed.

10

The Mother-Lovers

The criminal-addict usually arrives at Synanon with a drug habit, a tough-guy attitude, and a background of snarled and destructive past relationships. Many of his past associations had a negative effect on him. The parents, spouses, lovers, or friends with whom he was intimate before and during his addiction career were not able to change his self-destructive behavior. In some cases, their relationship to the addict encouraged or reinforced his destructive tendencies.

These past relationships will not be examined here in depth. They will be described in order to reveal the reasoning behind Synanon's strict policy for isolating newcomers from their past. Synanon takes the extreme position, based on its experience, that people from the addict's past can activate the newcomer's "addiction virus" by simple contact.

The parents of most addicts either contributed to or "hooked in" to their "child's" [1] problems. In some cases, they even used their "kid's" trouble as a rationalization for their own failure. One father, an alcoholic, vehemently claimed that he couldn't hold down a job essentially because of his "troublemaker" son. In another case, a mother seemed morbidly to enjoy the addiction antics of her "terrible daughter." It seemed to give her con-

[1] The parents of addicts often refer to their twenty- or thirty-year-old son or daughter as their "child" or their "kid."

siderable material for her daily ritual of commiseration with her alcoholic friends at a neighborhood bar.

Other parents of addicts present an exaggerated appearance of loving their child. A closer analysis often reveals that their "love" is a reaction formation to a deeper unconscious hatred and rejection. Many parents of this type reinforce their child's self-destructive addiction in subtle ways. Despite their claim of opposition to addict behavior, they may support the child's habit financially. When their addict seems to be "cleaning up," they sometimes do something (on an unconscious level) that helps get their child back on drugs. In several cases, this type of parent foolishly offers the child a few drinks to "cheer him up." Some leave money or pills around.

In another destructive pattern, the parent continually "picks on" the addict and repeatedly warns him of the trouble he will get into. This tends to produce and reinforce considerable guilt in the newly "cleaned-up" addict. The addictive personality's response to this nagging prediction is often a prophecy-fulfilling "fix." The child, in part, may feel helpless to change the *completely incorrigible* image of himself etched in stone by the parent.

It is difficult to pin down a parent's unconscious push of the individual back to drugs. Some manage, however, in a subtle fashion to press the buttons that trigger the destructive tendency. The destructive association is not usually apparent to the untrained eye, although the deadly *results* of this type of "loving-parent act" are clearly visible and apparent. The case of one mother who offered her child drugs rather than "mom's apple pie" illustrates a pattern of "mother love" that is more apparent than the previously described subtle forms. Her child (thirty-five years old) had been "clean" in Synanon for six months. This was the first time in fifteen years that he had remained "clean" for longer than a day in the open community. On her first visit (Synanon had not permitted her to visit him for the first six months), she was overheard telling him: "Please come home, dear. I'm dying of loneliness. I won't let you use heroin, but I'll give you all the pills you want."

Although it is somewhat sacrilegious in American society to view a "mother's love" as anything but pure and positive, the

Synanon experience has clearly revealed that this type of "mother-lover" is symbolically and realistically a deadly disease.[2]

The past spouses or lovers of newcomers are also apt to carry a mother-lover virus. In their past association with the addict, they were either destructive participants in his problem or, at minimum, helpless bystanders to his plight.

Some nonaddict spouses seem to select a dependent addict for a mate because of their own neurotic needs and feelings. In some cases, there is subtle evidence that they do not want the addict to quit his destructive behavior. This may stem from the fear of becoming unwanted and abandoned after the addict has recovered. The fear contains a measure of reality. After considerable self-examination and a better insight into their problem, many people who "grow up" at Synanon no longer want to associate with these people from their past. When the Synanon member changes and their spouse remains the same, the past connection is usually severed. Monica realized this "change of pace" after a visit with her husband about the time she had been "clean" two years. "He's like a stranger to me now," she said. "We really have nothing to talk about. I feel sorry for him and wish him luck, but I'm going to divorce him." (She finally did divorce him.)

Synanon, in its early experience, lost many newcomers back to drugs and jail after a visit from a mother-lover. Based on this experience, they developed a tough policy on early contact with newcomers. Visits are prohibited until there is sufficient evidence to indicate that the newcomer is strong enough to resist the mother-lover's potential "Circe" call to destruction.

This tough policy may seem cruel at first glance, but it is based on rather sound logic. An important aspect of many of

---

[2] The expression "mother-lover" will be used throughout to caricature the newcomer's past destructive relationships. In addition to identifying the destructive type of mother described in the case mentioned in this analysis, it will refer to the broader spectrum of rejecting, smothering, exploiting, or indifferent spouses, fathers, and lovers in the addict's past. (The term may be identified as a polite substitute for the expression "mother-fucker," an important term in the criminal-addict lexicon. In the underworld, it is used as a vicious epithet, implying in one interpretation that the person identified as such would "con" his own mother or even be "low enough" to have sex with her.) In brief, the term "mother-lover" will be used to identify people from the past who might cause the recovering Synanon member to relapse or regress.

these past relationships was addiction and criminal behavior. At worst, the past mother-lovers consciously and unconsciously reinforced this negative behavior. At best, they were ineffectual in preventing the person from acting out his destructive tendencies.

Synanon has sometimes found it necessary to perform major surgery on this kind of "mother love," at least in the newcomer's infancy in Synanon. The Synanon experience, to date, indicates that after about a year, if the individual has matured in Synanon, he either is able to handle or has outgrown his past negative emotional involvements.

Some Types of Mother-Lovers

Based on my studies of the relationships between Synanon members and people in their past, I have noted several standard types of mother-lovers. Their negative influence is, of course, only one force among the many that produce the criminal-addict. Yet, out of the variety of causal forces that shape an addict's personality, the following relationship configurations seem to be of considerable significance.

The Unconditional: The most common type of destructive mother-lover is one who gives "unconditional love" and rewards both "good" and "bad" behavior.[3] This nondifferentiating positive response to a child's behavior directly reinforces bad behavior.

The Rejecting: At the opposite extreme is a *totally* punishing or rejecting mother-lover. This type uniformly rejects the individual's behavior, whether it is good or bad. The destructive consequence of involvement with this type of person is very similar to the results produced by the "unconditional" mother-lover. Since the individual is punished for everything he does, he does not learn how to distinguish *emotionally*[4] between good and bad behavior.

[3] What is "good" or "bad" behavior is, to put it mildly, a controversial issue. For my purposes here, I refer to behavior that is considered good or bad in terms of the generally accepted norms of American society. (This "unconditional" pattern fits into the basic category of unconditional "mother love" described by Erich Fromm in *The Art of Loving*.)

[4] On a surface level, most people, including addicts, know right from wrong. This appraisal refers to the deeper emotional understanding—in Synanon terms, "the gut-level feeling."

The Indifferent: Another destructive pattern involves almost complete indifference. Here again, the victim of this treatment doesn't learn to distinguish between what is good and bad, since the response of the destructive mother-lover partner is indifference or neutrality. In this category, the mother-lover simply doesn't care what the person does. (Such mother-lovers may be bothered only by the inconvenience of appearing in court or visiting the victim in jail.)

The Vacillating: In another pattern, the mother-lover is inconsistent. The attitude may shift from total indifference to approval to rejection. None of the momentary and varied responses is especially related in any logical way to the victim's behavior. The shifting and vacillating response, like the other types, does not enable the subject to distinguish clearly between good and bad behavior.

In the complicated causal background of the Synanon newcomer, the mother-lover issue is only one of the factors which may have produced the addict's pathology. The evidence, however, reveals that most new arrivals have been exposed to either one or a combination of these self-destructive patterns. In many cases, the "significant other" in the newcomer's background (1) smothered him with indiscriminate approval, (2) totally rejected him and his behavior, (3) was neutral and indifferent, or (4) acted in an incoherent, vacillating fashion without logic or reason. Often, for the first time in his life, the Synanon newcomer is confronted by a consistent and firm reaction to his behavior.

In summary, Synanon attempts to heal the mother-lover problem with the introduction of a consistently firm hand and loving environment. It provides an extended family situation that clearly and systematically rewards good behavior and rejects bad behavior. This enables many people in Synanon to learn how to distinguish between the two and then to behave appropriately. Proper recognition and reward reinforces good behavior and seems to help the individual to grow up properly. Perhaps for the first time in his life, he finds himself in an environment where he is given direction and justice.

The Delicate Balance

The Synanon administrators are intensely aware of the potentially destructive mother-lovers in the newcomer's past and try to deter their potential for disturbing the delicate balance of attachment he may have acquired in Synanon. Synanon's policy of restricting visits by the former associates of newcomers is based on specified assumptions. They postulate that the newcomer is an emotional infant and that some of his prior human relationships encouraged, supported, or, at minimum, were incapable of deterring the individual's use of drugs. Based on this conclusion, in the early days at Synanon the potentially deleterious social forces are virtually eliminated from the newcomer's environment. The policy in part operates on the symbolic assumption that the healthy fetus of the newcomer has just become attached to the therapeutic environs of Synanon. Any shock to this link could destroy the newcomer's precarious balance.

Home visits as well as mother-lover visits to Synanon have produced destructive effects (people getting very emotionally upset and in some cases "splitting") and have in several cases almost "smashed" the individual. In one case, a young man who had been "clean" at Synanon for more than two years was granted a Christmas leave to visit his family in Texas. The results were almost disastrous. He came close to physically assaulting his father and almost shot dope. He still carried a time bomb of hate and grievances against his past mother-lovers, and it almost exploded.

He later worked out his feeling in a number of synanons and "came back." [5] But the destructive switch was almost turned on. One could infer from this case that the person wasn't fully recovered from his "illness." On the other hand, he was doing fine in Synanon. There does not seem to be any logical reason for

[5] In a psychodrama session I ran with the young man, he "acted out" several scenes with his father. (I ran about fifteen psychodrama sessions during my research in Synanon. The sessions revealed considerable data on various processes of Synanon and drug addiction.)

exposing the newcomer (or even a Synanon "old-timer") to some of the virus that originally made him ill or nearly destroyed him.

In spite of considerable evidence that they have failed with their "child," many mother-lovers try to get back into the destructive act. They try in various ways (prematurely) to renew the past relationship. Synanon, necessarily, attempts to block these efforts.

Synanon's policy and method of dealing with the problem is partially revealed in the following phone conversation I overheard between a Synanon acting director and a mother. She could not accept Synanon's refusal to allow her to visit her son. (I was able to hear only the director's side of the conversation and recorded the highlights.)

ACTING DIRECTOR: We don't permit parents to visit newcomers for at least thirty days. . . . I don't have time right now to explain our reasons in detail. . . . Yes, I know you always had visiting rights when Joe was in jail or prison. . . . We're trying to help him grow up and stay out of those places. . . . We can't help it if you don't like what we do and you want him back with you. Didn't he shoot dope and go to jail when you had him? . . . Well, I can't believe that you now know how to handle him. . . . Look, we're very busy trying to help young men like your son to grow up and stay out of prison. Some other time we will explain to you in detail why you cannot visit him now. For the time being, look at it this way. You failed with him, right? Well, we may be successful with him, and then we'll all be happy. . . .

You can make an appointment next week. I'll see you and explain in detail why you cannot see your son now. I'll also send you a package of our literature, which tells you something about how Synanon works. . . . No, you will not be able to see him when you come down to see me next week. . . . Well, if that's what you want to do, get a lawyer. Your thirty-year-old "child," as you call him, is here voluntarily and doing fine. And I repeat once more, you will not be permitted to see him for thirty days, perhaps longer. Thanks for calling.

Motivations

What do they want? Based on my observations of and discussions with a range of deadly mother-lovers and other parents and spouses who think more logically, I have concluded that there are four essential kinds of motivation. It is beyond the range of this discussion to go into the necessarily long analysis of the development of the mother-lover syndrome. The following categories attempt to explain and speculate on mother-lovers' motivations only at their point of contact with Synanon.

CATEGORY 1—THE DEADLY

They clearly and overtly do not want their "child" to get well. They want "it" home and under their control. A good example of this type is the addict's mother who openly and dramatically stated, "Please come home, dear. . . . I won't let you use heroin, but I'll give you all the pills you want." In another case, the mother of a Synanon female addict once smilingly told her on a jail visit, "I like to have you in jail, so I know where I can visit you regularly."

CATEGORY 2—THE FEARFUL

The "fearful" mother-lovers have an unconscious need to maintain and continue the addict's symptom. This need emanates from their own neurotic insecurity. For example, the nonaddict wife of a newcomer told me that she wanted her husband to quit using drugs. She admitted that she had often helped him to get drugs. Near the end of our discussion, she openly admitted her strongest fears: "If he quit using drugs, he would probably leave me. I would rather have him as an addict than not have him at all."

Most "fearful" mother-lovers will not consciously admit to these feelings. Their resistance to their "loved one's" growing up is more often reflected in a subtle attack on the therapeutic environment and an attempt to pull the "love object" out of it.

In one Synanon case, a young man who had been doing well and staying "clean" in Synanon for more than seven months received a letter from his wife. In the letter, she said, "Get well, baby," and then described in gross detail her erotic feelings and attractions. She described her black silk panties and her increasingly extreme passion. The letter was revealed by the young man in a synanon session. It was interpreted by the group as an apparent effort on her part to pull him out of his therapeutic environment and back into their past destructive relationship.

The group discussion concluded that if she really loved him, she would give him a chance to continue to grow. Later on, he could return to her as a capable adult.

CATEGORY 3—THE GUILTY

In this pattern, the mother-lover overtly wants the addict to get well, but unconsciously does not want anyone else to help him do it.[6] In the case of one mother who vigorously attempted to see her son against Synanon's advice, she expressed deep feelings in this area: "He came to me for help. I couldn't help him. I deserted him, and I don't believe that any mother should have to feel this way." (In a lengthy discussion, which will follow in this chapter, there was an apparent preoccupation with her own emotions, rather than her son's.)

One possible interpretation of this pattern is that it expresses a strong need on the part of the mother-lover *personally to expiate* the guilt felt for producing an addict son. In order to eliminate her guilt for producing an addict son, this kind of mother-lover feels it is necessary that *she* cure the addict. Because of her own selfish need to expiate her guilt in this way, she attempts to block anyone else from succeeding.

CATEGORY 4—THE IMPATIENT MOTHER-LOVER

Here, the mother-lover steps aside to permit the child to get well, up to a point. The "impatient" ones are more liberal than

[6] Some professional therapists react to the "Synanon cure" of their former patients in this way. When Synanon succeeds where they have failed, this is often unconsciously felt by professionals as an attack on their competence and on the validity of their professional vested interest. This partially accounts for considerable professional resistance to Synanon. See Chapter 16, "The Newest Profession," for a more complete analysis of this issue.

the "guilty" about permitting the therapeutic process to function for a time; however, they revert to type when they see the therapy actually starting to work. Then they, like the others, attempt to remove the individual prematurely from his beneficial environment. An example of this is the parents who wanted to remove their son after he had been "clean" about six months in Synanon. Their argument was: "He's gained weight and he's healthy again —we want him home with us so we can help him the rest of the way." They attempted to remove him from the beneficial environment of Synanon even though the past evidence of their inability to "help him the rest of the way" was crystal clear.

The Case of the Impatient Mother-Lover

An interesting Synanon case that reveals some dimensions of the mother-lover problem is what became known in the annals of Synanon as the "Gold Affair." A young addict's mother arrived from New York to "inspect Synanon" and visit her son. This, of course, was not permitted, because, as Dederich later told her, her son was "an eleven-day-old baby in Synanon and would not survive the visit." The mother caused a scene in the front lobby and hovered around the beach front, demanding to see her "child." Dederich privately interviewed the young man as a prelude to talking to the mother.

CHUCK: Hello, Jack. I understand your mother is down in our foyer demanding that she be permitted to see you. She appeared out of thin air without calling in advance, and we're not going to permit it. You're twenty-three years old, therefore a legal entity, and I wanted you to make up your own mind on this matter.

If you want to see your mother, you can see her—but then, of course, you'll have to leave with her. One of the things we have to do in here is train parents in proper behavior. So, if you want to see her, you can see her and go with her. If you wish to continue to enjoy the benefits of the Foundation, just tell us so and we will handle your mother. We'll point out a few facts of life. We don't permit parents to see their children here for at least thirty days. The longer we can stall this off, up to a point, the better it is for you. Before we talk to your mother, I want to find out how you stand on this.

JACK: I would like to continue here.

CHUCK: You want to continue here? Then we will explain this to your mother. I don't know how she got out here. She's from New York, isn't she? She came tearing out here to gobble you up again?

JACK: She came out to see me, and she has relatives out here.

CHUCK: She does? Well, maybe we'll suggest to her that she should go stay with the relatives for thirty or forty days. Later on, we'll permit her to call us up and ask kind of like a lady whether or not we will let her into our home. We're going to send her on her way. I hear she made a statement, "I will take him with me." Is this the way she treats you at the age of twenty-three?

JACK: This is one of the reasons why I don't live with her.

CHUCK: Very good. In other words, you were almost well when you got here, then, weren't you?

JACK: I don't think so. It had other results.

CHUCK: There you have it. All right, you run off and play with your blocks in the seminar or whatever the hell you're doing. We will handle momma. This is the way you want it? You want to stay here at Synanon, right?

JACK: Yes.

CHUCK: Okay, one of our rules applies to parents. All right, kid, go on and enjoy yourself, "find God," learn all about yourself, and we'll handle momma. We eat mommas around here!

JACK: [As he's leaving] *Good luck!*

[Now that Dederich has the consent of the twenty-three-year-old youth, he can, if it appears appropriate, treat the mother as an interloper into his therapy. Because of bitter past experience, he bases his approach on the assumption that the woman is potentially a destructive mother-lover.]

CHUCK: All right, Reid, let's get momma up here. Also, get Tootsie and Bettye [two women directors] to come in here. Frankly, I don't feel safe with this yiddisha momma around without at least two big strong women on hand. [Mother enters]

CHUCK: Come in. You're Jack's mother. What's your name, my dear?

MRS. GOLD: Sally Gold.

CHUCK: Sally Gold, this is Reid Kimball, Bettye Coleman, and Tootsie Davis. We comprise part of the Board of Directors at Synanon. Now, what is it you have in mind?

MRS. GOLD: Do you have to run the tape recorder?

CHUCK: Yes, indeed, that's what we do here.

MRS. GOLD: Well, these things are very strange, because when I enter any hospital, I investigate.

CHUCK: This isn't a hospital.

MRS. GOLD: Well, I say anything, anything that will help, I investigate.

CHUCK: Very good. Now you're not entering a hospital, are you?

MRS. GOLD: No, but my child is.

CHUCK: Child? You mean this great big twenty-three-year-old man that was just in here?

MRS. GOLD: I don't care if he was my grandfather. [Mrs. Gold begins with a tough attitude, and Chuck responds with a louder voice.]

CHUCK: Pardon me, Mrs. Gold, you're in my office. I will talk and you will listen, and you will talk when I want you to talk. You're talking about this great big kid I had in here two minutes ago—Jack Gold—as your [sarcastically] "child"? This may be one of the reasons why he's an addict, because you keep thinking of him as a child.

Jack has decided that he wants to stay here at Synanon, where he can stay clean and learn how to grow up and be a man. One of the rules we have at Synanon is that we do not permit relatives, particularly mothers and fathers and wives and husbands, to see any of our people for a minimum of thirty days. You evidently didn't bother to inquire about that before you came here.

MRS. GOLD: There were calls made. I will admit it was our fault the way the thing was done. It was done in haste, without checking. I may not be very smart, but I'm cautious. I did oppose sending anyone here or anyplace without checking it first.

CHUCK: Well, your opposition is understandable, but your having any control over a twenty-three-year-old voter in the United States of America, my dear, that is fantastic thinking. This boy came to Synanon, as far as I am concerned, in order to learn how to be a man; and we will, of course, teach him if he stays. He wishes to stay. I confirmed that, about two minutes before you walked in the office, so I'd be on safe ground. I didn't want to do anything he wouldn't like.

What you want with reference to the boy is of no consequence to us. We are in the business of curing narcotic addicts; we know how to do it. One thing that we insist upon always is that there be no contact with relatives for about thirty days. If you did make a trip all the way from New York to see your boy, this is unfortunate.

MRS. GOLD: Only because of the literature I received and because of the telephone conversation.

CHUCK: Did you come here for any other reason except to see your boy?

MRS. GOLD: To discuss it with him. We had not discussed it, and I felt he knew very little about it.

CHUCK: Well, it's too late for that.

MRS. GOLD: Is he in prison?

CHUCK: No, he's not in prison, he's learning how to be a man at this moment. Now, here's the way he put it to us. We told him that if he sees you, he can go out the door with you. He said, "I don't wish to do that. I wish to stay here at Synanon and grow up so that I can be an American citizen and can vote without being in jail all the time like addicts are." That's what he told us. He tells me that you're out here to see relatives or something of that kind. Well, then, if you're going to be out here for another thirty days or so, then maybe we can arrange a meeting at that time. Not today. Not now. Probably in around thirty days. If you want to do it this way, fine. If you want to do it some other way, then I don't know what you do. Maybe you get a lawyer.

MRS. GOLD: Why is he committed here? What do you mean get a lawyer?

CHUCK: No, my dear. He is here by choice. I'm trying to explain to you, you're not going to see Jack—your child, as you call him; this man, as I call him.

MRS. GOLD: I was under a terrific emotion downstairs which is over and done.

CHUCK: I understand.

MRS. GOLD: They kept asking me whether I heard what they were saying. I'm very aware of your organization. I'm very well aware of what you're doing. I think you're doing good work, but I think it should be voluntary. [Here Mrs. Gold shifts her approach, apparently in an attempt to gain her objective by more conciliatory means.]

CHUCK: One of these days—[Mrs. Gold interrupts; Chuck continues.] You're talking again; and when you talk and I listen, neither one of us learns anything about Synanon. If I talk and you listen, then, you see, we both learn something. You made an understandable mistake, as mothers do, when they keep thinking of the grown-up sons as children. This situation is emotionally charged for you. For me, it's old stuff. If your boy stays here at Synanon, I will make a prophecy that you and I will be very good friends one of these days. Right now you don't like what I'm saying to you because I'm trying to point out to you—

MRS. GOLD: No, I'm not opposed to you. I understand what you're saying. I understand what you're doing, and I understand what you're saying.

CHUCK: Very good. Now the thing for you to do—

MRS. GOLD: And I say it's just unfortunate the way things were done. He came to me for help. I couldn't help him. I deserted him, and I don't believe that any mother should have to feel this way.

CHUCK: You have finished doing the best thing you could do for your boy, by making it possible for him to come to Synanon, where he can grow up. I'm saying to you, don't make an effort to spoil it. Now, we have a lot of business to take care of.

MRS. GOLD: I know you're busy.

CHUCK: Good.

MRS. GOLD: I still feel that under the circumstances, my not knowing anything about the place, with Jack not knowing anything about the place, I should see him. I didn't know this was a jail and once he entered he couldn't get out and no one could contact him.

CHUCK: No, he's free to go at any time.

MRS. GOLD: It doesn't seem that way.

CHUCK: It may not seem that way to you.

MRS. GOLD: When someone walks out of this place, can they re-enter of their own free will?

CHUCK: Indeed not. An eleven-day-old-baby? No! Do you permit your three-year-olds to run loose around the streets? Didn't you try to keep him away from automobiles and things when he was three years old?

MRS. GOLD: No.

CHUCK: You didn't! You just let him run out in the streets? Look what you turned out; you turned out a dope fiend, didn't you? This time, when he grows up in our house, he will not be permitted to do things that are harmful to him. Now I know why he's a dope fiend. Because he was permitted to run the streets when he was three years old. You just said so. We can't afford to allow him to be exposed to this same influence that brought him to our door.

MRS. GOLD: Well, I still feel that I'd like to speak to him.

CHUCK: But, you see, you can't speak to him in our house at this time.

MRS. GOLD: No, I don't intend to do it in your house, but if there is an open door, then you should prove it.

CHUCK: No, we don't have to prove anything. There's where you make a great big mistake.

REID: There, you see, when I told her downstairs that she didn't hear, she got hysterical.

MRS. GOLD: I hear, I hear. I'm very well aware you just want me to hear what you want me to hear. You want me to understand your way.

CHUCK: Mrs. Gold, I just explained to you that you cannot see your boy in our house at this time.

MRS. GOLD: Can I see him outside?

CHUCK: I don't know how you'll accomplish this. He says he doesn't want to see you, and we will respect his rights as an individual. He doesn't want to see you at this time. There it is.

MRS. GOLD: I don't think he needs pressure from you whether to see me or not. If he is strong enough, if you have done anything at all with him, he should be able to see his mother.

TOOTSIE: Mrs. Gold, we told you downstairs that we have rules. Chuck just ran it down to you. Reid ran it down to you, and I ran it down to you. One of our rules is that the people who come in here have no contact with their people—wives, children, family —for at least thirty days. We have said to you we are not going to break this rule. Chuck even broke it down and said maybe at a later date, maybe thirty days from now, you would be able to see your son. Right now you are not going to see him. He called him in here and I suppose he ran it down to him just like he ran it down to you, and Jack agreed to go along with the rules in the house. He's only been here for just eleven days. There's probably something going on in his mind. He thinks that this place can help him. He knows more about it than you do. So why don't you take it that your son is trying to grow up and has a mind of his own? See what he can do for himself. He wants to obey the rules and stay. You want him to break them and leave. Why don't you leave it like he has it right now?

MRS. GOLD: No, because you're very principled, the way you're talking. If you feel that he cannot talk to his *mother* and make up his own mind, it's just too bad. He shouldn't be in this place. [Mrs. Gold uses the term "mother" the way one would refer to a "supreme being."]

TOOTSIE: Mrs. Gold, he has made up his mind.

MRS. GOLD: No, I don't know. I haven't heard him. I'd like to talk to him alone for a half hour.

CHUCK: There's no way of your getting to him, because he's in this house, which is his home. I would suggest to you that you write him a letter. We've done everything we can to communicate to you the way we run Synanon House.

MRS. GOLD: I am still opposed to your principle.

CHUCK: This is too bad. You don't have to live here, and we do. This is our house.

MRS. GOLD: That's right.

CHUCK: Our house is our castle and all that. Now, if you will excuse me, I've got a lot of work to do. I've got to work with young men and women like your son and give them an opportunity to grow up.

MRS. GOLD: Yes, I understand the work you're doing.

CHUCK: Very fine.

BETTYE: Mrs. Gold, has Jack ever been in jail?

MRS. GOLD: No. [This was later found to be untrue; Jack had been in jail.]

BETTYE: Never been in jail. Has he ever been in a hospital?

MRS. GOLD: No.

BETTYE: Then this is his first attempt at trying to do anything about his problem?

MRS. GOLD: I feel that this is a very severe thing to throw a youngster into, the sort of place this is, with these rules.

BETTYE: I think he's very fortunate that he made it here before he had to go through all of those different agencies in trying to find help. I think he's very fortunate if he never had to go to jail or to a hospital.

MRS. GOLD: You see, you know nothing. Yet you're arguing. You know nothing about him, and yet you did bring him in and pressure him into staying.

CHUCK: We what?

MRS. GOLD: *Any talking is pressure.*

CHUCK: Mrs. Gold, I'm going to repeat again, we are busy. Will you excuse us?

MRS. GOLD: I won't keep you. In other words, he is a prisoner here.

CHUCK: Whatever you wish to call it. If you like the word "prisoner"—

MRS. GOLD: Well, what is it when you're kept here against—

CHUCK: Against what?

MRS. GOLD: I wouldn't say against his will.

CHUCK: Against what?

MRS. GOLD: Keeping him against his parents . . . discussing it. Seeing the place. Interviewing the place. Having it investigated.

CHUCK: Mrs. Gold, this is a twenty-three-year-old voter in the United States of America.

REID: Mrs. Gold, may I ask you a question?

MRS. GOLD: Twenty-three-year-old voters do walk into trouble.

REID: May I ask you a question? I've been here for four years, clean all that time after eighteen years of drug addiction. If my mother took the notion tomorrow to pull me out of here and I did not wish to go, would you say I am then a prisoner here, or would you say I am being given my right as a human being?

MRS. GOLD: If your mother can walk in and discuss with you *man to man* and get your opinion.

CHUCK: Reid's mother is not a man, so she couldn't discuss anything with him man to man. She was permitted to come in and see Mr. Kimball when he had been here sixty days. His mother, of course, is now one of the best friends that the Foundation has. Now, if you'll excuse me, Mrs. Gold, we are very busy.

MRS. GOLD: I don't understand this. I really don't and I can't understand. If you really feel secure in the work you're doing, there is no reason why you should fear a parent. If I had been in here or if Jack had been in here and investigated and found out what the rules were and accepted them, then it would be all right.

CHUCK: Fine. Jack is a very happy young man. Coordinator, will you please escort Mrs. Gold downstairs?

Several key points were illustrated in this attempt by Mrs. Gold to see her son. Her strongest feeling was reflected in the comment, "He came to me for help. . . . I deserted him, and I don't believe that any mother should have to feel this way." It could be speculated that her essential reason for being on hand was an attempt to expiate her feelings of failure. Mrs. Gold later became a friend of Synanon and a financial supporter of the organization.

In the particular case of Jack, he remained "clean" at Synanon for more than a year as a functional member of the program. He left prematurely at the end of the year against the advice of the administration.

SYNANON'S ASSUMPTIONS ON MOTHER-LOVERS

Synanon obviously differs from other settings in their response to visits by relatives and friends. On the basis of the mother-lover concept, there is an effort made to protect the newcomer from formerly harmful relationships. In institutions, staff often join with parents vis-à-vis their child. They often commiserate about the difficulty of handling the person and how sick and helpless they find the "patient." This approach tends further to alienate the individual from the "helpers" and may support the mother-lover relationship that either caused or reinforced the original pathology. This is consciously *not* done at Synanon. Here "staff" joins in and supports their fellow members against the potential negative external influences of a variety of mother-lovers, who have already demonstrated their inability to help the person.

Synanon operates on the assumption that in his early days of exposure to the Synanon process, the newcomer is supersensitive and very vulnerable to his former associations. At that time, he is not capable of making too many correct decisions about how he is going to relate to these "significant others." Synanon, therefore, attempts to protect him from these potentially disturbing and harmful influences. At a later time, when Synanon assumes that the person's "self" and decision-making apparatus are in better working condition, they are allowed interaction with their past.

The Synanon "graduate" makes his own decisions in these matters. Some graduates have gone back into most of their old relationships, others to some; but in many cases, a graduate completely cuts off all past associations.

These relationship decisions are often crucial to the person's well-being and success. The Synanon organization attempts to be as helpful as possible in assisting its members to deal effectively with the potentially destructive past. Although Synanon's policy at first may appear to be harsh and unsentimental, their experience so far has proven that the approach is realistic and effective. It protects Synanon people from relapse and, most important, gives them an opportunity to grow up unencumbered by their past destructive associations.

11

The Criminal Mask

Protection from past mother-lover relationships is important for the newly arrived criminal-addict. In combination with this, an attempt is made to eliminate the newcomer's tough-guy pose. This sometimes produces a split personality for newcomers who have a heavy commitment to their past criminal-addict role. On the surface, they are "doing the thing." They talk "right" in synanons, act "as if" they have given up their criminal past, and, to the untrained eye, seem to be making healthy progress. Yet beneath this positive appearance, they maintain an underground involvement with their old, more familiar criminal way of life. They seem to hold on to their "criminal stash" and reference groups as an "insurance policy," in case Synanon doesn't work for them. A classic example of a successful Synanon attack on the "criminal-actor" pose is revealed by John's story.

The Criminal-Actor: John

John arrived at Synanon in 1962, at the age of twenty-two. John was a thin, baby-faced-looking young fellow. His pale, ascetic face had an almost religious quality. In his neighborhood on the upper West Side of Manhattan, he was known by some of his peers as Whitey the Priest.

He received this nickname from an addict who was kicking a habit. As John relates it: "Once, in jail, some Spanish guy who was kicking a bad habit came to for a minute. He saw me and began to scream hysterically in Spanish that I was a priest. Later on, it was picked up by other people who knew me around the city. Some of the whores on Columbus Avenue would even 'confess' to me as Whitey the Priest. First I made sure they gave me a good fix of heroin, or money for a fix, and then I would actually listen to their 'confessions'! They weren't kidding; they were dead serious. After the 'confession' took place, usually in some hallway or in a bar, after they poured out their tragic story, I would lay a concept on them. Something like 'into each life some rain must fall.' I'd bless them and cut out."

John, most of his life, worshiped gangsters and criminals. He wanted to be like them. In his neighborhood, there were many to imitate. A criminal he especially admired was Trigger Burke, who, according to John, "went to the hot seat without a whimper."

When John was twelve, he took his first fix of heroin in the course of his delinquent business. "I use to run dope and deliver heroin for some of the pushers in the neighborhood. One day, I delivered a package of heroin to some guy, and out of curiosity I asked him for a little. He fixed me, and that was it. I began using from then on. It's hard to describe my first feelings about heroin. The best way I can describe it is that it's like being under the covers where it's nice and warm on a cold day. Of course, I don't recommend it to anyone except as a mercy killing."

John was first institutionalized at the age of five by his parents. He doesn't remember the reason. From then on, however, he felt extreme hatred for his parents, especially his father. In the institution, he "always felt a need to protect the underdog in a fight." He had several fights each day and found the "home" a "house of horror."

When he left the institution at about the age of nine, he began running with various young kid gangs in New York on the West Side. They were involved in petty thievery and destructive acts. He remembered learning to hate his father more and more. "I always stayed out late, and when he would get me at home, he would beat me up pretty badly. Then he would actually sentence me, like a judge. For example, he would give me 'sixty days in the bedroom.' I began my jail time early."

John continued to run the streets, used drugs whenever he could, and received more training for a life of crime. "In my neighborhood, when I was twelve or thirteen, I was considered a 'cute kid.' The whores liked me, and once in a while, for a gag, they would turn a trick with me. I admired the stand-up guy gangsters. They were my idols. I had two heroes at that time, Frank Costello and General MacArthur.

"I took my first real fall at fourteen. I was sent to the reformatory at Otisville. I hated everyone there and wanted to kill the director and some of the guards. I was always fighting and spent a lot of time in the hole [solitary confinement]. This gave me a chance to think and plot different ways to kill the guards and the man who ran the joint."

From Otisville, John, at age sixteen, was transferred to another reformatory for older boys. From then on he went on to spend time in various institutions. These included several trips to Riker's Island Penitentiary, Lexington for a "winder" ("You wind in and out"), Riverside Hospital for youthful addicts, and various New York City jails.

John always considered himself to be a "stand-up guy" [a criminal with ethics] and had set his personal goal at becoming a professional criminal.

At one point, he tried to learn how to be a safecracker from an old-timer. "Somehow I wasn't very good. I did go on a few capers. But it wasn't right for me. Whenever I was out of jail, which wasn't too often, I would just use drugs and steal. I became a baby-faced stall for some cannons. The stall sets up the mark, and the cannon picks his pocket. I made a fair living in this business. I use to like to pick pockets in museums. In fact, I don't know why, but I spent a lot of time walking around museums. [Certain works of art would mesmerize the pickpocket's victim and render him oblivious to having his pocket picked.]

"The last time I got out of jail, at twenty-one, I degenerated into a vicious animal. I became ragged and dirty. With a knife, I preyed on anyone I could get to. I stole dope from other junkies. I broke into slum apartments and took toasters and radios in poor neighborhoods. I began to really hate myself and what I had to do to keep using shit [drugs]. I began breaking into four or five apartments a day. I remember, in some of them, seeing a shopping bag or a poor old lady's black coat, and it would kill me to steal their radio or toaster. I couldn't understand what had happened to me. I always thought I was going to become a big-time operator. I wanted to become a good, respectable professional thief, and instead I had to look at myself and admit I was a common run-of-the-mill street hype."

It seemed that when John could no longer maintain his illusion of being a stand-up guy and "boss" criminal, he tried to quit drugs and the life. In desperation, he voluntarily went to Lexington and then to the New York City Riverside Hospital for young addicts. Nothing worked for him. He heard about Synanon from a sociologist, Dick Korn, whom he had met at Riker's Island Penitentiary. Dick dispatched him on a plane to California with money out of his own pocket.

"When I got to Synanon and saw guys like the Greek, Middleton, and Reid doing something for themselves, it got to me somehow," John told me. "There were no authority figures I could really hate like I did in the joint. I immediately liked Chuck. Somehow he struck me as a nice guy. In a way, he became one of my heroes."

In his third month in Synanon, it was revealed that John had a court "hold" on him from a prior offense. He had to appear in court in New York City. Synanon and John's mother put the money together for his round-trip flight. I happened to be in New York City at the same time on other business, and I appeared in court on John's behalf. I told the judge about Synanon. I related that John had been "clean" for three months and that his prospects were reasonably good. John was given a suspended sentence and directed to return to Synanon.

Right after we left the courtroom, I knew I had a tiger by the tail. Synanon's hold was light and the lure of the streets was powerful. I could almost feel John salivating for a fix.

I decided to hang on to him any way I could manage it, until his scheduled midnight flight to L.A. To kill the afternoon, I called a radio announcer I knew and made arrangements for

John and me to tape a radio program. This held him for the afternoon, but he slipped away from me in the early evening to "attend to some business." I was helpless to hold him any further except by force. That, of course, was out of the question.

Somehow John made the plane to Los Angeles on his own and got back to Synanon. Of course, before taking the plane he "slipped." He said, "Yes, I got some money together, scored, and fixed. I couldn't control myself in New York. It was too much for me."

I asked him how he managed to make the plane. "The only thing that got me back to Synanon were the promises I made," he said. "I told the Greek and Jack Hurst I would be back." The same criminal loyalties and beliefs that originally almost destroyed John had, in this situation, helped him to return to his Synanon lifeline!

Despite John's overt appearance of joining the Synanon program in his first six months, he continued to hold on to what I previously referred to as a "criminal stash" (an emotional commitment to crime). He kept an "ace in the hole" for his return to a life of crime if Synanon failed for him. His "holding on" to his criminal image was dramatically illustrated by a group of letters he had written, but never mailed, on his arrival at Synanon. The letters were uncovered by mistake during a move. They reflect the pathological hold of his past criminal reference points.

LETTER TO: George M.   FROM: John
           Stratford Hotel   #19443
           New York, N.Y.

George,

I would appreciate it if you would be in a position to cuff me a couple of G notes. I hesitate to ask but you know my situation, all but one or two of us are dead or up above. That's what comes with losing those kind of arguments. I will be moving again shortly I'm afraid. I have no connections I know how to locate out here for help. Big Joe and I were discussing an either way draw.[1] You can count on being remembered. (If we make it.)

[1] This, in criminal vernacular, refers to a large-scale crime that would result in either a big "score" or a heavy sentence.

This Synanon is a very good place. I'll tell you where to send the dough when you answer this letter. Smile at all the pretty girls for me. My wishes to our mutual friends as may care.

Until I see you on 7th Ave. good luck. I'm acting as if you're sending the green and I promise I won't forget either way. You know my word is good.

                                                                    Whitey

LETTER TO: Sam B.   FROM: John
                Canal Street   #19443
                New York, N.Y.

Hello Moish,

I have been in California since I saw you last at a place called Synanon. A very good program exists here.

I expect to be back soon and have an idea of something to do with Joe and Jake.

I will stop by and see you as soon as I reach New York. Keep your old hands out of other people's pockets.

                                                                    Your friend,
                                                                    Whitey

P.S. Eddie Hill went to the seat in Sing Sing last month.

LETTER TO: Louis M.   FROM: John
                New York City Penitentiary   #19443
                1500 E. 134 St.
                Bronx 54, N.Y.

Hello fat Louie,

I heard about your violation. I'm sorry, but that's the breaks. I been to California for a while at the Synanon place. A good place believe it.

I will see you upon your release, I have some employment for you. Remember old pal Sam, well he has a small concern going.

                                                                    Good luck,
                                                                    Whitey

Of interest is John's use of "#19443." Synanon, of course, gives no one a number. John probably did not want to admit to his criminal associates that he was voluntarily in a "joint." The number implied he was doing time. At the same time, he felt compelled to make positive comments about Synanon. This reflected some partial involvement with the organization. John's Synanon split personality was manifested in the hidden letters. They revealed his conflict over giving up his "criminal mask" for the anticriminal view of life presented to him at Synanon.

The criminal self-image John held on to for many years had to be removed as a first step in his Synanon treatment. This was accomplished by a barrage of verbal surgery in synanons and "haircuts."

Attacking the Criminal Mask: A "Haircut"

The criminal-addict's self-concept makes him inept and keeps him on the wrong side of the law. A postulate at Synanon is that this face to the world must be changed and a new one developed. At Synanon, this is vigorously attempted. It involves a "180-degree" turn from the offender's past patterns of behavior. As John learned, criminal language, jargon, and values are viewed with disdain and extreme disapproval in this "new world." The newcomer is permitted to hang on to his past destructive mold for a brief period of time. In short order, however, new words and behavior patterns are ruthlessly demanded.

Chuck described part of Synanon's resocialization process in this area to my graduate class in Social Welfare at U.C.L.A.:

"First you remove the chemical. You stop him from using drugs, and you do this by telling him to do it. He doesn't know he can do it himself, so you tell him to do it. We tell him he can stay and he can have a little job. We tell him we have a lot of fun and he might get his name in the newspapers. We say, 'People come down and you can show off and have a fine time as long as you don't shoot dope. You want to shoot dope—fine—but someplace else, not here.' He stops using drugs. Then you start working on secondary aspects of the syndrome. Addicts live by the discipline of narcotics; therefore, they talk about this all the time. They discuss petty theft and short con; none of them is well enough for big con. Addicts never pull any big scores; they can't—they're sick people. They talk about this.

"The next thing you do is attack the language. Eliminating their criminal language is very important. We get them off drugs by telling them, 'Live here without using drugs and you can have all this.' We get them off the negative language by initially giving them another. Since there is some vague connection between their personality problem and the social sciences, we encourage them to use this language. The language of psychology and sociology is great stuff. Whether or not the recovering addict knows what he's talking about is exquisitely unimportant at this time.

"Very quickly, in a matter of about ninety days, they turn into junior psychiatrists and sociologists. They become familiar with the use of a dozen or twenty words and misuse them. Who cares! It doesn't make any difference. Now they're talking about 'hidden superego,' 'transferences,' 'displacement,' 'primary and secondary groups.' This is all coming out, and they're not saying 'fix, fix, fix' all the time. 'I used $20 a day.' 'I used $30 a day.' 'Joe went to jail.' 'I went to jail behind this broad.' 'Where did you do time?' and all that. They get off that, and they talk about 'ids,' 'superegos,' and 'group structure.' They make another set of noises.

"First, they substitute this sociological-psychological language wholesale. Eventually, when they come to learn something of the meanings of the words, they stop using them. Of course, like any intelligent adult, you don't interlard your social conversation with technical terms. No one does this if he's in his right mind."

Language is, of course, the vehicle of culture and behavior; and at Synanon, it is instrumental in shifting the behavior patterns that the addict has used in the past. He begins to use a new, still-undeveloped set of social-emotional muscles. This shift is not accomplished by loving and affectionate cajoling or by discussion of the criminal's symptoms of addiction and crime. *There is minimal symptom reinforcement of criminal patterns.* Behavior and thinking are modified by verbal-sledgehammer attacks. The attack is modulated and tuned by the expert synanist. The individual is blasted, then supported, and he seems to learn to change his behavior as a result of this *positive traumatic experience.*

A "HAIRCUT" FOR CHRISTMAS

An important method of attack therapy in Synanon is the "haircut." This form of verbal attack employs ridicule, hyperbole, and direct verbal onslaught. In part, the "haircut" attack keeps the rug pulled out from under the recovering addict. As Chuck describes it: "If he gets set, begins to feel a little complacent, and feels he's in control of himself—which, of course, he isn't—he may even think he can reward himself with a little dope or a pill. Then, of course—*BLOUIE*—he's dead again." This, of course, is also the classic pattern of the rise and fall of the alcoholic.

An important goal of the "haircut" method is to change the criminal–tough-guy pose. The self-image held by newcomers (like John) as big-time gangsters is viciously attacked and punctured in the "haircut." A case in point is the "haircut" that was administered, in the wake of bad behavior, to a group of twelve self-styled New York gangsters who had come to Synanon for help. John was in the group.

The group of so-called little gangsters was brought into Chuck's office as a result of "bad behavior" on the beach on a Christmas morning. They were called in for cursing and "crime talk" within the hearing of an elderly gentleman who was passing by the beach side of the building. (Chuck later told me: "Since Reid and I were already going to give our time to the youngsters who had committed the offense in question, we called in all the New York gangsters for a mass haircut. With the same set of motions, we were able to work on the larger little-gangster symptom we find in most of our young newcomers.") In addition to the relative newcomers "on the carpet," a six-month member and some older synanists were in the group to serve as role models. They represented models of the change that could take place in the little gangsters if they straightened out.

The elements of exaggeration and artful ridicule are revealed in this "haircut." In addition, the pattern of attack and then support is demonstrated. A typical "haircut" goes beyond the bad behavior of the moment and into a more serious problem, and this is also revealed in the session. Unlike synanons, it is not interactional. A "haircut" is usually delivered by several older Synanon members to younger members. Chuck and Reid dominate the following scene.

REID: I don't know what you'd call this meeting. I don't think you'd even call it a haircut. I think we're going to make some observations on stupidity—stark, staring, raving stupidity. Think about this—we actually have some guys in this room who are representing themselves to each other and other people as New York gangsters. I have an idea that Legs Diamond or Frank Costello would have never wound up in here even if they became junkies.

These punks sit around here and discuss in the back toilet how you hit a guy with a pipe. I doubt if any of you hit anybody. Maybe you've been slapped a couple of times and you think of this as gang violence.

This group was just out in the front of our building talking about boosting and dope and managed to say something like "I don't give a fuck" as one of our neighbors and taxpayers passed by. These little gangsters, all sent out here on momma's money, haven't even observed that their little clique is made up of dishwashers and service-crew men who haven't even been here long enough to get any of the treatment they so sorely need. They hit rock bottom and their mothers got some money together and sent them out there.

Here you are, little punks, representing yourselves as gangsters or hard guys. You get around our pool table downstairs and I guess you think you sound like Legs Diamond or Kid Weil or something. You sound like one of the cheapest, phoniest pool-hall gangs over on the East Side, where they chip in fifteen cents to play a short rack of pool. That's what you sound like.

This is really kind of funny. We always figure we have a disturbed ward. Part of the disturbed ward gets in front of the jukebox and they stick their ear against it and they snap their fingers. We stand at the doorway and we laugh. It's all right—they're insane. But when it starts messing with our business, we have to knock it off.

When the lunatic fringe stands back in the toilet and tells each other the best way to wield a pipe, because they read some pocketbooks somewhere, or when they get out on the ocean front with this gangster stuff, it's getting too absurd. It's all a part of the insanity.

For a short period of time, we don't mind if you stand in front of the toilet and signify to each other how bad you were or how much dope you shot. You were all such big shots that your mommas put you in Metropolitan Hospital [New York hospital for addicts] three or four times, then a couple of trips to Lexington, and then shipped you out here. We are not going to permit you standing out in front of our beach and insulting our neighbors. You are all so stupid that you don't even know how funny you are. You tell each other about all the dope, all the big scores, how bad you are and yell "fuck" out in front of our building. Your stupidity is pathetic. Boy, you're sad. I met a few gangsters. They used guys just like you to go get their sandwiches. And if they were big peddlers, they gave you a cap [capsule of heroin] for delivering something.

I really wonder if they get the message. Here's a bunch of punks whose mommas paid for them to come out here and they're talking tough. It's really fantastic! You're funny until you get out in front and say "fuck" in front of our neighbors. You're really funny. Anytime anyone with brains around here wants to get a laugh, we say watch some of those—they're hip and they're tough and they're sharp.

CHUCK: The lunatic fringe, the disturbed ward, the punks from the sidewalks of Azusa, New York, Akron, Ohio—they're all the same. They all read the same books off the magazine stand. When they came out here, some of them get with what we are doing, stay, and finally grow up. Others go back and wind up once again in Lexington or some penitentiary or the county jail or sitting in some filthy saloon. We know that we have to put up with this insanity for a period of time, until you work out of it. That's kind of like growing new hair when we cut all your hair off. It's like getting your teeth fixed or other things we have to do for you, like putting some meat on your bones. But as Reid explained to you, we will not permit it to get in the way of our business.

When you get out on our beach and can't behave yourselves like grown-up human beings, we have to take steps. You can't use the beach, you can't do this, you can't do that. You see, everybody else in the world that ever got into this business of cleaning up dope fiends and punks realized that they were bucking something that was absolutely impossible. There's one thing that's peculiar about punks like you—they inevitably foul their own nest. If you get them in a penitentiary and lock them up and you decide, 'Well, now, let me see; we'll try to give them just a little bit. We'll give them dessert on Thursdays, or we'll give them three eggs a week instead of two.' You know what they'll do? They'll throw the extra egg at each other. Not even at the guards!

This is the stupidity of the young punk that's made every single agency give up on this problem. Well, we're not at that point any more. The first two or three or four years were pretty rough. But we know now that some punks can grow up. We give them just so much time around here, just so much time! This time comes to an end, and you either fish or cut bait, you either grow up or get lost. That's the way it is in Synanon, and Synanon is the only place that works.

REID: Let's consider another angle. If this place was San Quentin or Sing Sing, I might agree with your tough-guy act. In prison, I suppose you have to let it be known that you were a hotshot on the street and that you're a bad guy inside the walls. This is what you do to get status in prison. But think of how ludicrous it is when you come here to this place and you try to be tough guys or gangsters. In this place, if you make progress, you act like an adult. If you are gangsters, let's at least concede this, you're the very dregs of gangsterdom—the very dregs.

CHUCK: When this thing hits you and you begin to just get a vague inkling of how absurd your behavior has been, you're liable to get hysterical laughing at yourself. This is the beginning of growing up, when you see how extremely and ludicrously funny you are.

This is kind of a young group. The old gangster, of course, went out of existence before most of you guys were born. There are very few of them left any more. I'm talking about tough guys that really made scores. I would venture to say that in the last five years, all of you in this room, if you took every dime that all of you scored and put it on the table, it probably wouldn't support Reid's old drug habit for six months. You see, the thing is too absurd if you want to use that frame of reference.

Let's look at some of the hipster's stupid behavior. We have the jukebox syndrome. That applies to people who use the jukebox not for what it's intended, not to listen to music, but to put on an act. The jaw kind of recedes and drops a little bit, and you have this bit [*snap, snap*]. That's the jukebox syndrome. Healthy people listen to jukeboxes to hear music.

Then there's the pool-hall syndrome. Men go to a pool-hall table to play a game of pool. Nuts go to the pool table to make shots this way [backwards], when it can be done much better the other way. They use it to give it this cigarette bit. They leave the cigarette there until the eyeball is all full of nicotine.

Then you have the toilet syndrome. Now, most people use the toilet to go to the john or wash their hands or face. No, not our lunatic fringe. They use the toilet to cut up jackpots of how tough they are and where to hit a man properly. I don't think you really know how to kill a man with your bare hands. You see, we have people around here who do. If you want to find out, we'll have a class in judo. We'll have a lot of fun and put some mats down in the basement. We can then get into that a healthy way.

We have the beach syndrome too. Healthy people go out to the beach, soak up some sun, go swimming, or look at the broads. What do the nuts do? The nuts use the beach to talk like ten-year-olds. "Mother-fucker," "cock-sucker," in loud ringing voices, so that our neighbors would like to have us thrown out.

What's your problem? What's your basic problem? You never know where you are, when you are, who you are, or what you are. That is what's wrong with you guys. You just don't know the who, the where, the what, and the why.

[The group sits morosely listening and appears to be somewhat disturbed by the apparent accuracy of the descriptions. I was later told by several that they felt Chuck and Reid had them cold. During the "haircut," some began to comment to the effect: "I've had to act tough to get by on the streets." This notion is quickly parried and then attacked by Reid.]

REID: I must have a Jimmy Cagney complex. When I see a Jimmy Cagney picture late at night where old Jim is taken after a terrific gunfight as a big-shot racketeer, gets sent to the joint, and then struts around the big yard, talking bad and commenting on the lames in our society, my heart goes out to him. "There's old Jimmy, boy; fuck those squares!" That makes sense to me in that absurd context. But if Jimmy's momma mailed him there to make it and he was walking around wisecracking about the lames of society, I'd think, "Why, that silly son-of-a-bitch!" That's exactly the position you're in. Imagine—acting tough in here, a place devoted to saving your life.

[The attack session is entered by Herb, a six-month resident at the time. Herb wrote the Synanon film *Some Sort of Cage*. Because he still harbors some of the feelings of the group, he is in a position to personalize his remarks. His position is somewhere between Reid's and the group's.]

HERB: I don't think they realize where they are yet. They don't realize that they're in California, they're on the beach, they're among people who want to help them. They just don't realize it yet, that's all. I know all the guys in this room very well. They live in here and they work in here. They're dug and watched all the time. They may think they're being cute, but they're not being cute, because we see them as they really are. After I was here about three or four months, I started to look at things objectively instead of subjectively, I started to look at things in a different way. It dawned on me, 'I'm not in jail and I'm not on the streets of New York. I'm at Synanon.'

[Herb is asked to tell the group about the "Basket-weaving" syndrome.]

HERB: All right. One Saturday night, I was doing the same thing as you guys; maybe my humor was a little more biting. You all have a way of rebelling, you see. Jimmy over there is the happy type. You know, cute. Raul walks around like a hip hard guy— and it looks ridiculous in the living room with the fireplace burning and a Christmas tree—laughing in that rebellious way. I can spot you all clearly, because I can identify with you.

One Saturday night when I first got here, I think it was right after the sing-along, I went to the john. I said to John, "The basket-weaving team will meet in the subbasement," and Chuck walked out of the stall. They called me into the office. He didn't yell or anything, but he made me seem like an idiot and a fool. I wasn't in a bughouse where they weave baskets, I wasn't in a jail where they press their pants by hanging them on the wall or tell what big gangsters they were. I'm in Synanon.

You may not believe it, but Chuck and Reid want to help you. You may not believe it, but Chuck is not the warden and Reid is not the deputy warden. You may not believe it now, but if you stay here you will. Chuck told the group this once; all you can do is take his word for it. Nothing else has worked for drug addicts. For thousands of years, this seems to be the only thing that works. All you guys come swaggering. Bill, you know when you came in, you had a broken leg; we had to carry you down to the basement. You were as helpless as a baby. . . . How effective were you out there as a dope fiend? Were you in charge of kilos of heroin, big-time gambling? I mean, what was your stick? You were a *gutter hype*, like most of us, 90 percent of us!

[Reid here appropriately sees fit to reveal again his own background. The newcomer may find it hard to believe that an intelligent, solid individual like Reid was himself once a "hype." Revealing himself is part of the method. Reid's emphasis on his own experience gives the newcomer something to shoot for. He is a role model for the group to emulate.]

REID: You guys aren't vicious or anything. You're like every one of us was. None of you in this room was as stupid as I was. I'll guarantee it. You couldn't have possibly been. I was so dingy and dumb. I still hold the goddamn record for working on the coffee counter. When I first got here, I was on the son-of-a-bitch washing cups for ten months. Nobody's talking about you as exceptional cases. When something happens, when you get over this idiocy, you will look back and think, "What were we trying to prove; what the hell is there to prove?" Nothing!

HERB: We've all been there, you know. People who have been

there with the same backgrounds, give or take a little. They're hip to you. What is there to say?

REID: Let's speed up the process. Everybody comes in here—they're stark, raving lunatics. They yell "fuck you" out front, they gather in the pool hall. Hopefully, many people are changing here. Why not speed up the process?

[Herb reveals his identification with the organization.]

HERB: You know what happens to that little man out there when he hears one of us say "fuck"? By the time he reaches that hill, he heard 140 guys say "fuck"; by the time he hits home, he'll probably say there was a sex orgy on the beach. They blow us up. They're just looking to blow us up. You guys and I came after Chuck had this hassle with the city authorities. What town accepts drug addicts, that society has washed their hands of? They put them in bughouses, get rid of them. Addicts ruin everything they touch. They don't produce anything.

REID: A year ago, Chuck was sitting in a jail cell for running this goddamn place. How do you feel about being out there ranking this?

DAN: Reid, I didn't mean that. It just came out of my mouth. It was in a conversation.

CHUCK: Let's not worry too much about these little details. Let's think in terms of an attitude. If you can actually get down through your funny little image and say "Where am I?" Let's list where you are not: you're not on the streets of New York, you're not in some big yard, you're not in the county jail, you're not in a private sanitarium, you're not in Lexington, you're not in a pool hall. "What am I? I am twenty-five years old, thirty years old, twenty-two years old." Whatever it happens to be. "I'm not a ten-year-old boy. What am I? Who am I? When am I?" You get those questions answered. This involves growing up. It's a much more comfortable way to live, boys, let me tell you. It really is.

REID: Let's look at the phenomenon of drug addiction. All of us, I think, in here are agreed that we might have had a delusion at one time that it's pretty hip to be a dope fiend. I think it's pretty lame to shoot dope now, don't you? In other words, you're kind of a lame if you're willing for three or four fixes to go sit in a cage for ten years. You know, real dunces and fools. Think about it. There I shot three weeks of dope, now I'm in jail for ten years. You're like a goddamn bird sitting in a cage. Okay, if that is stupid and lame, then you have a little period of perplexity.

When I came in here and I'd hear the Synanon Philosophy and the prayer read, I'd say to myself, "These fuckin' lames, I mean that's *square* bullshit." I guess you're in that area of thought for a while. Then maybe you see the contrast and how lame it is to sit around a cell for ten years for shooting a little dope. If you feel what the people are doing here is lame, maybe you better take a look at your hole card again. How lame are the people here? How lame is Arnold? How lame is Joe Pass? How lame is Herby getting to be? Not too lame, really.

HERB: You guys never gave yourselves a chance to see what you really could do. Maybe you can do an awful lot if you give yourselves a chance. Feel! You never give yourselves a chance to feel. That's the trouble with us dope fiends.

REID: Remember that everybody here was just like you, including me. As an example, I'll guarantee you I'm a hell of a lot further from ever sitting in a cell for the rest of my life than you are. I'm probably a hell of a lot more comfortable, and I'll guarantee I was just as nutty or nuttier than you when I arrived.

CHUCK: Let's accelerate this program. Would you rather be like Reid is today than like you are? [They indicate yes.] What's stopping you? You can beat him in this race for sanity, you know.

REID: Think about either lining yourself up on the side of sanity or lining yourself up on the side of insanity. You might say to yourself, even now after our talk, you may come out and say, "Well, I'm not going for that bullshit." Think about it this way. Are you going to be on the side of sanity or insanity? The nuts in here are in danger of returning to drugs, the street, and their cells. When you stand around and you listen and you don't make any comment when some real dingbat is raving and slavering, I guess you've got to face the facts that you are on the side of insanity. There are two camps in here, really. We've always had a bunch of lunatics at any given time. Are you with them or with the sane people who have given up the bullshit and are getting well?

[Chuck turns to a young man whose head had been shaved, a punishment sometimes used for bad behavior. The offender has the choice of leaving or having his hair cut off. One working assumption is that if he permits his hair to be cut, he becomes further involved in Synanon.]

CHUCK: When did you get your hair cut, son?

GEORGE: Last night.

CHUCK: What for?

GEORGE: I ran out and took a walk without telling anybody, just ran out.

CHUCK: How old are you?

GEORGE: Eighteen.

CHUCK: Eighteen? An eighteen-year-old man can go to war and fight for his country. He can reproduce his own kind. He can get his name in all the newspapers in any section of the country, in all states, as a high-school halfback. There's a lot of things an eighteen-year-old man can do, right?

GEORGE: Yes.

CHUCK: Is it true?

GEORGE: Yes.

CHUCK: Now here you are on Christmas Eve. Your way of thinking, acting, and feeling for eighteen years got you to the point where a bunch of guys just like yourself can say, "All right, Buster, we're going to cut all the hair off your head."

I was a nut like you myself. My own son never was. He's twenty-six now. When my kid was eighteen years old, he never had to put up with this kind of bullshit from anybody. A cop, his own friends, nobody. He was just lucky. A little bit luckier than you and me. You see, he has his troubles, like people have. But he wasn't so far gone that he had to be pushed around on Christmas Eve.

Of course, you're better off having your hair cut off Christmas Eve in Synanon than sitting in a county jail, a penitentiary, a bughouse or strung out [on drugs] in some back alley. Aren't you, really? As bad as it is here, see how bad it could be? Just think, you don't have to ever be in that humiliating position ever again as long as you live. Nobody can push you around if you try to become a man.

REID: Do you realize how funny it is? Nobody in this room ever again has to sit in a cell or stand on some cold goddamn bald-headed corner waiting for the man to come back with your bread [money] or your shit [drugs]. You don't have to go to any more lunatic asylums, you don't have to go through kicking another habit, you don't have to do any of these things. Nothing in the world is going to make you do these things if you don't want to. This is true only if you decide to give up the very actions [criminal image] that keep getting you back into trouble.

CHUCK: We can bring it a lot closer to the moment. Do you realize that you never even have to have another haircut in Synanon? I don't mean a physical haircut. You don't even have to have anybody talk bad to you. This session is business for Reid and me. This is work. Who wants to work? There are many more pleasant things that we can do than to pull a kid in and try to teach him how to save his life by cutting his hair or giving him hell. You don't ever have to be on that end of it again. You can keep your mouth shut, do your work, and try to behave like a gentleman. In a very short time, you're in a position of trying to help another guy who comes in here sick. Then you can turn to some other guy here and say, "Was I like that? Is that the way I acted? Is that the way I appeared to be?" And they will say, "Yeah, that's right— that's the way you were." You won't be able to believe it. You just won't be able to believe it. None of this stuff has to happen to you.

You know, a little humiliation in here is the highest price you can pay, a little humiliation. There is no punishment; we can't punish you if we wanted to. We can't lock anybody up, we can't strap you to a kitchen chair and knock out your teeth like it happens in police stations. We can't do that, and we don't want to. We *can* humiliate you, in an effort to save your lives. That is all. After you get a few of these haircuts, you'll learn how to do it pretty good yourselves, so that you'll be able to help some other guy. But you really don't have to go through this ever again. Keep your hair if you want to. You can live with a little dignity, you don't have to be degraded, pushed around ever again. I don't mean over a period of time. I mean at this moment, right here, you can walk out the door of this office right now and it can never happen to you again as long as you live.

There's something you guys don't know about squares, and it

took me a goddamn near half a century to discover it. Squares never put up with the shit that people like you and I have to put up with every day. Never!

I learned that from my own kid. A funny thing happened in the early days of Synanon at Ocean Park. Louie C., who worked for the Santa Monica cops, thought that my boy was one of the dope fiends living at Synanon. He braced him against the wall of the sidewalk out in the front of the place. Of course, he braced our dope fiends anytime he wanted to. He talked bad to them and sneered at them. He tried this on my kid. He was about twenty-four years old at the time. My kid got up on his hind legs and said, "Why, you fuckin' public servant, get out of my way. Don't you ever talk to me again." This is the way squares talk to cops. Do you know that? Do you tough guys know that? You see, it took me goddamn near fifty years to learn that. I didn't know. [Group laughs.]

REID: They tell guys like us, "Get up against the wall and put your hands up," and go for a gun like we're punks.

CHUCK: You know it yourselves. A nice kind of square guy, why—shit—some cop tries to step on his toes, he lets him have it. You know what the cop said to my son? "Jesus, I'm sorry—I thought you were a dope fiend from Synanon." What do you think about that? Now how do you like those apples? John's laughing. Isn't that amazing, isn't that funny? It really isn't, it's the truth.

[The group responds with laughter. Some shake their heads as if they are realizing and learning this for the first time. The anecdote appears to have great impact.]

HERB: When somebody like a cop pulls you aside, you know, all this guilt in you helps him. If there was no guilt in you, you'd say, "Why do you talk to me like that?" You'd have something to stand on, some kind of status. Dope fiends are always hung up with guilt and on the defensive.

REID: I'm a law-abiding citizen. I don't use dope any more. I don't pretend I do or that I'm a gangster or anything like that. I'm earning that much of a privilege. No narco bull better tell me to roll up my sleeves. Of course I won't roll up my sleeves, any more than Mr. Ralph, our landlord, would roll up his sleeves or turn his pockets out or put his hands up against the wall. But, by

God, if I'm out on the street yelling "fuck" and saying how bad I am, I guess I'd better respect their right to do that. When you claim to be a bad guy, a criminal, you know, that's what you are earning.

CHUCK: It's a nice thing to learn. It really is. Don't wait any longer. It's a pretty good lesson. If you can absorb this lesson, this could be the best Christmas you ever had. You really couldn't have a better Christmas present than this little mickey-mouse haircut we gave you. This is a good one. This is a Christmas haircut. Merry Christmas.

An Analysis of the "Little-Gangster Haircut"

Several weeks later, the "little-gangster haircut" was analyzed in an interchange with Chuck, Dr. George Bach, and myself. We listened to a playback of the session and then "cut it up," Synanon style. (Many tapes of synanons, haircuts, and lectures are played, replayed, and analyzed in different Synanon House locations. It is considered to be part of the educational process of the overall organization.)

CHUCK: First of all, let me make one point clear. This is not a regular synanon, this is a haircut. Attack is, of course, used here, and it is delivered against bad behavior.

GEORGE: I was impressed with the approach. However, there is a part of this that requires clarification. You had some warmth in your attack, Reid didn't. The others were even more severe. One can damage the ego if it's all attack and no support. How would you explain this angle of the haircut?

CHUCK: The extreme lead-hammer Synanist attack technique is a natural approach for an alcoholic or an addict fresh off his medicine. He is so frustrated and full of hostility that the lead hammer comes naturally. In training a Synanist, you have to make him clever at it. You have to teach him to direct his hostility properly. From my own experience, the haircuts that I gave four or five years ago were almost 100 percent totally vicious, with very little warmth. But as my own hostility diminished, I used the haircut as a teaching device, and I wouldn't, so to speak, black out personally in the middle of one. I would always have my eyeball rolling and reflect to myself, "I'm pushing this kid too far. I better come over here and lift him up." It's easier for me, because I do haircuts now with my ego. I don't do it out of my id or out of my personal hostility. Reid is almost as good as I am. And others, of course, will improve with time.

GEORGE: Why didn't you let the "little gangsters" speak or talk back?

CHUCK: Let me clarify that for you, George. Again, the important point is that this is not a regular synanon. Our people do their talking in a synanon interchange. This is a haircut. They have offended, they cursed on our beach. We don't want them to do this, so we communicate this in a one-way direction. It's from Synanon to them.

In the context of a seminar, a drama class, or a synanon, they can yell back and forth all they want. But when we are to correct bad behavior, we don't want to hear any reasons for it; this could become symptom reinforcement. We don't allow them to talk about or rationalize their bad behavior. We know that it's bad behavior to yell "fuck" on the beach. I don't want to hear any reasons why somebody did it. All we want to do is tell them graphically, clearly, with dramatic imagery, the way we want them to behave in the future. I'm not interested in why they want to behave badly. The way they behave is what brought them here in the first place. We attempt to correct stupid behavior. Call it therapy if you want to. We point out their stupidity in the hope that they will learn how to grow up and function like adults. We stress this education for life.

GEORGE: There is something I heard on the tape and would like to emphasize. It has to do with brainwashing. I think you use that technique in your approach. The word, unfortunately, has been given a negative ring. Jerome Frank, in his book on persuasion therapy, has a chapter on brainwashing.

CHUCK: Great stuff. When you clean a brain, you wash it. If you have a dirty brain, you wash it and make it clean.

GEORGE: The way you do this, I noticed, is to use a few principles from basic conditioning theory. First of all, you use the principle of repetition. Secondly, you use the principle of analogy, saying the same thing many different ways to avoid monotony. If you constantly said the same thing all the time, "You're a punk, you're a punk, you're a punk," you would soon lose them. Instead, you described their punk behavior in a variety of metaphors and very dramatically.

You also used what I would call a "relay system." I think it's a very important contribution to technique. Both you and Reid take up the ball in relays, each using his own strengths. In professional group therapy, we encourage our cotherapists to express different approaches. The reason for this is to tell a patient different things with different therapists. He cannot quite take all the dishing out from one therapist. When we sense that, we call one the "stick" and the other the "soft." You don't smash the ego; what you do is pare the ego down to the reality condition in which it is in.

L.Y.: You smash the irrelevant ego.

GEORGE: In other words, you are banging it down to the reality of the individual involved. You inform him of things he can't see for himself. You are really not smashing anyone personally, even with your lead hammer.

CHUCK: We let the gas out of the negative ego. We squeeze it down.

L.Y.: A good synanist is a master at smashing the *excess negative* ego. Without letting his own ego get in the way, he pares the person's self down to its reality. He also has to be an expert and master of uplifting the person. I believe there is a correlation between one's effectiveness as a smasher and as an uplifter. If we go on down the line from Reid to Jack Hurst to Bill Crawford and others [at Synanon], we find a close correlation between their effectiveness as smashers and their effectiveness as uplifters. I have observed that Synanon has a hierarchy of effective synanists. Chuck, Reid, and the other directors are at the top—with the newcomers at the bottom, in terms of their therapeutic effectiveness. The ability to uplift the person seems to be correlated with the Synanist's position in the hierarchy.

In one sense, you are not attacking the person himself or the ego, you are attacking the person's bad behavior. It's a subtle point, but you don't attack the person, you are dealing with the behavior that leads him in a destructive direction.

There is almost a self-regulation device operative here. A synanist near the bottom of the Synanon hierarchy isn't really a very good smasher, because it becomes apparent to the object of the session that the newcomer may be projecting, and that his own needs are involved. He's really not able to hurt anyone. At the same time, he's not very good at uplifting. At times, there is a little variance in the person. For instance, Reid, at this point, is a little bit better smasher than uplifter, but this will even out.

Looking at the continuum, at one extreme you will have the new-comer—he's yelling and attacking in the synanon almost completely from his own needs and problems. At the other extreme, you have Chuck and Reid. Most of their attack is technique for the purpose of benefiting the individuals. As they clearly said at one point, it is "work" for them.

CHUCK: There is another angle to be clarified. For example, one of the defenses which many addicts, drunks, and people like that develop is humor. If there is any spark of humor in the person, he will develop that facility to its fullest potential. Humor is one of the defense mechanisms that he used when he was a goof-up. When he begins to progress in Synanon, he does not automatically turn into a do-gooder or "find God" or lose his humor. He keeps this highly developed thing he used to defend himself with for years when he was sick. We can train him to use his humor and his sense of the ridiculous as a therapeutic tool.

Many alcoholics and addicts have developed exaggerated humor to a fine art for their own defense over many years. People who are subject to or washed in an environment of this kind are not going to lose this ability. I'm a very good fencer and bludgeon man because I had to use my tongue to keep me alive when I was a crazy alcoholic. The people that come in here are potentially masters of ridicule. But only potentially, you see; they need to be trained to use it as a therapeutic art. Not only have character disordered people developed the art of ridicule, they also led a pretty ridiculous life. They can draw from their absurd life experiences and use them, once they get past their pathology. The criminal addict's past absurd life provides a very rich resource of absurd situations which can be dramatically used to help others. The Synanist is the most important product of Synanon.

The Moral Position of the Synanist

Reid Kimball's power in attacking the criminal posture partially emanates from his own life experience. He has been in the "little gangster's" shoes and worked himself out of that situation. He has traveled the tunnel back and has necessarily learned something about the pitfalls that happen along the way. His own successful resocialization and honesty are powerful weapons. He uses them skillfully and effectively to attack the criminal posture.

Reid has a perspective on criminal-addict behavior different from that of most citizens or professional therapists. The "criminal-gangster" world holds no charm or attraction for Reid. As a Synanist, he has concluded from hard-won truths that the part of him (inside) that leans toward such behavior is stupid and immoral.

In part, Reid's approach in the "little-gangster" session serves to attack any latent negative beliefs in himself. At the same time that he goes at his "client," the process of attack clarifies for him where he has been and gives him still another look at his own past behavior. A Synanist like Reid sees nothing particularly attractive about his past "criminal–dope-fiend" pattern. He is inclined to be disdainful of this type of behavior and looks upon it as "stark, staring, raving stupidity." [2]

[2] John described an incident to me that occurred after he had been in Synanon almost a year: "You know, this old buddy of mine from the streets came into Synanon. I ran the streets, shot dope and even was in jail with him. At first, he couldn't believe what came out of my mouth about the 'stupidity of crime' and all that. Then he got me in the trap of cutting up [discussing] old touches, old dope-fiend friends with him and like that. Boy, it scared me how quickly I fell into my old way of talk. Since then, until he gets on his feet, I'm going to stay clear of him." John's anticriminal side was still weak enough to fall into the newcomer friend's criminal trap. At a later time, John was strong enough to talk his old crime partner "down." John's new view of the world comes closer to the one presented to him by role model Reid Kimball.

Reid has paid the dues of having "been there" himself. He feels fully entitled to view negatively criminal-addict behavior. Professionals and others who "work with" the criminal, in some respects have less of a right to attack the behavior in the same way as the Synanist. Too many professionals are, in reverse of the Synanist, intrigued by, and even take vicarious satisfaction in, their patient's criminal patterns. Professional opponents are necessarily more conservative in their judgment and disapproval, since they are only tourists in the foreign land of crime. Many professional therapists admonish each other in the literature on therapeutic practice with the dictum to "be nonjudgmental and withhold value judgments on deviant behavior." The Synanist, on the other hand, feels entitled to express a complete emotional and ethical response.

Reid's attack during the "haircut" was unalterably opposed to "little-gangster" criminal behavior. The objects of Reid's intense attack were receptive to his discourse. They were, at minimum, accepting of his right to attack them. The attack came from one of their own. (The "little gangsters" would probably not sit through the same kind of attack if it were to take place in a professional establishment and was administered by professionals.)

Synanists attempt to be completely honest in their approach, partially out of self-defense. They have learned by hard experience that they cannot afford to maintain a neutral position on dishonest behavior. A touch of it could fester and potentially destroy their home. In the philosophy and practice of Synanon, dishonest behavior is *totally* denounced. A simple incident illustrates this point: The directors learned that some of the "hustling crew," five of the fellows who collected donations from the community, were taking goods "off the top" before they delivered the sundry items collected to the Synanon warehouse. In particular, one took some shaving cream (which he probably would have received anyway in the normal course of distribution). All five were given a vicious haircut, verbal and physical, and "busted" from their jobs. They were pounced upon for behavior that is sometimes considered "normal" in the larger society.

In the larger society, expense-account cheating, kickbacks, and "taking a little off the top" are "standard operating procedure."

At Synanon, any indication of this kind of unethical behavior or corruption, at any level, is smashed. Chuck believes that "on an emotional gut level, there is little difference between stealing a tube of shaving cream or a thousand dollars." It appears necessary for the Synanist to swing completely to the "honest side" in order to survive. If he doesn't maintain this complete purity, he may fall (back on drugs) and pull others with him. *His total denouncement of bad behavior becomes an integral part of his own "treatment."*

The Synanist has a strong personal involvement with straightening out his "fellows." He begins to understand that it is for his own enlightened self-interest and benefit. If another person is helped, it also helps him, since the other is part of the same community. Attacking the "mask of crime" and resocializing his fellows are importantly related to his own personal-emotional well-being. This set of forces and attitudes necessarily produces in Synanon the posture of an anticriminal society that supports a high level of honesty and ethical behavior.

12

Growing Up

In the early period of growing up in Synanon, the newcomer is considered to be an "emotional infant" who requires protection and support. For a while, he is given a "pass" in the synanon sessions—the group goes easy on him because they recognize that he is "delicately balanced." This period of grace gives the newcomer an opportunity to become accustomed to the "new world." He opens his eyes to Synanon's possibilities, makes some friends, and becomes attached to the organization.

Attacking Old Patterns

In the next phase, after several months, the group in synanons and elsewhere begins to zero in on some of his emotional disabilities. They begin, slowly at first, to ridicule his tough-guy pose. (For example, the all-out Christmas "haircut" was given to a large group of young people who had been in Synanon only a few months.) They may begin to pick at the bizarre wearing apparel he affects or his slovenly work habits. An attack is made on profanity or "hipster talk."

As the synanons begin to reach him, the newcomer starts freely to express many feelings that were bottled up inside for a long time. Typically, he shouts and screams back at his "attackers," yet he begins to recognize them as real friends trying to help him "clean out his negative emotional insides."

He is encouraged to and begins to drop his tough-guy image. It is forcefully made clear to him that the hipster-criminal pose is a liability to him in making progress in Synanon. As his "front" drops away, the newcomer becomes sensitive and vulnerable. At times, he even feels free to cry and reveal the frightened child that usually hides behind the tough-guy façade. Childish tantrums are tolerated, sometimes even encouraged, in the synanons in order to release long-pent-up emotions. A shift toward adult work and responsibility is demanded, however, in other areas of Synanon life.

The development which takes place is best described as a "resocialization process." The individual is, in a fashion, "brainwashed" to give up his old deviant patterns. It is continually pointed out to him that these old attitudes were the ones that drove him to become and stay an addict-criminal. The evidence is powerful, since it is presented by people who themselves went through this phase but successfully changed over to a better way of life.

The Honeymoon Period

In a next phase, the individual goes through what is often referred to as a "honeymoon period" in Synanon. Here the newcomer has figuratively "found God," and he tends to accept all the Synanon concepts. He begins to parrot Synanon language. Everything he learns is "learned gut-level." He is given to say, "I feel comfortable for the first time in my life." He recites all the phrases that have evolved in Synanon to explain the new feelings experienced. Other examples: he "goes through the motions" (behaves properly even though he feels terrible), "gets gut-level insights" (sees himself on a deep level of understanding), "goes through 'things'" (anticipated emotional upheavals and depressions), and "does what he has to do" (behaves with great resolve to "straighten out" and grow up).

Although the newcomer's overt appearance may seem healthy,

to the trained Synanon eye he is still, beneath the surface, in Chuck's words, "a most sensitive new baby." His overt good behavior in Synanon is given a measure of unconditional love. This phase of growth in Synanon is considered a crucial and delicate period. The newcomer there fewer than six months may give a surface appearance of being adult and healthy; however, the Synanon administration is aware, based on past experiences, that, underneath, he is still a most fragile and vulnerable person. He is apt to "split" and go back to drugs if he isn't properly handled through this early emotional obstacle course.

The pattern of this dangerous period of more *apparent* than *real* early success is not a new experience for most newcomers. It is likely that at some time in his addictive history, before coming to Synanon, he was successful in not using drugs for a fairly long period (sometimes for several months). However, invariably when he was *on his own*, his successful abstinence would be short-lived. He would slip back into drug use, without really knowing how it happened.

There are several reasons why this appearance of success is dangerous. One is that it is deceptive. On the outside, the person may look strikingly healthy in contrast to his sick appearance when he arrived; however, his psychological dynamics have not had sufficient time to change significantly. Several months is not a long enough period of time to bring about any marked changes in a person who has had many years of destructive life experiences. Synanon people recognize this early overt change for what it is—a first awkward step toward a more stable personality development. The newcomer is given some modest approval for his advance. He may be assigned, in a carrot-before-the-nose fashion, a more demanding job than he is equipped to handle. However, he is kept under close appraisal, since this is a dangerous period in his growth process.

Breaking a Vicious Cycle

Although the newcomer may receive rewards for his early steps up the Synanon ladder, he is seldom given approval for *not* using drugs. This absence of approval for abstinence appears to be a key element in getting the person past his Synanon honeymoon period onto firmer ground. Chuck explains that this aspect of Synanon's treatment of addicts parallels a method that is also applicable to "drying-out" alcoholics.

Care is taken to not overapprove the Synanon base line of expected behavior: staying "clean." Most addicts have attempted to quit using drugs and have succeeded for a time. (The same pattern holds true for alcoholics and drink.) When they do this, very often they receive some approval for their abstinence. In Synanon, when they are voluntarily off drugs for a period of two, three, or four months, they begin to look around for the approval they have usually received for not using drugs. *It is not forthcoming.* The point that is driven home, again and again, is: "Why should we approve your *not* using drugs? Millions of people do not. You shouldn't use drugs, and there's no special reason for us to reward you in any way for not using them." This tends to break the vicious cycle that in the past put the addict (or the alcoholic) back on his "medicine."

The vicious cycle (in some cases) may have functioned somewhat like this with respect to the addict's or alcoholic's social situation:

Phase one involves the overuse of drugs or alcohol. There are no real rewards for this behavior. It is generally condemned and produces the painful results of jail, physical pain or discomfort, and so on. In any case, the temporary euphoria gained from the drugs or alcohol does not counterbalance the longer-term pain.

In *phase two* of the vicious cycle, the individual stops using alcohol or drugs for a time. He then begins to receive some approval or reward from some others for not carrying on his "bad" behavior.

Phase three emerges when the individual no longer receives approval or reward for *not* being an alcoholic or a drug addict. People, at a certain point, stop telling the addict or alcoholic what a swell fellow he is for not "getting loaded." When the former addict or alcoholic begins to be judged on the basis of regular adult demands (which he feels inadequate to fulfill), he often returns to drugs or alcohol.

One could speculate that, in some measure, the addictive person resumes the "bad behavior" so that he can later stop again and thereby receive *reward and approval once more*. Obviously, this vicious cycle does not operate with all addicts or alcoholics. However, it appears to be the case with many.

The departure or break from supporting this described vicious cycle in Synanon is that a newcomer does *not* receive approval for *not* using drugs. At Synanon, he is naturally expected to *not* use drugs. During this phase of development at Synanon, the newcomer is thrown for a bit of a loss when he does not receive his usual approval for *not* using drugs. This helps to break the vicious addictive cycle for many. Moreover, if he makes a childish threat to go out and shoot drugs, no one *overtly* seems to care. The Synanon position is that "if you want to go out and kill yourself or wind up in a cage, go ahead."

Synanon is aware of the delicate complexity of this stage of potential failure and consciously and unconsciously attempts to help the newcomer over this difficult early period of adjustment. Approval for *not* using drugs never fades out—because it is never given in the first place. Synanon's antiaddiction posture is clear and persistent at all times. Approval is given to the newcomer for constructive work habits and emotional growth. These issues are continually discussed, and talk about drug use is forbidden. (A member once told me in a discussion that "Synanon, like the old song, emphasizes the positive, eliminates the negative, and doesn't mess with Mr. In Between.")

SOMEONE TO TALK TO

Synanon helps many people who formerly failed to get past the difficult early phase of abstinence by providing a community of *understanding ex-addicts*. The newcomer in Synanon has people with whom he can communicate and who understand him during this trying period of transition from drugs to a "clean," constructive life. Monica related how her pre-Synanon attempts to quit using drugs always seemed doomed to failure because she had "no one to talk to" about her feelings:

"I remember one time, when I got out of jail, I went for three days without using. Then I began to get lonely. I suddenly realized the *only* people I knew to call and talk to were dope fiends. I didn't have any nonaddict friends, and I surely didn't know any addict who would admit to trying to quit using. Finally, I broke down and called some weed-head [marijuana smoker] I knew, out of sheer boredom and loneliness. Naturally, I was back on heroin in a few days."

In her first several months in Synanon, Monica found the change of language and discussions confusing but refreshing: "People were given a haircut for street talk or talk about dope. Not only was there a ban on talking this trash, there was a ban on newcomers' talking alone. Newcomers would sometimes be banned from talking to each other. I remember being told not to talk to Paula! 'She can't tell you anything but more street talk. Go talk to Bettye; she can tell you how it is in Synanon.' We were just not permitted to discuss drugs and all that gutter talk that was so common in Lexington. In Lexington, for one thing, most of the addicts were officially getting drugs. So, there you were, living in a place with many loaded addicts. Naturally, when you get addicts together like that, they'll talk about their connections, different scores they've made, and using drugs. I found that Synanon was a refreshing change. I always had an inner desire to talk about art and intellectual matters. Because of my past life, it was seldom appropriate, except in a phony way. In the dope-fiend world, in Lexington, and in jail, it was always the same monotonous garbage. Who you fixed with, how much time you got, the quality of junk, and all that nonsense.

"Not only did I have the freedom and approval in Synanon to talk about the better things of life; people would discuss their Synanon jobs and things like that."

Emotional Growth and Status-Seeking [1]

Synanon provides an atmosphere that points the addict in a new and constructive direction. He finds the new language and the new possibility for growth exciting and interesting. At about

[1] The issue of status-seeking in Synanon is discussed in depth in Chapter 13.

the six-month point, he becomes sufficiently aware of the Synanon environment to get involved in status-seeking and climbing the organizational ladder.

The person at this point finds himself in a position to look around and select some role model, a senior Synanist whom he would like to emulate. He begins to go after what appear to be interesting and worthwhile status jobs in Synanon. He is encouraged to do this and attempts to "manipulate his environment" to acquire status in the organization.

The successful manipulation of a social system requires knowledge of its structure. The newcomer is motivated to try to understand something in depth about Synanon. A healthy side effect of status-seeking in Synanon is that it is a useful learning situation for "growing up." Since the structure of Synanon compares in many ways with other human organizations, this is a healthy development.

If the individual is to succeed in Synanon, he has to learn how to relate effectively to others. This requires a degree of empathy, or the ability to put himself in another's place, to correctly understand him. He becomes freer in the world around him. He learns how to see himself as others do. This process takes place not only in the Synanon community per se but in the intensive synanon sessions. The newcomer's self-image begins to have a degree of reality. He begins to see his own weak spots and strengths through the group's eye. He tries to repair dimensions of himself that he feels and others feel are defective and self-deceiving. His work and personal development in Synanon are measurable by the progress he makes in the organization hierarchy. Synanon becomes a "real-life" training experience.

SOCIAL SKILLS USEFUL IN THE OUTSIDE SOCIETY

In most traditional settings, growth in the institution often disables the "patient" or "inmate" from developing successful social skills useful in the outside society. In contrast, social growth in Synanon develops the same perceptual and interactional capabilities that qualify an individual to be an effective member of the larger society.

The upper level of Synanon's organization comprises individuals who are potentially capable of functioning at the administrative level in other organizations. This of course includes the Board of Directors. They function at a level of work ability which appears to be transferable to administrative work outside the organization.

The fifty some "graduates" of the Synanon socialization process prove that Synanon people can operate effectively in the outside world. Among the Synanon graduates are successful salesmen, a publishing executive, a real-estate man, and several housewives. Synanon develops adult patterns of life that have broader application for functioning effectively in the larger society. This is attested to by the Synanon graduates who are successful outside Synanon and by the executive staff in Synanon.

WHEN DO THEY GET OUT?

A response from a person first introduced to Synanon is generally, "It sounds wonderful, but when do they get out?" This question is relevant to prisons, mental hospitals, and other institutions but is not appropriate in the same way to Synanon. The usual institutional setting is an abnormal way of life, and the individual who is placed involuntarily into a prison or hospital naturally desires his freedom. In such institutions, "newcomers," therefore, appropriately have less freedom to come and go as they please. However, most people who have been in Synanon more than six months are free to do their work either in or out of Synanon and to administer their own lives in the community.

Because of the intense interaction of Synanon people and friends of Synanon, in fact, roughly 80 percent of Synanon's residents live in the community, even though they may *reside* in Synanon. As previously indicated, people from all walks of life freely visit Synanon (several hundred per week), and many Synanon people live and work in the community. There is no sharp demarcation line between freedom and custody in Synanon. Each person has a differential and unique level of involvement with the outside society. This is correlated with his own personal maturity and ability to handle human relationships inside and outside Synanon.

Stages of Growth

For the purposes of analysis, an arbitrary division of *first-*, *second-*, and *third-stage* residence has been formulated. These levels of freedom are not nearly so cut and dried as they may seem, since each person's rate of growth in Synanon is different. Some people who have been around only a year are further ahead of some two- and three-year Synanon members. The person's level of freedom and his position in Synanon are different in each individual case; however, the three stages reflect the growth and status position of Synanon members.

First Stage: Here, the newer member lives and works in the main building. The newcomer is watched closely in order to ensure that he will stay "clean" and that a "mother-lover" doesn't tip him in the wrong direction with a phone call or a visit. When he goes on a walk, he is accompanied by an older member. It is assumed, "in front," that the newcomer at this time is relatively incapable of handling a productive association with "squares" and the outside community. His relationships are closely watched and regulated for his own benefit and personal protection.

Second Stage: Here, the member may live in a Synanon building and work or go to school in the community. If he works for Synanon, he has considerable freedom to conduct relationships outside Synanon. The second-stager is assumed to have learned how to conduct such relationships on his own. He is usually a year or two away from his problem and is considered to be unsusceptible to relapse. This phase of growth calls for considerable freedom and an enlargement of the scope of outside associations.

Third Stage, or Graduation: This applies to individuals who live and work in the community and to older Synanon residents who work for the Foundation. These members have complete freedom to come and go as they please. The graduate level of growth implies a sufficient emancipation and distance from the individual's original problem for him to conduct his personal life plan on his own terms. The graduate may choose to continue as an employee of the Synanon organization or to live and work in the community. Members of the upper-level management in Synanon, especially the Board of Directors, fit this category. Although they choose to work for Synanon, their personal friendships, relationships, and activities are developed as much in the larger society as in Synanon. Many such graduates "live out" and work in Synanon.

Chuck views the two-and-a-half-year point in Synanon as roughly the time of graduation for most members: "At about this time, there's little danger that the person will return to his past life. He then must make a decision to either work for Synanon or go out into the world. Of course, if he wants to leave, we'll help him all we can financially and with moral support.

"I, of course, want our best graduates to work for Synanon, and we try our best to make working for Synanon attractive. In this respect, we operate much like any other corporation; we want to hold our very best possible executive staff."

It should be emphasized that there is no special label or stamp placed on so-called first-, second-, or third-stage people. These are only convenient categories for descriptive purposes. As indicated, in Synanon, freedom is a correlate of personal responsibility. As the member grows and begins to move up both in Synanon and in the outer world, his increasing maturity is encouraged and rewarded. Graduate status does not usually involve complete disaffiliation from Synanon, even for those who choose to live and work outside Synanon. Almost all the people who have benefited from Synanon voluntarily maintain their affiliation. This involvement takes many forms, including financial contributions, providing goods and services, or counseling newcomers.

The type of comment often made by the graduates is, "I want my opportunity to put something back into the pot. Synanon saved my life, and I want to help in any way I can." What has become apparent is that this kind of "contribution" is as significant and beneficial for the "benefactor," who has matured in Synanon, as it is to the organization. His tie and involvement enable him to see the route he has traveled and indirectly to receive a continuing "physical and emotional checkup" by people who know him well, read him clearly and sharply.

It has been observed in some cases that when a person who

has "grown up" in Synanon moves too far outside the range of the organization, he sometimes regresses. There is some comparability between this phenomenon and the diabetic's being removed too soon from his insulin or a patient with a heart disease overextending himself physically. At some point, a Synanon person is free to remove himself fully from the Synanon environment. It seems indicated, however, even for those who move into the community, that some contact with the organization is in order. The contact helps the graduate maintain a perspective on his life style and seems to be beneficial to him.

One of the most important aspects about maintaining this recommended contact with Synanon is that the graduate is in a position to see newcomers. In meeting and talking with a newly arrived addict, the Synanon graduate sees himself as he was. Chuck describes this interaction as a necessary and useful continuing experience for all graduates: "The old-timer sees in a discussion with a newcomer the gross manifestations of his own past insanity. Seeing this glaring past picture of himself enables him to remain aware of the possibility of vestiges of destructive behavior in himself. Even when these negative forces are dormant or latent, they might flare up." In the process of talking to newcomers, the older member not only sees himself as he was, but is in a strategic position to attack any negative components in himself that may still be potentially operative. This is useful even though these negative aspects are latent and held in abeyance at the time.[2]

Growing up in Synanon has been described as a "circuitous and tortuous route back." It seems to be different for each person. Some stumble on the way, "split," come back, and finally make it. Others join Synanon, stay, hold on tight, and travel the route back from their past life in a steadily rising curve of growth.

[2] Graduate Synanon people who live or work in the community are encouraged to maintain some type of affiliation with the organization for their own self-interest. When they do not fulfill this requirement, they run the risk of regression. Only a few graduates have regressed to drugs. These were people who, in Synanon terms, "cut off their lifeline." It may seem to some an unnecessary dependency to maintain a lifelong tie with Synanon. However, using the medical model as a parallel, it seems necessary for many diabetics and heart-trouble patients to keep in communication with their doctor. In a similar fashion, at this time a "lifeline" with Synanon seems indicated for people who have arrested a problem that many experts consider to be a "terminal disease."

Zev "Grows Up" in Synanon: A Case in Point

Some of the processes, characteristics, and phases of "growing up" in Synanon were articulated by Zev Putterman (when he was a one-year Synanon member) in a lecture to my graduate seminar at U.C.L.A. For his lecture, I asked Zev to compare his past role as a "patient" in a variety of treatment settings with his Synanon experience. Also, I asked him to relate this to his growth process in Synanon.

Zev was thirty-three when he arrived at Synanon, in 1962. Partially because of his upper-middle-class background, he had managed to complete a college education. After college, Zev had some success as a producer and director in the theatrical profession. Zev's unique ability and background as a student, a producer-director, drug addict, and patient are clearly revealed in his personal description of his early encounter with Synanon. His statement documents some of the phases of "growing up" in Synanon. Zev describes the experience felt by many Synanon members. The unique quality that differentiates Zev from the others is his exceptional ability to articulate the growth process: "I will try to give you the benefit of my contact with various institutional approaches to my disorder, which has been labeled by psychoanalysts as 'constitutional psychopathy, complicated by drug addiction.' I guess in your frame of reference, 'sociopath' would be more applicable. At any rate, this diagnosis was made fourteen years ago, by Dr. Abraham Kardiner, a pretty reputable Freudian psychiatrist, after I spent eight months with the man.

"Over a period of thirteen years, I wound in and out of private, public, state, county, and federal institutions for drug addicts; also private hospitals for people with the whole spectrum of emotional and psychological disorders. What I think is relevant to examine here today, in the light of my experience, is what happened to me in the thirteen months that I've been at Synanon that has made it possible for me not to behave as I did previously.

"There is no evidence, as yet, as to whether I have been changed on a deep and meaningful level. But there is plenty of face evidence that my behavior has manifested a change so drastic from what it was thirteen months ago that, to me, and people who knew me before coming to Synanon, it's almost unbelievable.

"What I wanted to point out to you, in brief, is that what *happened* at Synanon did not happen at the Menninger Clinic, in Topeka; the Institute of Living, in Hartford; three times at Lexington, Kentucky; New York; Metropolitan Hospital; Manhattan General; the Holbrook Sanitorium; or the Westport Sanitorium. . . .

"When you think of an addiction history of fourteen years, people have the image of fourteen years of constant drug use. The thing that makes a person a drug addict, to me, is the equation that they learn after their first detoxification. A drug addict becomes a drug addict not when he just becomes addicted to drugs, but when he learns this equation. They kick their habit physiologically; they have decided consciously to change their behavior; they are going to manipulate themselves in every way that they know, in order not to repeat what they've been doing, and—*bingo* —they repeat exactly those *processes* which got them to the point that they didn't want to get to. This, to me, is when a drug addict becomes a drug addict. The drug addict, to me, is the person who has taken his first cure and then *gone back* to dope. *The institution he goes to is part of his addiction process.*

"Now, let's discuss institutional settings and their differences. I think the very first difference between Synanon and other setups is that the addict on the outside has heard something about this thing called Synanon. He knows that it has something to do with drug addicts and that there are no psychiatrists there. He hears that they're all drug addicts and that they're not using drugs. Of course, the drug addicts don't believe this—not for a second— this is absurd! 'Of *course* they're using drugs. If they are a group of drug addicts, they're using drugs; and if they are not using drugs, they're *not* the kind of drug addict that *I* am. Because if they were the kind of drug addict that I am, why, they would use drugs.' So this is the first impact that Synanon has. In other words, you're convinced that this sounds very nice but that it's not true.

"Certain circumstances force people to come to Synanon. The A.A. always uses the phrase, 'You reach your own bottom.' So, let's assume that I had reached a 'bottom'; I had tried everything else in the Western world, I think, just about everything else; you know, chemical cures as well, which I didn't bother to mention.

"Anyway, I came to Synanon. At first, something very strange happened to me. I came into this place early in the morning. I had just gotten off the plane; I'd flown three thousand miles. The usual reception at a place where a person has volunteered for a cure is, 'Welcome aboard!' This was not the case. I was told to sit down and shut up, in just about those words; you know, literally, 'Sit down; shut up.'

"I figured I was talking to a disturbed person who didn't understand who he was talking to. In the first moment of contact, instead of being told 'Welcome aboard,' you're told to shut up and sit down. Whereupon, being loaded on a variety of opiates, I explained that I had just arrived in California; that I flew in from New York; and that I had talked to a board member; whereupon the magic words 'shut up and sit down' were readministered. I began to realize that reason has nothing to do with the behavior of these people; these are not reasonable people, obviously; because I was being perfectly reasonable. So I shut up and sat down, because I had no alternative. If I'd had an alternative, I would have said, 'I'll come back another time.' But I was three thousand miles away from my connection. I didn't have that resource.

"I sat down for a number of hours, and then I was called by some people into a room. Oh, first of all, my luggage was taken away from my possession. And one of my pieces of luggage contained a variety of drugs, nonnarcotic in nature, that were prescribed for me by my psychiatrist. When I left New York I said, 'I'll be gone for six months,' and he wrote five prescriptions for six months' worth of five different kinds of medication . . . you know, to ease withdrawal . . . nonnarcotic: psychic energizers, tranquilizers, sleeping medication—a whole satchelful of it.

"The intake interview . . . I've been subjected to many intake interviews, by social workers, psychiatrists, psychologists, and charge nurses, you know. And I was usually asked a variety of questions, and I had my pat answers; you know, am I white or black—'I'm white.' In this instance, I wasn't asked anything. They didn't even want to know my name. I mean, literally, they did not say to me, 'Who are you?' They proceeded to tell me who I was.

Their only contact with me had been a phone call from Westport, which lasted maybe a minute, and then my contact with the guy at the desk, who didn't listen to what I was saying. So they were telling me who I was.

"They told me things like I would 'never make it,' I was a 'momma's boy,' I was 'spoiled,' I was 'a compulsive talker,' I was 'unable to learn anything,' I was 'probably incurable'; that if I didn't shut up they would throw me out; that they were not interested in learning anything from me, because I had nothing to teach them—which, of course, to me was absolutely absurd, because, you know, I had come there to enlighten the West Coast. This is a shocking experience. I'm making it humorous, but it shook me up; it shook me down to my feet.

"After being screamed at by Reid Kimball, who has tapped sources of rage better than anyone I've ever met, and being thoroughly humiliated by six dope fiends staring at me . . . He would use devices like this: he said, 'There's an accumulative thirty-seven years of sobriety in this room and eighty-two years of dope addiction in this room; so, therefore, your fourteen years of addiction and three seconds of sobriety doesn't count.' Now, that was reasonable to me. So you see, I was being hit on a reasonable and nonreasonable level as I saw it.

"So, they were talking about me as if I wasn't there, after this thing happened. You know, 'Let's take him downstairs, let's do this to him. . . .' I wasn't being consulted, and the first thing I thought, when I heard about Synanon, was, 'There won't be any "we" and "they" alienations, because these are folks like me, and they know how sick I am.'

"I was then taken outside by a man by the name of James Middleton. A gargantuan character that I would never have an opportunity to communicate with—even shooting dope. It would just be a matter of conning him, or him hitting me over the head. And he proceeded to take my little satchel with medicine in it— you know, he looked to me like Alley Oop—and he took this satchel of medicine and led me downstairs to the basement, which is pretty grim, and looked like the Twenty-third Precinct in New York. He took the satchel and opened the bottles and proceeded to pour them into the toilet. I said, 'Now, wait; you see, you don't understand; these are nonaddicting drugs—none of these drugs are addicting drugs, and they're legitimate. See, my name is on them.' And while I'm saying this, he is like grunting and pouring my medicine out.

"This is another important aspect of Synanon as different from another institution. The first thing I picked up in this indoctrination, being a manipulative type of guy, was this: when people didn't want me or didn't seem to want me, I, of course, wanted them. The appeal to me was somewhat like a fraternity appeal in a college. The fraternity which is most difficult to get into is naturally the most desirable.

"Well, what had been communicated to me immediately by 'sit down and shut up,' you know, as if I were rushing the house, was, 'This club is rather exclusive. They're not particularly impressed with me, so naturally they must be pretty good'—because my self-esteem was pretty shitty, although it didn't look that way.

"Then, my personal property . . . I think a person's property represents who you are—you know, your resumés. For people in my business, your 8 by 10 glossies [pictures] and your theater programs—you know, this is who you are. I had a few pieces of clothing and an electric shaver—things you picked up that are pawnable. These things were taken away from me—brusquely. And I was given—'schmatas' [rags] is the only word I can think of—I was given unseemly clothing.

"There was nothing institutional about the clothing. There was a plaid shirt which didn't fit. And I was very specific in asking for cotton, because my skin gets sensitive during withdrawal. I was given a wool plaid shirt, because I asked for cotton, and a pair of khaki pants that didn't fit, and rubber go-aheads, or flip-flops, or suicide-scuffs, which were very uncomfortable. And then I was taken upstairs.

"There I was. My luggage was gone, my resumés, my identity, my drugs . . . my pride. I also got a haircut, just because I protested too much. I had my hair cut off rather short, and by a guy who didn't particularly care for the cosmetic value of a haircut. I didn't need a haircut. The day before, I had been to Vincent of of the Plaza and had a haircut.

"I went into the living room and was introduced to a few people. I recognized a couple. I recognized a couple as drug addicts. Like I saw scar tissue on their arms. I saw that they were— like maybe they really were drug addicts.

"Kicking my habit at Synanon had a big effect on me. It was a process which, again, was very different from the institutions. The institutions I had been to all had detoxification procedures of one kind or another. All the detoxification procedures that I've ever been involved in, although they may be medically necessary for people with a heart condition or people who are over ninety-three, really were *not* necessary, I discovered at Synanon. In all of the settings I had been in, the bit was to exaggerate your symptoms so that you could get medication. Because if you get medication, you feel better. Which is very simple: if you get medication, you feel better; if you don't, you feel badly. I don't think there is anything pathological in this kind of behavior. So the thing to do, of course, is to get medication.

"Well, at Synanon, of course, I was told, with the flushing down the drain of the medications I had brought, that I was not getting any medication. And I said, you know, 'I'm going to get quite sick—I'm not feeling very good.' 'You will not get any medication.'

"I said, 'You don't understand. You see, I'm going to be *really sick*. You see, I'm from New York, and they've got *good* dope in New York, and I'm strung out—and I'm going to really get sick.'

"They again repeated, 'You will not get medication. If you want medication, you can *leave* and get medication. But here, you won't get medication.'

"This immediately stopped a whole process which would have gone on for two or three weeks if medication were given. This is another important thing: I had my biggest manipulative device taken away from me, because there was nothing to manipulate for, except maybe a glass of water. That's about it, you know. And how much of a con game would I have to run down to get a glass of water?

"Then Candy Latson [at that time a coordinator at Synanon] started his therapy. The second day I was there, I started to get sick. The drugs held me for twenty-four or thirty hours. He came up to me and said, 'Little brother'—he referred to me as 'little brother,' which offended me to the quick—'when are you going to get sick?' I *was* sick, and he *knew* I was sick. So he come over and he says, 'Little brother, when are you going to get sick?' Now this is significant. Do you know what this did to me? I wouldn't give him the satisfaction of knowing that I was sick. Because his attitude was ridiculous, as far as I was concerned. So I said, 'Oh, I'm all right.'

"Now, what he had done by this simple little intuitive thing, 'When are you going to get sick?' is that he let me know that he knew that I knew that he knew. He immediately stopped the possibility of—you know—he didn't give me sympathy; he didn't give me any kind of 'understanding'—and yet he gave me understanding on a very deep level. Like it became a challenge to me to see how *unsick* I could be in withdrawal during the next four or five days. And I noticed another thing. There would be some people in the house who would come over and kind of be concerned about me. I'd get a back rub. If I wasn't vomiting, I'd get a milk shake, and sometimes I would drink the milk shake so that I could vomit and show them how sick I was. There were still these things that were going on that weren't getting me anywhere. This is very important in understanding why Synanon seems to work.

"And then Candy did something to me that was very important. They made me think they had a secret. They made me think that they knew something that I didn't know. I snapped to this, and it was quite true; they *did* know something I didn't know—as they *still* know many things I don't know. It wasn't just a mystique. They really had information I didn't have. And they weren't willing to share it with me, particularly. This got my nose open. I became quite curious about what *is* it. Candy would drop a concept on me—you know, an incomplete statement—like a Zen cat and run off in the other direction. He would say something like, 'Just stay.' You know, like a Zen master would clap me on the head and I'd have enlightenment.

"Well, this is what was going on during the period of detoxification, Synanon style, which is a cold-turkey withdrawal, which is unlike any other cold-turkey withdrawal, because it's bad and it's wretched; *but* it's not all *that* wretched and not *that* bad. And no one is terribly impressed with it—no one is very impressed with it. You're hit with ridicule; you're hit with shots like Candy use to do every morning. Every morning he would come over and say, 'Hey, little brother, when're you going to get sick'—with a little grin, you know? And I wouldn't cop to being sick. I just wouldn't.

"Now, what happened when I wouldn't cop to being sick was that I wasn't as sick as I usually had been. In other words, my nonpurposive symptoms went right along; but my purposive symptoms were destroyed by the Synanon context, the purposive symptoms being the symptoms that a person unconsciously manifests in order to get dope, approval, sympathy, understanding—a fix. But, you know, the other things—the nausea, the diarrhea—that go on for the best part of this thing continued.

"I was up off the couch in four days. Now, I had been kicking habits. I was a specialist in observing myself kicking habits—you know, reading Cocteau as another frame of reference in kicking habits . . . how he kicked his habit—and all of my evidence crumbled. You see, all of my evidence was destroyed by the experience that I was sleeping by the seventh day—I hadn't slept without medication, in or out of a place, in seven years. I had not been able to sleep. I was now sleeping within seven days.

"On the fifth day, I was rewarded for kicking my habit by receiving a mop! I thought the least I deserved—you know, the *least*—for what I'd been subjected to was a week at a country club. Instead, I was not rewarded at all. Because there really was not any reason for a reward. I heard things like, 'Not shooting dope is not worthy of a reward. People don't shoot dope! Therefore, *not* shooting dope doesn't earn any reward.' It's like saying, 'Congratulations for not beating your wife,' or, 'Thank you for not murdering my sister.' You know, one doesn't do this, so naturally you're not going to get a big hand.

"No one at Synanon is going to applaud you because you're not shooting any dope and you're mopping the floors. Somebody's got to mop the floors, and you're constantly told you don't know how to do anything else. You begin to think that maybe they're right—because at this point, you're pretty broken, psychically and physically—so you find yourself mopping a floor.

"And then the magic thing begins to go to work, this thing about the secret. I think this is what motivates you to mop the floor *well*. You begin to see that if you mop the floor well, you won't feel as guilty as if you mop the floor badly.

"In most institutional settings, and in most psychoanalytical or socially oriented or tradition-directed treatment centers for dope fiends, your guilt is usually ameliorated: 'You're a sick fellow; you can't help yourself; you have an acting-out disorder; together we'll work this thing out, resocialize you, and everything will be "crazy." ' So, of course, what people like myself do is, they take all this ammunition, they fuel themselves with the fact that they are acting out a disorder. What can they do? They have all the data, so they go and act out.

"You see, at Synanon, they lay guilt upon guilt upon guilt. In other words, every time the energy flags a little bit—like mopping the floors and the corners aren't done—instead of being told, 'Well, you know, he's still sick; he hasn't really kicked yet; he's new and he hasn't done much floor-mopping in his time,' you are made to feel that the dirty corner represents a dirty corner in your psyche, your gut. You think that you really are ridiculously bad at mopping floors, and you get guilty, you see, and your guilt is fueled.

"Now, whenever you are in an institutional setting, your guilt is explained away—it's lightened. The burden of guilt is lightened. In Synanon, whenever things begin to get buoyant and you permit your insanity to return as self-compensation for your low self-esteem, you're told you're *not* unique in nature and get smashed on the head with a velvet mallet. If it doesn't crush the tissue, you still feel the impact of it, which is an important thing.

"Now, by this stage in Synanon, you are beginning to learn something. You are beginning to find out that everybody there, from the members of the Board of Directors down to yourself, has had a history akin to your own, somewhat akin. In other words, most of them came in and kicked their habit. Most of them came in and anticipated something completely else. You know, *no* drug addict anticipates being humiliated because he has decided to kick a habit. He does not conceive of this. I conceived maybe that because these were other drug addicts, maybe they'd be kind of tough. But I did not expect to be laughed at for doing the right thing, like kicking a habit.

"Now, how much of what I'm saying is exaggerated because I'm that type of person? There are people who come to Synanon *without* the resumés and the 8 by 10 glossies . . . who are not smashed quite as hard as I was. They came in with a birdcage on one foot, a boxing glove on the other, and, like, they are in bad shape. You can see that they don't have any totems of success or any illusions, so there's no reason for them to be ridiculed the way I was ridiculed. But they still will not be able to get rewarded for bad behavior.

"For instance, I thing this is significant in looking at the total Synanon picture: A friend of mine arrived from New York about three months after I got here. My friend, Herb, was addicted to barbiturates as well as heroin, and he got pretty damn sick and began to act pretty crazy. This is interesting. Reid Kimball, who is one of the directors, came down and told Herb that if he acts like a nut, we'll have to throw him out, because we can't handle nuts. In other words, 'Herb, you'll have to go to Camarillo or someplace where they handle crazy people. We don't handle crazy people, *so you're not allowed to be crazy here.*' Now, I've been in three hospitals with Herb, and I know how crazy he is. Now, literally, this happened to work. '*Don't be a nut.*' And, you know, he wasn't! He just couldn't act crazy if he wanted to stay at Synanon, so he didn't.

"Herb was a pretty sick guy physically, but he was able to curb his emotional symptoms because of the Synanon approach to him. Candy would not go over to Herb and say things like, 'When are you going to get sick, little brother?' But, you know, he also didn't go over to him and say things like, 'Aw, poor boobie-baby-baby-boy,' so that Herb would act crazy to get some more 'poor boobie-baby-baby-boy,' which is symptom reinforcement. Instead, he got what he could get. There were three or four other guys over there who had themselves convulsed when they came in, who said, 'Well, man, you go into one of these wingdings every eight or ten hours; and you know, we're all here, and you'll be cool, and don't worry, and stay away from the furniture so you won't fall off.'

"Here is another significant thing in terms of an institution, and in terms of understanding the Synanon thing: About this time . . . about three or four weeks after my arrival, I began to notice that the place was full of *me*. The place was full of *me*. In other words, in every other institution I had ever been at, I had had a very schitzy feeling. There were the doctors, and I was kind of like them . . . but by some fluke, they became doctors and I was a dope fiend. And I'd look at them, you know, and I felt like I kind of had a foot in their camp. And then I was with the dope fiends, and there, you know, I'm a dope fiend. And there was kind of this 'we-them' thing, and I kind of felt that I was straddling them both; and I really knew that my soul was with the dope fiends, because the doctors did not know where it was *at*. They really didn't!

"At Synanon, in contrast, I saw a million manifestations of *me*—in everyone—even the guy I called Alley Oop, Jimmy Middleton, who's extremely different. Candy's different. He's colored. Yet Candy can spot things in me so quickly that are exactly me. He knows when I'm gaming; he knows when I'm conning, when I'm lying to myself. I can't do this when he's around, because he sees himself in me too.

"The contract that had been set up all my life, the 'we-they'—my father and me, my psychiatrist and me, the warden and me, the teacher and me—you know, this contract was smashed by Synanon. I became aware that the place was run by a hundred Zevs—different aspects of me. Different aspects of me were all there. So when I hated somebody's behavior, I hated me; when I approved of somebody's behavior, I approved of me. My sense of alienation with the 'we-they' equation—the hip and the square, the culture and the subculture, the ingroup and the outgroup, the Jews and the Gentiles, the white and the black—all of the 'we-they' equations that we had learned, primarily for me *they* had been a square . . . *they* had been destroyed.

"I began to see that if I mopped a corner right, first of all I wouldn't be so guilty. Even if nobody saw the corner, you see,

I felt funny. Secondly, I didn't have to be afraid of being busted by people like me if I did the corner right. And thirdly, I'd probably be able to stop mopping soon; I wouldn't have to mop for the rest of my life. Because, it seems eternal—absolutely eternal. You know, they'll tell you, 'You'll be mopping for the next three months, brother,' and it seems like a long period of time. A long period of time. Since then, I have moved up into more important jobs in Synanon.

"I begin to see what Lew Yablonsky articulates as 'social mobility' at Synanon. We don't have a caste system. We have a kind of class system, based on clean seniority, productivity, mental health, talent, and so on. I've just begun to climb this status ladder, and I'm beginning to understand now that I'm hooked into the organization and want to move up. The side effect may be getting well and growing up from being a baby to my thirty-four chronological years of age." [3]

[3] Zev has "grown up" in Synanon in a striking fashion. He is now functioning as an acting director of Chuck's administrative staff. He was recently married to a Synanon girl, Anita. Although Zev maintains an interest in his past work in the theater (he has produced several plays and other productions in Synanon), his central work now is as an executive in the Synanon Foundation. He recently assisted the producer on the movie on Synanon, filmed by Columbia Pictures, Inc.

13

Status-Seeking

The administration attempts to manipulate the class system in Synanon for the therapeutic benefit of its residents. Each individual's status in the Synanon society is complex and depends upon many variables. These include the member's length of residence, work skills, and ability to communicate. Of all the factors of status in Synanon, the most important one emphasized is the individual's social ability or maturity. Some members grow up and move up in the hierarchy rapidly. For others it is a long, hard battle.

Implicit in growth or social maturity in Synanon is the member's perspective on the world around him. According to Chuck: "The newly arrived addict is blind. He's encapsulated. He's only capable of menial work, cleaning the building, or washing dishes. As he matures, his line of sight broadens. He is capable of doing more demanding jobs, and he can advance as fast as he grows."

One parallel that seems to apply in Synanon is what Chuck refers to as an "out-of-the-womb" movement toward maturity. "Although an addict may be six feet tall and have hair on his chest, when he arrives he's an infant that has to grow up emotionally. Don't be fooled by his physical appearance or his ability to make some noises like an adult." As the individual matures and his vision enlarges, he moves up in Synanon's status system.

A "Status Probe"

An important assumption made about the Synanon hierarchy is that a resident's position is closely correlated with his knowledge about Synanon. The individual's position in the stratification system corresponds with length of time "clean," social maturity, ability to understand the organization, and effective work ability in the system. In many respects, the elements important to status in Synanon are comparable to the attributes useful for acquiring status in the outside society. Synanon attempts to utilize "status-seeking" drives in Synanon as a constructive and useful device for manipulating members toward maturity.

The following "educational synanon," focusing on the status-seeking issue, provides some insights into the process and its meaning inside Synanon. The group comprised members in various status positions in Synanon. Chuck ran the session and asked me to sit in and comment whenever I felt it was appropriate.

CHUCK: Here is what this meeting is going to be about: We're going to investigate the phenomenon of status-seeking in Synanon. Emotion cannot be kept out of our discussion, and I would not want it to be even if it were possible. Let's recognize, in front, that status-seeking is neither good nor bad. Status exists. There is nothing we can do about eliminating it even if we wanted to. It would be kind of silly inasmuch as we are a status-type animal. If there is a status that people will be most comfortable in, then maybe we can determine ways and means of achieving this spot in the status system.

I am a status-seeker myself. I'm pretty good at it. You folks here are picked for various reasons. The reasons for my selecting you will come out as the meeting progresses. Nobody is being criticized in this room, although it may sound like it to some of you. This is definitely *not* a haircut session. It is a status probe, a probe into the issues of status in Synanon. Don't be frightened or enraged, don't allow your emotions to affect your happiness pro or con because you hear some critical noises in the room. You must know by now that noises don't hurt people.

We have here in this room some interesting subjects for the study of status. Notice I didn't say objects. We have some people here who are not proceeding to fulfill their needs for status in a satisfactory way. Satisfaction with one's status is something that most of us had to stumble into. When we have achieved status satisfaction, we may be able to give something to other people so that they too can attain or achieve this goal.

We have some people in here that have gone after status consciously and unconsciously, even ruthlessly, and have failed. I know some secrets about status-seeking, since I have myself had a terrible massive dose of the status-seeking virus all of my life. Only recently, through Synanon, have I acquired status satisfaction.

Let's touch briefly on some of your past problems and recent approaches to status in Synanon. Arnold is an interesting specimen. He has a normal need for status peculiar to the loud and overweight type like myself. He investigated status through many years of addiction, using as a vehicle his very fine talent as a pianist. He stumbled around Synanon banging his head against various walls. He felt out of things, and rightly so. He couldn't get into things, because he was somehow always walking in the wrong direction, about 5 degrees off, and 5 degrees off is just as far off as 180 degrees. He fell into various creative vacuums, ran into pressure points in Synanon, and a lot of other crazy things. Somehow, he moved his sights over or got them moved for him. He is now a big shot in Synanon.

[Arnold is an acting director. He ran the San Diego facility, with a residency of more than 150 members, and has also been in charge of the Santa Monica Synanon House.]

Let's look at some others in this group. We've got a powerhouse in this room. We have a powerhouse of people with ability, great potential, and creativity.

I've seen Jeanne here, not even knowing how to type, prepare somehow by blood, sweat, and tears legal briefs that were so terrific in their execution, stenographically, that a former attorney general of the state of California commented enthusiastically about her work. When she got here, fresh off the streets and after several tours of duty in nut houses, she weighed around eighty pounds and was literally raving for several days. Somehow,

Jeanne has taken hold and climbed the Synanon ladder to the point where she can run one of our houses and our warehouse at the same time. We have manipulated her into this position. It's good for her and good for us.

We want to release some of these positive emotions, collectively and individually. I feel, somehow, if we can get a better understanding of the phenomenon of status and its many implications as applied to our human situation here in Synanon, we might remove other blocks in your path to growing up—and we can also improve our work with other people coming into Synanon.

I want to tell you why I picked this particular group. I picked Dave because he has an overjolt of status. It's so ridiculous. His inner drives and his ability bang up against this thing so strong that it's set up a block and actually makes him tremble physically.

Jeanne has a status problem in reverse. She is always in this condition: She always thinks that something is trying to push her down the drain. She is constantly struggling to get on the first rung of the status ladder. She started to climb three years ago in Synanon and is already up twenty rungs, but she's still reaching for the first rung of the ladder. She can't reach it, of course, because she is way above the first rung that she's trying to reach. It's fantastic!

Bloomfield over there seethes with status needs. So much so, that in spite of the fact that he's only been here a hot minute [one year], he thinks that no matter where he is, he's frozen and hopelessly locked in position. The only thing he can ever see for himself is a rather limited use of his opposed thumb, as a building fixer [carpenter]. He doesn't realize that he is a senior coordinator! I tell him this and he doesn't hear it. Even now, he can't hear it, and I'm right across the room from him. He thinks of himself as a putty spreader and a nail driver, and yet he doesn't want to be these things. Of course, he *isn't*.

Zev has a massive status drive. With him, it's a dangerous disease, and this is very interesting. To Gordon [an ex-alcoholic and writer who lived in Synanon for a time], Zev is Synanon. Gordon looked up like worms do and stopped right there at Zev. Zev's partially conscious and partially unconscious gut-level need for status is so unhealthy that Gordon couldn't even see beyond it. He watched Zev twirl around in a circle for a time and then begin to move in the right direction, straight up.

Bill was kind of a last-minute choice for this meeting because he happened to be a fresh demonstration of the status problem. He was a salesman, on the outside. I am a salesman. I became a professional salesman when I got out of college, and it's been my career. Salesmen try hard to attain status, and what they can't get, it's their business to fake—as if they have it. This is what Bill does. Only he doesn't know what he has and what he doesn't have in the business of status.

Arline has turned around and inverted herself. She currently has an unsung job as woman's counselor. However, if she stays in this business, she should be a director in the Synanon corporation. It's almost a self-evident thing. Her problem lies in another area. She knows all about it and knows what it is. She has abilities that cannot be denied, but within the framework of Synanon, something makes her dry up. She loses control of situations that she could handle standing up in a hammock on her head. Yet she allows them to blow up in her face, and she falls down.

There was a classic example at Terminal Island when she lost control. [Chuck is referring to a Synanon prison project.] There was absolutely no reason for it at all. There is a fear which is standing in the way of her drive for status, which is almost pathological because she had this terrible status thing as a youngster. She was the only Jew in her school and the only fisticuff exponent and a lot of other crazy things that don't have too much to do with anything. She experienced so much reverse status in and out of jails, her story makes most of yours look like amateurs'. She has a greater need for status than anyone here, but must always deny it, because she has this fear of reaching for it. [Arline now helps run the Reno Synanon House with her husband, Gary, whom she met and married in Synanon.]

Terry here is all confused about her status needs. Maybe it's beginning to dawn on her. She has to play two roles. She never seriously used any drugs, but she was crazy enough to marry Jack Hurst and to do a lot of crazy things which she and I know all about. None of them were as crazy as the things I did, but she's not a square. She once smoked some pot, but never really had an addiction problem. She never had guts enough to go all the way and get thrown in jail. God knows, maybe she should have, because she can't somehow reconcile her two roles. The first role is being the wife of Jack, a director of the Synanon Foundation, and the second is as a person with no status vested in herself. Of course, all she has to do is be the person she is—that is, Terry Hurst, who is married to Jack Hurst. If she would get this on a gut level, then, of course, she would have her own status, which couldn't possibly fall any lower than Jack's. Naturally, she rides there as a fact in nature, the wife of a director. Anything she does for herself puts her a notch above that. [Terry currently, after clearly accepting the role of Jack's wife, has made considerable progress in Synanon.]

Now that I've run through most of the group, I would like to hear some comments. I would certainly like to hear some points of disagreement. Remember, this isn't a haircut. We are investigating the phenomenon of status-seeking. Lew, for openers, why don't you comment on the process of status-seeking?

L.Y.: I'd like to make a few commonplace observations about status. First of all, from a sociological point of view, if there is one law that has been established in the field of sociology, it's this: wherever a human collectivity exists, some kind of status system emerges. However you label the rank order—for example upper, middle, or lower class—there is a system of human strata. These positions or classes are levels acquired by certain qualities people basically have or acquire that are considered important to the organization of the society.

For example, a doctor may be more important in our society than a laborer. This is partially because there are fewer doctors and the time and ability required to become a doctor is greater. His skills are therefore more important to the society than the laborer's. For this reason, he has greater prestige and receives greater rewards. There are certain rewards built into different status positions.

In all human societies, there is a stratification system and people are rank ordered in terms of the values important to the group. For example, being a hunter may be important to a more primitive society. A good street fighter is a "big man" with "rep," or status, in a gang social system. There is always a rank ordering of people, and there are rewards that accrue to certain statuses.

Despite the fact that seeking status appears to be a normal human condition in all societies, "status-seeking" in the United States seems to be a nasty term. Why should it be a negative idea? "Status-seeking" is often considered a negative and critical expression in American society because there is the implication that the person who has status acquired it by foul means. There is an implied assumption that the status-seeker on his rise "stabbed someone in the back" or "stepped on" someone else to move up in a power struggle. This is often true, but the destructive practice of beating someone else out of a position to get yours is not a necessary practice.

For example, in Synanon, when people rise in the system, they also become or are more mature. If your fellows are growing up and maturing, this is good for Synanon and good for you. Even if you are standing still, when a colleague of yours gets better, you benefit from it. In the same way, as you mature and move up in the hierarchy, it benefits everyone, because it helps Synanon grow.

Consequently, at least in Synanon, personal growth is an attribute of higher status. I see nothing negative about developing and unleashing your status-seeking motivation here in Synanon.

Another dimension of status relates to the intensity and degree of *existence*. If you are higher up in the hierarchy, if it is equitable in its system, probably you have more ability and power. You probably also accomplish more things. In this respect, you are *existentially* more alive.

For example, within this organization, Chuck has the highest position. He is importantly involved in the lives of every person in Synanon and with many people in the outside society. As a consequence of his status, he lives an extremely intense and gratifying life. He is a "boss" status person and status-seeker.

At the bottom of the ladder in Synanon is the newcomer, who has limited status. Many people devote time and effort to reach him. In a sense, he is an infant that you are trying to bring up in the world. At first, he has difficulty even relating to others, because at the outset he is an alienated social isolate. The newcomer sitting in the corner of the living room is close to being literally dead and buried. In fact, symbolically speaking, when he was using drugs he was close to death and almost a hopelessly egocentric alienated person. When he grows up in Synanon, he has status and power. What is wrong with being on the "alive" end of the human life-death continuum?

In another dimension, the person who thinks he has something to offer the world wants to be in as powerful a position as possible to make his contribution. He has a healthy desire for status, and if he gets the right position he can be a helpful human being. I suppose John F. Kennedy sought the position of the Presidency of the United States for a variety of reasons. He, of course, no doubt had personal ambitions, but there is nothing wrong with that. He also seriously believed in the high principles he wanted to put into practice. President Kennedy's status-seeking drives and his human accomplishments were healthy, constructive, and benefited millions of people in this country and all over the world. Also, his management of the Presidency no doubt strengthened that status position and helped the nation grow and become more powerful.

zev: In spite of what you say, I've identified status with every sick thing I've ever known or done. It would seem to me that I would be a healthier person and my disorder would somehow be changed into something else if I were no longer status-seeking. Without getting too psychoanalytic, I was always told by my parents to be the best. I never asked why; I was just told, "We're not telling you what to be Zevvie, but we're telling you to be the best. If you want to be a shoeshine boy, be the best shoeshine boy." I've always accepted this, because I was told about being the best before I had any ability to decide about or discern its validity. This "be the best" has almost taken the form of a mystical yen. It ties right in with my fixing and shooting drugs.

I tried to be the best in college. I actually became the best in a college of fourteen thousand people. I did everything you could do—absolutely everything, from getting kudos from the

Governor all the way down—in a big school, and it was all a lot of bullshit.

When I came to Synanon and was here about three months, I felt the sickness crawling up on me again. "Go ahead, get ahead!" What Lew says about status mobilizing someone in the Synanon situation in a healthy manner, I don't understand it. I hold it up for scrutiny and I doubt it because of my own history. Status-seeking for me is deadly. I shot dope behind it.

L.Y.: When you talk about your status-seeking in other types of situations, it doesn't necessarily compare with your status-seeking within Synanon. Here, it could be a positive impulse for you to have. It could help you grow up. What are the goals of this society? They are positive. This is an anticriminal, antiaddiction society. Think about that.

ZEV: That's true, but all status-seeking for me is the same. Whether it's status in Synanon or status in Hitler's Youth or status in the theater. I don't think my gut knows the difference between moral status, amoral status, Synanon status, and Red Chinese status. Status is status on an unconscious level, and therefore I question its value to me. Therefore, I hold in disrespect people who are status-seekers. It is an indictment only because of my own self-hatred.

L.Y.: You seem to revel in being fouled up about this.

DAVE: Lew, you mention the goals of this society [Synanon] as though they were a set of clearly defined goals that everyone is aware of or becomes aware of. I wonder what they are?

L.Y.: I guess one of the goals of Synanon is self-maturation.

DAVE: What the hell is that?

CHUCK: Let me see if I can answer that with something that is probably not going to give you any satisfaction at all. I'm going to have to cornball it up. I'm going to have to say that a goal in Synanon is to find yourself. I'm damned if I know what the status goals are in Synanon. They seem to go in some kind of a creative direction. Hank Anderson, for instance, set up a new status in Synanon. He did something that was nonexistent at the beginning of Synanon. He has become a photographic kind of fellow, and he makes a tremendous contribution to the archives of people's ego satisfaction by taking their pictures and getting them filed properly. Up until the time Hank Anderson was impelled to take an electric shaver, two dollars, and go to a pawn shop and get a camera with it, there was no status goal of photography in Synanon.

One can, of course, add to one's status in Synanon by putting together a choir group to the best of one's ability. One adds to one's status in Synanon by wiggling a bookkeeping system around to the point where even I can understand it. One adds to his status here by demonstrating, without ever knowing anything about it before, that he can be the stage manager sort of a fellow, like Frankie Lago did under the instruction of a professional in the stage business.

L.Y.: I think Chuck is hitting on something very important. Synanon is flexible enough to allow different people, with varied motivations, to satisfy their needs for status in different ways. In Synanon, you can create a new status constellation. The organization is new and unique and malleable enough for you to create the particular role you would like to fill. Most roles in the larger society are predetermined. Among the factors that make Synanon work are the new statuses and roles provided here for people who were formerly alienated and without status.

Also, the work you can do in Synanon is somehow compatible with your personality. Many people in the larger society use something, alcohol or pills, to keep them attuned to job roles which are alien to their inner motivations. The afternoon and evening cocktails, the pills to sleep. These little escape patterns are all humorously accepted as part of the normal scene. Jokes are made about drunks, possibly to rationalize away the pathology of alcoholism. There is really nothing funny about a sick drunk or a dope fiend stoned out of his mind. These patterns are about as funny as cancer. It may be that the pain of an unsatisfying job or role necessitates the excessive use of chemical lubricants and supports. It may be precisely these difficult and painful roles that caused some of you to turn to drugs for a way out. Synanon somehow helps you get into a position or role you like. And if you don't like Synanon's available status role, you can make your own.

CHUCK: Let's look at status and shooting dope on the outside as Lew describes it. Take Arnold Ross as an example. He was a topflight pianist. Arnold made more money than most people see in a lifetime. The acclaim of the crowd—Christ, we're juke-box crazy; we're dope-fiend-musician crazy in our society. People have been applauding Arnold since he was a little bit of a slob with an Eton collar getting up on a piano stool. These normal status symbols didn't work for him out there. He had to use dope along with his status.

Finally, after he was here for a while, he said, "I've got to get into the Synanon dynamic and get away from drugs and all that crap." I said, "Okay, forget the lousy records and piano playing for a while." He said, "Fine!" and he's been doing great ever since.

There are as many status goals in Synanon as there will ever be people who try to do it our way. I am living it. Synanon has given all of us a position in the world. Zev wants to take his drive and do away with it, simply because it has been pointed in the wrong direction. It took me all these years to find myself a direction and a job I could live with. Why eliminate an important part of your character, your drive? Why fight your own nature? It's easier to find the status symbol or position you want in Synanon. Once you do that, you will probably find the one you want in the world. It's that simple.

Status and Personal Growth

Status-seeking and assuming responsibility in Synanon appear to foster a personal growth transferable to life in the larger society. Status in Synanon seems to be correlated with the enlargement of social perception and empathy. At the top, Chuck and the Board of Directors can see more dimensions of the organization than the people further down in the pecking order. At the bottom, the newcomer is emotionally and socially blind. The job he gets when he arrives corresponds with his narrow outlook and his low position in the hierarchy. He is usually assigned a simple task, such as cleaning. ("A newcomer said he came here to clean up in Synanon. So we gave him a mop and he began.")

In the beginning, Synanon has little to work with in the newcomer. Often all he has is the momentary drive to escape from the end point of his problems and addiction. He is physically sick, alienated, and wants a temporary respite from his problems and confusion. He is amenable to accepting "the end of a mop" or another simple job. A menial task at the time is often a welcome relief from his past painful life.

Moving him from this basic level of functioning to a higher level of aspiration is a subtle process. It essentially involves whetting his appetite to grow. Zev's description of an early work experience he had on the cleaning crew gives some insight into the way he developed a greater involvement and identification with Synanon. It was his first confrontation with status manipulation in Synanon:

"It went like this. At first I was on the service crew, and the guy who was the head of the service crew was promoted. Naturally, I figured they would pick another head of the service crew. Naturally, it was going to be me. You know, I'd learned to mop the corners and I knew how to organize the work schedule. Instead, they took a kid by the name of Dave S., who was a wino—a *wino*. What can be lower among the poppy-worshipers than a wino. They made *him* the head of the service crew! I was smashed. I wanted to be the head of the service crew.

"This was the important learning thing. At *that* time—when I wanted to become head of the service crew—at that time, I became a member of the staff of the Synanon Foundation, Inc., because I was shooting for a job in the Foundation. I wasn't shooting for the mop when I got off the couch, but I was shooting to be head of the moppers; and at that point, my identification with *them* became complete and I became involved in status-seeking at Synanon."

The process of involving Zev and others like him into Synanon in a healthy fashion takes time. At first, the new status-seeking member of Synanon is almost completely egocentric about his drive for position and power. He may employ the "dog-eat-dog" method so typical in the larger society. His motives, at first, are essentially to prove his ability and to get what he can.

As he becomes more deeply involved in the organization, he begins increasingly to believe in Synanon's life-giving power. First, and most important, he is experiencing the Synanon effect himself. He sees and feels a personal change in his attitudes and behavior. His work necessarily involves helping other people, since this is what Synanon does. This new attitude toward life has to reach the individual on a personal level, after several months. He automatically, as a normal part of his job, reverses his exploitative approach and assumes the Synanon role of a person helping others.

At a later phase, he begins to get some perspective on his world. He has increasing confidence in his ability to lead a drug-free life, and he has *existentially* experienced the rewards of (in the words of the "Synanon Philosophy") "seeking and assuming" responsibility. Perhaps for the first time in his life, he has had the experience of seeking a realistic status—in a society in which the means for achievement are available. Most important, he has had an experience of success in a positive role that he approves of, and the achievement was rewarding.

The Synanon member also discovers that the personal growth of anyone in the organization is closely associated with his own development. And any setback he has is also felt throughout his community. The awareness of this new tie to others implies feelings of empathy and sympathy. This experience, with all its implications, is one of the most important lessons Synanon has to teach its people.

Synanon reveals that status-seeking can foster self-maturation. In its first phase, it motivates the alienated person to aspire for position. There is visible proof that others like himself have succeeded. His method of status-seeking may at first be ruthless, but it is bound to become increasingly altruistic as he benefits from the Synanon experience of helping others. In the mature phase of status-seeking, he learns that his fate is tied in with the emotional life of all his peers and the Synanon organization. He begins to recognize that his personal growth and status are entwined with Synanon and, through Synanon, the larger society. The complex human forces of status-seeking, commitment to others, and assuming responsibility foster personal growth and maturity in Synanon.

14

The Management of Crisis

Synanon attempts to attract as many individuals as possible away from leading a criminal-addict existence and into its constructive pattern of life. As Synanon grows, the criminal-addict population decreases. The counterepidemic force of Synanon also helps to reduce the contagious spread of addiction and crime.

The newcomer's attachment to Synanon is quite fragile. The longer he stays in the Synanon environment, however, the more he is drawn into and becomes attached to the hard core of older residents who are devoted to Synanon's philosophy. Chuck believes that, at first, it is important to "buy time" for the newcomer. If he gets past the three-month mark, he is more apt to "make it." With Chuck at the center of the circle, diagrammatically Synanon seems to have several concentric circles of involvement. At the core, with Chuck, are the older members and leaders, including the Board of Directors.

The commitment of the leaders is great, and they are further away from a criminal-addict existence than the newcomers. The newer people are closer to the periphery of the circle. People at this outer fringe tend emotionally to have one foot in and one foot out of the organization.

Involvement in the organization appears to be positively correlated with the member's potential for staying and being successful in Synanon.

Increasingly, the percentage of people who enter Synanon and stay is greater. According to Chuck: "With time and the development of our method, our holding power has improved. Using a strainer as a parallel, over the years the holes through which an addict might fall out have become increasingly smaller." Despite the fact that Synanon's ability to attract, hold, and treat the addict has increasingly improved, individuals do "split." [1]

The newcomer is apt to be shaken by a "split" more than an old-timer, since his more limited involvement in the organization is quite fragile. The member who leaves Synanon prematurely produces a measure of crisis for those Synanon members who have an emotional tie with the "splittee." A *split results from crisis and also produces varying levels of crisis in the organization.*

The "Splittee"

Newcomers fail and leave Synanon for a variety of reasons. One type of potential "splittee" is the person who cannot be induced to "believe" that the new environment in which he finds himself is "for real." This "limited-belief" feeling is often found in the criminal newcomer who has considerable prison time in his background. When he arrives at Synanon, he is apt to encounter many individuals with whom he did jail time. Despite the overwhelming weight of visual evidence of the differential quality of Synanon as an organization, he still "in his gut thinks he is in jail." This type of splittee sometimes becomes so engrossed in perceiving a jail or prison structure that he may leave in a ridiculous fashion. For example, one such person left by way of the building fire escape in the middle of the night. He could, of course, have walked out the front door.

The case of Bobby further reveals this "jail syndrome." In a synanon, it was pointed out to him that he acted like a prison psychopath. He continued to have a self-image of being a "stand-up guy" (someone who upholds criminal values). Refer-

[1] "Split" is the term used to describe the action of a person who leaves before the directors and the group feel he is ready. In almost all cases, when an individual "splits," he returns to drugs and his old criminal way of life.

ence was made to a situation in which he withheld information about another resident who had confided in him his intention to "split." His confusion about "squealing in prison" and telling the truth in Synanon was pointed out to him by Reid Kimball in a synanon session: "I would agree with you that maybe a guy should not be a stoolie in prison. In the cage he gets few enough privileges. So if he has some contraband in his cell or has some mickey-mouse homosexual deal going for him, why snitch? Life is hard enough; why should he have to go to the hole? However, in Synanon, when you tell about someone's bad behavior or, in the case of Joe, his plan to split, you're *helping the person,* not squealing on him. It may be a kind of therapeutic first aid. The minute his symptoms begin to flare by bad behavior or a desire to leave the place that can help him, your revealing this fact may help save his life. Instead of his splitting, going back to drugs and jail, if we learn about it, someone may be able to point him back into the right direction!"

The newcomer who has not established any significant relationships with other people in Synanon is also a potential "splittee." The "loner" has less chance of "making it." The relationship he vitally needs may come from an old-timer, another newcomer, or a clique of several people. He needs to find someone or a group in the organization with whom he feels free to discuss his momentary or long-term problems. It is of particular importance to have this kind of "therapeutic friend" when an inevitable personal crisis appears. Crisis of this kind is par for the course of a newcomer.

A POTENTIAL "SPLITTEE"

The following slice out of a synanon session depicts an individual close to becoming a "splittee." It reveals some of the cross-pressures that the relative newcomer faces and how he discusses them. In the session, Al appears to be "in trouble" because of an extreme concern for his wife. Al wanted to stay and "do something for himself" in Synanon. Outside pressure, however, was building. Al's "mother-lover" problem with his wife was not resolved. He later "split" and returned to his past drug-addiction existence. The impending "split" was evident in this synanon; however, the group was unable to help him resolve his "crisis." (Note that "hip talk" and jargon are still part of Al's speech pattern.)

AL: Since I came here [to Synanon], I keep thinking of my wife and I can't handle it. I'm always considering my wife. I'm always considering her, man—like in the future, you know? I can block her out of the now for a while, but I'm always considering her, man. She's on my mind—I feel like I got to do something about her.

NANCY: What does she want you to do?

AL: Well, she wants to be with me. You know, here.

NANCY: Here in Synanon?

AL: Yeah, she wants to come here, and I guess I want her to. I really don't know; I know that this is the only broad I think about. I ask myself how bad I want her here. Do I want her to come here and see how I really am? I know she's got some real distorted image of me. To her, everything looks real swinging—beautiful. And right now I feel pretty shitty about myself.

It's pressing me, man. Sometimes I feel like the only way I'll ever make it with my old lady, without thinking logical, the only way I'll make it with my old lady is to cut out—to split. Then when I think about that, you know, I realize that it wouldn't work, that what I want is just like momma.

I just want somebody with unconditional love and to cool my guilt and have her think I'm sort of a great cat, you know—who is curing himself or whatever other corny number there is. I want this, I think, but then I know I can't have it.

NANCY: How much do you tell yourself that you can't?

AL: Oh, I tell myself; yeah, I tell myself I really can't all the time. It never worked when I was with her. *I used drugs when I was with her and probably would again. But I still want to be with her.*

PETE: You know what? I think you're some kind of morbid asshole or something, man. About three months ago, you were telling me the same goddamn thing over at the dorm next door, when we were living over there. . . . Your wife and all those words that you said tonight. You've been carrying this on for three months. You know—she's on your mind and blah, blah, blah, you know, on and on and on, man. How long are you going to carry this shit on?

AL: Well, that's the point.

PETE: Yeah, it is the point.

AL: Well it hasn't been no three months; that's bullshit. But it's been recently. I feel that I've got to get it straightened out somehow. It's in my gut—I can't understand it—but, you know, I got to get it straightened out somehow in my gut.

WILBUR: Al, you don't have to feed yourself a lot of bullshit. You want your old lady?

AL: Yeah.

WILBUR: Start from there.

AL: Yeah, I do, but then I always go through the same shit—I can't help that, man. That's how I think, man. I go into a real long extended trip—the pros and cons—and I argue with myself.

WILBUR: After six months in Synanon?

AL: Since the day I walked through the door, if you want to put it that way. Yeah, I got a tie with the broad, man.

PETE: Why don't you do what you got to do? Evidently you can't cut her loose—you've been longing for her all this time.

AL: I couldn't cut her loose without a demonstration, you know. I'm a little afraid of the demonstration—that's what it is.

PETE: Well, why don't you work towards getting her here to see how you feel about that?

AL: I am. I've got it worked out. I can't.

PETE: No, why don't you do something towards getting her here?

NANCY: I thought she was coming over for the summer to stay?

AL: Well, that's a possibility.

NANCY: Is it all right for her to come here?

AL: She's working.

PETE: You see, as long as she's in Chicago and you are here, you think about her. You can't hold all this conflict in your gut—you're not doing nothing about solving this problem. Wait a minute—to me, if you get her here where you're at, then you have the problem with you and you can work on it. As long as she's thousands of miles away, you can't do a goddamn thing about it.

AL: Well, that's how I feel about it. That's how I feel about it.

I feel that I've been carrying this—especially lately it's come up—as a decision, you know? I gave myself like a minimum of a year, you know, before I would see her again; or, you know, when I have my year birthday, I thought maybe she'd come down again. The thing is, I want her very much, but what I want is for her to come and live at the club, man. To be with me. This is what I want. All the other problems are secondary. But I also feel that it's an awful short time, and that's where the conflict comes up. I'm afraid that if she comes down in a year, I don't know what I'll do—I went into a hell of a nut when she was down for a week. And I got both of these directions pulling at me. I can be logical on one side, but both of them are really pulling at me—I'm afraid to have her here, yet I want her here.

WILBUR: In the meantime, you're in pretty bad shape.

AL: Not really. I think I'm making out pretty good, you know? . . .

PETE: Yeah, but the pressures are building. . . .

AL: You see, they don't build—they build at *times*. . . .

WILBUR: You're lying to yourself, Al. Anytime we got something tied out there that we're holding onto . . .

AL: Well, it's . . . pressure, you know. You see, I just don't walk around and don't talk about it—you know, whenever it gets up to a pressure point and I have an inkling of it . . .

PETE: But did you hear Wilbur? Anytime anyone in the house has something out there that they're tied to emotionally, man, you know anytime this happens in this house, man, it's going to eventually pull him out or do something to them.

WILBUR: And in the meantime you're under constant pressure.

AL: Well, I'm going to have to get her down here within a year—I've just about reached that decision, anyway—and see what happens.

[After examining the possibility of his wife's coming to Synanon, they explore the other alternative: "cutting her loose."]

WILBUR: Why can't you cut her loose, Al?

AL: Man, I couldn't answer that, Wilbur, and make any kind of sense. I just can't.

WILBUR: You can't think of one? You got yourself an intellect you know. You've been around Synanon a while. You've got a lot of answers, you've got a lot of information that is valid, and you can't come up with a valid reason why you should cut her loose?

AL: Oh, I can give you a lot of valid reasons why I *should*, but I can't give you a valid reason why I *can't*.

WILBUR: Not me—yourself.

AL: Well, I give myself valid reasons why I should all the time.

PETE: Why should you?

AL: Well, going by Synanon information, here's a broad, man, I probably don't really want; I was forced to marry her because she was pregnant. Most of it is just guilt, and it's going to drive me out the door. I'm trying to fulfill my guilt with her, and I can't do it. I probably resent her.

I know this, that every time I look at her I always get the feeling that I should be something for her. When I'm reminded of the fact that I'm not, it makes me feel like splitting. Most of the square broads on the outside pull their old man out anyway, because it's one frame of reference that's opposed to another. I've got to sort of start over again.

I can't have the ties of the past and all that shit. I'm not old enough and strong enough, synanon-wise, to even attempt to handle a wife and a child. The only thing that I would do would be destructive to me. But at the same time, I can't cut her loose.

PETE: And in the meantime, you defeat yourself day by day by day.

AL: I work with it, man—I don't think I defeat myself. I work with it as best I can.

WILBUR: You know what you're doing, Al? You know what it sounds like you're doing? You're right in everything you said. You realize this. You also realize, out of your own mouth, that at this time the situation will pull you out the door. Maybe subconsciously you're just waiting for this to happen. You're looking for some excuse. When something happens, the pressure builds up—boom—you can tell yourself, "I knew it was going to happen. I knew it was going to pull me out the door." And you'll be right back out there shooting dope.

Unfortunately, nothing worked for Al during this difficult period. He "ran out the door" and returned to drugs. Obviously, this result was damaging to Al, his wife, and child. Most newcomers successfully resolve the crisis by becoming effectively involved with Synanon and its method.

AN ANALYSIS OF THE "SPLITTEE"

Chuck and I discussed, in detail, the issue of involvement with Synanon, "splitting," and the crisis produced by a "splittee."

CHUCK: Let me diagram the crisis issue with a circle, which will represent the Synanon organization. In the early days of Synanon, any kind of crisis dissected the circle somewhere near its middle. Let us say that at that time, 52 percent of the population represented a force for "good," or staying, and 48 percent of the population represented "evil," or "splitting." The line representing the crisis was approximately in the middle and bisected the circle.

It was actually true, in this way: in the very early days, a particular crisis dramatically split the club into two parts. Many of the people who went away from Synanon at that time have never been heard from again. Most of them are locked up, although a few have come back over the years.

At the end of our first two years we had about fifty people, and it was quite possible for the "good" and "evil" forces to do battle. The "evil" 10 percent would be maybe five people who couldn't make it, and they might all leave in one day. Or one person would start and several others would split with him. This was, of course, in the early days.

Here's the phenomenon we have in Synanon right now. There is now a hard-core center of the circle. There are concentric circles and an ever-widening core of people who we are sure will stay no matter what happens. You could call these core people "positively cured," although I do not like to use the concept of "cure." Let's say, the core will, at minimum, never use drugs or get into trouble again. These graduates are our healthy center, and their numbers are growing all the time.

Let's look at Synanon as a dynamic organization that whirls like an atom or a molecule. The centrifugal force of this whirling dynamic may throw off a chip, but this has no particular effect on the stationary core. Crisis today at Synanon affects a little segment of the perimeter. It usually consists of one person. Crisis is now represented by all the members of Synanon trying to hold the one chip, the newcomer who has not yet properly been integrated into the organization.

A crisis can be resolved in two ways, either the chip that wanted to fly off is drawn back in somehow, gets anchored again, and becomes part of the core or hub of the wheel or it flies off. The splittee, the recalcitrant addict, goes back into the streets and into the drug and jail culture. Our job is to keep pulling more and more people away from that way of life to ours—back into the center of our dynamic.

In the early days of Synanon, when two or three or even one person split, it would be discussed for days. People would be upset about it and it would constitute a real crisis. The organization was threatened, since they thought, "If Joe failed, I might too."

These days, the situation closes up and reintegrates immediately. When somebody splits out the door, the core realizes nothing more can be done for that person till he comes back and is able to negotiate a new therapeutic contract. This is now transmitted out to the perimeter, and in a very short time, like an hour, the outside of the perimeter closes up and the cohesion of the group is restored.

L.Y.: Let's examine some of the forces at work here as they affect individual and group cohesion. The terms "evil" and "good" symbolically can relate to centrifugal and centripetal forces, respectively. The positives and negatives are reflected in the individual and in the group dynamics.

CHUCK: Starting with the group first, let's look at things that can happen here to cause tension and pressure on the perimeter. This can result in people's being thrown off the dynamic's wheel. Synanon can become too lax. It can get away from its central values. Any group of people can lose sight of their basic principles. Ours are our *truthfulness* and basic motivation to *help others*.

When the synanons get too routine or when these vital sessions are not used properly, there is an important loss of necessary self-examination. We all need to attend synanons to keep our battery charged. This, of course, includes me. Another problem we have to stay aware of is an overconcern with good or bad publicity. We get a little bit too rigid about what we want our Saturday-night meeting to accomplish. The meeting becomes more of an entertainment situation. It loses some of its therapeutic value for our new-comers. This is the night our people interact with the outside world, and this is highly important. We begin to worry too much about the fact that we don't have enough automobiles. We worry too much about material possessions. When we get off kilter about these various matters, a crisis is more likely to happen.

In other words, the dynamic itself and the core group begin to get a little off-balance. Using the parallel of a flywheel, when you move the axis over a bit, off its basic center, it doesn't run smoothly. It begins to vibrate and shake itself. I like the idea that a flywheel twirling around a dead-center point rather smoothly could go up to 500 r.p.m. and be balanced right on a little point. But if you add a little unnecessary weight over here, or slightly off its base, it gets way out of line on the perimeter. The whole dynamic begins to vibrate and wants to shake itself to pieces. The more fragile peripheral person may fall off.

A return to first principles is always good to get back into the center of things. We begin to reassess our posture, our emotional condition, and get back on the track of our main job in Synanon: helping people help themselves.

Say we take in a new girl. We overwork her at ironing shirts. Maybe she shouldn't iron shirts at this time; maybe she should be sitting in Synanon reading a book, playing the hi-fi, flirting, or playing volleyball for her own personal development. We shouldn't work her too hard on the ironing board. We are getting four shirts out of her in four hours. Let's make an adjust-ment. Let's send those four shirts out for twenty cents apiece; and with the eighty cents, we buy four hours of freedom of ex-pression and growth for our new "child." We did this recently, by the way. We are now sending the bulk of our laundry out.

When we emphasize the wrong things instead of our basic emphasis being placed on helping people grow up, the group can become too concerned about looking good. For example, in the beginning we never buffed our floors at all. We began to polish our floors. Then we buffed them every day. Some leisure for a new-comer to think may be more important than floor buffing. Work is not necessarily good for the soul. If we overconcentrate on work, at the expense of the newcomer's emotional needs, we are doing him and Synanon a disservice. After all, the person came here to learn how to live. Work is only a means, not an end in itself.

L.Y.: This issue is almost a joke in the field of penology. It's almost axiomatic that when you visit a prison with well-manicured lawns and an overemphasis on its physical appearance, it's often rotten inside. This may be all the institution has to present. When the cells are immaculately clean and everyone's lined up just right at attention, this often turns out to be an attempt at compensating for no human-rehabilitation activity or program. The tone of human relations is always more important than the physical condition of the establishment.

CHUCK: There is a great big contradiction and a paradox in our society. When one walks into a home where three of the pillows on the two couches are all crumbled up, you know that living has gone on in that house. If there is a magazine on the floor that fell off the coffee table you know that somebody has been reading a magazine. If three of the ashtrays are cleaned and two are dirty, full of cigarettes, then you know that somebody has been smoking. Life has been going on.

The fact that sterility is virtuous is a descendant of the old Puritan idea that work for work's sake is virtuous. Synanon questions whether work is intrinsically virtuous or not. Work is either virtuous or not depending on the setting, the person, the time, or the place. Some newcomer may do a beautiful job on a buffing machine five days a week or in the office and suddenly out of a clear blue sky run out the front door and use drugs. When we overemphasize the wrong things, we help produce crises and splittees. Our first job is to involve our newcomer emotionally into the marrow of the organization as soon as possible.

L.Y.: In studying violent gangs, the "level-of-involvement" idea of concentric circles was most helpful to me in analyzing a gang's structure. Obviously, the goals of Synanon are the reverse of the violent gang: Synanon is constructive rather than destructive. Yet there is a parallel in terms of group organization. Somewhat like the "Synanon gang," the violent gang has different levels of membership and involvement. The core gang leaders were most committed and involved, whereas increasingly as one moved out to the periphery, the members had less attachment.

In an analogous way, at the center of Synanon are the more core leaders, heavily committed to the goals of the organization. We can predict that the larger Synanon's core of dedicated people becomes, the greater will be its holding power.

Also, paradoxically, the more involved an individual becomes in Synanon, the closer he moves to an active participation in the larger society. In other words, the further he moves from the periphery of Synanon, and the possibility of splitting prematurely, the more integrated he becomes in Synanon and, along with that, the outside society. He is more capable of interacting with squares; he almost has to in the course of the required leadership roles he has to assume in transacting Synanon business.

CHUCK: Most of our two-year people begin to sprout some leaves into the larger society. They go on speaking engagements, some work outside for a while and become friends with many squares. Our directors—Reid, Bill, Jack, Bettye—can be put on an airplane to go to New York on business, as we did for the White House Conference on Addiction. They can shoot their branches out and go out and stay for months with no danger of getting loaded. They can carry on the world's business.

On the other hand, the addict in the outside society is totally encapsulated in the mucus of his addiction. He's not usually a member of any group. He comes into Synanon and puts a taproot into the core of the Synanon society. After he has been here a year or two, he begins to put his branches out into the larger society and becomes a part of that group too. Essentially, however, his taproot is in his family group, the extended family tribal group of Synanon, with its values, its philosophy, and so on.

This situation is illustrated beautifully by the group of people we sent to open the Westport branch. It would never cross the horizon of my brain that Jack Hurst would someday casually go down to New York and get a fix or go and do some stupid thing like that. We know of course that Dave, in Synanon only nine months, might do this. Jack is a core leader in the overall Synanon organization and concomitantly has his feet firmly in the larger society.

As our Westport resident director, Jack is recognized by the community. He goes on TV, gives lectures, and meets the public.

Jack now has his secondary roots in Westport, Connecticut, kind of like a good general in an army. His main roots, of course, are in the Pentagon here; but he is also out in the operating theater, "the European theater," of Westport.

The Crisis-Makers

The "core leaders," or directors, are considered by Chuck to be on firm ground both in and out of Synanon. As a clique in Synanon, the directors are not likely to become involved in crisis situations or produce them. This is not true of other cliques. It is from these more marginal entities and newcomers that crises and problems emanate.

Such "negative gangs," or as Reid Kimball calls them, "the vicious little kids," are closer to the periphery of Synanon and, unlike the directors, are closer to the criminal constellations of prisons and the "streets." In a noon seminar, Reid describes this Synanon problem to the entire Santa Monica group, in a talk on the "code of the streets." In his talk, Reid cites John's "criminal stash" as an example of the problem. (This noon talk took place during John's early days in Synanon.)

THE CODE OF THE STREETS

"Today, let's examine a subgroup of people in Synanon. It's senseless to name them; you know who they are. We have a gang here that maintains a code of the streets. If there is such a thing among dope shooters, these are probably the guys who upheld it the most outside. They've brought it in here. You see, they won't bust their own people or jeopardize their own gang.

"These punks come in here with their distorted thinking and do the following: They may approach you and say, 'Let's get some shit [drugs] in here,' or, 'Let's violate the rules.' When they do this, they're insulting you. I wonder if you know they are insulting you? A man who assumes that you would go along with helping to bust this joint or jeopardize it is assuming that you are some kind of a rat, you know, some kind of a real louse. A person who discusses his destructive plans with you assumes, in front, that you're his kind of punk.

"Let's look at this so-called code of the streets. I want you to get a look at someone who believes in this firmly. We've got one kid here, John, whom we have never been able to cure of the illusion that he observes some ethical criminal code. He is a good example of the insane way of thinking which kept us all on dope and in jails and still produces problems for Synanon. He's been here now for eight or nine months. We have fed him, cigaretted him, therapied him, sent him to school, babied him, everything else. . . . If someone is trying to destroy this place by working against us from the inside and throwing us all back into the pens and institutions, tell us about it. Good God, please give us a hand with our business. Let us know what's happening in the minds of the insane, vicious young punks we're trying to save from themselves.

"The night before last, two residents in Synanon, on a presumably supervised trip, were necking on our beach. Think about this. If it had been discovered on this carefully patrolled beach, it's the one circumstance, I guess, that would have given our enemies fuel to close us down. If this happened, some of us would have to go back to the street or be Court 95ed [the new state "prison-treatment" program] or sent to Camarillo or something. Because, you see, we would have demonstrated to the outside nuts that there is the kind of sexual promiscuity in this place that they hallucinate about. They would further say, with this evidence, that there is no supervision of our residents.

"This situation came to the attention of Peggy Logan, who is a comparative newcomer. Unfortunately she has had some negative attitudes instilled in her by John's lunatic fringe. Namely, if you talk and protect your home, you're a rat. Peggy wrestled all night in her mind with this situation, and she finally decided that she had to protect this place. She couldn't help kill all these people. When she told us about the incident so we could do something about it, John, who was not even involved in the episode, told her that she was a goddamned fink.

"John, who helps to stir up our troubles here, is still affiliated with the New York mob. You've read his letters. He writes to Fat Louie in New York, 'Cuff me a couple of C's. We're the last left—they've burned Blue-Tooth Eddie at Sing Sing.' I want you to consider how valid this man's observation is about what a fink is. He must really think he and Blue-Tooth Louie, or whoever it is, are all that's left of the Syndicate. After all, they're deporting Costello, and Luciano just died. Here's this baby, whose momma phones him every week—she phoned him last night—who's going to school as a schoolboy on our dough, who we're feeding and everything else, calling the people who try to protect the place finks.

"Here's the position he puts us in. Chuck and many members are overworking to keep the place properly going and on its feet. In the meantime, the opposition, John, has set up his gang downstairs. The code of his gang says that if you protect Synanon, you're a fink and a rat. I guess he still thinks he's in jail or on the streets of New York. He doesn't call the people who work hard for Synanon, like Greg or McDermott or Arnold, finks—of course not. You know why? This tough gangster may have a fear down deep somewhere that he might get slapped in the mouth.

"The reason I'm belaboring this situation is not simply because of John. John has graduated from a vicious little kid to a vicious little punk. He's been here all these months and he still maintains his destructive ideas. The reason I'm belaboring it is that I want each of you to get a clear look at, to examine, which side you're on regarding the code of the streets. The code to destroy this place is reflected by John of the New York mob. The Board of Directors and many others in our group want to protect this place.

"Why don't we throw this gang out? I suppose because they are our main work here at Synanon. We really do not want dope-fiend punks in here—that's exactly how we have to view them—*but these are the people we treat here!* We have a disturbed ward, a revolving dishpan, a lunatic fringe. For a while we have to view them as the vicious, nasty little punks they are when they arrive. We have to do two things with them at the same time: we have to protect ourselves against them, and we also actually have to do the thing for them that they said they wanted done—clean them up and straighten them out where all others failed. Everyone else has failed with this kind of punk. But they will not win here! You can believe this. They will not win here! We'll cure them in spite of themselves, as we've done with others like them.

"We have to assume, in front, that their actions and behavior at first will be pretty vicious, petty, and crummy. All of us, when we were out there shooting dope, did anything and everything. For a dope fiend, you know, nothing is too low. We therefore cannot assume that just because they walk through this door, all of that is dropped. No, of course not. The only thing that I'm submitting to you today is this: how long do you want to be a member of that gang? Every one of us was a member of that group at some point. I was as crazy as any one of them.

"Every one of us came in intent on destroying the very tit we're feeding on. You know, smashing this house. Today, there are a considerable number of people who can stand with me and Chuck and other people in the doorway and watch losers' corner. We watch the lunatics plot and call people finks and try to smash this joint. There are now many people here who can watch this behavior and see it for what it is—disturbed, mixed up, and destructive. The people who have a perspective on this negative pattern are the core of the sensible group in this house. We want more people in this positive group so Synanon can grow.

"I wonder when the truth will come out about why John fears the terms 'fink' and 'stool pigeon' so bad? You know, we've all read about how psychologists discovered why certain people hate homosexuals so bad, or the word. You know, it's almost classic. I guess we all know that if you're afraid enough of your unconscious thoughts about homosexuality, you've got to hate homosexuals, don't you? I wonder why John and his gang are so rabid on the subject of finks? Think about it."

The Crisis of Regression

In his lecture, Reid points to a crucial cause of crisis and "split" patterns. The "crisis-makers" he describes are those who bring with them into Synanon their "code of the streets." These same crisis-makers at first mistakenly perceive Synanon as a "we-they" institution, rather than as a community of their peers. After a time, they learn to accept the organization *as their own*.

Synanon comprises several different population segments in transition. At one extreme, there are the John-type newcomers, who are in a minor state of transition from old criminal-addict behavior patterns and values to more constructive living. At the other extreme are people like Reid, the Board of Directors, and upper administration, those who have made an almost total shift to positive values and behavior.

In most cases, when an individual has passed over a line, roughly after a period of two years' involvement in Synanon, there is an assumption, with evidence to support it, that the individual has "made it." In some cases, however, older members regress and cause crises. As might be expected, a "slip" by an older member has a great impact on the equilibrium of the total organization.

A FIREPLACE SCENE: THE CRISIS OF
AN OLDER MEMBER

Ted, a two-year Synanon member stole some pills out of the medicine cabinet of a donor's house while visiting to collect a donation. This was reported by the donor, and upon intensive cross-examination by Reid and others, Ted admitted to the act. A general meeting was called, and the offender, head shaved and contrite, was placed before the entire group, in front of the living-room fireplace. This form of all-out "haircut," the "fireplace scene," is seldom used except for extreme misbehavior. The "fireplace scene" involves a situation where the group can choose to impose its ultimate punishment and eject the "offender" from Synanon. The offender, Ted, was "presented" to the group by Reid for their consideration and decision.

REID: We have to expose people in this house who are working against themselves and the organization, the people here who are carrying on all the phony-baloney stuff that kept us all in jails and nut houses. This has been going on with this nut here. This is going to be a good opportunity for everyone here to examine his part in this type of behavior. Examine whether you are contributing to this by your apathy or just what is your role in this. *We have all failed in some way with this guy.*

You can learn a lesson for yourself by looking at this guy's problem. You can derive a benefit from it. You can get a good clear look at the vicious disease that you suffer from if you're a dope fiend, and perhaps you can make an even more determined resolution or effort to get away from anything that is that depraved or that has a hold on you and can cause you to do such things.

I am going to enumerate these things in a moment with reference to this guy. Some of you will use his vicious behavior as a rationalization to go shoot dope. You may think, "What's the use trying? If a two-year man can't make it, neither can I." I suppose if you want to do this you are a loser, in front, and you're only waiting for an excuse. You will then not be directing your attention to the winners, the people who are making Synanon a success.

We sort of anticipate losers and take for granted the fact that in this particular corporation or factory that produces clean-man days, we have, at different levels, people who cannot make it. We have some poor devils who have been here for a long time and are back in the dishpan because they couldn't abide by the simple little rules of good behavior we lay down here. We do not shoot dope or use physical violence. We ask for good behavior whether or not you feel like it and whether or not you place any value on it. We ask you simply to conduct yourself sort of like a human being. The ones you see back in the dishpan with their heads gleaming can't even do this. Well, God bless them, we lose some of those.

The same thing, apparently, can happen to older persons who are over the honeymoon. They are over the thrill of not being socked around by cops, living with a big knot in their stomachs, or waiting for the police to knock at their door. For them, the enjoyment of living like human beings has lost its initial impact. It becomes sort of ashes in their mouth; the honeymoon is over. They have become blasé about living like human beings.

We have some people in this group who have never really made it. Any improvement, change, or reformation in them was really only on the surface. We lose some of those. These are some of the calculated losses that we have to operate with. I guess we have to expect it.

Some losers have in inherent viciousness. This viciousness is manifest in this guy Ted. We took him in here a couple of years ago when he was flat on his back. The state parole department jerked him out, because to them we were out of bounds on a zoning violation. We fought like dogs for him. Chuck sat up night after night composing letters, making phone calls to all the authorities, and knocked himself out trying to save this guy's life. The parole department put him back in jail for a year. When he came out, we took him right back in and started him all over. We greeted him like a returning hero.

After a time, we gave him some responsibility and the privilege of getting his driver's license back. We insured him for driving one of our vehicles and entrusted him to visiting our donors—the people who keep us alive, who feed us, who pay our rent, who put food in our bellies and clothes on our back.

Ted here chose to go into one of our donor's houses the other day and steal some pills out of a medicine cabinet. I don't know if this is the first time. He claims it is. He's, of course, only copping to what we absolutely have on him. He stole some pills. He did this while, at the same time, we have people out all over this country knocking themselves out for Synanon. These citizens have come to our aid and defense. Donors like this lady and her sister go out on a limb for us and this punk violates their home. She's a registered nurse, and she has been telling other people of the miracle they've found and the good work that's being done here at Synanon. Teddy robbed this woman and put her into such a state that she hasn't been able to sleep.

Teddy said to me before, "I don't know, it just happened. It's just one of those things." You know, kind of an all-inclusive cleanup. You know, like a blackout; he doesn't know what prompted him. I was explaining to him before that this behavior happens mainly to dirty, backbiting bastards.

I don't believe it would happen to Arnold Ross, Jimmy McDermott, Jack Hurst, or a lot of other people in here. It happens to just one kind of bastard in my estimation, a real vicious ingrate. I don't know how else to describe him.

This woman suspected her pills were missing on trips prior to the other day. As painful as it was to her—and she was very distraught about it—she said she had to know. So she put an exact number of pills in two different bottles. Four were missing out of each one. Ted denied everything when he came up to my office; but after I told him the exact facts, he copped to that much. We don't have any more details, so I guess he's not copping to any more at this time; but I guess you all know now what kind of a situation he puts us all in. Tell us about it, Ted.

TED: I don't know what to say, Reid. I guess the reason I'm still here is because it's not easy to be here right now.

[The group shouts, "We can't hear you!"]

REID: You didn't miss anything. He said something designed to make him look pretty good. He said probably the only reason he's here right now was because it isn't easy to do this. He's some kind of hero now.

TED: Well, I made a mistake. Here I am. Thank God for that. Thank God for the opportunity to be here. That's all I can say. I don't know what else to say.

REID: Why don't you go into more detail about how it just happened. . . . It just happened that you went into this woman's home, asked to go to her toilet, went into her medicine cabinet, and stole her medicine. To you it's dope, but to her it's medication.

TED: I went in and took the pills. I took the pills. The state of mind I was in, Reid . . . I don't know what state of mind I was in.

[A lot of accusing questions are now asked at one time by the group.]

JEANNE: I want to ask you some questions, Ted. I'd like to ask you how you could take any pills at all, being completely clean, and come home and not be totally wiped out [loaded]? I'd like to know how you could do this?

TED: Jeanne, I don't know.

JEANNE: I don't see how you can be clean, Teddy. I don't believe that you just got loaded once yesterday. I'd like you to tell me if there is anything stashed [drugs] at our house, where we have children and four other people who could go to jail?

TED: No.

JEANNE: I don't know whether I can believe you or not.

TED: I didn't know what I took until I was told. I didn't know what they are. I don't know now.

RAY: How many times did you beat [steal from] this woman?

TED: This is the only time.

TOOTSIE: You were asked a question—how did you know where the pills were?

TED: I went to the medicine cabinet.

ARLINE: Do you check every medicine cabinet in every house you visit?

TED: I don't make a habit of it, Arline.

REID: Are you telling us that you didn't know what the pills **were** when you took them?

TED: No, I did not,

REID: They could have been vitamins. You just dropped some pills?

TED: I knew they were pink ones, but I didn't know what kind of pills.

HENRY: Ted, you went into the toilet when we were there?

TED: Yes, and washed my hands.

HENRY: You didn't open the medicine cabinet then?

GREG: All of a sudden you started to look into medicine cabinets yesterday, and yesterday you got caught.

MCDERMOTT: Well, Teddy, I guess these people thought, "Some people from Synanon are coming; I better lay a trap?"

TED: That's possible.

CHARLIE: [Another "hustler" who was with him] Teddy, was I sitting in the living room when you were doing this?

TED: Yes.

CHARLIE: Thanks, thanks a whole lot.

BOB: You haven't got guts enough to make it out on the streets. You've been sucking on this tit around here for two or three years. Don't tell us you're here for any other goddamn reason. You're just here to whine and cry a little bit longer.

TED: What I've done concerns everyone here, and I think I owe myself and everyone here this much—to stay.

JEANNE: You don't owe me anything, Teddy, except a big fear that I've got junk in a house with four or five children and other people who could all go to jail. [She lives in the same house with Ted.]

REID: Let me get one thing clear. Your inclination is to leave, but because you think that you can make a contribution to us by this demonstration, you're staying? Is that what you're saying?

TED: Reid, I'm thankful for the opportunity to stay.

REID: Why don't you leave? Let's hear the truth.

TED: I don't want to go. I'm afraid. Look at me. Where could a guy like me go? For Christ's sake.

[The group shouts, "Back to jail!"]

REID: How come this is a different answer than the other one? "I felt I owe this to you to stay."

TED: I'm pretty confused right now.

[There are a lot of questions and shouting at this point, two or three or more people talking at the same time. Ted is accused of other offenses. He is accused of different "funny" actions at his home.]

DAVE: I was sitting right up there where you are six months ago, and I know what you're thinking. You're thinking, "If I just cop to just one little slip, I'll probably be able to make my recovery a little bit faster." Yeah, don't deny it, buddy. I've been there. You're thinking, "This is just one little thing. If I make it look like I just got out of touch this one time, they won't all hate me out there quite so bad." That's what you're thinking. I want to tell you something, buddy. You better get it out. You better use this opportunity to get all that shit out of you or you're a dead son-of-a-bitch. If you don't cop out, you have about as much chance of making it as a snowflake in the Mojave Desert. You better pour all that shit out of you.

REID: You remember our contract upstairs, Teddy. If we find out anymore you're lying about, we're going to throw you out of here.

[There are more questions, more accusations, and there is more defending by Ted.]

ARNOLD: I'd like to say one thing. This is a good time for anybody else who wants to say something and save their lives right now. I know there are people in here who think they are putting something over on us. Now is a good time to save your life by getting any crap in you out in the open.

GREG: [Heatedly] I would like to ask everybody to hear this here right now. If there is anybody in here that has anything going on, let's hear it. I don't care about saving lives and all that. That's good for Arnold or others. But, you know, do us a favor. There are some of us here who would like to go ahead and do what we are doing and make Synanon grow and help ourselves. Do us a goddamn favor. Either get up and do the thing and maybe save your life or, you know, *walk!*

Please! This is an appeal from me. I don't want anybody to smash this house. We've got bastards like Ted running around in here stealing dope out of medicine cabinets and thinking he can get away with smashing people in the face.

REID: The people who are playing funny little games in here—the tough guys in the halls, the people who are stealing from each other—you jerks, here's your end point right here [points to Ted]. Here's your end point! You know who you are, the ones that are playing these funny little phony-ass dope-fiend games in here. Asking for our help, professing to be one thing, then trying to rank it. You start with these small phony games, but here's your end. Ted here is a real big punk. You little punks keep it up. You can grow up to be Ted's size before too long.

I hope you don't cop out to your phony nonsense. I hope some of you make a decision to end it right now. You know who you are. Just ask yourself, "Am I playing this funny little shit in this place of all places? Am I so goddamn hopeless that with the whole world out there, I come in here to rank this place?" This is the only place left in the world for dope fiends to make it in. Boy, you're a real son-of-a-bitch if you're playing any phony little chicken-shit games in here. Don't call it by any other name. That's what you are. The people pulling this nonsense in here are real punks, believe me.

REACTIONS TO TED'S CRISIS

There was a range of reactions to the "fireplace scene." For many, there was a feeling of threat and fear that Ted did not "come clean" about all his "offenses." It seemed that he was still lying. An underlying fear expressed was: "If Ted could lie like a dope fiend, I could too."

An assumption in Synanon is that if an individual does not clean out his emotional wounds by telling the truth, his guilt and anxiety will fester and eventually "kill him" by driving him out to the streets—back to jail or to an overjolt of dope. The notion is that no Synanon member can handle any degree of dishonesty at all. They must tell the truth completely.

Here was a two-year failure. Some old-timers were disturbed on the grounds that if it happened to Ted, it could happen to them. Some newcomers expressed the fear that they might not "make it." It also gave some newcomers the possible excuse they sought to quit Synanon and validate the "once-a-dope-fiend-always-a-dope-fiend" assumption that they still believed in.

Ernie, a thirty-five-year-old past offender with more than ten years of jail time, expressed another type of reaction: "How could a guy two years in Synanon do that? If I was going to shoot dope, I would go out of the building." In part, he was expressing his fear of the possible spectacle of himself as a ridiculous "shaved-head." At the same time, he was expressing a loyalty to Synanon. He indicated in his comment that he would not "foul up" the organization that had provided so much hope for him and others like himself. If he were going to shoot dope, he would go else-where. (Ernie is still in Synanon, "clean" more than two years.)

Ernie somewhat reflected the position of the "older-criminal" ethos by identifying with the group. His "moral commitment," despite the fact that it involved illegal ends for many years, was to *his group*. His reasoning was that since Synanon was now "his gang" and since its existing norms were "no dope shooting and no violence," he would cooperate and adhere to these norms while in Synanon. If he were going to misbehave, he would go elsewhere.

One female newcomer used the episode as a possible rationale to "split." Her comment was that "if this type of slip could happen to a two-year person, it could easily happen to me." She appeared extremely disturbed and discouraged by the event, and this shock stayed with her for several days. (She too is still in Synanon at this time, two years later.)

Even one of the directors admitted to a feeling experienced by some other senior Synanists. She admitted that during the "fireplace scene," she regressed in her thoughts to feelings of self-inadequacy: "I identified right there with him as a lying dope fiend, unable to cop out. It shook me." Although this director had been at Synanon more than three years, she still found a part of herself identifying with Ted.

The fireplace mass meeting appeared to be a learning experi-ence for many members. For some, it helped to clarify their posi-tion vis-à-vis the organization. The episode produces a greater motivation to work harder for themselves and the "club." They attributed Ted's failure to their own unawareness: "We should have been aware of his problem and helped him." Many felt that they had let Ted down by not being aware enough to have prevented his "slip."

Greg's comment, "If there is anybody in here that has anything going on, let's hear it," revealed his concern and motivation for Synanon. Greg, in addition to his dedication to the club, was getting married at the time. The experience of his fellow two-year member shook him deeply, since it threatened his newfound home. The incident clarified for him the fact of his close tie with the organization. The "no-man-is-an-island" theme was proven to be a reality in Synanon that could go two ways: a person who made progress helped all, but a member who failed in some way diminished everyone.

Over the long run, the impact of the incident on Ted himself had constructive results. At this time, he has been "clean" for more than five years. (He first entered Synanon in 1959.) He seems to be functioning well in various assignments within the organization. His later comments reveal how deeply affected he was by the "fireplace scene": "I was never so humiliated in my life. I felt terrible at the time. You know, I've done lots of prison time—Chino and San Quentin. Nothing like this ever happened to me before. One thing I felt was that it couldn't happen to me ever again. I knew for sure I wanted to stay at Synanon and it was my only hope. I look back at it this way: I paid the small price of being humiliated in exchange for my life."

Controlling Regression

Regression on the part of older members is not always as clear-cut as it appears in the case of Ted. It is rare for a Synanon "graduate" (members more than two years) to revert to drugs. (There have only been a few cases out of more than a hundred graduates.) Signs of emotional regression are sometimes subtle and not always apparent to the untrained Synanon eye. The Synanon administration maintains a "roving eye" that attempts to help older members over potential periods of regression.

In situations in which blatant signs of potential regression appear, a member may request a counseling session, or he may be called in and given an "extreme haircut," as Chuck puts it, "in an effort to save his life." The tools of attack therapy or gentle counseling may be brought into play to help the person see the light. The Synanist decides on the approach that is appropriate for the person's momentary emotional needs.

(Chuck and Reid do not usually administer these "first-aid" sessions any more, since they are heavily engaged with overall Synanon administrative work. The techniques have been transmitted and are currently administered by other executives.)

EL GATO

The following portion of a longer session is an example of the kind of "haircut" that is administered to older members who show subtle signs of regression. It was delivered by Chuck and Reid in the earlier days of Synanon to two married "second-stagers" (living in Synanon and working outside), Bill and Marion.

In his criminal-addict past, Bill ran with a Mexican gang and was know as El Gato. The nickname was earned by him in the criminal culture because of his proficiency as a "cat burglar." Bill had a long record of addiction and burglary and had spent a considerable length of time in different prisons and jails. He entered Synanon in 1961, and at the time of this "refresher haircut" he had been "clean" about one and a half years. He married Marion in 1962. (She entered Synanon in 1959.) Both Bill and Marion worked, and they were doing reasonably well. Bill had a job as a cab driver, and Marion was a hairdresser. At the time, although they both worked outside, they lived near the main Santa Monica Synanon building. The session was requested by Marion, who saw signs of regression in Bill. Her concern led her to seek help from Chuck and Reid. (After about a half hour of discussion, the session seemed to arrive at the crux of the problem.)

MARION: First of all, I am concerned about his not attending synanons. To him, I'm just kind of a nut. I have to avoid arguments or discussions of this kind with him. Then he began to grow his thick Mexican moustache. The first thing that hit me was that it was a throwback to his old Mexican-gang environment. I couldn't discuss this with him. I said I didn't like it, and he got annoyed with me. When he said, "I'm going to grow a moustache," I made the mistake of saying, "No, you're not!" About an hour or two later he said, "*Nobody tells me what to do!*"

CHUCK: You have to be awfully careful about how you handle this dope fiend. There are many things that you can't talk with him about in the privacy of your own home. You can't even bring them up in synanons, because he doesn't attend them any more.

I can understand, it must be a very tense business over there. Can you talk about politics in your *home*, or does he forbid you talk about politics, too? He says, "*Nobody tells me what to do!*" Well, there you have it, the classic remark of the dope fiend. This is his great cry as they bust him, lock him up, put him in jail, shake him down, and delouse him. He stands at attention and shouts, "*Nobody tells me what to do!*" You are a figure of fun, Buster, you really are!

"*Nobody tells me what to do!*" This is the one that I like better than his brush, when somebody comes up with that perfectly ridiculous comment.

Now, Buster, I'm going to tell you what to do. And I'll show you. You either do it or you'll get the hell off Synanon property. [Bill and Marion live in an apartment rented by Synanon.] You shave off the moustache, you attend synanons, and you behave like a gentleman as long as you live here. You don't like it here? God bless you, I'll give you the same good wishes that I gave other people like you when they left and went off to jail.

That's the way we operate in Synanon; you see, you're getting a little surgery. If you don't like the surgery—fine—go and do what you have to. Maybe we'll get you again after you get out of the penitentiary or after you get an overjolt. "*Nobody tells me what to do!*" Nobody in the world says that except dingbats like dope fiends, alcoholics, and brush-face-covered El Gatos.

That's an ultimatum; there it is. We know what we are doing, and if you don't think so, test it out—test it out. Try it your way and see what happens to you. We'll pick up a statistic. That's what we'll do.

What a magnificent atmosphere that must be to live in over there. "We don't discuss my moustache." What else don't you discuss over there because nobody tells him what to do? Do you have other verboten topics? Dare you discuss his drastic need for synanon? You can't do that, can you? Things are getting pretty tight over there, aren't they?

I wonder if he's been messing around with an occasional little Benny [Benzedrine]? You know, to keep awake while he's driving his cab. A little phenobarbital at night, you know, kind of to ease the tension, to clear the head so he can be very careful of picking out the things that they can discuss between themselves? It's real funny; we seldom miss. Maybe an occasional little shot of vodka to kill those long hours at night when he's wheeling his little cab around? Actually, all of these things I'm mentioning are symptoms. They are actually no more dangerous than the symptoms we've been discussing, like the fuzz on your lip and your attitude. *"Nobody tells me what to do!* I'm going to grow a Pancho Villa moustache." You have a dope-fiend attitude. You belong leaning up against the wall tickling your ribs. You know, "Get over here, get over there, get out of the car, come with me,"—the history of your life. You're headed for it. That's what's happening to you, Bill. Boy, I hate to see it. It's such a waste, such a complete waste. You have the world by the ass and you're throwing it out the window.

Let's get with it. Find out what the hell's going on over at the cab company where you work and get a day job instead of working nights. Let's have a nice, courteous report of the status of your progress toward a day job delivered to Reid in the next week. Reid likes to hear these things. And get that damn moustache off.

In the meantime, while you're trying to get your day job, you better scurry around here and see if you can get together a synanon in the afternoon. We have a lot of newcomers down here who would be tickled to death to have a little afternoon synanon once or twice a week under the auspices of a boss Synanon diagnostician like you. You know, they are just longing for this.

You know, there are ways and means of not shooting dope.

You see, we know what they are. I know what they are. You don't. You know all about the cab business. I know all about the dope-fiend business. When I want to ride in a cab or take one apart, I'll call you. We have a cab expert. But you are not a diagnostician. You are not a dope-fiend expert. I am.

REID: We'll make use of our synanon mechanism to find out in synanons how much progress Marion has made in bringing subjects up to be discussed in her home with this other dope fiend. Let people ask her in synanons what is no longer verboten as a topic of discussion in your home.

MARION: I know I probably could discuss things with him. It's my own fear of getting into an argument with him.

CHUCK: I don't see why there should be any argument; a little yelling in a fresh marriage is natural.

MARION: There may not even be an argument, but I just have the feeling that there will be.

CHUCK: Are you afraid of this guy? Maybe you won't be so afraid of him when you see his whole face. Well, let's play it that way and take another look at it in thirty days. It would be very helpful if he could discuss all subjects with the woman he's married to, kind of like a human being.

The sharp "haircut" appears to have helped Bill and Marion over this difficult period. They later saved enough money to buy a modest home and move out on their own. They recently had a child and appear to be doing fine at this time. Bill and Marion maintain a continuing affiliation with Synanon even though they now "live out" completely.

THE RETURN OF PRUDY

In dealing with "regression," the "haircut" or counseling session is tuned to the needs of the person. In the case of Marion and Bill, Chuck believed that a tough line was required. The later evidence of Bill's "straightening up" supports Chuck's hypothesis in that case. On other occasions, a softer approach is used in coping with the crisis of potential regression, especially when the person involved is "delicately balanced." The handling of the following situation reveals another quality of approach for resolving a personal crisis.

Prudy, now in her late twenties, began using drugs in 1951. Her addictive way of life put her in California's women's reformatory, Camarillo State Hospital, Lexington, and a county jail. She spent approximately seven years in these various prisons and hospitals prior to arriving at Synanon's door in June of 1961. In the Synanon community, for the first time in more than ten years, she was "clean" voluntarily for several months.

In September, 1961, The California State Parole Department pulled her out of Synanon, where she was staying "clean." The parole department sent her back to prison to fulfill the balance of her sentence. The day she was released from the women's prison at Corona, in December, 1961, she returned to Synanon. She stayed for six months and then "split." She returned to drugs and spent another year in jail.

In January of 1964, she showed up again at Synanon's door. After three weeks of being on time for appointments and after several discussions, she fought her way back into Synanon. She began to kick her habit on the couch. On about the second day of kicking a difficult habit, she told the Synanon person assigned to her that she was "icky," couldn't "make it," and had to "split." Several members tried to talk her out of it, but her compulsion to leave and get some drugs was powerful. As a last resort, Chuck and Jack Hurst talked to her. Chuck used a different approach, in a compassionate effort to help her resolve her strong drive to leave.

CHUCK: I'm kind of at my wit's end, Prudy; but I'm going to try somehow, if it is possible, to help you through this rough spot. You're pretty sick now. You're not as sick, of course, as you would be if you got picked up by the police and had to face five or ten years in prison. You made a real all-out effort to get into this place over a period of something like two or three weeks. You came down repeatedly. You really knocked yourself out. Now you want to throw that all away and go running out into the streets again. You're playing with death, baby. You keep doing this over and over again. You're going to reach the end of the line, and this could be it. You're in no danger right now, except you don't feel very good. You've felt worse in your life, haven't you?

PRUDY: Yes.

CHUCK: Did you live through it?

PRUDY: Yes.

CHUCK: This is ridiculous. Nobody's mad at you here. We want to help you do something for yourself and you won't let us. What the devil did you want three days ago when you made it . . . when you finally got what you apparently wanted? You got back into Synanon, to us. Prudy, when you said that you wanted to do something to take care of yourself, we believed you. Now we believe you again; we act as if we believe you, and we hope.

We can't turn it over to the gods. What we do is turn it over to you. It all depends on your guts; we can't give you anything . . . nothing . . . nothing . . . you have to give it to yourself. Now, I understand you want to run off again.

If you're trying to prove that you can get along without Synanon, you can prove that too. Of course you can. There are people all over the country just like you getting along without Synanon. They're shooting dope and they're locked up, but they get along. They dream for a while. But it's very unpleasant. You're the big-yard broad, the toughie; but, you see, you're not very tough, and we know it. You're not tough enough to show some guts. Why don't you grab your liver in one hand and just hold on? We have things all over the place saying, "Hang Tough," and all this corn-ball stuff. It works, it works.

Why don't you stop fighting? Why don't you let other people do your thinking for you for a while? Look at the mess that your thinking always gets you in. You keep trying to use that decision-making mechanism of yours, and, baby, it's no good at this time. You're not a bad person. You're like someone they send to the hospital. They take everything away from him. They put him in bed. They bring food and drink. They tell him when to turn the lights off and go to sleep. They give the person a little pill and say, "Now go to sleep," and then they wake him up. This is the way they treat an illness, my dear. Just because you're ambulatory and you can walk out of here doesn't mean that you're not helpless. You *are* helpless.

Why in the name of God don't you let somebody help you? That's all anybody here wants to do for you. Why do you want to go back to prison? In another four days, you'll kick your habit and you can begin to eat and live again.

It's at times like this I almost wish we could confine you and make you kick your habit. You know, tie you down, and then in three or four days it would all be over. But, you see, it wouldn't work that way. *This you've got to do for yourself.* Nobody can do this for you . . . nobody. Nobody can have a baby for you. There are certain things people have to do for themselves, and this is one of them.

I don't know why in the devil you have to keep punishing yourself. What are you so guilty about? Why do you have to go out and try to kill yourself all the time? You don't have any fun out there do you? Do you have any fun out there?

PRUDY: No.

CHUCK: Are you living when you're out there, Prudy? I don't think you are. You're just a sick little helpless girl at this time. And you want to go out there in that jungle again.

Give yourself a chance, Prudy. Why don't you do me a favor? I think we've all been pretty good to you. I'm going to put you on the spot, and if you turn me down, you can just add this to your ball of guilt. I'm asking you, as a favor to me, to stay here one week. Pay me back for everything that I've tried to do for you . . . the lawyers, feeding you, and everything else.

You stay here one week for me and you can wipe the slate clean. Then you can go. You can either face up to that debt or put it down with all the rest of the unpaid debts that you've built up in your life. You can wipe this debt clean in one week. In seven days, we'll be even.

If you walk out of here now, too bad . . . too bad. On the other hand, if you pay me back, it would be the first person you ever paid. There's a deal for you. Stay here a week for me and we're all even. You can go now, you know, and say, "Thanks, Chuck, but I don't want it." Or we can make a contract and start in even across the board. That's all I have to say. I'm asking you to stay one week. Go on downstairs, think it over, and make your own decision.

Prudy went out, thought it over, and stayed. Chuck traded on the relationship he had developed with the girl. It was possibly the only approach that would have kept her from going back to the streets. (At the time of this writing, Prudy had been in Synanon for over ten months, working in the business office.) She recently told me that Chuck's contract offered her a challenge she had to accept: "I felt for the first time that someone actually cared about what happened to me. I think I'm going to make it this time."

The Value of Crisis

The Synanon person may "live or die" on the basis of a crisis. It is often a situation in which all the positive and negative forces at work in himself and in the organization are marshaled. In some respects a "fireplace scene" or a "haircut" is a battle between these constructive and destructive forces. In the "fireplace scene," Reid was the protagonist for positive behavior; Ted, by the nature of his act, played the role of an "evil, lying dope fiend." This combination of forces existed in all the people involved in the general meeting.

Many people who participated in the "fireplace scene" later told me that some of their inner feelings were clarified by the "crisis." Some came away from the session with a greater resolve to succeed. In the various "group haircuts" in which John was the central target, others felt the sting of barbs thrown at him and learned something for themselves. Prudy told me that the counseling session with Chuck convinced her for the *first time* in her life that someone cared. Crisis situations help to articulate and surface new information and emotions, both for the central figures in the crisis and for others less involved.

A side effect of many crises appears to be a greater insight into the dynamics of Synanon and a closer identification with the total group. Crisis situations often force an examination of each person's degree of commitment to Synanon. In many cases, after a "slip" on the part of an individual, he "grows up" and becomes more involved in the Synanon organization. (This has happened to Ted over the past several years.) The person involved attempts to "demonstrate" his dedication more intensely and, at the same time, places himself more firmly under the group's guidance, scrutiny, and evaluation. This increased attention is often useful.

Some slips or signs of regression are flares put out to get attention. (Bill's moustache, which he has grown and shaved off several times since the "haircut," seems to be a barometer of his emotional condition.)

The misbehavior of a member sometimes (as in the "fireplace scene") also gives the overall group a right to react as "righteous nonoffenders," attacking bad behavior. This somewhat "holier-than-thou" position seems to reinforce the group's own positive behavior. Witnessing the ridicule to which they themselves might be subjected if they misbehaved serves as a partial deterrent of negative behavior.

The total process of crisis and response appears to identify the group more closely with values and behavior patterns of importance. The "haircut" or "fireplace scene," in effect, is only partially a punishment situation. It involves an intense and sharp appraisal of the rules of the Synanon community. The group's solidarity in attacking bad behavior gives it an opportunity to examine its norms and usually results in a greater *esprit de corps* and a more cohesive Synanon group structure.[2]

Crisis also raises a significant question for all group members to examine: "What have I done to help produce this failure?" Individual failures or crises are considered to stem from dislocations or from problems within the total Synanon society.

In the wake of a crisis, the administration and many members review and analyze the group's patterns in an attempt to locate the source of the failure. All related Synanon people are asked to examine their role in allowing the person to "slip." The reasoning is based on the assumption that no person in Synanon is a separate entity, that everyone has a responsibility to everyone else.

The criminal-addict characteristically is not excessively disturbed by crisis. In his past life it was almost a normal situation. His arrests, jail, and a whole host of breaking-point emotional experiences were par for the course. The crisis episodes in his past,

2 This community response pattern closely approximates the relationship of punishment to group cohesion as described by Emile Durkheim in *The Rules of the Sociological Method*, New York: The Free Press of Glencoe, 1950.

however, usually pushed him further down and were deleterious. He had a limited ability to learn from his crisis experience. In contrast, in Synanon, an attempt is made to explore and exploit crises fully for each member's and the group's therapeutic advantage.

The Synanon assumption is that human growth almost naturally involves a series of crisis incidents. (A basic one often cited by Chuck is the "birth trauma" or "crisis of birth.") The standard phrase in Synanon during a crisis is, "Let's examine it; we may grow up behind it." Crisis situations are manipulated and used in Synanon to help the person grow. The process of growth is recognized to be a natural cause of crisis. Giving up one attitude for another entails a degree of disturbance. An attempt is made to convert the crisis situation from a destructive to a constructive experience.

In two of the cases presented, the behavior of John and Ted was held up for the total group's inspection. Ted and John, however, were not really the focus. They were, in a sense, a mirror for the group. Each person was explicitly or implicitly asked to examine the failure as it related to his own behavior. As Reid said, in effect, in the case of Ted: "If you were a dope fiend, here is an opportunity to look at the symptoms of your vicious disease." The examination of Ted's crisis was exploited and gave all the members an opportunity to check themselves.

The methods may appear brutal and harsh. However, the end point of regression, when there is no intervention (or the wrong kind), can be deadly. The only price the Synanon member has to pay for growing up and being "saved" in Synanon is the price of group ridicule. And this is inflicted on his *behavior* not his *"self."* Bill, Ted, Prudy, and John, among many others, paid the modest fee of humiliation. In all their lives, the reward, so far, has been a life free from the enslavement of drugs. The cooperative group effort of helping others, "Synanon style," over a crisis period seems to effect an increasingly productive and happy new existence for all the participants in the Synanon society.

Part III

The Professionals

I suppose a professional is someone
who is trained and professes to do
something. Right? The professionals
haven't cured any addicts, and Synanon
has. I guess we have as much right to
be called professionals as they do.
Right?

Reid Kimball

15

Breakthrough in Correction

There has been little significant progress in the management of prisons since man first incarcerated man. "Progress" has essentially been measured not from the inmates' point of view, but from the position of prison administrators, the press, and the public. To the large majority of prisoners, being physically unchained and receiving humane treatment are only minor mitigations of the problem of being *deprived of liberty and placed in a homosexual environment.*

It is not my intention to go into the overall issues of when, how, and for what reasons we deprive people of their liberty by imprisonment. Suffice it to say that we do. Nor am I necessarily advocating that we "break down the walls." The important point is that no matter how society "slices it," from where the prisoner sits, not much has happened to this human condition in several hundred years.

Historically, a few landmarks have been cited as "breakthroughs" in penology. Southern chain gangs have been, to the best of our knowledge, abolished (although chaining men to walls and manacling them has not disappeared). In 1913, Thomas Mott Osborne, then chairman of a New York State prison-reform committee, spent a week (incognito) in the Auburn, New York, prison. He later published a book (*Within Prison Walls,* 1914) based on his prison experience. The book was important, setting off a chain reaction of public sentiment to make prisons more humane. To a great extent, this has been accomplished. The brutalities of whipping and torturing inmates have virtually disappeared from the contemporary prison. The modern prison is reasonably humane, in the sense that sanitary food and living conditions usually prevail.

A recent trend has developed, since World War II, involving efforts at therapy behind walls. Various treatment approaches, with group counseling and psychotherapy in the foreground, have been implemented. There are some indications that these new approaches have had some impact. However, most of the evaluations of "success," "landmark," or "breakthrough" in the treatment of prisoners are those of the "enlightened outsider."

The first real breakthrough in the history of prisons, from the viewpoint of the prisoner, has come from Synanon. The first report on the project appeared in *Time* magazine (March 1, 1963):

MUTUAL AID IN PRISON

Since Synanon House set itself up in Santa Monica four and a half years ago as a mutual self-help cure station for drug addicts, it has seen its fame spread across the country. And for good reason. Addicts given intensive treatment at special federal hospitals have a relapse rate as high as 90 percent; Synanon, which models itself on Alcoholics Anonymous and uses ex addicts to give junkies the support and understanding they need to kick the habit and stay clean, has cut the relapse rate to as low as 20 percent.

Most striking outpost for the addicts' mutual-aid method is Nevada State Prison. Authorities invited Founder Charles E. Dederich, 49 (never a drug addict himself, but a graduate of A.A.), to set up Synanon's system in the cell blocks and maximum freedom honor camp at Peavine, northwest of Reno. The result has been an unexpected bonus. Not only is Synanon taking hold with 18 addicts, but because the same personality weaknesses that drive some people to narcotics are also present in many non-addict prisoners, the Synanon program at Nevada now covers twice as many convicts with no addiction history.

The Unconnables. At the prison, Warden Jack Fogliani has

set aside a whole tier of cells for Synanon. Occupying it are men who normally would be under maximum security. Yet this tier is the only one in which the cells are left unlocked at night. Each 4-ft. by 8-ft. cubicle is spick-and-span. On the walls, instead of calendar nudes, are reproductions of Van Gogh and art work done by the inmates. Neither Fogliani nor the prison guard captain visits the Synanon tier unless invited.

"Punishment is not the answer, nor keeping a man locked up," says Warden Fogliani. "These Synanon people can approach the convicts in a way that we can't. They've been at the bottom of the barrel, too, so other convicts listen to them. It's the voice of experience." Bill Crawford, one of the Synanon leaders who moved to Reno, and an ex-addict himself, goes further: "The prisoners suddenly found they were with guys who, like themselves, have conned people—and therefore can't be conned by the prisoners."

Socrates in the Cells. Synanon depends heavily on group therapy, and it insists on a tough regime. Since both addict and non-addict cons have made lying a way of life, absolute truthfulness is demanded. Any hedging, any attempt to shift the blame for their plight to others, is ruthlessly torn apart within the group. Even foul language is banned, because it might snowball into a rumble. And the ultimate punishment is expulsion from the program. But in return, Synanon gives the addict, often for the first time, a sense of belonging to a group. Instead of a "fix," it offers by the example of the ex-addict leaders, hope that a cure is possible. And because the group governs and disciplines itself, it gives the addicts and other convicts a jolt of self-respect.

Often the starting point for hope is a timeworn epigram that is chalked on a slate, such as Socrates' "All I·know is that I know nothing," or Emerson's "Discontent is the want of self-reliance." From there the prisoners take it on their own, analyzing themselves and one another. But the strongest prompting toward cure is the living example of the ex-junkies themselves.

Such a one is Candy Latson, 26, a Houston-born Negro who started using dope when he was 15. He has twice done time in Los Angeles County jail. "I got to the honor camp once there.

I went in clean, but I came out hooked again," he says. Through Synanon, Candy learned insight: "I kept telling myself I had four strikes against me: I had only a seventh-grade education, I was black, I was a dope addict, and I had a record. I was using my misfortunes for an excuse to keep using dope." Last week Candy Latson was in Nevada State Prison—not as a prisoner but as an honored guest and Synanon counselor. He has been clean now for three years, and is working full time for nothing more than his keep and $2 a week spending money, to help others kick the habit and stay clean.

The Origins of Synanon in Prison

The first Synanon prison experiment began in the federal prison of Terminal Island, California. The project ran for two years. Part of the limitation of the T.I. project was that it was restricted to once-a-week synanon sessions in the prison. The sessions were directed by Synanists from the Santa Monica House. The administrative structure of the federal prison did not facilitate the expansion of the program deeper into the prison structure. There was resistance from the administration about permitting inmate Synanon members to live together in a cellblock or carry on sessions more than once a week. Limitations placed on the natural development of Synanon in the prison were the apparent cause for the program's drying up. It ended two years after it began.

The T.I. project was valuable in that it served as a warm-up and as a springboard for a more ambitious and far-reaching program in Nevada State Prison. The T.I. program highlighted the necessity of having room for expansion as more inmates became involved. There were practically no restrictions placed on Synanon's development in N.S.P. As a result, a successful program has been built into the total N.S.P. social structure.[1]

[1] The development of Synanon in the N.S.P. is due in large measure to the progressive correctional philosophy of the Governor of Nevada, Grant Sawyer. Synanon also had the full cooperation of the N.S.P. warden, Jack Fogliani, and Captain Orville Jackson. Chuck Dederich put in many hours on

ORIGINS OF THE NEVADA STATE PRISON PROGRAM

The first contact developed between Synanon and the N.S.P. in November, 1962, when I presented a paper on Synanon to the Western Psychological Association, in San Francisco. In the audience was a Dr. Wes Hyler, who was at that time the N.S.P. psychologist. He was intrigued with the idea and was stimulated to consider the possibilities of Synanon at N.S.P. With the support of Warden Fogliani, and Chuck's approval, Hyler moved into Synanon at Santa Monica for four days. He became enthusiastic about what he observed and reported back to the warden.

Within several weeks, arrangements were made for a contingent of Synanon people to go to Nevada and attempt to open a Synanon House as a base for the prison work. In the original group were Jimmy Middleton and Candy Latson, both of whom had participated in the T.I. project. Also in the group was Gerry Brod, who had been in Synanon only several months, fresh from a prison term in Sing Sing.

The Synanon House in Reno became a base for the prison "work." The Synanon House group, led by Candy, first introduced synanon sessions into the prison environment. This later evolved into a more developed Synanon community in the overall prison system.

LAUNCHING THE PROGRAM: EARLY IMPACT

Most inmates in N.S.P. are from out of state. Their offenses usually occurred in either Reno or Las Vegas, the two urban gambling centers of the West. The inmate population at N.S.P. comprises individuals who had committed the gamut of offenses, including theft, robbery, homicide, addiction, and burglary. Since

---

planning and developing the program, at various phases, in collaboration with the prison officials. His continuing "talks to the inmates" have had a profound impact on the men in clarifying their involvement with the program and in keeping the men "fired up." (In researching the N.S.P. program, I did a twenty-four-hour tour with Synanon members in the prison and slept overnight in the Synanon cellblock.) Many Synanists have helped the development of the N.S.P. program. Among the pioneers of this project are Gary Gutierre, James Middleton, Ron Pacifici, Charlie Hamer, Ronnie Clark, Billy Miracle, Arty Whitehead, Gerry Brod, and Zev Putterman.

the N.S.P. is the only prison in the state, it has a total range of offenders, both young and old, under one roof.

The Synanon group at first met with some resistance. According to Candy: "We were booed in the yard, the guards were suspicious of us, and it was real tough at first. The warden was tremendous. He really helped us get started. The first group sessions we ran were attended by inmate curiosity-seekers. They didn't believe we were clean and all that. We spent our early sessions just talking about Chuck and Synanon, how we couldn't get anywhere unless they helped us and all that. Some of the guys began to get with it, including some of the prison guards. We mainly had to rely on Synanon's record, to start out. Then some of the synanons began to kick off and do something for the guys who got with it."

When some of the inmates who participated in the early sessions began dramatically to change their behavior, the resisting factions started to reappraise their initial negative reactions. Inmates who at first blasted Synanon people as "do-gooders" and "snitches" began to reverse their field, and many joined Synanon. This accelerated when they saw some of the "big-yard tough guys" responding with enthusiasm. The guards, who at first feared that Synanon would produce a laxness in security, later revised their opinion in the light of a sharp reduction in fighting and other inmate problems. Doubts in the upper administration's mind were dispelled by the spirit and effort of inmates to change themselves. They began to change their usual side-of-the-mouth talk about past "scores" and "capers" to discussions of personal problems. Intellectual seminars on Synanon, correction, and philosophy began to infiltrate the cellblocks.

The new dimension that Synanon added was an actual change of behavior within the walls. The usual inmate ploy of swearing to reverse their criminal and deviant pattern when they left the institution was also present, but this was not the dominant theme. According to Captain Jackson, in charge of disciplinary problems, "We began to see fewer black eyes on the big yard." This meant that the fighting problem had decreased. Many former hard-core candidates for solitary confinement began to work, maintained self-discipline, and became concerned with the fate of their Synanon "brothers." From the inmates' point of view, for the first time, many saw the vague possibility of a future without crime.

One inmate, who thought that he was going crazy before Synanon arrived, joined the program as a last resort. He later told me, "If it had not been for Synanon, I would have really gone crazy. Synanon gave me something new to think about. Wh. Candy and Jim told us about how Synanon came to be, it excited me. I saw some hope for the first time."

On a less dramatic level, many Synanon members reported their feeling that Synanon's complex of activities and thought patterns gave them a hook for transcending the grim environment of the prison. In one seminar discussion that I directed in the cellblock, the men told me that Synanon stimulated their otherwise vegetable-like existence. They began to read more, think more, and "moved toward life rather than away from it." Synanon also provided a connection for many of the men with the outside world. They hung on every sentence when I told them about Synanon's overall development and plans.

Although we were definitely in a lockup (three sets of "bars": the cell, the tier, and the outside wall), in the three-hour session I ran, the involvement was so great that we transcended the condition of being imprisoned. I remember telling the men at the time, "Here we are in the joint, all stretched out along the prison tier. No chairs and the rest. Yet as we talked, we could have been anywhere: in a college, a library, or an auditorium." Our discussion was intense and rather than being devoted to crime and prison, it was devoted to life.

Synanon and the "Doing-Time" Problem [2]

Almost all prisons have in their structure a disease that impedes rehabilitation. The problem of a "doing-time" society exists in even the most progressive institutions. My observations during

[2] Parts of the discussion in this section are derived from a pre-Synanon article entitled "Correction and the Doing-Time Society," published by the author in the September, 1959, issue of *Federal Probation*.

my early visits to N.S.P. confirmed the existence of this problem in its social structure. Although Synanon was making progress, I was concerned with the need for Synanon to overcome the usual "doing-time" malady found in N.S.P. and in most prisons throughout the country.

In order to understand the obstacles encountered by Synanon in the N.S.P., a fuller description of the "doing-time" issue is necessary. This will be described first in general terms and then as it applies to Synanon's intervention in the N.S.P.

INMATE-STAFF DIVISION AND CONFLICT

Most prison social structures are divided into two generally hostile factions: the inmate population and the institution's personnel population. Each "caste" is clearly and easily identifiable. Each tends to view the other with mingled feelings of distrust and suspicion. There is a reinforcement of mutually hostile attitudes between prison personnel and inmates through the stereotyping and distorting of perceptions according to special needs. There is a tendency to praise one's own group and to deflate the other. The prisoner points to the prison doctor as a "sawbones" or "croaker," to the warden as a political "hack," and to the psychiatrist as a "headshrinker." Institutional personnel, in response, generally view prisoners as stupid, shiftless, never-changing, immoral, and recalcitrant "hoods."

Some inmates and staff attempt to walk the line between these two divisions; however, this is usually a precarious position. They find at one point or another that it is necessary to take sides; and it is too difficult, if not impossible, to leave one's defined membership group.

The offender, when sentenced is, in effect, being rejected by society. He must make some adjustments in terms of his self-concept as opposed to his custodial status. He can accept his sentence as being "just what I deserve" or he can begin to rationalize and project the blame for his incarceration onto the "unfair" society.

One characteristic response of the inmate is to project and channel his hostility upon the nearest analogue of society. The nearest objective representative of the outside world, to the inmates, is the institutional staff. They, therefore, tend to reject the outside social system and its values through negative stereotyping and rationalization, responding to the guards and prison administration as symbols of a society that has "wronged" them.[3]

THE PRISON "ORGANIZATION MAN"

In prison, there are advantages which accrue to the prisoner who becomes an "organization man," sticks to his group, and conforms to inmate values. The prisoner who continues to accept the outside society and its values through not being hostile toward the prison administration (the inside-the-walls symbol of the outside society) may find himself in the difficult situation of being rejected by both worlds—the prison and the outer society. Few inmates have the resources or courage to stand up against these expectations of the prison system. These norms are imposed by fellow inmates with persistent force and clarity. In some instances, their norms are more precise than the regulations prescribed by the administration.

The enculturated, or conforming, inmate does better in prison. He becomes, as Donald Clemmer (author of *The Prison Community*) has termed it, "prisonized." If he accepts "stir" rules, he is accepted not only by his fellow inmates but also by custodial officers, who have learned to expect this type of negative behavior on the part of the inmate. The maintenance of this equilibrium is reinforced by all factions in the "doing-time" society.

STAFF ATTITUDES

There is a similar pressure on guards. They too conform to certain generally accepted negative attitudes and "doing-time" goals of the institution (negative in the sense that they militate against correction). The new guard is quickly instructed by the old-timer about the "correct" attitudes to have toward "shiftless, recalcitrant, no-good hoods," who will "never change." This negative attitude is especially enforced against addict inmates. The correctional officer, at whatever level up to warden, who enters the prison social structure with a degree of correctional idealism

[3] Lloyd McCorkle and Richard Korn, "Resocialization Within Walls," *The Annals: Prisons in Transformation*, May, 1954.

will soon be cajoled or forced into submitting to the shared "doing-time" norms of both personnel and inmates. He is quickly admonished by both fellow officers and even some old-line inmates, with such expressions as, "You'll learn"; "You'll see what I mean about these characters"; "No cons really change." He, like the inmate, is encouraged to "do his own time and stay out of trouble."

To resist these pressures to conform to the "we're-all-doing-time" philosophy takes more courage and strength than most new correctional officers can muster and still do their difficult, demanding, and, at times, dangerous job. Moreover, to do their work, they require the cooperation of their fellow officers (particularly in dangerous situations), and this may not be forthcoming to "eager beavers," "rate busters," or "inmate fraternizers."

THE MUTUAL "DOING-TIME" AGREEMENT

If either the administration or the inmates shift their responses or attitudes about the prison as a "doing-time" society, it may become a threat to the other faction. For example, an inmate who sincerely defines the prison as being a therapeutic community, and wants to change his illegal behavior, may make the custodial officers and the administrators feel uncomfortable. They then have to reshuffle their stereotyped view that prisoners never change. And, in fact, they then might have to provide therapeutic services. This would be viewed as a real threat. It might add burdens to an already demanding job and impose demands on the administration impossible to fulfill in terms of budget, staff, and therapeutic resources.

In reverse, if the prison administrators take a definite view that the prisoner's behavior can be modified, that he is reachable and can "straighten out," this may produce great anxiety in the offender, who will have to modify his rationalized view of society as being unfair, disinterested, and unable to help him. In addition, if he accepts help, he is forced to admit that there is something wrong with himself, something that should be modified. This is something not easily accomplished by an inmate with a calcified set of rationalizations about himself and society. The *status quo*, although painful and self-defeating in many respects, is less anxiety-producing for him than the drastic changes required in accepting efforts at modifying his personality. Life "as is" is more comfortable. Given this described set of conditions, there is a silent agreement on the part of both staff and inmates to maintain the equilibrium of the existing social system.

The Synanist Attack on the "Doing-Time" Problem

The *status quo* system described is committed to failure. Synanon's intervention into the prison situation tends to disrupt the variety of contracts that support this defeatist structure. The Synanist shakes up the calcified images of both "prison officialdom" and "convict personality."

The Synanist is difficult to assess. He is neither administration nor con, yet he is both. Both staff and inmates tend to react to him with an interest mingled with suspicion. In the "we-they" situation of inmates versus administrators described, the newly arrived inmate is quickly incorporated into the inmate social system. Also, a newly arrived prison administrator or staff member is quickly incorporated into his faction. The Synanist represents a new element to be absorbed.

The staff may view him as a potential helper. At the same time, they want to be convinced of his dedication and honesty. They may fear that he will identify too strongly with the "inmate enemy." Even so, they may try to use him for advancing their power and control. At the same time, the inmates tend to view the Synanist with a degree of criminal suspicion. They might be "snitches" sent in by the prison "establishment."

The prisoners wonder whether the Synanist is a stool pigeon or a very shrewd operator who has managed to worm his way into the prison administration. They quickly discern that he is neither of these things and yet is both of them. The Synanist entering a prison has the advantage of being both staff and inmate, but not really either one. He has the unique new role of Synanist.

The Synanist in prison is an important new link in the rehabilitation hierarchy. For one thing, he is in the process of recovery himself. By demonstration, he asserts to the inmates,

"I'm doing what you are attempting to do. The only difference is that I am ahead of you, at this time." The Synanist also lets the inmate Synanon member know that he is aware of the emotional bumps, jars, depressions, and problems that the prisoner will inevitably face in changing his life's direction.

The Synanist has already traveled part of the road. He can almost predict the problems that the inmate will confront in the process of rejecting one way of life for another. This fact of hav-ing been in the same position himself is a continual reference point used in the intensive synanon interaction. The Synanist recognizes that he is accepted to some degree as a role model for the prisoner. He serves as an image of what the prisoner can become. The fact that he was once himself in the inmate's shoes, of course, facilitates his being "listened to" and has great impact.

The Synanist almost automatically injects a disturbing abrasive into the "doing-time" con culture. He is inviting the criminal to change, and he provides for him an "in-person" example of the fact that this is possible. The Synanist is "walking the talk." He hobnobs with the prison administration and is apparently enjoying the rewards of his changed way of life. This is disconcerting to all segments of the inmate system, since it begins to crack up many long-established rationalizations and beliefs about being a con "forever."

It affects various kinds of inmates in different ways. The extreme "big-yard" psychopaths at first may attempt to smash Synanon, since its approach contradicts and implicitly attacks their tough-guy attitudes and rewards. The half-indoctrinated inmate-criminal finds himself in a new type of bind. His formerly "satis-factorily" resolved prison way of life becomes complicated. The sheer existence of Synanon produces a complicated new dilemma. He knows he has to hate, distrust, and not become part of the administration. That is a clear-cut case. Yet, how should he handle his relationship to Synanon? If he joins Synanon, he's in trouble with a segment of the inmate community. If he doesn't join Synanon (when it looks logical to him as a life direction), he may be in a bind with himself. He is then not moving in a direction that seems most appropriate to his own enlightened self-interest.

The inmate's first step in taking a stand against the criminal code and on the side of Synanon requires considerable courage. In fact, attending a synanon, even if nothing happens to the inmate personally, is a difficult step forward. Even without directly affecting the synanon inmates, the mere presence of the synanist has, in a prison, a powerful impact. Synanon shakes up the "doing-time" society and offers an alternative, positive life direction for those who want to travel this new route to freedom.

Paths to Freedom

Synanon, the inmate Synanon members, and the prison administration have created some new paths within the overall system of N.S.P. Some new cultural patterns have been firmly imprinted and built into the N.S.P. social system. These new paths have revolutionized N.S.P. to the point where both inmate and administration roles have been deeply affected.

An inmate can now "graduate" from the isolation of the "hole" and work his way up the Synanon ladder to increasing levels of personal freedom. For every increment of responsibility and freedom he achieves, he must demonstrate by behavior a measure of responsibility and commitment to his freedom. This "social growth" must be proven not only to the prison administration, but to the tougher, more demanding jury of his Synanon inmate peers and to synanists. Proof of his growth is evaluated by his participation in a variety of Synanon activities: synanons, lectures, educational seminars, and work.

As the inmate develops and moves up the Synanon ladder, he receives increasing freedom and access to a "better" way of life. An inmate can move from participation in synanons in maximum security to living in the general prison and attending synanons to living on a Synanon tier to the Synanon Honor Camp and, finally, to parole into a community Synanon facility.

SYNANON'S POSITIONS IN PRISON

Maximum Security: The N.S.P. prisoner in maximum security lives in his cell almost twenty-four hours a day. He is usually in "max" because of his incorrigibility and inability to function without violence in the overall prison population. About twice a week, the Synanon participants from "max" are permitted to leave their cells for synanon sessions.

The "max"-security synanons function on almost a "grunt-and-groan" level. Prisoners in "max" are heavily caged most of the time. They become unaccustomed to communication, except through the walls of their cells, with other inmates. In the synanon session, it takes a while for the men to warm up to adequate communication and interaction with one another.

The actual physical posture of the "max" synanon group is interesting and reveals something about their emotional condition. Some individuals sit on their haunches, as if they were still in their cells. They are reduced by their life situation almost to the fetal position. (One individual, in particular, who had been in maximum security for six years, until he was released to the yard through the Synanon program, fit this description.) Their primary topic of discussion is the fact of their custody. This is the most dominant and pervasive factor in their life. The synanons tend to revolve around the possibility of "going crazy in stir." (One youth in the "max" session that I attended showed how he had pulled out his eyebrows out of boredom. He also showed a slash on his chest from a suicide attempt.) The individuals living in maximum security are obviously under heavy emotional strain and have difficulty seeing very far beyond their immediate situation.

Given this backdrop of circumstances, the context of the "max" synanons revolves around fears of going insane and the pain of "custody." Another theme is the attempt to "con" the synanist into getting them out of "max."

In "max," the inmates hew closely to the "mask-of-crime" line. Such criminal-code matters as snitching, being a stand-up guy, and fighting are major issues in the session. They often discuss the "hole" (total isolation). In fact, most of the individuals, immediately before movement to "max," had been in the "hole." The possibility of return to solitary confinement appears to be one of their fears.

Another dominant theme in "max" synanons is rebellion. One twenty-one-year-old youth, who according to the warden, "got into a fight every day he was in the yard," described his reasons for rebellion in a synanon: "I look at myself as a wild horse. You have a bunch of wild horses running wild on the plain. They try to tame them. They saddle them and they break them. Everyone respects the horse they can't break. They'll never break me. I'll be respected; I'm the wild horse that can't be broken."

A member of the Synanon group pointed out an idea that was not acceptable to the youth at the time. He commented that the horses that were broken and saddled were able to participate in something constructive. They were well fed and lived better than the wild horse. The "wild horse" stuck to his guns—at least in that synanon. This "tough," rebellious youth was, however, at a certain point in the session, in tears. (He later succeeded in Synanon and was released to the Synanon Honor Camp.)

Another inmate in one "max" synanon that I attended was Arty Whitehead. Arty, a Negro, was clearly a rebel against society and had been a street fighter all his life. In a later talk with him in Synanon, Santa Monica (Arty "went the distance," from "max" to Synanon parole), he told me: "Most of my life, I've been in fights. I never knew what I was fighting for—I just had to do it. Outside of being a good fighter, I always felt I wasn't shit. The only thing I had going for me was fighting. Before Synanon came to the prison, I kept up my image as a tough guy for six miserable years. During that time, I spent a lot of time in maximum security and the hole. Somehow I got into Synanon, and my whole life changed. In the synanons, I learned that I fought because I was always afraid. I was afraid for anyone to get near me and see what a punk I really was. I would almost have a fight a day.

"Since Synanon, I've moved up. I now live here in Synanon, Santa Monica, and I'm going to make good. I prove myself now by hard work." (The warden confirmed for me that Art had been a troublemaker for six years in the N.S.P. According to the warden, "The change in Arty is a true miracle.") [4]

General-Population Synanon Participants: The next level or

---

[4] The last time I heard Arty speak was at a lecture I gave at U.C.L.A. He rose and proudly told the group of students and professors of his progress. I vividly remembered him crouched on his haunches, a short year before this time, in maximum security.

path to freedom involves participation in synanons while living in the regular prison cellblock facilities. The individual who proves himself in "max," both to the administration and to Synanon personnel, may be moved to general population and is eligible to continue in Synanon. Others may come from the general prison population and apply for entrance into Synanon.

In the first several sessions, the prospect is verbally hammered. This is an attempt to get him to fight his way into Synanon. It is a "check on his sincerity." This approach to indoctrination somewhat approximates the pattern of entrance into a community Synanon House.

Some prospects have jobs in the prison, and they all have access to the prison yard. Many of them participate in synanons with a thought in mind of becoming more firmly involved and moving on to the Synanon tier.

These men participate in synanon sessions in the so-called cave. This structure is literally a stone-roofed cave carved into the mountain right off the prison yard. Synanons in the cave are attended by members of the Synanon tier, as well as by synanists from the general prison population. The sessions are manipulated and run by the synanists living outside the walls, in the Reno Synanon House.

A Classic Prospect—Shotgun: A newcomer off the yard who was attempting to obtain membership in the cave Synanon was an inmate known as Shotgun. The dialogue between this "prospect" and Candy Latson, in a cave synanon of the older members of Synanon in the prison, went as follows (I happened to sit in on the session):

CANDY: What do you want in here, Shotgun?
SHOTGUN: Well, man, I thought I might change myself, you know —do the thing. I know there's something wrong with me. [Shotgun's comments are accompanied by the snarl and shoulder-shrugging of the "hip" tough guy.]
SYNANIST: Well, what's wrong with you, man?
SHOTGUN: I don't know—you know, I'm pretty crazy sometimes.
SYNANIST: Yeah, we know that, but what's wrong with you?
SHOTGUN: Well, I figured I could do something for myself. But if you don't want me here, well, I'll just go.

SYNANIST: No one said they didn't want you here. We want to know what you want to do.

SHOTGUN: Well, I'm always getting in trouble—and I want to do something about it.

CANDY: Why do they call you Shotgun?

SHOTGUN: [Brightening up] Well, I pulled lots of robberies with a shotgun.

He then proceeds to describe in detail, and with glee, how he would carry out a robbery. He waits for the subtle approval of the usual criminal group after he has told his crime story. None seems to be forthcoming from the Synanon group. As he becomes increasingly aware of the fact that his story isn't a big hit, he becomes more nervous. The Synanon group lets him go on until his story runs out. They then drop him cold with what was for Shotgun an unanticipated reaction: "You mean you ran around with a shotgun like a nut, scaring people and stealing dimes and quarters, and that's what you want to do something about?" Shotgun is a little baffled by what he considers the wrong response. He defends his "big-shot" past. The group laughs at him and ridicules his claim to fame.

The Synanon group then moves to another level of attack and appraisal. "Who do you hang with in the yard?" "Well, my best buddy is Joe." "Why do you hang with Joe?" "Well, he's a pretty good guy; he's a good thief." "What is a good thief?" Shotgun falls back on his criminal track and says, "A good thief is a guy who knows how to rob and will burn through anyone that gets in his way."

The group begins to ridicule his relationship with "good-thief" Joe. They again allude to robbery of this sort as "insanity." Shotgun becomes increasingly hostile under the attack. This may have been the first time in his life that he had experienced an attack of this kind from his criminal peer group. The attack was a double whammy, because it was against the very basis of his "reputation."

Later in the session, I decided to test a hypothesis. Although it was not my role as a sociologist-observer to get into the Synanon act, I measured Shotgun for the comment that I speculated would blow him sky-high and "dropped it on him":

"According to what I hear around the yard, you are the biggest snitch in this joint. Is that true?" This question threw Shotgun out of his seat. He snarled at me and the group that he was not a snitch.

This response produced considerable laughter from the group. Candy then said, "Why does that word make you jump so hard? It's just a noise. Maybe you *are* a snitch." Candy then told him that if he wanted to grow up in Synanon, he was going to have to be able to take this kind of attack.

Shotgun settled down somewhat as he was taken off the hot seat. The discussion moved to an individual referred to as Louie the Punk. Louie was accused of being a "boss faggot" (homosexual). The group began to zero in on him and his problems.

The cave synanons involve many Shotgun and Louie types. They are essentially managed by Synanists from outside the walls, like Candy, although these Synanists receive considerable cooperation from the tier Synanists. The tier level is the next step in Synanon growth and development in the N.S.P. program.

The Synanon Tiers: There are several Synanon tiers, with about twenty-five men living on each. These are special cellblocks set aside for Synanon members. The administration acknowledges that they are the cleanest, best-kept tiers in the prison. The individual cell doors are never closed over the twenty-four-hour period, so that members can circulate within the physical limits of the cellblock.

There is Synanon literature at the end of the tiers; there are pictures of significant people in Synanon and Synanon Houses. In general, there is a great involvement with the overall Synanon movement. The men on the tier know directors Reid Kimball and Jack Hurst. Chuck is well known to the men and is looked up to as the hero of the Synanon movement.

The men seem concerned with Synanon's activities in Westport, San Diego, and beyond the immediate situation. They feel they are part of the overall Synanon program. This is, of course, true, and the identification is encouraged.

Generally, discussion on the Synanon tier is at a higher level than the usual crime and "caper" talk found throughout the prison. Discussions of "capers" or criminal behavior are heavily ridiculed in the synanons.

The men on the tier exude an air of a commitment to a different way of life. They look forward to living in a Synanon House upon release. As one man expressed it: "Synanon is my new family. These are my brothers. Synanon has given me a lift. Life is miserable behind walls, but Synanon lifts me out of here when I'm with it. I'm going to stay in Synanon when I get out."

The Synanon Peavine Honor Camp: Clustered on the side of a desolate mountain, two miles off a main road, is an encampment of several huts, tents, and a mobile kitchen: the Synanon Peavine Honor Camp. The facilities house about twenty men. Unlike the usual prisoner who acquires honor-camp status, most Synanon members *were* hard-core offenders and inmates. Only a few were addicts; the rest are in for a variety of offenses and lengths of sentences (some up to life). According to the warden, "Ninety percent of these men would ordinarily be ineligible under usual conditions for transfer to an open honor camp."

The main daily work of the group involves preventing and fighting forest fires. The civilian director of the government firefighting unit is a man who is not affiliated with prisons. He supervises the Synanon group of fire fighters and told me: "These men are the most effective and dedicated group of fire fighters I have ever supervised. They have real spirit and work hard."

In addition to their basic work, the men of Peavine are intensely involved in the Synanon program. They hold synanons three times a week, have educational seminars, and maintain a Synanon structure of coordinators and other positions. Their organization is modeled as closely as possible to the outside-the-walls Synanon. Discipline and behavior are self-regulated. The men, when it is indicated, give one another vicious "haircuts." Their own regulations in this respect are often more severe than the prison's.

A token security is maintained by one guard around the clock. On my visit to the camp, I was astonished by the following situation. The single guard on duty wanted to go to town for a pack of cigarettes. He asked Candy Latson to "Keep an eye on things," and then went off into town in the N.S.P. car!

Synanon Parole: The next and last phase of development and freedom is Synanon parole. About twenty men have been paroled into Synanon Houses at this time, and most seem to be doing fine.

Some of these men received their Synanon parole in advance of normal parole expectations. The preparation of Synanon in prison helps develop the individual's ability to make the transition to this kind of parole. This latter phase, like the rest of the program, is highly experimental. The success of the men who have made the trip from the "hole" to freedom points up a hopeful future for many other N.S.P. Synanon men and for several hundred thousand inmates in prison today, throughout the country.

Phases Involved in Introducing Synanon into Prison and Speculations on Synanon's Impact on Prison Structure

Based on the T.I. and N.S.P. experiences, there appear to be several marked phases in introducing Synanon into a prison structure. These do not take place as smoothly as will be described. However, based on the experiences to date, the following phases seem to occur:

Phase 1—Party: At first, there is a large attendance of inmates at the synanon sessions. In part, there is a curiosity to see so-called live ex-addict criminals. (Some addict inmates later said they didn't really believe that the Synanon people were "clean" and came to see whether they could "score"!) Most prisoners look for some activity to relieve the monotony and boredom of prison life.

The party phase is the initial situation. It rapidly becomes apparent to many of the "partygoers" that the Synanists "mean business" and will not be deterred from their goals. Resistance is thrown up by the Synanists, and many members of the original "party group" disappear; they were not serious in the first place. Some of these men withdraw, take a "wait-and-see" attitude, and then attempt to get back into Synanon at a later time.

Phase 2—Early Attempt at Inmate Take-Over: The "prison politicians" and upholders of the most negative inmate creeds attempt to take over the Synanon intrusion, since it may interfere with their "game." This phase of possible "take-over" is permitted by Synanists to operate for a short period of time.

After synanon gets its foot firmly in the door, the take-over contingent is openly challenged by Synanists. They get this faction to reveal its real motivations. This quickly builds up into a "join-us-or-get-out" attitude on the part of the Synanists. In the N.S.P. project, several take-over individuals were tolerated for several months and then the vise was tightened. Some stayed in the program, and several "split."

Phase 3—The Battle: In the next phase, a pitched battle develops between Synanon values and the "doing-time-society" elements in the overall prison. The fact that the Synanist is free, leading a "clean," constructive life is the most powerful demonstration of the Synanon argument.

It requires considerable strength and belief in the Synanon position for an inmate Synanist to stand up against the criminal code. Synanists are normally accused by many inmates of being snitches, of selling out, and being tools of the administration. As described by Candy, in the early days of Synanon at N.S.P., synanists were "booed" by inmates as they walked through the prison yard. One synanist, a relative newcomer, eight months in Synanon, revealed how, when he first "went to work" as a Synanist in the T.I. project, he had considerable guilt about pushing the Synanon idea. He revealed how, at first, he gave in to a type of apology. In effect, he was at the outset saying to some of the inmates, "Forgive me for being free and happy."

The dynamic of Synanon conflict with one destructive "doing-time" faction was revealed in a report on the female inmates in the T.I. project by the director at that time:

"For the first time, the girls have done a little organizing. They now have a Synamaster and an operations girl, someone to do all the book work, and one to call the meeting to order and to do all the voice work. They took care of a few things they had been neglecting. They are also using the regular members to help in their work. They have two girls who talk to new girls coming into the prison. Next week I am going to play a tape for them. Probably an indoctrination tape. They are very eager to hear it.

"I feel fearful at times, but I think of Chuck and all that he has gone through in getting Synanon started, its hassles, and so on. I know what I have to do, and I'll do it. Some of the institution girls are trying their best to smash Synanon right now. They won't even allow our [Synanon-inmate] girls to put their articles in the prison paper. I talked to Miss C. about this, however, and our girls are going to print their own paper. They say that all day long people are calling them snitches and giving them a hard time (mostly the girls that used to go to synanons but dropped out after we made the change). It reminds me of the resistance we got from the City of Santa Monica." [5]

Phase 4—The Showdown: The inmate resisters are culled out of the program when they do not cooperate properly in this phase. The Synanist shakes the group down to those truly involved in the program. After the showdown, it might be expected that a select group of inmates would remain. The evidence is to the contrary. At N.S.P., the Synanon group (of about a hundred) contains a "random sample" of the prison population.

Phase 5—"Opening Up": After the Synanon group has solidified, many inmates begin to feel free and "open up" and reveal their inner conflicts and feelings. A real step forward then takes place. Unlike the professional institutional group-therapy situation, where, for the most part, "opening up" is geared toward impressing the administration, in Synanon the inmate is doing it for himself. (No prison staff members are allowed in the synanon sessions.) The Synanon groups become almost a family association. At N.S.P., the Synanon-tier members refer to one another as "brothers." Practically all secrets, problems, and feelings are revealed to one another in this phase of growth. This "opening-up" process must constantly be pushed. After a time, if "therapeutic contracts" develop, the Synanist has to shake the situation loose.

Inmates who remain with the program into this last phase

[5] In a discussion with this Synanon person, we explored the possibility that introducing Synanon into a correctional institution is very much like introducing Synanon into a new community. Often the most pathological members of the community respond with tremendous resistance. Their unconscious fear is that Synanon might reach and expose them and their underlying disturbance. Some of these resistant factions have a thin mask of sanity that may be stripped away by the Synanon approach.

seem to benefit maximally. In the process of reaching this position, inmates, Synanists, and prison administrators necessarily have to batter down some of the destructive "doing-time" conditions. Many of the participants learn something useful about themselves and the institution in the process of getting Synanon in prison organized and under way.

THE INMATE-LEADER SYSTEM: SYNANON IMPACTS

It is an accepted fact of prison life that there is an inmate power structure, with certain types of criminal leaders at the top. The variety of "inmate leaders" operate in different ways. There were three usual types of leaders in the N.S.P. when Synanon came on the scene. In one category was the "prison boss," often referred to as the "prison politician." This type of inmate leader acquires a degree of power from "playing ball" with the administration. He is usually in a position to trade to the administrations the commodity of "good inmate behavior" in exchange for special privileges. (The privileges usually include contraband and guards looking the "other way" during a fight or a homosexual tryst.)

Another type of inmate leader has status because he is feared for his ruthlessness and strong-arm ability. This type of leader is the "prison tough guy."

Another type who plays a leadership role is a long-termer with much "time" in his background. His power comes from an intimate knowledge and close understanding of the way the prison works. He is "con wise."

Three N.S.P. inmates fit these leadership roles. They will be called here Big Joe, Duke, and Danny. Synanon's effect on them personally, on their "power" and their response in Synanon, reveals something of Synanon's impact on the prison power structure.

The "Prison Politician": Big Joe was doing life for murder. He had been in the N.S.P. for nine years prior to Synanon's arrival. He was a recognized political-boss leader in N.S.P. He ran the mess hall and, in effect, had a staff position with the prison administration.

Gambling is legally permitted in the N.S.P. (This condition

may stem from an extrapolation: since gambling is legal in the state of Nevada, why not in a Nevada prison?) There is a large gambling hall in the middle of the big yard of the prison, replete with the paraphernalia of blackjack, roulette, dice, and so on. (It is a fantastic sight to walk off the big prison yard into what looks like—and, I suppose, is—a movie-style "Wild West" gambling casino.)

Big Joe, in addition to his position in the mess hall, had a large interest in the gambling situation and controlled several tables. This situation bolstered his position as a somewhat wealthy, powerful inmate. Big Joe was known as a soft touch for a loan or a free cup of coffee. He enjoyed a reputation as a "friend of the inmates." (He somehow did not consider himself truly an inmate.)

As a prison leader, Big Joe had to cope with Synanon in some fashion, since he quickly saw that it could affect his empire. When Synanon first came into N.S.P., he made the decision to support Synanon. At the same time, he took the position that the program wasn't for him personally. (He may have intuitively recognized that condemning Synanon would not serve his own interests.)

The "Ice-Cream Rebellion": As Synanon grew in power in the prison, Big Joe became increasingly interested. He saw the evidence of its effect on his power through a peculiar incident. What might be called the "ice-cream rebellion" is described here by a prison official. It provides some clue to the shift in Big Joe's power produced by Synanon:

"Joe runs the kitchen, and, of course, he still holds considerable power as an inmate leader. On one occasion, on the Fourth of July, we were to give the inmates a half-pint of ice cream in their cell. This, of course, was a big thing in the institution, and everyone was in his cell anxiously awaiting for delivery of the ice cream. When the ice cream was delivered to the prison, our man in charge noticed an error. The ice cream was quarter-pint Dixie Cups rather than the half-pints expected.

"Big Joe, as head of the kitchen, was directed to have his staff deliver the ice cream to the cells. What we had in mind was that we would get another batch of these Dixie Cups to make up the half-pints at some later date. Big Joe refused to have his men deliver the ice cream. He said he wouldn't be a party to the delivery, when half-pints were expected throughout the prison. Big Joe was asked again to deliver the ice cream by a higher official, and again he refused. As a last resort, we went into a tier and asked some inmates to volunteer to distribute the ice cream. Surprisingly they cooperated with no resistance, even though they had heard about Big Joe's rebellion.

"Before Synanon, if Joe had rebelled against an order of this kind, no one else would have jumped in to undercut his authority. Since Synanon, there is a greater direct cooperation between inmates and staff. This allowed the inmates to cooperate with us, even though they all knew about Big Joe's rebellion. It is clear to me that a measure of power has slipped away from some inmate leaders and that there is a greater inmate cooperation with our officers."

Shortly after this incident, Joe applied for admission to the Synanon program. He began to attend synanons on the yard and became a Synanon fan and booster for several months. For a time, he was given a "pass" by the group in the sessions and was allowed to "get by" without the group's "opening up" on him.

Joe applied for and was accepted into one of the Synanon tiers. On the tier, the group began to cut loose on him in synanons. His homosexual "contracts" and carryings-on with younger inmates was brought out in the open. "Synanon style," the group also began to attack his gambling and other political interests. Big Joe could go only so far at that time. He quit Synanon, *even though he remained a booster*. Big Joe is at this time back in Synanon and has assumed an important role of leadership.

The "Prison Duke": Duke is a full-blooded American Indian. His criminal pattern consisted in getting drunk and then violent. He received a life sentence in N.S.P. for an atrocious homicide that involved dismembering the victim's body. The Duke hated most non-Indians and believed in the need to "stick with his own people."

Duke's power in the prison came from brute force, mainly his own. He also had a group of musclemen as satellites. He was considered "the toughest, most feared person in the prison, and no one fooled with him."

Duke became involved with Synanon when the project first

arrived in the prison. He participated in quite a few synanons and appeared to be making some progress—until the group began to attack him as they would any other member. "I just can't take anyone calling me a punk or pushing me around in any way at all," he said. "I blow up and am ready to tear them apart." Duke, after several months, left Synanon. This was partially because of his inability to take the synanon hot seat, but it was also because of some pressure from the clique of Indians in the institution who were his followers. He later returned and was accepted back into the program.

Duke, despite, or perhaps because of, his power, was elected to the important and respected ("It is no sellout job.") Inmate Council. One of the responsibilities of his position was to counsel new prisoners. He invariably recommends to the newcomer that it would be good and useful for him to join Synanon. For Duke, Synanon is an important reference point, one that affects his behavior as a leader. Synanon has had the effect of almost eliminating his past violent way of life in the prison.

The "Long-Termer": Dan was a drug addict and a thief whenever he was free on the streets. He had not had much freedom in his thirty-four years of life. He had been sent to various juvenile institutions at an early age and had spent almost eleven out of the past fifteen years in prison. He had "convict savvy," as a result of his lengthy prison experience, and knew how to manipulate his way around the prison. This gave him a leadership quality and a degree of power. He was a "hip" inmate.

Dan, at first, saw Synanon as just another gimmick to ease the difficulty of life in prison and perhaps earn some "good time" (quicker parole). Gradually, he became involved and worked himself up in Synanon to become one of the leaders in the prison tier. Despite his basic underlying disbelief, Dan was "doing the thing" in Synanon. He looked and acted dedicated to Synanon. He stood up to the derision hurled at him by other convicts in the yard. The necessity of standing up for Synanon against the negative attitudes of other inmates helped him to become increasingly involved in the organization. He had continually to examine his new association and learn more about Synanon in the process of defending his position.

Dan's commitment to Synanon developed despite his underlying belief that he was "a righteous dope fiend" for life. He has changed considerably as a result of Synanon, and as a role model for other long-termers, Dan has appreciably affected the power structure by his positive Synanon leadership. (Dan received a Synanon parole and is currently living in a community Synanon House.)

THE PRISON "FISH" (NEWCOMER)

Another type of Synanon member in prison is the "first-timer." Gary found himself in a long-term prison for the first time in his life, doing ten to twenty for possession of narcotics. On entering prison, he admitted to a great fear. He decided to handle the situation in a particular fashion: "I had never done any big-time, and I was scared shitless. I felt I better not show any sympathy or inner feelings. I had seen plenty of movies—you know, like, 'We'll rub out this squealer,' and all that. I decided I was going to get in with the big-time cons and work things out that way."

Gary had no real position in the prison power structure when he arrived. He was set to join the inmate culture and do whatever was necessary. He heard about and joined Synanon. His entrance into the prison Synanon *before* he received the usual negative convict indoctrination protected him from this potential contamination. *Synanon for Gary was a shield from negative prison influence.* At the same time, Synanon enabled him to attempt to grow up, in preparation for release.

The foregoing examples reflect only a few of Synanon's impacts on and rearrangements of the N.S.P. leadership and power structure. They depict some of the influence of Synanon on different types of inmates. A most important new dimension that Synanon introduced into N.S.P. is the possibility of inmate status for *good behavior*. This is a profound reversal of the "requirements" for being a Big Joe politician, a Dan old-time know-the-ropes con, or a Duke muscleman. Getting prison leaders to "go straight" inside the walls is a major accomplishment. Synanon has done this and has also begun to help prepare some of these same men to "make it" outside.

There are currently over one hundred prisoners in the N.S.P.

Synanon program. Many of these men serve as significant "heroes" for both "old" and "new" prisoners to use as positive role models. Synanon provides both an avenue and a method for change.

Impacts on the Synanist

Of as much importance as its potential impact on the inmate is the effect of the Synanon prison project on the Synanist. The Synanists working in N.S.P. can see themselves and the position they formerly occupied in life in a different perspective. They can see the ridiculous nature of the set of rationalizations that they had as inmates, and they have an opportunity to deal constructively with their own past fear of prison. This complex of factors tends to stiffen the back of the Synanist in his difficult work. The point-counterpoint of the Synanist position versus the prisoner's recalcitrant tough-guy approach (exemplified by Shotgun) is a continuing battle.

Typical of the feelings expressed by several Synanists who have worked on prison projects are those revealed in an article that appeared in the *Terminal Island News* in January, 1963. The following excerpt was written by a Synanon member. (The Synanist is Frank Lago's wife, Carmen.) Although this statement was written by a female Synanist in the T.I. program, it is relevant to and reveals the views of Synanists working in prison in general:

> I have a history of drug addiction—and what that entails—
> that goes back ten years. Through a fortunate set of circumstances, I found my way to Synanon twenty months ago and have been free of drugs ever since. My first impression when I was asked to go to Terminal Island was one of fear and reluctance, because the idea of going to prison again triggered off old feelings. In spite of this feeling, I know that for me, personally, working at T.I. has been fulfilling experience and has benefited me tremendously.

Another participant in the Synanon prison program, a man who had spent four years in San Quentin, described his reactions to the experience as follows:

"The first time I entered a prison other than as an inmate was an experience I won't forget. The first prisoner I saw (I met many others later on) was someone I had served time with in the state prison and used dope with on the streets. The shock of seeing me coming into the prison with a group of ex-junkies, who were unquestionably clean and healthy-looking, had a tremendous impresson on the men who showed up for those first synanons.

"I understood their suspicions about us, but at the same time, I was anxious to let them know that there really was information available and that we were experiencing a new life through Synanon. The strongest feeling I had was that here was the opportunity to help someone who wanted to help himself—inside the walls or not."

Impact on Administration-Inmate Relations

The warden, other prison administrators, and many inmates are in general agreement that Synanon has produced some remarkable changes at N.S.P. Many dramatic developments have occurred in the prison since Synanon "moved in."

There has been a decrease of tension in the prison yard and in the general prison environment. This has produced a higher degree of communication and interaction between inmates and guards and has resulted in a considerable breakdown in the "we-they" situation.

There have been fewer prison offenses in general and a reduction of severe disciplinary problems. In particular, prison officials have observed fewer battle scars on inmates, a "quieter prison yard," and the virtual elimination of knife fights. This general reduction of hostility in the prison has been attributed to Synanon by Warden Fogliani. The fact that the men can fight their battles verbally in the synanon sessions may help prevent their carrying out the actual physical fights.

Synanon has produced a greater emphasis on inmate self-discipline. According to the warden, this is "particularly true of the Honor Camp situation." The state official who administers the forestry-camp part of the Honor Camp operation commented favorably on the spirit, behavior, and self-discipline of the Honor Camp men. When there is any infraction of rules, the Synanon men take care of their own problems in the synanons. This seems to foster the development of the inmates' "inner controls." They also realize that their behavior reflects on and affects the men back in the prison.

Participation in Synanon has become a factor in parole consideration. Inmates have come to recognize that there is something to be gained from Synanon participation. (There is a paradox in this situation. When the men sincerely involve themselves in Synanon, they are, in fact, increasingly better parole risks.) Progress in Synanon is determined by the judgments of prison officials, by Synanist analyses, and by the opinions of Synanon-inmate peers. This appears to be a most useful collection of opinions and analyses for determining who is "ready" for parole. (In some respects, it is a new kind of parole prediction method.)

The sharing of opinions among these different, yet cooperating, factions seems to have a side effect of bringing staff and inmates into greater harmony.

Synanon's apparent success has a degree of positive fallout that has affected the therapeutic action of many guards and other prison personnel. Synanon has somewhat smashed the "doing-time" myth of the "tough con who cannot change." Startling changes in behavior have already occurred in many former "hard-core, difficult inmates." This has resulted in a greater staff belief in the possibilities of rehabilitation in general. Some of the formerly "unsolvable" problems have been mitigated somewhat by Synanon's entrance into the prison. This has stimulated the overall rehabilitation approach of the prison staff.

The Small-"S" Synanon in Prison

Since life in a Synanon House in the community is closely linked with life in the larger society, many of the items of discussion in synanons relate to the problems of life in society.

However, prison synanons, as might be expected, usually relate to the problems of life in the institution.

The synanons facilitate verbal communication. This is an important learning experience for individuals whose usual approach to interaction or to "making a point" was an act of violence. The synanon sessions seem to help the inmates communicate better verbally, rather than with the usual violence.

Status in prison is usually acquired by toughness and a criminal reputation. The synanon sessions tend to undercut these surface symbols of status and place a value on personal development. In a synanon group, the most "humble," weak con can attack the "mighty" one without fear of physical reprisal. This enables both to grow. In the synanon, they can both discard their general "tough-guy" pose. The physically weaker inmate, under these conditions, is in a position to help a "tough guy" with attack therapy. Prior to Synanon, he would have found it almost impossible to tell a "tough guy" anything useful about himself.

When a synanon is operating effectively, it is dealing with the range of human problems. In a synanon, the individual is dealing with good and bad feelings, with negative and positive attitudes. The fact that he is black or white; was a junkie, a murderer, or a rapist; is young or old is irrelevant in the synanon situation. The synanon functions at a "gut level" and helps to break down existing prejudices and fears among many kinds of prisoners.[6]

Synanon helps to make the inmate more aware of his problems—as a first step in solving them. One prisoner in a session made the following comment: "When I first heard about synanons, I thought it was only for junkies. I didn't think it was for me. I thought I didn't have a problem. You see, I'm a murderer." This individual, in most of his prison career, had actually minimized the fact of having committed a homicide. He didn't believe he had a problem—after all, he had only committed murder! (One possible explanation for this unusual belief system is the fact that many long-termers in N.S.P. are in custody for murder. Being in prison a long time, usually for life, they have

[6] One interesting side effect of Synanon's entrance into N.S.P. is Negro-white integration. Pre-Synanon, *de facto* segregation existed.

to learn to live within that system. Consequently, the people in for homicide achieve a great measure of power and status. If the status individuals in a group have a certain attitude toward a particular offense, it may carry throughout the rest of the prison population. The leaders in N.S.P. thus tend to minimize homicide as an offense, in order to rationalize their guilt.)

The content of a synanon in prison very often relates to the level of development of the Synanon inmate. From the maximum-security group on through the Honor Camp, there are definite changes in the quality of articulation and communication. A trained synanist could listen to a tape of a synanon and pick out the locale of the session by the voices and what they say. The maximum-security boys mutter and moan, whereas the Honor Camp and tier synanons are more productively related to higher-level life problems. The cave synanons are for both "Synanon yard people" and "tier people." A trained Synanon ear can pick out differences of Synanon performance between the two categories of members. Tier individuals are more developed, more articulate, and more knowledgeable about Synanon than yard people, who do not participate as totally in Synanon.

Synanon sessions in prison are a focal point for personal development in the same way that they are in community Synanon Houses. They are used in prison to promote communication, to analyze the individual's problems, to deal with organizational issues, and to facilitate the inmate's growth as a person.

The General Prison Population

Synanon has a considerable effect on inmates who are not direct participants in Synanon activities. They see the strange spectacle of their former hard-core criminal buddies getting involved in Synanon and changing their attitudes and behavior. This has caused many nonparticipant inmates to examine themselves and their "hole card." For some, it is a disturbing experience. Their "doing-time" rationalizations, "rejecting the rejecters," hatred of middle-class squares, assumptions about being helpless to change their lives, and other false notions are sharply challenged by the Synanon demonstration. If, in fact, some of the prison leaders and old cons are beginning to modify their behavior and if, in fact, the synanists "are for real," something has to be wrong with their own criminal rationalizations and values.

The values, rationalizations, attitudes, and patterns of the convict are threatened by the Synanon program. This has the effect of dislodging some of the fiercely upheld beliefs of the recalcitrant criminal whether he joins Synanon or not. All these forces help to destroy the "doing-time" complex and facilitates correction in the total N.S.P. system.

Back to Reality

The new "prison-to-freedom" tunnel carved out by Synanon in the N.S.P. program may very well represent the opening of a new "trail" in American correction. Taking the Synanon path, a prisoner can move from complete custody to freedom. At each turning point, he must positively affect the critical judgments of his inmate peers, synanists, and the prison administration.

The paths of transition available through Synanon provide several more "gateways to freedom" for the offender—not only a personal freedom but the freedom to learn how to live effectively with others. The inmate has an available set of achievable goals that can transport him from the "hole" to life in a Synanon in the community.[7] He progresses through these levels as he outgrows his apparent need to live in the womb-like atmosphere of the cell and demonstrates an apparent ability to assume greater responsibility at a higher level of life.

The movement is analogous to movement from the womb (solitary confinement) into various stages of life. In the "hole," the inmate vegetates and is almost totally inactive. The "hole"

[7] In the administration of the Synanon prison movement, there is a lag for certain members. Some inmates stay behind a rung in the process in order to maintain themselves as a role model for others. Thus Synanon "max" has one or two people ready for the yard or tier level and the tier has several individuals eligible for the Honor Camp. By agreement, these inmates stay back one rung to serve as examples for other men on the move. This maintains a continuity and flow of potential Synanon development.

is dark, and there is no interaction or communication with other people. In maximum security, he functions like a child. He begins to make sounds and mutterings in synanons, which are usually concerned with his physical comfort. At another Synanon level, he is beginning to interact with others in the yard (adolescence). On the Synanon tier, a still higher level of expectations and demands, he assumes a more adult role, although he is still in a protected environment. In the Synanon Honor Camp, he more clearly demonstrates his ability to function as an adult. He is given and assumes responsibility. He does significant work and begins to interact with people in the society at large. In the next step, living in a Synanon community, he is to a great extent on his own and has earned the right to function on the outside as an adult. There he can round himself out and grow up, along with his hundreds of newfound "brothers" and "sisters."

Starting from inside the walls, Synanon has carved a path back into a world of new reality. The only price the formerly encapsulated inmate has to pay is clearly stated in a brochure written and printed by N.S.P. Synanon members: "The only requirement for new members is honesty, for this is a basic necessity in making the concepts of Synanon practical."

16

The Newest Profession

Perhaps the most controversial element of the new Synanon society is its profound belief that people can help themselves without standard professional therapy or therapists. The organization has developed an independent approach to social problems and their solution. Synanon draws its concepts from many quarters and works in somewhat the reverse fashion of the usual professional approach. Chuck once gave me a summary of Synanon's "professional" position: "We use as much knowledge from as many sources as possible. In Synanon, we quote and use the ideas of Freud, Ralph Waldo Emerson, Lao-tse, and many of the pronouncements of Christ. We use any system of ideas that helps us to better understand the human condition.

"We use self-training; you know, 'going through the motions.' We deal with the person's identity in the here and now. We use brainwashing and attack therapy here to peel away those parts of the self that haven't been too effective—in fact, have put the person in the mess he's in. We make him aware of new ideas and ways of behaving. By getting the person to go through certain behavior motions, he is somehow euchred into constructing his own approach to life.

"We work backwards from psychoanalysis. They begin with the id and the unconscious. We get there, too, but we begin with behavior and the superego.

"We do not reward bad behavior here, and we always try to reward good behavior. We give the people here information about themselves and life, and this seems to equip them to construct their own superego. We just provide the tools for learning and a direction. The person does the rest himself."

Professional Monopoly, Resistance, and Attack

Over the past fifty years, the treatment of social problems has been dropped into the professional lap and has been held on to tightly. The propaganda about the professional's exclusive right to treat social problems has reached its high mark. The professionals, the public, and even patients are firmly convinced that the only "bona fide" treatments and "cures" available come from "legitimate professionals" with the right set of degrees.

The sheer existence of the Synanon approach is considered by some professionals to be an attack upon the *status quo* and vested interest of their professional domain. Synanon's position that some of its "patients" can become therapists seems to draw fire from many professional quarters.[1]

The Synanon organization has not gone out of its way to counterattack. It has been too busy developing its own method. Synanon's independent self-help posture, however, has caused much negative professional direct response and, in some instances, indirect attack. (For example, the California State Department

---

[1] The absurdity of some of the professional attacks on Synanon is exemplified by the following two cases. A Santa Monica baby doctor declared himself an expert on drug addiction and wrote a lengthy article in the *Santa Monica Evening Outlook*. The article was hailed by the newspaper as a "penetrating analysis" and cross-comparison of Synanon and the federal hospital at Lexington, Kentucky. The fact that this doctor had never visited either Synanon or Lexington did not deter him from his *total* condemnation of Synanon. On the basis of his "knowledge" and "expertise," he never missed an "attack-Synanon" opportunity in their many judicial battles.

In another case, during Synanon's attempt to locate in Malibu, the president of the Bay Area branch of the L.A. County Medical Association was quoted in the *Evening Outlook* as stating that he was opposed to Synanon because it had not helped any addicts and had no scientific validity. Both these professionals condemned Synanon on "scientific grounds," yet neither utilized the most basic tool of scientific investigation: firsthand observation.

of Parole and the Los Angeles County Probation Department placed Synanon "out of bounds" for their parolees and probationers.) [2]

To balance the scale, it should, of course, be noted that many professional people have supported Synanon in principle and with direct psychiatric, medical, dental, and other professional services. The more absurd professional enemies of the Synanon movement, however, do slow and impede Synanon's natural thrust and growth. Their unwarranted destructive attacks have helped block aid to untold numbers of addicts. Many more addicts might have availed themselves of the Synanon program if it had been accepted and permitted to grow large enough to accommodate more people.

This kind of bureaucratic and unwarranted professional opposition is directly and indirectly responsible for deterring many addicts from joining the Synanon program and benefiting from its proven life-giving approach to their problem.

[2] In 1960, the California State Department of Parole ordered seven clean Synanon members back to the streets and still does not permit state parolees to participate in the Synanon program. Several tragic cases highlight the destructive quality of this bureaucratic blindness. When Ted Sondergard (one of the unlucky seven and the only one to get back) returned to Synanon after a year in prison, he was more than bitter about the "correction department's" assault on him. His fiancée, who was staying "clean" in Synanon, followed him out when he had to leave. She returned to her addict life and died several months later from a possible overdose of drugs. (Ted, free from state parole, is currently doing fine in Synanon.) In other cases known to me, several parents of addicts petitioned the Governor and state agencies to allow their sons and daughters to enter Synanon when they were released from custody. This has been to no avail. In all cases, the addicts who sincerely wanted to try Synanon were denied this right.

For five years, the L.A. County Probation Department bureaucracy has played a merry-go-round game with Synanon and the courts that cost the taxpayers many thousands of dollars and some lives. In phase one, Synanon accepts the probationer. In phase two, the probation department charges violation of parole (for staying "clean" in Synanon!) and returns the probationer to the courts. Fortunately, eight Superior Court judges are on Synanon's side. These judges have overruled the probation department in seventeen out of nineteen cases and sent the probationer back to Synanon. Among this group saved by the judges (in spite of the bureaucracy) are such important figures in Synanon as Bill Crawford and Candy Latson. Bettye Dederich was almost destroyed by the probation department's action. She was ordered back to the streets; however, she somehow managed to get back into Synanon after her probation hold was released.

Beyond the bureaucratic explanation, I find it difficult to assay the professional resistance to Synanon. This opposition is unfortunate not only for the addict who is blocked in his efforts to save himself—the ignorant judgments of some professional enemies slop over into the community and give intelligent potential supporters of Synanon pause.[3] An even more damaging result of irrational professional negativism is that it provides fuel for many elements of the community viciously opposed to all "mental-health" efforts.[4]

Part of the resistance to Synanon may stem from the fact that Synanon has been modestly successful in an area where most professionals have admittedly failed. Moreover, this success, in part, has resulted from the "patient's" reversing roles with the therapist.

The examination and clarification of Synanon's position on a variety of issues that relate to "professional" Synanist work may help to delineate some of the boundary lines that exist between Synanon and orthodox professionalism. In passing, these "essays" may reveal some of the overt and covert professional conflict with and resistance to Synanon.

The Antidrug Posture

Synanon is totally opposed to the nonmedical use by Synanon people of any "drugs, alcohol, or chemicals" that modify a person's emotional, or feeling, state. The reasoning behind it is that the use of drugs or alcohol might affect the person's self-control and propel him into using stronger and stronger drugs, up through heroin. Chuck considers drugs to be exclusively the province of the medical profession: "Drugs are properly used by

---

[3] One absurd psychiatrist, who never visited Synanon and knew nothing about it, testified against Synanon in the court trials that put Dederich in jail. In a private conversation with a psychiatrist friend of Synanon, he said he really liked Synanon and thought it was effective. He was opposed to Synanon because it was unorthodox!

[4] For example, many branches of the John Birch Society have been extremely opposed to almost all "mental-health" programs in different communities throughout the country.

medical men in the course of their work. We do not believe in the use of any kind of drug outside the realm of proper medical practice. As far as alcohol goes—the great big standard American social lubricant—we do not permit our people to use it in any form. There is a flat-out alcohol-prohibition policy in Synanon. One reason for this is the bare possibility that residual proneness to an addictive escape might rear its head if a person starts fooling with a few cocktails every night for dinner or even every few months.

"Another reason for this prohibition throughout the organization is that the leaders of a business based on strict abstinence on the part of its rank-and-file members should also forego this pleasure, if it be pleasure. We in the upper reaches, as part of our job, serve as role models—clean examples to our newcomers. I seriously doubt whether I or some of the directors would get in any trouble if we had a drink now and then, but we just make a policy of not doing this. We insist on Synanon people conforming to this posture.

"We do not care whether our square friends are drinking or not. However, when any have the poor taste to show up at our home loaded, we would have to kick them out. We have enforced this policy with several people, and a few of these were important donors."

Synanon is uncompromising on the issue of drug and alcohol use. This "moral position" regarding drug and alcohol use seems to disturb many "hip-square" friends of Synanon. (The "hip square" would be a person who has dabbled with drugs or had some association with the criminal-addict world in his experience.) Many "hip squares" are attracted to Synanon and its members because they (mistakenly) believe that there is a kinship between their own beliefs and the viewpoint of Synanon members. The "hip squares" (and this includes some professionals) who visit Synanon often use such "hip talk" as the greeting, "Hey, man, what's happening?" They are somewhat surprised and often chagrined when this talk is, in their own hip language, "put down" (verbally crushed).

This brand of hipsterism and the Synanon response are illustrated by a "hip" young couple who visited Synanon. The wife thought they would be real "in" (accepted) by her comment: "Yeah, my old man and I blow some pot [marijuana] occasionally—just for kicks—nothing serious." She and her husband were quickly escorted to the front door with the admonition, "We cannot afford to have any using dope fiends on our premises." (The expression "using dope fiend" is Synanon's standard hyperbolic "put-down.")

The moral attitude of *clear opposition* to drug and chemical use, and accompanying "hip talk," is an attitude clearly taken by the *Synanon* professional, but not necessarily by the *professional* professional. Many professionals join the criminal culture, if not behaviorally, at least with subtle approval. Many New York psychotherapists I have known have "worked with" [5] drug addicts and taken no really negative position on their use of drugs. Their working assumption is that if they can successfully treat the psyche, the addict will eventually abandon the use of drugs. I do not know of one case where this professional position has succeeded. Synanon, in contrast, seems to have an approach with a strong measure of moral fiber built in. Synanon works, "in front." They don't *hope* that the addict will stop using drugs— they *demand* and *get* abstinence.

The Professional Hipster: A Case in Point

My own hipsterism, when I first arrived at Synanon, clarified a "professional disease" that facetiously became known in the Synanon administration as the "Yablonsky effect." In my past research, pre-Synanon, in "working with" and doing research on violent-gang youths, prisoners, and drug addicts both in lockups and in the community, I had acted on my belief that the best way to "establish rapport" (social-work jargon for "get next to") with my subjects was to "talk their language."

---

[5] Chuck, on one occasion when I used this term in reference to a parole officer's "working with" an addict, commented: " 'Working with' really describes what they do. They lock up the addict, then turn him loose—they continue to 'work with' him. He shoots drugs and they lock him up again. They don't treat him—they 'work with' him."

This I began to do in my early Synanon research days. In particular, I began to "hang out" with Frankie Lago and Jimmy Middleton. (Both Lago and Middleton had, in their pre-Synanon past, been "boss dope fiends." Their combined jail and prison time totaled almost twenty years.) We were "buddies"; and, in fact, the association (in addition to being personally gratifying) produced for me some useful knowledge about Synanon.

At about a six-month point in my association with Synanon, in one of the so-called big-shot synanon sessions that I attended (comprising the executive staff), I was "brought up sharp." In that synanon, my "appalling, atrocious behavior" was pointed out by Chuck. He said that there was a "bare possibility" that my hip talk and manner might very well be reinforcing Middleton's and Lago's criminal components. It was pointed out to me very forcefully that my "buddy approach with the patients" was harmful to them. Chuck and other members of the executive staff gave me a vicious "haircut," and it hurt.

But I began to see something. True, I was gathering some useful information, yet I could see that my response to Lago's and Middleton's revealing to me the details of their criminality was in some ways giving approval to this component—the very dimension of their personality that Synanon was trying to change.

I was asked or, better said, was told, "Why don't you talk to them sometimes about sociology or academic life or world politics?" "Why not indeed," I began to think.

This personal (and somewhat painful) experience caused me to review the overall professional posture toward criminological research and treatment. In fact, it now seems to me that professionals who glory in hearing crime stories can, by tacit approval, negatively influence individuals attempting to "put down" their past (and future) criminality. The wrong approach seems to reinforce the symptom of criminal behavior.

There exists in many criminologists whom I know an intense interest (and perhaps vicarious satisfaction) in the criminal exploits of their subjects. Many are intrigued voyeurs of the criminal world. This inclination and involvement are in some measure reflected in many professional publications on the subject. For example, in the drug-addiction field, my cursory review of recently published conference reports and papers reveals a tremendous preoccupation with the symptoms and various patterns of destructive drug use and with the hallucinatory effects of drugs. In comparison with the symptomatic destructive aspects of addiction, there appear to be fewer publications concerned with the causes and cure of the problem.

There seems to be, among many professionals, almost an admiration of the "interesting, exciting world of crime and addiction." In my past work, I found this to be true among professional "gang workers" in New York City. They would almost brag about how tough their gangs were. In response to a question I asked of a New York street-gang worker (a professional social worker) about his gang's criminal-addict behavior, he commented, "Oh, man, this is a real down ["sharp"] group of kitties. We have all kinds of weapons, and they'll use them at a moment's notice."

Then, laughingly, about drug use, he said, "All the kids fool with some drugs—not much H [heroin], but, you know, smoking pot and pills. The other day they wanted me to get high with them. Naturally, I wouldn't, but I think I lost status because I acted square." This type of blatant symptom reinforcement is quite prevalent among many professionals, including the objective, nonjudgmental breed of therapist.

A more subtle support of the criminal-addict position is found in an early criticism of this manuscript by a sociologist-editor. Although he makes many useful points, his annoyance with Synanon's antiaddiction posture shows through his appraisal. His position is the typical "hip professional's" view of drug use and reflects a subtle support of drug addiction:

> . . . If the author wants to say that anyone formerly addicted to drugs should never, absolutely never, take drugs again because of the danger of reawakening old addictive behavior patterns, etc., he can make out a case that for good therapeutic reasons the former addict should learn to get along without any chemical escapes from reality, etc. (Note I say he can "make out a case"—not, I think, prove it.) For some former addicts, at least, there seems to be no such danger; I know two former junkies who have been completely clean

of hard stuff for four years and over ten years respectively but who *do* smoke pot and who, despite such marijuana use, meet all the usual "square" criteria of doing well at their jobs, raising their families well, etc.[6] But it's quite another thing to claim, as he does and Synanon does, that no one should use drugs. First of all, every, repeat, every society, not just modern ones and not just capitalist ones, has recognized that most people occasionally need some escape from reality—some aid to fantasy, etc.—and every, repeat, every society has permitted some sort of chemical aid to such escape.

If the author wants to say that some chemicals are better than others (some are addictive and some not, some physically damaging and some not, etc.), okay. But everyone does, in any society known to man, have to escape occasionally and if the drugs are useful in this regard and otherwise not harmful— why not? Why should the *non*-addict forego use of *non*-addicting drugs?

In claiming that they should, Synanon goes beyond the point it needs to make vis-à-vis the proper therapy for addicts. In this respect Synanon seems too "square," *needlessly* moralistic, indeed puritanical. . . . Nor is it possible to defend the notion that the use of addicting drugs necessarily *transforms* even the healthy personality so that it becomes "character disordered." Again, this is a matter of social circumstance. It's too bad for Synanon's thesis—but unfortunately true— that when addicts have easy access to the drugs they need (as in the case, in the U.S., with many upper-class people and many people in the medical profession), they usually do *not* manifest so-called "character disorder" traits, are not the little punk failures that Synanon would like to believe all addicts are. Where the laws are tolerant, as in England, the *large majority* of addicts get along quite well in their jobs, in raising families and otherwise being respectable members of the community, etc.

This is a matter of proven fact, not opinion—and it's a fact

[6] Smoking "pot" (marijuana) is definitely illegal, and an offender can receive a stiff prison sentence for its use. More than that, as I have indicated, there is clear evidence that it makes the user vulnerable to the use of more addicting drugs, such as heroin.

that Synanon ducks. What Synanon idiotically refuses to accept is that if U.S. addicts could get their drugs without having to steal, go to jail, etc., most of the so-called "character disorders" would disappear overnight . . . perhaps the weakest part of Synanon's "anti-criminal" stance is the refusal to see any difference between law and justice, i.e., its easy assumption that because the individual conflicts with the law of his society re drugs, it's the individual who needs changing (brainwashing), not the law that should be changed.

Changing the laws to fit the needs of self-destructive behavior patterns seems patently absurd. The so-called British system, which permits medical doctors to give addicts drugs legally, is much more complex than described in the foregoing criticism. There is evidence (and I have corroborated this myself in a visit to London) that England has a more severe drug problem than the American "experts" who advocate free and legal drug use in the United States know about. (I personally and professionally feel that it is totally absurd to give an addict drugs. It's like giving a person dying of cancer more cancer!)

Synanon does not take a militant position about the so-called British system or the use of drugs for withdrawal in hospitals. However, within its framework, the rigid policy against drug and alcohol use has been developed on the basis of considerable sober thought. According to Dederich: "We do not have any dope problem in Synanon or any drinkers. We do not raise our eyebrows or judge others. Of course, we have our opinions. We don't think that the so-called British system would work in the U.S. I've read about its claims—and the contradictions in the British press of arrests for drug peddling. Recently, several Americans were arrested for controlling a large black-market drug-pushing business in London. We do not have the time to address ourselves to this paradox, since we are busy with our own work. The British system has no more to do with Synanon than Chrysler Motors. We can't really get involved with these other approaches. We're too busy strengthening and developing our own, which seems to be rather successful in controlling criminal and addictive behavior.

"In Synanon, we don't violate the law or use social lubricants, and we are opposed to this type of behavior. We are more square than our square friends. Perhaps we have to have a more rigid moral fiber than is believed to be necessary in the larger society."

The antiaddiction, anticriminal posture is crucial to the Synanon method. Although many members are past the need for this extreme attitude, it seems important to maintain the pressure in this direction for the sake of the newcomer, who is always looking for a chink in the armor. In spite of the sociologist-editor's beliefs and in spite of the opinions of some professional therapists who have failed, I still hold to the position that there is nothing wrong with *not* using alcohol, drugs, or other artificial stimulants or depressants. This Synanon position, which I share, seems to disturb many professionals who believe in giving addicts drugs.

"Mental Health"

An issue of disagreement between some professionals and Synanon is what constitutes "mental health." To many professionals, a true "cure" can be accomplished only by a "bona fide" professional therapist. Some professionals say that Synanon works "up to a point." When that "point" is reached, they contend, a "real professional" should be permitted to take over for a "real cure." One psychoanalyst friend of Synanon described it this way: "Synanon is fantastic in bringing the person to the level where he can be reached by psychoanalysis. Because of Synanon *we* [professionals] are now in a position to cure the addict."

This covert residual of resistance, even by enthusiastic pro-Synanon professionals, reflects a generally held belief that, in an "underground" way, blocks Synanon's forward thrust. In my view, on a deep level, many professionals and fund-granting agencies (government and private), and even some Synanon members, firmly accept this sneaky propaganda that "mental health" can result only from the aid the "patient" gets from "bona fide" professional agencies or people. This viewpoint is, I believe, one of the greatest and most persistent blocks to Synanon's acceptance and growth. It is the position that prods the more irrational professionals and lay citizens to attack Synanon.

Despite these overt and covert resistances, Synanon continues to produce, if not "bona fide, legal mental health," at least healthy behavior. Synanon maintains a relatively liberal view of what constitutes "mental health."

At Synanon, "mental health" (a term often facetiously used: "He thinks he has 'mental health'") is associated with rational behavior. Important among the characteristics of "mental health" is a high degree of predictable and consistent behavior. A basic specification for "mental health" in Synanon is a freedom from the use of alcohol and drugs. This abstinence is the starting point for the growth and development of Synanon people.

According to Chuck: "If one gives off an aura of enjoying life more than not and has the ability to do his job and conduct his human affairs rationally, we would say here he has 'mental health.'

"We don't subscribe to the idea, which I find so extant among professionals, that everyone is sick. They look at everyone in terms of his personality weakness. For example, they'll say, 'George X, the car dealer whom I met the other day—boy, is he crazy.'

"We would ask, 'Why is he crazy?'

" 'He plays golf every Sunday, he works five days a week, he has a family. . . .'

"There's too much of this 'sick' labeling in society. As far as some people are concerned, I'm considered a megalomaniacal nut; of course, this is true, but I'm not so crazy. I've helped make hundreds of people who formerly acted like nuts act quite rational, as human beings should. Synanon doesn't want to fall into this labeling trap. The professionals perpetuate this false notion. Synanon believes people are people. Some like to wear their hats sideways, or even their heads; but if they do their jobs and get along (even if their heads are on crooked), why does this make them sick?

"One of the forces at Synanon which helps our people's growth is that they are judged by their present behavior. They are appraised at Synanon by what they do now, not in the past. The upper half of Synanon people function as well as people in the larger society in the course of their work and relations with others.

"One can only speculate how this group would do in terms of 'mental health' outside of Synanon. We have some bellweathers, of course; there are currently over thirty of our people working and living outside and doing quite well."

One of the dimensions of the Synanon community that may foster "mental health" is its emphasis on cultural activities. There is an implicit encouragement to participate in a semantics class, a band, a dance class, or almost any other kind of cultural or intellectual activity. There is little boredom at Synanon, because of the variety of available "healthy" activities.

"Attack Therapy"

Some professionals who have been exposed to Synanon's "verbal-attack approach" to therapy find it highly unorthodox. Some consider it destructive; others, supporters, believe that it gets to levels of human problems that have not been reached by other approaches. A first encounter with Synanon's hard-hitting approach to therapy is often shocking. A close appraisal of the method reveals some sound underlying logic.

In a forthright statement on some aspects of this "hard line," Dederich commented: "Dope fiends shoot dope. As long as they are dope fiends, they are not much good; they are slobs and thieves, with the temperaments of nasty little children. When they stop using dope, they're something else again. They need self-respect and then general respect more than they do sympathy.

"This will send them running for a fix. Too much laxness with them—particularly in the early stages—makes them take their adjustment problems too lightly. At Synanon, we may seem rough on the newcomer at times, but we have to be their guts, until they develop guts for themselves."

Synanon sessions and verbal "haircuts" are powerful forms of attack therapy. During my first synanon session (even though I had been exposed to fourteen previous years of work in group psychotherapy), I too was shocked by the brutal treatment of individuals when they were placed on the "hot seat." (The "hot seat" consists in the entire group's vicious cross-examination of a person's behavior. He has to defend himself, since no one else will. In the process, his negative behavior is exaggerated, caricatured, and ridiculed. It seems as if his self is being psychologically damaged.)

My first reaction to the rugged synanon was to conclude that the attackers were after "blood" and that somehow this "fixed" their own emotional, sadistic needs. I also feared for the victim of the mob. I could see some of the therapeutic rationale for attacking "bad behavior"; but at that time, I felt that the group was "rat-packing" a "victim" and was going too far.

However, on the basis of my participation in about a hundred synanon sessions and "haircuts," I have revised my early personal opinions about what some professionals have labeled "verbal brutality." [7] (I personally was a "victim" and target in about a dozen sessions.) My recognition of the validity of "attack therapy" was gradual. At first, it surprised me tremendously, after a rough session, to see two or more "bitter enemies" come out of the session laughing about their synanon experience and discussing it in a friendly, jovial manner. After one session that I attended, I remember an individual who had been on the "hot seat" (accused of "goofing off" on his job) telling his antagonist later, "You son-of-a-bitch, you really exaggerated my work out of sight—I did most of that work. . . ." The former antagonist, now friend, said, "What did you expect? We were in a synanon."

I began to learn the rules of the synanon game and that almost any kind of verbal tactic is legitimate if it helps a person to look at his behavioral soft spots. The issue of how far one goes in a session is not precisely spelled out. It varies with the person involved, the time, and place. An old-timer in the Synanon de-

---

[7] It is important to point out that by no means do all professional therapists oppose the attack kind of therapy. My colleague Dr. George Bach, who works with more middle- and upper-class patients, has recently concluded, on the basis of twenty years' practice, that the attack form of therapy is functional and effective. He has developed a training center for "constructive marital fighting." He more fully describes the process in a forthcoming book called *Intimate Enemies*. Bach's method is also the subject of an article entitled "The Marital Fight Game," *Life* magazine, May 17, 1963.

scribed it this way: "I've known Chuck to give people haircuts for giving haircuts and not knowing when to knock off. Chuck can make a man literally climb walls, but he will never push him over the edge. I mean, Chuck somehow has the sense of timing or understanding or feeling—whatever it is—that all of us needed to be pushed up against the wall when we came here. We needed to be pushed hard and have our thinking turned around. Chuck somehow has the exquisite sense of knowing just how hard to go, when to quit, and, of course, to pick up a man after he's run the man up against a wall. He doesn't leave him depressed after a haircut—he'll give him something to pick himself up with."

The "pickup" after a man has been verbally attacked is crucial to the method. I have observed that this invariably occurs at some point. More often than not, it doesn't occur in the same session in which the person was pushed hard to "examine himself." The "pickup" may occur right after the session, over coffee; or the victim of a verbal attack may be "fixed" by a compliment at a time when he least expects it. The approval or compliment is given at a time of maximum effectiveness.

Dederich looks at attack therapy as a necessary approach in Synanon: "Of course, some synanons are brutal. So is surgery or amputation. The process of cutting out an emotional element which might turn into a deadly gangrene tends to be brutal."

In synanons, I have noted that each member, almost in turn, takes the hot-seat position and gives the group the right to hack at his disability. The underlying assumption seems to be, "If I'm strong in that emotional area, no screaming at me can hurt; and if I am supersensitive, then, good—point it out. I better examine what you say, even if you grossly exaggerate the problem."

Some people would, not too surreptitiously, draw the group's verbal fire because they wanted and needed attention. For example, El Gato would use his Mexican-style moustache to draw critical attention to himself. The moustache seemed to grow in proportion to his need for help. Another individual would bring up a personal problem he had that he knew would attract the group's attention. As the Greek put it to one member, "You like to be hollered at, don't you? I guess it makes you feel good to know someone cares."

After my first twenty-five sessions, I began to feel that, in many respects, the synanon "attack" was an act of love. Entwined in an attack was the assumption: "If we did not care about you or have concern for you, we would not bother to point out something that might reduce your psychic pain or clarify something for you that might save your life." In this context, the verbal "attack" seems to be an expression of great sympathy.

Since Synanon does not permit the use of chemicals or violence, the participants in verbal-attack therapy have to confront their problems in the "raw." They cannot threaten another person, even if he is physically inferior, to "lay off" or else face the consequences of physical retaliation. (In contrast, violence is one of the problems in much professional prison group therapy.) Nor can they avoid the impact of what is being said by making use of the sedative qualities or escape qualities of alcohol or drugs. Brutal truth is the keynote, and it must be candidly faced and examined.

In this manner, people who formerly used violence and drugs to "protect" themselves are thrown onto their verbal resources for relating to others. They learn to interact with words. This facilitates their ability to communicate through this mode of expression rather than with their fists or other possible "weaponry." [8]

The power of the individual's attack in a synanon appears to be correlated with the emotional strength of the attacker and his position in the Synanon hierarchy. Old-timers in Synanon have developed more powerful verbal weapons and speak from a more powerful status position in the hierarchy. Their sword has a sharper edge; but at the same time, they have learned to level their attack with more precision. They direct their attack at the person's problems rather than his "self," and seem to know when to pick him up again. (Moreover, they are less apt to be doing it out of their own need to attack another person.)

One of my conclusions about synanon attack therapy is that a skillful Synanist batters the individual's emotional flab rather

[8] These rules would provide a set of interesting conditions for international relations. If, in fact, physical violence was banned, verbal battle might become as "brutal" and sharp as that in synanons. (In some measure, the so-called cold war and the existence of the means of total destruction has set up these conditions.)

than his "self." The newcomer is much like a ten-year-old with twenty-three-ounce padded boxing gloves. He can't hit too hard or hurt too much. The older members have eight-ounce gloves and seem to know when and where to hit at the person's hypocrisy, emotional blindness, and problems.

As Dederich put it: "There is much truth in the child's 'sticks-and-stones' poem, which ends 'but words can never harm me.' Of course, words can hurt—but so can the set of delusions a person carries around with him that formerly required drugs to control."

The question of whether verbal attack is valid is confirmed, according to Chuck, by Synanon's positive experience: "Look at our record. What appeared to be a grand slide toward self-destruction for many people with the terminal disease of drug addiction has been halted. We stepped in and diverted it by using this method, among others."

In response to the accusation that there is a "sadistic gratification" for the purveyor of "loving brute force," Dederich commented: "I guess you just have to believe me when I say my motivations are pure. When I attack, I can't prove I'm immune to sadistic satisfaction. In the early days, I was probably less immune than I am now. I can tell you this—I don't particularly enjoy having to give anyone a haircut. It's hard work." This viewpoint corresponds with that of other older members of Synanon.

Part of the rationale for attack therapy is that the recipient doesn't "hear properly" in areas in which he is emotionally blocked. In fact, in sessions that I have been in, the group often gets a good laugh because a problem that has been pointed out several times to someone is often *literally* not heard. "Attack," in a sense, is a misnomer, even though it appears to be "attack" to the untrained eye. It is more accurate to view the "attack" as an effort to communicate some information useful to the person, information that he appears to have an emotional block to hearing. Consequently, ridicule, caricature, exaggeration, analogy, repetition, and other devices are used. The volume of the attempt to communicate is turned up high (almost to the point of screaming) at times and down low (when the person is apparently "rationally" listening to the group's opinions) at other times.

In some cases, what has become known in Synanon as the

"carom shot" is used in a synanon. This involves telling person A what you also want person B or C to hear and learn. In the middle of delivery, a comment may be made to emphasize the point ("Do you hear what is being said to Joe, Jack?"). In fact, many people appear to have obtained therapy in synanons from listening closely to what another person is receiving. And at times, a person who is "screaming" at another is also talking to himself.

The use of ridicule and exaggeration in synanon sessions appears to be an important tool in the system. The rationale for using ridicule, which also appears brutal at first glance, is that "ridiculous behavior deserves to be ridiculed." Behavior (*not* the "self"!) is examined, and if it is ridiculous, the person is ridiculed. He is often laughed at by the group for certain acts. When he begins to laugh with the group at himself, he is considered to be on the road to recovery. In Dederich's view, exaggeration is a way of holding "magnifying glasses up to the person's behavior so that he can look at himself more clearly."

Some different viewpoints on the drug-addiction sympton serve to highlight Synanon's approach to ridicule. On the one hand, the professional and public view of addiction is that it is a serious and disturbing symptom formation. And, of course, this is true. Most intelligent people have a sympathy for the victim and a compassion for his painful plight.

Synanon people deeply share this sympathetic viewpoint. However, they are convinced that this kind of commiseration or sympathy does the addict no good. In fact, it often backfires, reinforcing self-pity and continued drug use. At Synanon, they reverse the field and take this posture (which at first glance may seem cold and unfeeling):

"You stupid slob—you've run yourself into the ground by your behavior. Your tough-guy–dope-fiend style keeps getting you dropped off in a cage. You're not really bad; you're just stupid and ridiculous. Look at how ridiculous you are: like a rat, you ran up and down alleys stealing; you buy some white powder, and then you jam a needle with some fluid in your arm, conk out, and go back for more. Of course, you are killing yourself. You will either die by being locked up for life or die from an overdose in a back alley. Your *behavior* is ridiculous!" (Thirteen addicts died from an overdose of heroin in Los Angeles in the summer of 1964!)

This is cold, hard talk—on the surface, lacking in sympathy; yet in a definite way, it is realistic. More than that, it doesn't support the old pattern, which considerable unrealistic affection apparently does. The proof is that the standard, generally sympathetic counseling approach has not done the job that Synanon has accomplished with its attack therapy. Love, affection, and involvement are also certainly practiced in the organization, but these approaches have to be assessed in Synanon as they are used in conjunction with the (seemingly) tough approach. The combination of tough and soft—in proper proportion, at the right time— seems to do the job.

ONE PROFESSIONAL VIEW OF "ATTACK THERAPY"

Despite the apparent success of Synanon's "attack therapy," it is negatively evaluated by many professionals as a "destructive approach to human behavior." An interesting vignette related by Reid Kimball reveals the paradox of professional resistance to "attack therapy":

"In one synanon session, we had with us a visiting clinical psychologist—a Dr. Gold—a Governor's man (evaluating Synanon), and several parole officials. This visiting group had expressed a great interest in being in a regular synanon session. They agreed, in front, that they would participate like anyone else. We happened to have some of our toughest guys in that particular synanon. In the group, among others, were myself, with eighteen years of addiction behind me, before Synanon; George the Turk, with fourteen years behind him; Phil Hunt, with twelve years; and Jack Hurst, with nine years of past addiction. I think Charlie Hamer and Jesse Pratt were also in the session.

"We had a rugged attack-type synanon, but a usual one. All of the Synanon people went at each other, but we also went after the visitors. We attacked the Governor's man for not doing his work in evaluating Synanon. We could never get to talk to him about Synanon, because he was too busy chasing one of our broads around the building. We went at the psychologist, and one of the parole officers was even attacked.

"But here's the point. At the end of the session, the psychologist made the flat statement that this was the most 'destructive approach to human behavior' he had ever witnessed in his twenty years of practice. I said, 'But we're all clean, and nothing else has worked.' He stuck to his guns. This man, whom I liked, who is probably intelligent in all other areas of life, could not see any *non sequitur* in his thinking!

"Now, dig this. The event I described occurred back in 1960. When Chuck and I attended this gathering of drug-addict experts at the U.C.L.A. conference in 1963, I ran into the same psychologist, Dr. Gold. I put him on. I said, 'You remember George the Turk, Jack Hurst, Jesse Pratt, Phil Hunt, and, of course, myself? You know, we are *all* still clean. Do you still think this is the most destructive therapy you've ever witnessed?' You know, his answer was still yes!"

Professional Therapy and Synanon

Many professionals become interested in Synanon and visit for the purpose of adapting some of Synanon's methodology to other therapeutic settings. Synanon has developed some treatment approaches, especially the small-"s" synanon, which seem to be transferable. However, Dederich believes that the utilization of Synanon's methods in another setting tends to fragment the approach and renders it less effective. More than that, it is his view that Synanon has very little to do with the standard professional schools.

"We have no argument whatsoever with the professional fraternity doing whatever they do," he said. "It's none of our business, really. However, we do not want them interfering with our business. When they attack what we do, of course, we become defensive and in some cases have to institute a counteroffensive. We do not want or need interference from professionals.

"Some pros have been most valuable to Synanon, and this seems to be in direct proportion to their ability to relate on a human level first and on a professional level secondly. After a professional finds out what we're up to, he can then offer us some help from his trade.

"We ourselves have been guilty, along with professionals, in thinking that Synanon had more of a connection with the professional—sociologists, psychiatrists, and so on—than with real-estate people, lawyers, bakers or truckers. This isn't true. Our needs are even more in these other areas. For example, we have more problems with real estate than with the 'head business.'

"We ourselves made the mistake of thinking of Synanon as therapy rather than education. We are more of an educational enterprise than a therapeutic one, more of a learning process than a therapeutic process. We don't presuppose sickness as much as we presume stupidity. We say, 'If you weren't so dumb, you wouldn't be in jail all the time. The hell with your being sick.' Our starting point is not a hospital but rather a school. We currently have several hundred Synanon graduates, and we plan to graduate several hundred more.

"Synanon has run head on into several professional systems. Some have helped, others have opposed. One thorn of opposition has been the California Department of Corrections. They pulled seven parolees, Synanon residents who were staying clean and doing well in the program, out of the building. With one exception, Ted, who returned to Synanon after his parole hold was over, they are either in jail or using, and Ted's girl friend died of an overdose of drugs."

Dederich believes that the negative feelings about Synanon projected by some professionals and some professional bodies are manifestations of their fear of losing their vested interest in the *status quo*: "I think it's mainly subliminal. We don't really constitute a threat to the California Department of Corrections, even though their efforts to smash us reveal that they seem to think so.

"We keep plugging away at our work, which seems to be hailed by many as a breakthrough. Yet, there is a cultural lag of recognition in certain quarters, particularly from the professionals. We've had all sorts of National Institute of Mental Health people and pros come through here, but nothing comes of it. We keep getting turned down on our requests for funds, even though we submit well-developed plans, in the form they seem to want them. Senator Dodd recommended that we receive federal help over a year ago, but nothing has happened.

"The California Department of Corrections, we know, tries to stop our natural growth. They have sidled up to judges and other people who want to help us in San Francisco and bluntly told them to back off. We just want these public servants to stop interfering with our business."

My own observations support Dederich's conclusions. There is no reason for the California Department of Corrections to impede the progress of Synanon, other than a subliminal resistance. The state of Nevada, in contrast, has legislated funds ($24,000 for two years) for Synanon work in their prison. The program appears to have all the earmarks of success.

Even some professionals who are friends of Synanon and think they know better often tend to distort the picture. They perceive Synanon from their own limited viewpoint. The psychiatrists see a psychiatric process; the correctional people see a "halfway house"; the psychologists, depending on their school, a therapeutic process. The "friendly" professionals tend first to heap praise on the organization and then to conclude that Synanon has inadvertently stumbled upon their magic professional secret. One very friendly, enthusiastic psychiatrist, after a two-week visit, concluded that Synanon had inadvertently developed an extension of Freudian psychoanalysis: "Many of your people are now ready for the ["true," "bona fide," "legal"] therapeutic experience of psychoanalysis," he gleefully announced and then went on to publish his "discovery."

In another case, a prominent sociologist, wedded to a learning theory of crime causation, coauthored an article that ignored most of the Synanon process. The article essentially attempted to prove that Synanon had "unwittingly" implemented the theory he supported.

(A younger sociologist published an article in an important criminology journal in which he attempted to prove that Synanon made people dependent and was not applicable to treating criminals other than addicts. He had never visited a Synanon House or the Nevada State Prison project!)

In the meantime, Chuck Dederich watches with some amusement (and, occasionally, chagrin) the varieties of professional response. As indicated, there are two dominant professional responses. One is the attack on a methodology that appears to be, by its sheer existence, a threat to the *status quo* and vested interest.

The other is the "friendly" professional's ploy, which is to be extremely laudatory, even indicate that it is some kind of break-through—but one that is, "of course," within the framework of his professional school.

Neither professional response honestly gives Synanon its proper due: the recognition that Synanon, as created by Dederich and his able assistants, is a *new* methodology and social structure, administered by a *new* breed of professional people. An attempt to jam Synanon into other molds clouds the issue and produces false appraisals.

"A Lesson from History": The Imitators

A professional problem that looms large on the Synanon horizon is the potential threat of a peculiar brand of professional take-over and neutralization of Synanon. Walker Winslow lived in Synanon for a year and is eminently qualified to relate Synanon to the larger "mental-health" movement. Winslow is author of *The Menninger Story* and *If a Man Be Mad* and has been an observer and practitioner in the field of psychotherapy for more than twenty years. He has witnessed the historical development of the "mental-health" movement in the United States from several points of view. He was at one time a patient and later became an important lay therapist at the Menninger Foundation.

His incisive observations on a complex bureaucratic professional pattern were presented in a special Synanon issue by the publishers of the journal *Manas* (1963).[9] In Walker's article "A Lesson from History," he predicted one of the "professional problems" that currently confronts the Synanon movement.

> Sooner or later in the life of any new and advancing organization some "authority" studiously dusts off a tired cliché and announces that it has "reached the crossroads." Usually this prefaces a suggestion that the time has come to embrace

[9] I am deeply grateful to Walker Winslow and also to Henry Geiger, the editor and publisher of *Manas*, for permission to use this excerpt from Winslow's insightful article.

some sort of institutional respectabiliy that can only be reached through accredited conformity. Such a day will come for Synanon Foundation, if it has not come already. At such a point it is to be expected that the status- and degree-seekers, bureaucrats who have piloted the failures in the same field, foundation men, representatives of project-hungry seats of learning, and the like, will be invited to crawl on board. Such crossroads are in fact but loading terminals for people who can bring in some money and status, or the promise of it, in exchange for an authority they can earn in no other way.

I don't think that anyone needs to warn Charles E. Dederich, the founder of Synanon, of this possibility. He was born with a good, healthy *no* in his throat and has anticipated such an event from the night he held his first tentative synanon meeting. He has been helped, figuratively and actually, by the fact that the uniqueness of Synanon has been such as to place it in uncharted territory where there literally can be no crossroads. Such is the wilderness into which the route of Synanon led that it had to spend its first three years fighting a legal battle for survival while at the same time moving forward to the point of recognition. Legalistic aborigines didn't deter Synanon's progress, and by single-minded dedication and quiet demonstration of worth it has now won the assistance of the legally sophisticated and more humanistic group in repelling the earlier sort of war parties that were out to take scalps at any cost.

As the result of its success in really doing somehing for and with drug addicts, Synanon already has various imitators, and in the future will have many more. This imitation is a form of flattery that Synanon, and the drug addicts it can help, can well do without. It is the beginning of the adulteration of an idea and one that even friends of Synanon can unthinkingly accept as a victory of some sort or the other. When the state, for example, announces that it is opening houses where addicts can live together and help each other, it is too easy for the uninitiated to think that here is the Synanon idea spreading out effectively under auspices that should make for even greater success. Few will recognize the great possibility that such places will be run and dominated by the same people who failed so dismally with addicts in the past and that these new houses, under whatever name, are a means of perpetuating a bureaucratic and emotional investment in drug addiction. Even if good intentions are granted, the methods of application will drag in archaic survivals of the old punitive controls. *The greater menace is that these places, as they spread and get publicity in indirectly borrowing Synanon's reputation for success, can divert support from the genuine Synanon Houses and thus isolate and circumscribe the great work that Synanon has just begun.* [My emphasis.]

The history of mental health has an analogy for the dilemma which will confront Synanon more and more. Well over a hundred years ago, a schoolteacher, Dorothea Lynde Dix, happened to visit some of the jails and alms houses in which the mentally ill were kept in chains, often without heat, fed like hogs, and tormented by bored and sadistic keepers. When people higher up in the community were told about this they often righteously inferred that there was something morally wrong with anyone who went crazy and fell back on some variation of "Once a nut, always a nut," repeating it in the same singsong cadence heard from their equivalents of a century later, who say, "Once an addict, always an addict." This cultivated ignorance has remained operative for nearly 110 years.

However, Miss Dix, like Dederich, decided that there was something she could do about the situation. Her demand was for hospitals for the mentally ill where they could be accepted and treated as the sick people they were. Suddenly this woman became a force such as this nation or any other rarely encounters. She was seen anywhere and everywhere, taking in England as well as the United States. She was fearless and she knew how to apply pressure where it was needed. Ruthlessly, she exposed those who were torturing the sick in mind. Where she could, she proved that understanding, acceptance, and kindness would work where chains and lashes wouldn't. Certain of the New England states saw the light and built hospitals, some which are famous today. . . .

But while Miss Dix was crusading, reputations for humanitarianism were being harvested by the administrators, doctors, and politicians who had climbed on her bandwagon—even as it passed its "crossroads" and the climax of her effort was being vetoed. Long before the sign "Hospital" over the gates of the mental health institutions had taken on a patina, the wardens and keepers from the jails and alms houses were in charge. As citizens drove by, pulsing with the warm virtue of having done good, patients in chains were being fed slop and were beaten in a setting that gave their tormentors a protection they had never had before. Moreover, the public had purged its conscience and didn't want to be bothered again. For all Miss Dix's dedication and high intentions, her eager "helpers" and sponsors may have set the treatment of mental illness back for nearly a hundred years.

Synanon and Chuck Dederich are determined not to be caught in the trap that snared the first hospitals for the mentally ill and Miss Dix. However, a knowledge of what has happened in the mental field in the past may help the friends of Synanon and all who are sympathetic to the movement to understand why at times Synanon has seemed grossly egocentric in its insistence that it *go its own way*, even to the extent of spurning apparently friendly offers from institutions, agencies, and individuals. Its destiny has to be its own, and unadulterated. Another point is that practically no one can come to Synanon with experience in the field of drug addiction and really offer its people anything. A history of failure is all such visitors have to offer and unless they are addicts Synanon has nothing it can honestly offer them. Only research that in no way interferes with the Synanon process can be condoned, and only for the purpose of furthering the work of Synanon. In any case, the spirit of Synanon defies analysis. Help given on faith —goods, services, and money—is all Synanon really needs anyway. That and friendship that will assert itself whenever the peculiar integrity of Synanon is threatened. Synanon itself gives lavishly. Visit the house or go to a Saturday night get-together and see how much you take away with you. You might even wistfully think that you would have been fortunate to have been an addict. The individuals you meet will be as unique as the organization that gave them back their lives.

The imitations of Synanon that spring up, leaning heavily on Synanon's success and at the same time bathed in an aura of institutionalized respectability, are not a threat to Synanon but only to the addicts it could genuinely help. How easy it is for what appears to be a house with an open door to become a psychological prison where the aim is serving out parole or evading an outright commitment. The open door can very well be an entrance to prison for parole violation. Almost certainly, the supervisors will be those who have failed with addicts before.

I'm speaking of possibilities and probabilities, not indicting any present institution. My experience in the mental health field has taught me the hard way just how difficult it is for the old masters of failure, window-dressing and deceit to let go, and that they will make any compromise in order to retain their positions. To let go is an admission of failure. For the penal-minded, it would even be an admission of failure to admit that a drug addict can get well and stay well.

The attempt to destroy Synanon has pretty well passed. The thing to watch for now is the "If you can't lick them, join them" phase. It is during this period that the strength of Synanon can become most apparent. There is nothing on earth less susceptible to fakery than the Synanon principles. The imitators' great mistake will be in forgetting that comparisons can be made from day to day, without waiting a hundred years.

Nevertheless, it will do no harm for students and friends of Synanon to be aware of some of the factors involved in the next stage of the game. There is a chance to chuckle with Chuck as you observe that history need not repeat itself. I doubt that Chuck Dederich himself could imitate Synanon, if he were starting over again, and I think he would agree with me.

Some of the problems that Winslow predicted have already taken place.

The public's confusion about "Synanon-style" programs was partially revealed in a comment by one of my students. He was aware of my great interest in Synanon and approached me after class one day with the following remark: "Professor Yablonsky, have you seen the good news in the newspaper. The state and the federal government have finally approved Synanon!" The student was referring to an article on the Governor's approval of a new California State Department of Parole "halfway house" and prison program for addicts. Here a bright young man, better informed than the average person, was deceived by bureaucratic camouflage. The deception is a tragic game that in some cases costs lives. Walker Winslow saw the problem clearly: "The imitators of Synanon that spring up, leaning heavily on Synanon's success and at the same time bathed in an aura of institutionalized respectability, are not a threat to Synanon but only to the addicts it could genuinely help."

At the same time that this student mistakenly believed that Synanon was being accepted by the state, its Department of Parole was enforcing its policy of barring parolees from entering Synanon.

As Winslow so clearly pointed out, the major menace that the "imitators" pose for Synanon is that "as they spread and get publicity in indirectly borrowing Synanon's reputation for success, [they] can divert support from the genuine Synanon Houses . . ."—the same community understanding and support that Synanon needs for its development and very existence.

An example of this problem is illustrated by the following: Personnel from an East Coast probation department visited Synanon. One of these people, the chief of probation, became enthusiastic and his Department applied for a "Synanon-style" demonstration program grant from the federal government. (Their limited knowledge about Synanon came from several short visits.) The National Institute of Mental Health accepted their "bureaucratically kosher" proposal and granted $390,000 for the implementation of a "Synanon-style" probation program.

The program began about a year ago and, as might be expected, has shown signs of imminent failure. Walker Winslow anticipated the reason for its potential failure: ". . . such places will be run and dominated by the same people who failed so dismally with addicts in the past and . . . these new houses, under whatever name, are a means of perpetuating a bureaucratic and emotional investment in drug addiction."

The capper to this bureaucratic tale is that the grant application of the genuine *product*, Synanon, was *rejected* by the same bureaucrats in the National Institute of Mental Health! (I am familiar with this bitter paradox firsthand, since I helped to draw up Synanon's application for funds.) In spite of this bureaucratic hyprocrisy, Synanon, with no government support in the year 1963, *successfully* treated more than 150 addicts (mostly from the East Coast). In this same period of time, the "government-approved" project, the pseudo-"Synanon-style" program, according to several reports, has failed with about twenty addicts!

This case sheds some light on some old and new wrinkles of bureaucracy. Why should a bureaucratic structure like the N.I.M.H. grant funds to a *potential imitation* instead of to the genuine, already proven product? One possible answer to this question is that the bureaucratic mind, by definition, is more interested in *form* than *results*. *The real Synanon was implicitly "punished" because it did not fill out its application forms as well as the potential imitation.*

The fact that the genuine Synanon organization knew less about properly filling out forms than about treating addicts was apparently of crucial significance to the bureaucratic decision-makers.[10]

Synanon, although it keeps some minimal records on its people, will never be as "good" as the traditional agencies and institutions at filling out forms. Nor will they permit their "addicts" to be shot with drugs, which happens at Lexington and in the California State Department of Parole Nalline test.[11]

Chuck and the other administrators of Synanon also reject the "urine test" of addiction. (This is part of the East Coast

[10] The East Coast probation department, which was an admitted failure in the treatment of addicts, seemed to know intuitively the right "buttons to push," and more important to the bureaucratic game, they knew how to fill out the forms properly. Since they were themselves a bureaucracy, they naturally knew how to successfully carry out this procedure. This simple episode highlights an important sociological hypothesis that deserves further investigation: *bureaucracy begets bureaucracy and feeds upon itself.*

[11] The California State Department of Parole uses a Nalline test as a deterrent to recidivism. This involves injecting a paroled addict with a drug to test whether or not he is addicted to drugs! (Many addicts have told me that Nalline gives them a real "fix.")

probation department's method of checking whether someone is using drugs.)[12] Synanon, in fact, eschews most of the bureaucratic tests of respectability and validity. All that Synanon seems to know how to do is get addicts off drugs and then get them involved in a more constructive way of life. I do not believe Chuck Dederich will permit Synanon to become "bureaucratically kosher." If Synanon reached that state of being, it would probably fail as miserably as its imitators.

Professional Evaluations

Many professionals have taken a "wait-and-see" attitude about Synanon. For them, it is "an interesting experiment, but nothing has been proven until adequate statistical measurement has been applied." The fact that there are hundreds of "clean" addicts in Synanon, who repeatedly failed in other settings, does not seem to alter the position of these professionals. For these "social scientists," Synanon has not proven itself until it has been rigorously subjected to and validated by the standardized tests and measurements applied to the prisons, hospitals and other systems of admitted failure.

It may very well be that it is precisely the "scientific research" demanded that is a major hindrance to treatment success in other programs. Running addicts through professional mazes, measuring their heads and their I.Q.'s, and testing their urine may very well be the methods that impede therapy. I do not share the extreme position taken by some Synanon members that "research kills," but I do believe that the professionals who have failed ought to respect and listen to the voice of success.

The kind of "rigorous scientific evaluation" demanded by some professionals could possibly ruin Synanon, at this time. One of the reasons Synanon works is that the people are treated like *people* and not like inmates. Another is that "professional probing" (I can't forget the "Yablonsky effect") could be especially harmful to delicately balanced "newcomers," who might run out the open

12 A financial appropriation for testing the addict's urine is part of the N.I.M.H. grant of $390,000 to the Eastern project.

door and shoot dope. According to Dederich: "In the early days when we let visiting professionals loose on our addicts, somehow we would lose many of our people. They would run out the door. We're not sure of why, but that's what happened."

Another factor that would tend to invalidate standard research practice for Synanon is that unless the researcher understood the *new* social organization called Synanon, he would be inclined to project onto it concepts that apply to the traditional institutions. Since Synanon is not a prison, a "halfway house," a hospital, or A.A., it would be inappropriate to evaluate it by many of the traditional research methods.

The standard evaluations relate more appropriately to the type of institution in which a "ward" of the state goes through a painful process of involuntary incarceration (as in a hospital or prison) and then attempts to succeed outside the walls. The usual chain of events involves getting "into" the ward, "cured," and then "out" of this abnormal (homosexual) life situation. In contrast, life in Synanon is pleasant (involving many aspects of "club" living), and there is no great impatience to leave this situation and return to the same environment that originally produced the problem.

Although some Synanon "graduates" return to the "open community," many others (more than half at this time) continue to work as "professional Synanists." They like the work and seem to want to repay the organization that "saved their lives." Even after "graduation," they may choose to stay on the Synanon "faculty."

Because of some of these issues the problem of counting a "cure" is complicated if we use standard professional criteria. In professional terms, even if the individual has been "clean" one, five, or ten years, it could be argued that he has not been "cured" until he has left the institution in question. Since Synanon is not an institution but a way of life, there is no special pressure to leave, and this makes the standard professional concept of "leaving the institution and not becoming a recidivist" an inappropriate measurement of success.

Another possible danger in using standard methods of research on Synanon is that the approach could conceivably impair the aura of positive expectation and success that surrounds Synanon.

(Recent research into therapeutic success has revealed that an important element in "mental-health cure" is a *strong belief, at the outset, that the method will work*.) The image of Synanon as a hopeful organization contrasts sharply with the "hope-to-die addict's"[13] pessimistic opinion of various hospitals and jails. The Synanist looks upon these other institutions as failures, "in front." (In fact, he probably failed in one or more himself.)

Chuck has concluded that: "addicts are emotional children who won't gamble. Addicts, like children, want a sure thing. Let us assume that at Synanon there is a 60 percent chance of success. Better than half of those who come to Synanon will never use drugs again. Some addicts will seize immediately on the 40 percent failure rate and use it as a rationalization for continuing their use of drugs. They would say, 'I'd be among the losers.' As of now, the percentage of people who come here and of those who remain is not published. I have the data, but I won't release them to general public attention. It might present a rationalization for some newly arrived addicts and might interfere with their potential success in Synanon. Our batting average for success with the people who come here has climbed progressively each year we've been in business. Our holding power has gone up! I'm not going to mess with this delicate instrument—it works.

"Perhaps the reason why Lexington and other similar institutions fail—with, as I understand it, a 95 percent recidivism rate— is that the addict goes there essentially to clean up. He does not believe he will fully quit using drugs as a result of the treatment. Many addicts who have been to Lexington or to Fort Worth [Federal Hospital] tell me the professional therapists tell them, in front, that they are incurable.[14] Synanon, however, has set a tone of success, which is part of our method. Along with this, we have, of course, been modestly effective in producing clean-man days—our measure of success.

"There is a vast national drug-addiction problem. Let us assume that the fifty- to sixty-thousand figure on the number of

[13] The phrase "hope-to-die addict" is used by many addicts to signify their belief that there is no cure and that "once an addict, always an addict."

[14] Almost all (more than 90 percent) Synanon residents have attempted to quit using drugs in other settings—voluntarily and involuntarily.

addicts, according to the Federal Bureau of Narcotics, is somewhat accurate, although I believe it is a minimal figure. Our goal is to remove as many using addicts from drugs as possible. If there is an epidemic of drug addiction, we try to operate as a counter-epidemic force.

"Every addict not using drugs each day he is affiliated with Synanon represents one clean-man-day unit. If these clean-man days build up in one individual, this is fine; however, our goal as an organization is as many total clean-man days as possible. Right now [June, 1964], we are achieving well over four hundred clean-man days each day. In another ten years, I predict we will be producing thousands of clean-man days each day. The more clean-man days we achieve in Synanon, the greater our counterepidemic force. This approach also reduces the contagious spread of the drug-addiction epidemic.

"If an addict uses on the average of $25 a day for his habit, keeping him clean in Synanon saves the community at least this amount each day, which he would almost necessarily steal. [The addict usually has to steal about $100 worth of merchandise to realize $25.] Using the four hundred figure as a base, keeping this many addicts clean each day in Synanon, as we do, saves society at least $10,000 each day, or around $3,500,000 per year." [Addicts do not take "vacations" from drug use except when they go to prison and become financial wards of the state.]

Chuck sees Synanon as an enterprise with its roots in the community. He believes that the average citizen has a clearer image of what Synanon is and does than the professional. The layman's vision is not complicated by "unwieldy jargon and methodology." Chuck considers the community's dominant response to Synanon, as reflected in concrete moral and material support, a better "evaluation" of Synanon than the complicated pronouncements of the professional.

"People like what we do. Last year [1963] they gave us a million dollars. Two hundred thousand of this figure was in cash donations, and the rest was in goods and services. Our donors include citizens from all socioeconomic classes. We have received donations ranging from several dollars to a few large contributions in the thousands.

"Izzy Cohen, who comes down with his family every so often, is a baker. He provides us with hundreds of dollars' worth of bread and cakes each month, and he's been doing this for several years. One of our members, Ron Pacifici, has a father in the trucking business. His father, Jack Pacifici, channels large amounts of dairy products into our organization. We have several new sets of choppers [teeth] around here thanks to some dentists who like our work. I suppose these people do this because they like what they see.

"You don't have to show Jack Roberts the results of a Rorschach or a psychiatric test to prove to him that Synanon works. Jack is in the advertising business and has given Synanon materials and knowledge of inestimable value to our public-relations work. He does this in addition to giving us money out of his own pocket. Jack sees a sick, skinny kid come in our door running from all orifices. Six months later, he sees this same kid running an office or a service crew. Two years later, this young fellow is running one of our houses or working outside. The average intelligent citizen, like Jack, can see this clearly. He likes what he sees and supports us to do more of the same."

The Professional Bias

Synanon seems to go against the grain of many prejudiced members of the community, who have an aversion to ex-criminal-addicts and interracial living. On another more complex level, the prejudgments of many professionals (both friend and foe) reflect another problem with which Synanon must cope. First, Synanon finds itself in the necessary position of proving to the professional community that a therapy "of, by, and for" the people works. This must be done despite the fact that there is already ample evidence (five hundred people) that Synanon *does* work.

Another attitude that Synanon has to battle repeatedly (especially with Synanon's professional friends) is the illusion the professionals have about Synanon's "fit" into their pet theory or institutional image. They refuse to accept the organization on its own terms; as a unique therapeutic system. The clamor of many professionals for more "scientific proof" when there is an obvious prima facie case of hundreds of ex-criminal-addicts who are now leading productive lives, is a smoke screen for a more subtle form of bias. I believe that the most important element of professional resistance to Synanon is the widely held belief that the professional superstructure is the only feasible one for the "bona fide," or "legitimate," treatment of emotional problems. The professional, the average layman, and even the "patients" have been convinced on a deep emotional level that only the properly schooled *professional* is qualified to understand and help people.[15]

The lack of proper recognition of Synanon is tied in with the controversy over the professional therapist's acceptability and respectability.[16] Synanon has the audacity to proclaim, by its sheer existence, that the "patients" can do the job themselves! This may be a new therapeutic revolution. It is to be expected that professionals, especially the conservative wing, will increasingly attempt to put this "uprising" down. Among other reasons, their fear may be related to a financial threat. This fear (already registered by some professionals) is, of course, absurd, since the increasing complexity of our world and social problems demands increased help from all quarters—professional therapists included. The only fall professionals may take by the ascendancy of the people's therapy role is one in status. The professional therapist (with the psychiatrist at the apex) may find the Synanon revolt of several hundred former "patients" most distressing, because it is possible that eventually many patients may be regarded as his therapeutic equal.

[15] One error in the logic of a devout belief in professionalism is a subtle one. In the process of selling the field of increased psychological knowledge about human behavior, the purveyors of this new understanding of psychodynamics imply that they are the only ones qualified to deal with the emotional problems encountered in this sphere. I buy one, but not the other. I accept the new insights into human behavior, provided by Freud and the many who have followed him, but not the second element of the package: that the new "priests" are the only ones qualified to treat the problems they describe.

[16] Psychiatrists, social workers, and clinical psychologists are currently fighting among themselves about status and about who is or is not accredited to do the various kinds of therapy. If they can't be sure of who among them is qualified, naturally they would tend to oppose non-professionals. But in the face of Synanon's therapeutic success, the resistance is apt to be covert.

Professional criticism of Synanon often takes the form of what Dederich has called the "orthodoxy effect." Dr. Gold, described earlier by Reid Kimball, evidenced a typical professional response. He reacted negatively to what he considered to be an unorthodox method. *He was more concerned with proper method than with results!* Despite the clear, live evidence, in the person of Kimball and others, that the synanon session was constructive, Gold believed that it was destructive because it was unorthodox. Perhaps professional therapy has reached the bureaucratic stage in which orthodoxy of method is more important than the achievement of concrete therapeutic results.

Merit and logic inhere in the Synanon methodology, and this is confirmed by considerable evidence. It rests on (among other principles) *the logical foundation that if a particular social configuration of people and beliefs can produce a person's problem, another constellation of people operating within the framework of a constructive social system can ameliorate the same problem.* Such a social system for positive living has been developed by Dederich and his associates. (It may be that they have succeeded in an area in which the professional has failed because they were unencumbered by the vast body of complicated and often conflicting theory and research found in the professional therapeutic field. Moreover, Synanon was certainly not plagued by the "orthodoxy effect.") In any event, Synanon works, and the existence of hundreds of "clean" ex-addicts and criminals should be clear evidence of success to any logical, unbiased person.

Based upon the foundation of its successful work with the hard-core criminal-addict, in response to a community demand, Synanon has recently embarked on a more ambitious program for working with a wider range of human difficulties. This new direction includes individuals who were never criminals or addicts. Most of these people are reasonably successful members of the community. For these "members" of Synanon, synanon sessions and overall involvement with the "movement" appear to be resolving a variety of frustrations, feelings of loneliness, alienation, and relationship conflicts. This part of the program, for people with "average" human problems, has been incorporated into the overall Synanon operation and seems to be functioning with a considerable measure of success.

The belief of some professionals in their *exclusive right* to treat human problems is no longer logical or practical in the light of Synanon's success. Greater cooperation between the professionals and the Synanon community of "professionals" seems clearly needed. A first step in this potentially productive cooperation would be for the orthodox professional and the public to understand Synanon, not as an extension of older institutional models, but as a new therapeutic system with a viable structure and integrity of its own. From this more logical starting point, the public and the professional community, in cooperation with Synanon, can forward the natural thrust of this vital new *social movement*.

Index